A FIGHT FOR THE SOUL
OF PUBLIC EDUCATION

A FIGHT FOR THE SOUL OF PUBLIC EDUCATION

The Story of the Chicago
Teachers Strike

**Steven K. Ashby and
Robert Bruno**

ILR PRESS

AN IMPRINT OF

CORNELL UNIVERSITY PRESS ITHACA AND LONDON

First published 2016 by Cornell University Press
Printed in the United States of America

Library of Congress Cataloging-in-Publication Data
Names: Ashby, Steven K., author. | Bruno, Robert, 1955– author.
Title: A fight for the soul of public education : the story of the Chicago teachers
    strike / Steven Ashby and Robert Bruno.
Description: Ithaca ; London : ILR Press, an imprint of Cornell University Press,
    2016. | Includes bibliographical references and index.
Identifiers: LCCN 2016030324 (print) | LCCN 2016030946 (ebook) | ISBN
    9781501704918 (cloth : alk. paper) | ISBN 9781501706486 (ret) | ISBN
    9781501705939 (pdf)
Subjects: LCSH: Strikes and lockouts—Teachers—Illinois—Chicago. | Education
    and state—Illinois—Chicago. | Teachers—Political activity—Illinois—Chicago.
Classification: LCC LB2844.47.U62 A75 2016 (print) | LCC LB2844.47.U62
    (ebook) | DDC 331.88/1137110977311—dc23
LC record available at https://lccn.loc.gov/2016030324

Cornell University Press strives to use environmentally responsible suppliers and materials to the fullest extent possible in the publishing of its books. Such materials include vegetable-based, low-VOC inks and acid-free papers that are recycled, totally chlorine-free, or partly composed of nonwood fibers. For further information, visit our website at www.cornellpress.cornell.edu.

To educators who are changing children's lives and reinvigorating the labor movement

Contents

Acknowledgments ix

Introduction 1

1. Education Reform from Washington to Chicago 10

2. The Era of Mayoral Control Begins 28

3. Chicago School Teachers and CORE 46

4. Evaluating Teachers and Political Opportunism 73

5. Senate Bill 7 88

6. The Contract Campaign 105

7. Emanuel Provokes, Teachers Prepare to Bargain 134

8. The Start of 2012 Contract Negotiations 151

9. A Breakthrough and Prelude to a Strike 168

10. The Strike 185

11. Bargaining during the Strike and a Deal Reached 211

Conclusion 230

Notes 257

Index 301

Acknowledgments

We are very grateful to the educators who agreed to be interviewed for this book. Our work was greatly enhanced by the teacher interviews conducted by Roosevelt University Professor Stephanie Farmer as part of her *Sea of Red* report. Additional interviews with charter school teachers added an important dimension to the story.

We are indebted to Chicago Teachers Union (CTU) President Karen Lewis and Vice President Jesse Sharkey who found precious time in their schedules to participate in multiple discussion sessions, and to all the CTU leaders and staff who shared insights. Karen and Jesse also shared pertinent documents that helped us to illustrate the events and issues important to the contract bargaining and strike.

Both labor and management have a voice in our account. We are deeply appreciative of the time former Chicago Public Schools (CPS) Board President David Vitale, former CPS CEO Barbara Byrd-Bennett, former mayoral staff member Beth Swanson, and CPS Chief Labor Relations Officer Joseph Moriarty provided.

A big part of the story involved the negotiations and legal strategies of the parties. In this regard we were most fortunate to have the cooperation of CTU counsel Robert Bloch and CPS attorney James Franczek. Both lawyers participated in numerous interview sessions and were very generous in providing documentation.

We are also thankful to the many elected representatives, news reporters, representatives from other teacher unions and education groups, and individuals affiliated with the State Board of Education who shared their perspectives. We are grateful to labor arbitrator Edwin Benn, who shared his insights and made available his records from the fact-finding process.

It was also very helpful to have the comments of the anonymous reviewers who took the time to read drafts of our work.

We have a special affection for ILR Press Editorial Director Fran Benson who worked tirelessly to ready the manuscript for publication. Additionally, we are very grateful to Joy Sobeck, who did a wonderful job as our copyeditor.

Finally, we'd like to thank our spouses. Dr. Lynn Bruno, a retired middle-school language arts teacher, and Rev. C. J. Hawking, executive director of Arise Chicago, spent hours reading drafts of the manuscript. The book bears their gracious imprint.

Introduction

For seven school days in September 2012, approximately twenty-six thousand members of the Chicago Teachers Union (CTU) walked picket lines in front of 580 schools. The Chicago school strike was the first the city had seen in a quarter century.

This book offers an analysis of what happened during the strike and why it is important for public education and the common good. We aim to tell two interwoven stories.

First, we provide a rare look deep inside the contract bargaining process, based on extensive interviews with both management and union bargainers. For roughly ten months leading up to the strike, union and management teams enveloped themselves in the minutiae of more than one thousand contract proposals. A labyrinth of procedures governed the bargaining activity, and two major state education laws needed to be incorporated into the contract. Bargaining continued throughout the strike, and the parties eventually produced a labor agreement whose proteacher substance few had predicted possible.

Second, we seek to tell, through the teachers' and staff's voices, the story of how the CTU was transformed from a top-down, bureaucratic organization into one of the most member-driven unions in the United States. In this process, a labor conflict focused solely on compensation at the start developed into a challenge to a national education reform movement that, teachers charged, was systematically destroying public education and using Chicago as its test case. Unlike in past strikes, tens of thousands of teachers, clinicians, and paraprofessionals marched repeatedly in Chicago's neighborhoods and downtown. Thousands of community members and parents joined the demonstrations. Crowds swelled, shutting down streets in the city's Loop district. Instead of accepting the loss of classroom control and corporate style-management of schools, which teachers had been told for decades was "inevitable," the CTU reinvigorated a national teachers movement by fighting back. The ripple effects of the 2012 strike are being felt in school districts and union halls across the country.

The strike occurred in the context of a decades-long political and economic struggle where probusiness forces maneuvered against teachers unions, often with bipartisan support from Democrats and Republicans, for control of the country's public education system. Public schools have always been the subject of intense scrutiny, but, beginning in the 1980s, they became the institutions over which the continued prosperity of the United States was bitterly fought. Education was the democratic means for allowing any citizen, rich or poor, to live a prosperous life.

For many years prior to the events in Chicago, Illinois politicians and business leaders had pushed education reforms that blamed teachers for all the problems in Chicago's schools, sought to break the ability of teachers unions to negotiate over classroom issues, and prioritized the systematic closing of public schools and their replacement with privately run but publicly funded and often for-profit charter schools.

By the time unionized teachers and staff in Chicago walked picket lines instead of hallways, a deep economic recession had normalized the idea that school districts should function with steadily less taxpayer support. At the same time, a corporate ethos had eclipsed the democratic ideal of public education. Central to the effort to remake schools in the image of the free market was the need to break the power of teachers unions. As contract talks in Chicago approached, the nation's political and education policy landscape had provided encouragement and funding to forces coalescing under the deceptive banner of "reform." With few exceptions, the burgeoning education reform groups had two things in common: they embraced market solutions to school improvement and viewed teachers unions as the major barrier to change.

Following a pattern that had been unfolding in other large urban school districts, in 2012 in Chicago multiple groups contested for the right to shape what kindergarten through twelfth grade (K–12) education would look like. On one side was a seemingly invincible coalition made up of Chicago Mayor Rahm Emanuel, the Chicago Public School (CPS) system administration, the Chicago Board of Education, several well-funded anti–teachers union organizations, charter school entrepreneurs, and national foundations such as those run by billionaires Bill Gates (founder of Microsoft), the Walton family (owners of Walmart), and Eli Broad (a construction and insurance magnate). Also aiding their cause was the president of the United States and his education chief. In 2011, Rahm Emanuel was elected mayor on a platform that included a strongly stated commitment to improve the education of school children. To his allies the mayor was a pragmatist ready to invest in any form of school that produced results. But to his detractors Emanuel was an ideologue prepared to abandon neighborhood schools and privatize public education. Unlike previous Chicago mayors, he relished using blunt political force to get what he wanted.

On the other side of the conflict stood the CTU. To the CTU's cause came a large number of neighborhood and community groups, parents and parents' organizations, some supportive unions, high school students, and a grassroots teacher support network. First elected in 2010, the CTU union leadership was principled, democratically oriented, unconventional, innovative, and militant. The Caucus of Rank and File Educators (CORE), born and developed as a study group within the CTU, was an extraordinarily progressive type of union body. Nothing about it was routine. Before and after being elected to office, CORE leaders were class-conscious proponents of social-movement unionism. They held that teachers, as professional workers, were part of a US working class whose interests aligned with their students' economically marginalized families. CORE leaders believed that preserving public education and promoting social justice would require uniting with other private- and public-sector workers struggling against the interests of the country's economic and political elite. Where past union leaders had largely ignored the CPS administration's and the mayor's trampling on teacher professionalism, and union leaders had disavowed membership mobilization to counter corporate reform measures, the CORE activists seemed fearless in their willingness to educate, organize, and mobilize CTU members and their allies to resist.

A CORE-led teachers union deeply worried the mayor. Only one year into his term as chief executive, Emanuel did not relish the idea of a strike and school system shutdown on his watch. There would never be a good time for a school strike, but the fall of 2012 would be the worst possible moment. The Democratic Party Convention would be renominating Barack Obama for president. Obama and Emanuel were members of Chicago's political class, and the city was a Democratic and union stronghold. So the mayor aggressively took steps to prevent what he most feared. Ironically, his every step, enabled by the CTU's enemies, made a historic strike more likely. In the end, a combination of the perceived danger of a CORE-led CTU and a failure to realize that the new union leaders were not like their predecessors seduced management down a fateful rabbit hole. The mayor, school board, and school administration badly mischaracterized the people now leading the union.

A confrontation between Chicago's mayor and a school district representing nearly four hundred thousand children, on the one hand, and the nation's third largest teachers union, on the other, was in itself high drama. But on this occasion, external self-styled education reform organizations, well funded by the business elite, would both push and negotiate their way into the fight for public education. They would overtly align with the school district and the mayor and pursue an uncompromising political path to dictating education policy. Unlike in past school labor-relations struggles, in this instance the CTU would be supported by thousands of parents and neighborhood school–based community groups.

One other thing was different. Chicago school-reform efforts had been imposed on school employees for nearly a quarter century. During that time, with rare exception, the union membership was mostly passive. But in 2012 CTU leaders developed and executed a multidimensional, electrifying contract campaign to engage its members in a fight "for the soul of public education."[1] The objective was ostensibly to negotiate a new labor agreement, but the bargaining was as much a platform for educational justice as it was a process for reaching a contract.

Teachers unions have been buffeted by powerful national reform headwinds for decades. Both Republican and Democratic officials have largely adopted a narrative that public schools, and particularly public school teachers unions, are the source of the educational and economic malaise in the United States. While standardized testing has dictated classroom activities and school districts have required lesson plans that were more scripted to accommodate the country's assessment mania—a typical student takes 112 mandated standardized tests between pre-kindergarten and the 12th grade—teachers unions have made compromises with the prevailing wisdom.[2] They have done so with reservation and they have expressed opposition, but in the face of the bipartisan demonization of schoolteachers and their unions, some believed tactical retreat was prudent.

While the claims of negative educational impacts associated with teachers unions have been misguided, they most often take the form of polemics that characterize collective bargaining as the principal agent of an alleged public school crisis.[3] Aided and abetted by nearly three decades of corporate financing, a cacophony of strident anti–teachers union voices have influenced national education policy. Their message has been simple: public school children will never get the education they deserve as long as teachers unions, like the CTU, continue to operate. Against the rising political tide clamoring for reform, some teachers unions repeatedly asked that their members have a say in how schools were reorganized. In cities like Chicago and most everywhere else, their requests to be part of the change process were rebuffed. Denied a partnership in educational decision-making and fatefully concluding that resistance was futile, teachers unions reluctantly accommodated to changes they knew were wrong. Surrendering to reforms that were ill designed, badly theorized, and unsupported by data was an enormous psychological blow to teachers. But, under attack from both political parties, teachers unions most often tried to move delicately between accommodating some modest level of forced change (e.g., reduced bargaining rights) and outright capitulation (e.g., the loss of tenure, the guarantee that after a lengthy period of employment a teacher cannot be fired without strong just cause). The strategy was at best a rearguard action that did not prevent defeats from piling up or deter additional assaults and setbacks.

The nonpartisan disregard and defunding of public schools has largely happened without teachers strikes, but not in Chicago in 2012. The CTU case is an anomaly. The union's membership mobilization also addresses a question raised in the national fight between the political and corporate class and teachers unions: What should be the role of teachers unions in education? For an answer we turn to one of the founding mothers of teachers unions. Not by chance, she is a legendary Chicago heroine. In 1897, Margaret Haley was a Chicago school teacher and an organizer for the Chicago Federation of Teachers (CFT, which later became the CTU). Haley was the nation's leading proponent of teacher unionism, and her tireless activism made the CFT the country's strongest and most militant teachers union. In 1904, she traveled to Saint Louis to be a keynote speaker at the National Education Association's (NEA's) annual convention. Haley titled her brief talk "Why Teachers Should Organize"; it delivered a powerful manifesto for teachers unionism that embodied the values, ideals, and goals that the CTU exemplified in 2012.[4]

Haley began by arguing forcefully that teachers must "assume the role of educating citizens about their political responsibilities."[5] To her, public schools were beacons of democratic potential, and, critically, unionized teachers were in the best position to prepare students for democratic citizenship because "organization is itself educative." The CFT had "given to the teachers a practical knowledge of civic conditions and civic needs," and, in fighting for better working conditions, it had contributed to democratic engagement.[6] Haley insisted that only with thorough unionization would teachers be independent and capable enough to "democratize the schools," thereby enabling the "schools to democratize society."[7] Teachers had no less an existential burden than securing democratic practice within civil society.

Haley went on to argue that there was no discernable difference between what was good pedagogy for students and what was good for teachers. In her words, there was a correspondence between "the principles underlying a rational system of teaching and those underlying the movement for freer expression and better conditions among teachers."[8] Teachers were professionals and, as such, needed to focus on classroom instruction. But professionalism was impossible if administrative, political, or corporate influence threatened teachers' professional autonomy. "To know the better way and be unable to follow it is unfavorable to a healthy development."[9] Professionalism and teachers unions were perfectly compatible. "The success of one is dependent on the success of the other."[10]

Finally, the CFT organizer situated teachers unions at the intersection of two worldviews competing for dominance at the turn of the twentieth century. One she called the "industrial ideal," which prioritized commercial activity and culminated in the supremacy of the private market. The other was the "democratic ideal," which placed humanity above profit and demanded that all human activity be the expression of a meaningful life. For Haley, public schools should advance the latter ideal, and there was no one better equipped to do the job than unionized public school teachers.

> If there is one institution on which the responsibility to perform this service rests more heavily, it is the public schools. If there is one body of public servants of whom the public has a right to expect the mental and moral equipment to face the labor question, and other issues vitally affecting the welfare of society and urgently pressing for a rational and scientific solution, it is the public school teachers, whose especial contribution to society is their own power to think, the moral courage to follow their convictions, and the training of citizens to think and to express thought in free and intelligent action.[11]

Haley also fought and preached for thirty years against the "factoryization" of the schools and the increasing constraints placed on teachers by rigid school and political bureaucracies. A teacher, she insisted, needed to be in a union in order to be treated as an educator and not as a "factory hand."[12] For thousands of teachers across the United States, in both 1904 and 2012, she could not have been more prescient. Consider the four areas of labor relations that Haley identified as most in need of improvement more than a century ago: "(1) making wages correspond to the cost of living and the educational requirements for teaching positions; (2) improving job security and pensions; (3) reducing class size; (4) making the teacher a participant in school decision-making."[13] Haley vociferously argued the point made by other NEA members that strong teachers unions were needed in order "for the teacher to call her soul her own."[14]

More than a hundred years after Haley's address, in 2012, individual teacher's souls coalesced in a battle cry echoing out of Chicago. Now it was public education's own soul that needed saving, and where more appropriate than Chicago for a labor confrontation with national implications for teacher dignity, the welfare of children, and educational policy? This book explains how efforts to diminish the value of the classroom teacher and professional staff inspired the fight whose climax was a community-wide school strike.

The Chicago story illustrates from multiple vantage points how the CTU attempted to harness and unify different forms of power in a rapidly deteriorating political environment. The 2010 midterm elections had brought a historic number of Republican governors and state representatives into office, and public sector unions had come under unrelenting assault. Aware of the contemporary realities of labor organizations, CTU set out to redefine itself as an institution committed not only to protecting teachers but also to advancing the public good.[15]

To move from a strictly workplace-based organization to a champion of public good required that CTU adopt a social justice orientation. It also demanded that the union develop relations with community allies and use different modes of mobilization to collectively contest forces that had seemingly greater capability to assert their will. Articulating an idea of collective bargaining power, which embedded the teachers' interests within community concerns about educational justice, the union became the fulcrum of an emergent social movement around public schools. Advocating for ways to improve schools, CTU drew the backing of crucial stakeholders such as parents, students, and the many community groups that focused on quality neighborhood schools. By aligning their bargaining interests with the common good, CTU generated significant public support for their goals and were able to assert an analysis of why Chicago schools were under duress that effectively contradicted the reform narrative.

In addition, while restrained by oppositional political actors in the state capital and Chicago, the union and its allies framed the contract fight so as to legitimize to the voters of Chicago the possibility of a more progressive policy environment once the strike was over. CTU built upon its heightened workplace and community power to advance more socially egalitarian political goals. The street-level power the union displayed during the strike was translated into bargaining power that energized a greater defense of neighborhood schools and fueled an electoral organizing campaign. How CTU positioned itself within a restrictive legal framework to use bargaining, coalitional, and political power is a critical element not only of this story and for public-sector collective bargaining, but also for the future of the labor movement.

Once again, the timelessness of Haley's manifesto is illustrative. When she spoke to NEA meeting delegates shortly after the commencement of the twentieth century, the CFT leader articulated a synergy between teachers, their unions, and organized labor. These three forces shared three common struggles. One was the fight for "greater political and social emancipation waged by citizens." A second struggle was to improve the material and operational "conditions of public schools." And the third was to advance the "economic and social well-being of working people."[16] In retrospect, little separates these early goals from the CTU's 2012 objectives of delivering publicly valuable goods. Likewise, just as Haley warned against an alternative siren song leading schools toward commercialism and influence by corrupt "good business men," the CTU leadership campaigned against the commercialization of public education.[17]

In assessing the overall threat to education, CORE concluded that the democratic promise of the United States was being undermined. Public education was the country's most secure promotion of citizenship, and for generations it had greased the wheels of social mobility. It was more national myth than reality that anyone with an education could grow up to be whatever he or she wanted to be, but it was true that an education could lift a person's fortunes beyond his or her station at birth. But now the public schools' ability to function as a national corrective to racism, poverty, and political self-interest was at risk. Schools, as championed by the CORE-inspired CTU, were bulwarks of healthy neighborhoods, which were the building blocks of citizenship. In this way collective bargaining intersected with community mobilization and public policy. CTU was not just representing its members but fulfilling public education's promise of recreating the democratic polis for every generation.

During her union career, Haley felt similarly about public education; she closed her NEA speech with a call to arms. "Today, teachers of America, we stand at the parting of the ways. Democracy is not on trial, but America is."[18] The battle, she explained, would have no middle ground. Teachers would have to choose between a narrow vocational curriculum serving the profit motive and a humanistic education enriching democracy. When advocating for educational justice, the CTU also presented teachers with a choice. One option was to accept the movement to align public education with what Haley objected to as the "industrial ideal," and what in the twenty-first century would be called the neoliberal school project. (Neoliberalism is a set of political behaviors that translate human interactions into market transactions.)[19] There was no better place to investigate the penetration of market dynamics into public schools than in Chicago.[20] The alternative to the neoliberal option that CTU offered in 2012 was an overwhelming embrace of Haley's democratic ideal. Educated by its CORE leadership, rank and filers had a sophisticated appreciation of the relationship between the possibilities of collective bargaining and the need to rein in neoliberal practices. By choosing to defend their schools instead of surrendering to a corporate-style transformation of public education, CTU members committed the ultimate act of resistance, demonstrating an alternative vision of education that could inspire teachers everywhere.

In choosing to fight, the union also activated public consciousness and offered community advocates a voice at the bargaining table. Haley would have certainly approved. What happened in Chicago in 2012 may not have been literally inspired by Haley's vision, but the CTU's strategy was powerfully animated by her organizing principle. The concept of a democratic teachers union fighting for the common good is the unifying theme for the story that we tell in these pages.

1

EDUCATION REFORM FROM WASHINGTON TO CHICAGO

The Chicago Public School (CPS) system is the third-largest school district in the country. Its educational, political, and socioeconomic imprint on the Illinois landscape is enormous. For example, more than 550 Illinois school boards—64 percent of the total—oversee school districts that enroll fewer students than the average Chicago high school. Nearly 400,000 students, or about one in five of those enrolled in Illinois public schools, attend one of 660 Chicago schools, a number that accounts for 17 percent of the state's total. The student population is overwhelmingly children of color (84 percent) and "economically disadvantaged" (86 percent). CPS employs approximately 40,000 people, and teachers in Chicago represent about one-quarter of the number employed in Illinois. The system's operating budget is roughly $5.6 billion. If CPS were a city it would be the second-largest in Illinois.[1]

Size and racial and socioeconomic composition are not the school district's only defining characteristics. Teachers strikes, some in consecutive years, have been frequent, and as bargaining for a new contract in 2012 approached, the system was primed for a fight. Adding to this local dynamic were an intensifying conflict between the Chicago Board of Education and the CTU and a national attack on public schools.

In 2012, labor relations between the CTU and CPS would be redefined as more than a narrow technical exchange limited in its impact to the parties of a contract. Extending deep into Chicago neighborhoods, the school dispute offered a vision of collective bargaining that associated workers rights with elevating the public good. Teachers across the country were fixated on Chicago because they, too, were the victims of an educational reform movement that was tearing up the roots of public education. Teacher anger had grown to dangerous heights, but the seeds of the dispute were planted three decades before. To understand why the CPS-CTU conflict mattered beyond Chicago requires first examining how a Washington political consensus converted public education into an investment opportunity.

A Nation at Risk?

By the early 1980s, Chicago had become the symbol for a frenzied anti–public school movement that blamed public education for putting the nation's security at risk. In 1981, at the direction of President Ronald Reagan, Secretary of Education Terrence Bell appointed the National Commission on Excellence in Education and directed it to examine the "quality of education in the United States." The commission was created to address the public perception that the nation's educational system was falling short of expectations. In the opening paragraph of its 1983 report *A Nation at Risk: The Imperative for Educational Reform*, the authors sent a clear distress signal: "We report to the American people that . . . the educational foundations of our society are presently being eroded by a rising tide of mediocrity that threatens our very future as a Nation and a people."[2]

As evidence of decline, the report pointed out that millions of adults, and perhaps 40 percent of minority youth, were "functionally illiterate." On one academic test after another, Americans were found to trail most other developed countries. The report also addressed the need for more stringent high school graduation requirements, higher academic performance standards, additional time dedicated to classroom instruction, and increased teacher salaries. Critics of the report, however, pointed out major flaws in the statistics used to document alleged educational failure and in the quality of the overall assessment, the questionable link between student achievement and the national economy, and how politicians shamefully used the bad news to "manufacture a crisis."[3] Whatever the legitimacy of its content, the report fueled a national debate about school performance and launched a multibillion-dollar high-stakes testing industry. A crusade to reform public education was begun, and critics of the public schools quickly jumped to the front of the line.

Schools were accused of being captured by vested interests, including "teacher unions and myriad associations of principals, school boards, superintendents, and administrators," who were "beneficiaries of the status quo."[4] To break the hold of what Connecticut Senator Joseph Lieberman called "ossified bureaucracies," public schools, it was claimed, should operate in a competitive environment disciplined by market incentives.[5] Conservative economist Milton Friedman had first laid out the proposition that schools should be driven by market principles such as consumer choice, and his disciples published books, funded conservative think tanks, and recommended national education policies.[6] Decades later Friedman continued to carry the reform flag by escalating the rhetoric that boosters adopted as if it were a divinely inspired creed. "Our elementary and secondary educational system needs to be radically restructured," Friedman pronounced with certainty. To bring about this reconstruction required "privatizing a major segment of the educational system—i.e., by enabling a private, for-profit industry to develop that will provide a wide variety of learning opportunities and offer effective competition to public schools."[7]

After a fitful start, the market found ardent proponents in both the Republican and the Democratic parties. George W. Bush, a self-declared "education governor" and, in 2001, a president committed to the principle "No child will be left behind," revealed his own plan to reform US education. Promising higher school standards, increased testing, stricter school accountability, aid for struggling schools, and options for children in failing schools, his No Child Left Behind Act (NCLB) won broad bipartisan support, becoming law in 2002.

According to education reform critic Diane Ravitch, Republicans and Democrats enthusiastically embraced NCLB because they "believed that accountability was the lever that would raise achievement."[8] Intentions aside, more than ten years of trying to implement the law's provisions have revealed that little of NCLB's promise was fulfilled. Student scores at best inched up.[9] But by one measure NCLB was a huge success. The time withdrawn from the instructional school day to test students and to prepare children to take tests of questionable value had expanded exponentially. As Washington was incentivizing the states to squeeze the time that teachers could teach by tying federal aid to student test scores, school districts were being asked to do more with less.

State financial support for public schools was diminishing at an alarming pace. By 2010 the states' contribution to public education had slipped to a near fifty-year low of 43 percent, and education became the biggest victim of the 2007 banking recession. When the economic downturn hit, schools got punished. Between 2008 and 2013 more than two-thirds of the states cut their K–12 per-student education spending. State cuts to education spending in 2012 and 2013 exceeded more than $10 billion; many states reduced spending by double digits. Illinois slashed school appropriations by 11 percent and, in 2010, contributed a smaller share of revenues to education than any state except Missouri.[10] The reduction represented a dramatic withdrawal from the United States' historical commitment to schools.

After *A Nation at Risk* was published and widely popularized, it became conventional wisdom that education was in crisis. Task forces and commissions claimed to have evidence of failing students, obstructionist teachers unions, and poorly performing teachers. The public was saturated with negative school head-lines, and its approval rating of public schools fell from 58 percent in 1973 to 29 percent in 2012.

Across the nation school districts were reorganizing and closing schools. The upheaval of school reform may have been necessary collateral damage if indeed there had been a crisis that needed fixing, but just as there had been questionable evidence in 1983, there was little to be found twenty years later, after the latest "education president" had left office. According to long-term trend results, read-ing and math tests scores had improved.[11] Additionally, based on national com-parisons, US students were scoring above the international average.[12] Graduation rates mirrored testing results.[13]

Taken cumulatively, since the 1970s, student standardized tests scores did not reveal evidence of anything approaching a national crisis in public education. Undeniably, since 1992, at least for elementary students, modest improvements in math and reading test scores have occurred. But the growth was actually faster in the decade before NCLB was authorized than since the law went into effect. Additionally, even these small gains cannot be strongly correlated with any re-form measures. Instead, numerous studies have documented that test score and graduation rates are much more strongly predicted by the socioeconomic status of students' parents than any other particular variable.[14] In other words, when you take into consideration a student's family economic status, little improve-ment is seen for low-income children. The wealth effect holds for international comparisons. For example, based on test results from at least 1999, when so-cioeconomic characteristics are controlled for, the discrepancy between US test scores and those in other wealthy nations disappears. Comparing a middle-class suburban US school with its counterpart in Europe reveals no differences in test scores.

The strength of the relationship between students' socioeconomic class status and school success has not only effectively explained achievement disparities, but it reveals a growing problem that reformers have been hesitant to acknowledge. Beginning in the late 1970s, economic policy in the United States had the effect of concentrating wealth at levels not seen since the Great Depression and over-turning three decades of a roughly shared prosperity.[15] As economic inequality between the late 1970s and the second decade of the twenty-first century reached historic highs, the achievement gap between the wealthiest and poorest students nearly doubled. Consequently, as explained by Sean Reardon, the "achievement gap between children from high- and low-income families is roughly 30 to 40 percent larger among children born in 2001 than among those born twenty-five years earlier."[16]

It does not seem coincidental that at the same time that income inequality was rising, family economic stability was weakening, and social mobility was faltering, reformers popularized a new notion of what constitutes education success. By any measure, since the early 2000s, test scores have become increasingly central to the purpose of public education. Teachers express deep frustration with the escalating time they spend preparing for and giving standardized tests. As student assessments have come largely to define how schools are performing, the widening class differences between students suggest that the achievement gaps are likely to worsen. Families with greater economic resources will continue to invest more in test preparation than those with fewer financial means. In 2013, high-income families were already spending approximately seven times as much on their children's educational development as low-income families. By comparison, in 1972 the ratio was only four times as much.[17]

The stubborn consistency of long-term educational performance trends should have prodded school administrators, school board members, big city mayors, and legislators at all government levels to rethink the idea that "school-based strategies alone will eliminate today's stark disparities in academic success."[18] But the rethinking never happened. So in 2008, progressive educators and defenders of the public school system believed they had finally brought some rationality to the reform movement. They had helped elect an ex-community organizer, college professor, and best-selling author to the nation's highest office. But they could not have imagined how much more irrational things were to get—a process that started with the new president's first educational decision.

Barack Obama's Race to the Top

When Illinois Democrat Barack Obama was elected president, Chicago teachers and advocates for public schools around the country were rightfully hopeful that Washington would adopt a different approach to improving education. The CTU was in an unusually aspirational mood. It was one of the first labor unions in the city to endorse Obama's 2004 primary run for the US Senate. Another, more experienced prolabor candidate from a political family, Dan Hynes, was preferred by a large majority of the state's labor movement. Backing the unheralded junior state senator over the familiar Hynes earned the CTU a terse retort from the American Federation of Teachers' (AFT's) president at the time, Sandra Feldman, who asserted that in this race Obama was not "labor's guy."[19] But, once elevated to the White House, instead of leading a movement that would raise the nation's respect for the only people who could make schools better—the teachers—Chicago's native son doubled down on a plan with a track record of failure. To further the sense of betrayal, he did so with an ex-CPS CEO who was anathema to Chicago teachers.

Arne Duncan was confirmed as US secretary of education in 2009. To the disappointment of teachers all over the country, Obama did not nominate Stanford education professor Linda Darling-Hammond. She was considered one of the nation's most influential people on education policy and headed the president's education transition team. Darling-Hammond also had a distinct record of negatively evaluating NCLB.

Before going to the nation's capital, Duncan did not have a leading academic record in education research, but he had been the Chicago schools' chief from 2001 to 2008. To teachers, school activists, and community organizers, he functioned largely as the caretaker for city hall's education agenda. They pointed out that whoever the mayor appointed to oversee the schools was the "central messenger, manager, and staunch defender of corporate involvement in, and privatization of, public schools, closing schools in low-income neighborhoods of color with little community input, limiting local democratic control, undermining the teachers union, and promoting competitive merit pay for teachers."[20]

Obama and Duncan called their version of education reform "Race to the Top." The reform was less a plan than a threat wrapped in a bribe. Washington would dangle billions of dollars in front of resource-needy schools operating at the height of the nation's worst recession in half a century if they agreed to comply with two conditions. First, states would have to eliminate any caps on the number of charter schools that could be opened. Second, any state that legislatively or by school code prohibited "a linkage between teacher and principal evaluation and student test scores" would be ineligible for the extra federal dollars. To win one of the Race to the Top grants, states like Illinois were forced to surrender their control over public education policy to the charter school and testing industries.

While NCLB had situated student testing as the primary mechanism for measuring school accountability, Race to the Top twisted the use of test scores to determine the employment status of teachers. Elected with overwhelming support from the teachers unions, Obama empowered Duncan to entice states and school district leaders to increase the job vulnerability of the nation's teachers. The message was blunt: if a school's test scores were inadequate then it must mean the school's teachers were inadequate. To win grants, states would have to act as if it were true that a student's test score was an honest measure of a teacher's worth. Tools never designed to assess pedagogical practices would thenceforth be used to evaluate a teacher's job performance. Education reform had veered far from *A Nation at Risk's* holistic focus on a more rigorous curriculum, additional time for instruction, improved methods for training teachers, and higher teaching salaries, and had devolved into an abusive employment and labor relations system.

By creating a tournament for federal dollars, Obama abandoned the traditional goal of equal educational opportunity in favor of picking winners from a field of competitors. Race to the Top created millions of dollars of incentives for consultants to offer their services to fund starved school districts. The plan's profitability for private educational entrepreneurs was not a mere by-product of a commitment to the education of children. People were supposed to make money on education. A 2012 Reuters story described the education market that had formed for private investors:

> Indeed, investors of all stripes are beginning to sense big profit potential in public education. The K–12 market is tantalizingly huge: The US spends more than $500 billion a year to educate kids from ages five through 18. . . . Traditionally, public education has been a tough market for private firms to break into—fraught with politics, tangled in bureaucracy and fragmented into tens of thousands of individual schools and school districts from coast to coast. Now investors are signaling optimism that a golden moment has arrived. They're pouring private equity and venture capital into scores of companies that aim to profit by taking over broad swaths of public education.[21]

As *Chicago Magazine* trumpeted, with Obama and Duncan, "two Chicago champions of the charters," in Washington, opportunities for profit would abound.[22] Some of the activity would be a response to the creation, separately from Race to the Top, of a national assessment to measure compliance with national education standards. Known as the Common Core, for the first time in US history a set of national standards for English/language arts and mathematics would be developed for school children. Ostensibly proposed by the National Governors' Association, development of the Core was funded by the federal government and the Bill and Melinda Gates and Walton Family Foundations, among other private donors.[23] Nearly all the states agreed to adopt the standards. School districts were expected to apply the standards in the 2014–15 school year.

But then Race to the Top happened. In order to be eligible to compete for the grants and be exempt from NCLB school performance targets, school districts had to agree to adopt "college and career-readiness standards." No one said that the standards had to be Common Core standards, but most states acted as if they were. Legislation was introduced and passed in many states to create for-profit charters, reduce teachers-union bargaining rights, modify or eliminate tenure, and establish new protocols for evaluating teachers based on student achievement.

The laws passed often resembled those written by a corporate-funded private organization, the American Legislative Exchange Council (ALEC). Founded in 1973, in Chicago, on free-market principles and opposed to public sector unions, ALEC became the bill-writing wing of the school reform movement.

Laying the blame for the decline of the United States at the schoolhouse door fed an inevitably irrational bipartisan opposition to the teachers who committed their lives to what unfolded inside the classroom. The narrative held that teachers caused low student achievement and that teachers unions protected selfish institutional interests at the expense of students. Revealingly, despite the large quantity of useful content found in *A Nation at Risk*, it was what was intentionally left out that mattered more than teachers' flaws. "We addressed the main issues as we saw them," the authors acknowledge "but have not attempted to treat the subordinate matters in any detail."[24] Among those other matters, for example, were seismic job loss in urban areas, increased rates of poverty, and crime. Public schools were struggling, but not more so than the communities in which they were embedded, where the "subordinate matters" were being transformed.

Chicago's Economic Transformation

Nationally, after the publication of *A Nation at Risk*, teachers increasingly felt that they were being scapegoated for the problems schools were facing. Poverty, teachers insisted, was the major culprit, and Chicago schools, like those in other major cities, were a microcosm of the communities in which they were located. They knew that in the 1970s and 1980s, massive deindustrialization had driven an exodus of urban manufacturing jobs into the suburbs, sunbelt, and across the nation's borders. Economic contraction in metropolitan areas then inspired destructive antitax movements and gave birth to an ascendant politically conservative ideology that was hostile toward public education. Urban schools were soon struggling to operate with the dwindling resources coming from financially distressed communities.

In the period pointed to as the time when public education was "failing," life for the families of school-age Chicago children underwent a severe coarsening. The city of Chicago, according to a Federal Reserve Bank of Chicago paper, experienced "some very painful years of restructuring that took place during the 1970s and 1980s."[25] Academic researchers Marc Doussard, Jamie Peck, and Nik Theodore found that a savage reduction in manufacturing work beginning in the 1950s produced, by 1980, "an entrenched and deepening pattern of wage inequality in Chicago" that permanently reshaped the fortunes of the city's working class. According to the study, Chicago had become "the epicenter of *deindustrialization*, the capital of the 'rust belt.'" Shuttering factories was a sign that deindustrialization was ushering in a "wrenching period of socioeconomic dislocation" with dramatically uneven consequences for different populations. Between 1980 and the 2001 recession, new jobs were created, but the majority of those jobs paid "40 percent to 50 percent less per hour than those the economy was shedding."[26]

Not only were available jobs paying workers less than the ones that were quickly disappearing, but remaining production employment was becoming more contingent. In 1990, less than 1 percent of the region's production workers were temporaries. However, by 2002, a third of Chicago's temporary workforce were industrial placements, and, in 1998, "9 out of every 10 [manufacturing] employers were using temporary workers."[27] After two decades of transformation, full-time service and contingent workers were trapped near the bottom of the labor market, where because of reduced unionization the "terms of employment deteriorated significantly."[28]

Viewed from the vantage point of a largely working-class and minority population, the city had abandoned its industrial infrastructure and displaced those who once had held decently paying union jobs. No longer "hog butcher for the world," Chicago was quickly becoming a modern tale of two cities. One city glistened with professionals able to pay for privately provided services; the other was toiled by workers on the fringe of middle-class status, utterly dependent on public institutions like their neighborhood schools.

Those schools had become decidedly more populated by black and Latino children. Between 1970 and 1980, citywide white residency had fallen from 65.6 percent to 43.7 percent. In contrast, the percentage of black residents had grown substantially, from 34.4 to 56.3. Whereas, in 1970, roughly 40 percent of CPS students were white, by 1985, the proportion of white students had fallen dramatically to 13 percent. Conversely, the proportion of Latino students more than doubled, to 23 percent. By the mid-1980s more than 61 percent of schools had more than 85 percent minority enrollment.[29]

Job restructuring had another deleterious effect. As economic conditions deteriorated, getting an education came with increased risk. Crime in the city, and especially violent crime, went up in the 1980s and peaked in 1991. The total number of "index crimes" (i.e., murders, criminal sexual assaults, aggravated assaults and batteries, burglaries, thefts) grew continuously until 1991 and did not start falling until the end of the decade.[30] With crime going up and the availability of well-paying middle-class jobs falling, school dropouts, particularly for minority students, increased.[31] The disparate test outcomes for students based on race, income, and geography was an unacknowledged dynamic happening in plain sight and weighing more heavily with each passing year. With the loss of union-supported middle-class jobs, the reading and math scores of working-class and poorer students tumbled.

Chicago's schools were struggling, in turmoil, targets of massive media attacks, and ripe for marketization. The school system stood at the precipice of transformation.

Chicago Style Reform: "Peoples' Democracy"

In April 1987 a broad-based alliance of parents and community activists decided to do something about Chicago's schools. Organized as Chicagoans United to Reform Education (CURE), they held a forum at Loyola University. In front of a crowd of approximately four hundred people, the group unveiled a proposal for "A New School System for Chicago." Joan Slay, one of the attendees, summed up the participants' aspirations: "We're going to start a city-wide peoples' campaign like nothing you've ever seen before around the public schools in Chicago."[32] A few months later, President Ronald Reagan's Education Secretary William Bennett labeled Chicago's massive school system the "worst school system in the nation."[33] Bennett's broadside came shortly after the end of the city's longest teachers strike and a massive school reform rally convened by Mayor Harold Washington. The combination of grassroots organizing, national shame, a school shutdown, and the election of a black mayor with progressive allies provided Chicago with a historic moment for transforming how its children were educated. It also left the city's teachers union unprepared for the imposition of a school governing structure that at first honored parents' input to determine school budgets, the hiring and evaluation of principals, and the formation of school improvement plans, among other things, but later centralized decision making in city hall. It is significant that at no moment did any version of education reform represent the strategic thinking of the union. Operating as an insular institution focused on promoting its members' economic interests and largely indifferent to community pressures, CTU was immobilized by external demands for reform. Uncertain about how to respond to an assertive community coalition of parent groups and a new political leadership attentive to educational performance, the union left the design and implementation of reform to others.

Elected in 1983, Harold Washington brought to the mayor's office, for the first time, a fierce interest in improving the city's schools. His educational advocacy had initially earned him the strong support of the CTU. On July 4, 1986, at the Hyatt Regency in Chicago, Washington attended the Sixty-Ninth Convention of the American Federation of Teachers, speaking at the opening. Appearing with the mayor was CTU's first black female president, Jacqueline Vaughn. Elected in

1984, Vaughn used her credibility as a strong union leader to help Washington overcome some initial racial tensions between the black mayor and a largely white union leadership and to develop stronger relationships with organized labor.

The mayor's attention to education won the favor of the teachers union but, as the 1987 school year beckoned, a new contract was being negotiated. Teachers demanded a pay increase; the school watchdog group that was created as part of a fiscal crisis in 1979, the Chicago Panel on Public School Policy and Finance, agreed that a small hike was doable. This fiscal oversight body, consisting of nineteen civic and community groups, had been aggressively documenting incidences of school mismanagement. In a series of devastating reports, the panel found that a "disproportionate share of job cuts during the financial crisis had fallen on teachers and system employees that worked directly with students, rather than on administrative staff." The report went on to state that while "total school enrollment was dropping the administrative bureaucracy was growing."[34] But when the panel pointed out cuts that could be made to administrative areas, which would have freed up funds for modest teacher salary increases, it was viewed by CPS officials as just one more outsider assault on CPS's command and control edifice. Instead of using the panel's findings to negotiate a settlement with the union, the school board suggested that a lack of funds would require teachers to take unpaid holidays. Vaughn dismissed the board's proposal as "unrealistic."[35] CPS finance chairman Clark Burrus aggravated the bargaining relationship by using an insulting metaphor to describe the teachers' demands. "I am tired of raping the system to satisfy the desires of employees."[36] Infuriated by the board's position, the union began threatening to "get out the picket signs."[37]

Washington's favored status with the union was tarnished when he agreed with the board and asked the teachers to forego a pay increase. They promptly rejected his appeal, and for the ninth time since 1970, shut schools down. As striking teachers marched in front of school doors all over the city, various public and private entities opened alternative places for children to learn. Teachers and parent organizations formed educational groups in day care centers and churches, but the volunteer efforts only affected a small percentage of students and, as the strike dragged on, community attitudes hardened. "Something snapped during the strike," according to education researcher Mary O'Connell. "Something that broke up the business-as-usual mood." This strike, the longest in the city's history, would turn out to be different from the previous eight. "Nobody can pinpoint what it was or when it started," O'Connell recalled, but "everyone agreed that it was the accumulation of anger and frustration" that ignited a community drive to take control of the schools.[38]

In every section of the city, parent groups sprouted, with names like Parents United for Responsible Education, People's Coalition for Educational Reform, and Believe in the Public Schools, signaling the formation of a grassroots move-ment. They held rallies, marches, and teach-ins, but the strike went on. Mayor Washington was sympathetic to these groups, but he rebuffed their demands that he intervene in the strike. To do so, he claimed, would be to interject politics into "complex labor negotiations."[39]

In truth, education reform was a delicate issue for Washington. His electoral strength came from black and Latino voters, but CPS employed a lot of minority residents, including teachers and principals. African American teachers outnum-bered whites, and 35.4 percent of principals were black, as were 45.4 percent of office administrators.[40] The Board of Education president and school superin-tendent were black, as was the CTU president. Changes backed by white business leaders that would weaken CPS authority or reduce administrative employment would have a disproportionate impact on the base of the mayor's constituency. Hal Baron, Mayor Washington's policy advisor, admitted that school-based em-ployment was a "tremendous political problem."[41] Schools remained closed into a third week and "everybody all over the city was raising hell."[42]

Around the city, public "stop the strike" sessions were organized by parent and civic groups. Organizers issued statements claiming that children were vic-tims of the walkout and a failed school system. Demonstrations by "hundreds of parents and busloads of children" occurred at board headquarters. As nego-tiations dragged on, Vaughn accused the board of "bad-faith bargaining" and feared that CPS was ready to accept a lengthy strike. "I don't think the public will stand for that," she said, acknowledging that the public was "exasperated" with the shutdown.[43] Still, the strike continued, entering its fourth week. In response, a massive rally occurred on October 2 in front of city hall calling on the mayor to "settle the strike." Pressured daily by parent organizations and African American community leaders, Washington vowed the strike would end by the following Monday. It stopped over the weekend when the board and the teachers union agreed to terms nearly identical to the ones recommend by the Chicago panel nineteen days earlier. Teachers got an 8 percent pay increase over two years, added sick days, and improvements in their health coverage.[44]

The nineteen-day shutdown in 1987 followed a fifteen-school day walkout in 1983, and a ten-day stoppage in 1984. In each strike, teachers strengthened their financial standing and stirred up community opposition. None of the strikes was framed or understood as improving the quality of education for city kids. Teachers had material grievances, but these work stoppages were blunt forms of economic pressure designed to raise pay. After the 1987 stoppage, the *Chicago Tribune* ran an editorial under the headline "A Dismal End to a Sorry School Strike." The paper left no ambiguity about what it believed was the impact of yet another school shutdown. "Given the militant teachers union, the beleaguered board, the intractable financial shortfall and the dismal academic performance of so many students, what hope is left for the school system-and the city?" There was, however, one thread of hope. "Perhaps the only encouraging result of the strike was the turnout of angry parents demanding that their children's education resume."[45] Not wanting to allow the organizational imperative to dissipate, Washington also "harnessed the energies stirred up by the strike" and announced an October 11 School Reform Summit to be held at the University of Illinois at Chicago. Long-time local education reporter Linda Lenz explained that the "teacher strike was a blessing because it gave a boost to expand the Summit."[46]

Washington's summit drew more than a thousand people. Those attending were largely nonprofessional representatives from community groups formed during the strike. However, the event also attracted a diverse group of prominent civic, business, and labor leaders. Fearing, in part, a community backlash due to the work stoppage, a large contingent of teachers participated, and Vaughn addressed the assembly. The large turnout surprised the union. John Kotsakis, a CTU representative, admitted, "We were shocked at the number of people who showed up and at finding so many groups that agreed with us."[47] Having potential allies was promising, but the size, composition, and energy of the crowd made union leaders nervous. Upon noticing the congregation of community organizations, Kotsakis turned to Vaughn and said, "This is the Coliseum and I don't want to be the Christians."[48]

Teachers' relationships with parents and school governance had never been a union concern. Community mobilization around school-based change developed in social spaces outside the union's comfort zone and frightened the CTU. Suzanne Davenport worked nineteen years for the community education group Designs For Change (DFC), and her recollection of the union was that it was strictly "interested in protecting union interests." School reform measures that invested authority in parents "looked like an infringement on union collective bargaining rights."[49] Years of grassroots organizing and Washington's summit had helped to destabilize the status quo. Change seemed imminent but pregnant with uncertainty. The CTU had forfeited an opportunity to be an equal partner with the parent groups leading the movement and found itself desperate not to be relegated to an interested bystander.

Unlike the research-driven focus on school organization and governance promoted by school reform groups, the union kept its distance from "educational issues, such as curriculum or school design."[50] Ironically, the CTU endorsed much of the critique leveled against the school system, and it was eager to have the yoke of Pershing Road (then the location of CPS headquarters) administrators removed. The union had actually proposed a reform idea built around "school-based management." Despite the CTU's support for greater decentralization of authority, the public consensus was that in 1987, while the union had won a modest pay increase, they had "lost face" with the community. The school board and CPS fared even worse. Many community organizers blamed the school board for provoking the strike and identified school officials as the primary obstruction to better schools. Frustrated by the school board's past failure to initiate fundamental changes in school management, a coalition of reform groups participating in the summit began to advocate for external intervention.

Washington had charged the summit with development of a "compact" that would commit school leaders, the teachers union, parent groups, and business heads to construct proposals for comprehensive school reform. The effort was a chaotic, noisy affair, but the outlines of a reform agenda emerged. Pushed by the ill feelings about the 1987 teachers strike, a coalition of parent groups formed CURE (Chicagoans United to Reform Education). Its purpose was to develop a strategy, based on ideas from the summit's proposal, to persuade the Illinois General Assembly to pass reform legislation. CURE fashioned itself as a pressure group that could insure that an education bill with parental oversight of schools would emerge from the legislative process.

Tragically, one month after the summit took place, while working in his office, the mayor suffered a fatal heart attack. Washington's death left a power vacuum in city hall and denied the reform movement the force of the mayor's office, but it also inspired community activists to make school reform part of his legacy. A rush of bills sponsored by various components of the original groups aligned at the summit flooded the state capitol. In the spring of 1988, CURE deployed a multipronged strategy to win approval of a "satisfactory bill" with "twenty-nine key elements."[51] At the center of the bill were mechanisms for giving parents more control over their local schools. It also contained provisions for equitably disbursing school resources to all schools.

Despite elements of the law that were protective of teachers' interests, the CTU was not enthusiastic about going to the legislature. The union suspected nefarious machinations behind one of the early proposals. Downstate Republicans had advocated for a plan, modeled after New York City's school system, to break up the massive Chicago school district into forty smaller jurisdictions. While legislators outside Chicago had complained for years about the governability of the city's schools, CTU and its parent body, the Illinois Federation of Teachers (IFT), suspected that the decentralization plan was really a cover for destroying the third-largest teachers union in the country. Their suspicion increased when they realized that the Illinois Education Association (IEA), another teachers union representing mostly smaller suburban school districts, was lobbying for the breakup plan. If Chicago were carved up, the IEA would have a chance to compete against the CTU for the right to represent Chicago teachers.

An additional provision that alarmed teachers was a "school choice" option that would expand the ability of parents to enroll their children in select schools through a lottery system. The option of attending a school other than a neighborhood school was not new to Chicago. In fact, by the 1970s, a dizzying amount of formal choice had been introduced into the system. Parents could choose from an array of vocational, magnet, and selective schools with "distinctive educational philosophies."[52] Most options, however, had strict academic criteria for admissions, and each school had its own particular application process. While the idea of choice proved popular, and thousands of parents attempted to enroll their kids in alternative schools, "the majority of students who applied were turned down."[53] After all parental options were exercised, few children found their way into one of the alternative schools.[54]

Chicago's poor record of creating alternative public schools only invigorated its advocates to push the idea forward. With each new plan, teachers raised their voices in opposition. Unfortunately, bitterness over the 1987 strike had moved union-friendly Democrats to join union-hostile Republicans in demanding a reform law, including one that provided for more school choice. Facing the inevitability of legislative action, the Chicago teachers union agreed to join with school system representatives, business leaders, and reform groups to "hammer out a school reform bill."[55] The CTU's support of the reform was buttressed by Vaughn's presence in Springfield but did nothing to deter *Chicago Tribune* and *Sun-Times* editorials warning of a union plot to prevent a law from being passed.

The pounding out of a consensus bill began in an extraordinary public session with legislators and all the interested parties participating. Subsequent meetings to "work out the details" were held by an ad hoc committee, chaired by Representative John Cullerton at the direction of House Speaker Michael Madigan. Formulating the actual line-by-line language of the law, according to Cullerton, required "sixty hours of meetings."[56] All of them were spent in Madigan's office. Republican Senator Robert Kustra, the sponsor of the decentralization bill, referred derisively to what was happening inside Madigan's office as "these mysterious meetings."[57]

However, after writing a bill that Democrats would vote for, the committee ran into Republican opposition. Republicans insisted on changes that would have reduced teachers' job protections. Every year CPS reduced the number of teachers needed within each school based on revised enrollment figures. The teachers who were displaced due to falling enrollments had a contractual right to trigger a "bumping process" that would ultimately lead to the school's most inexperienced teacher being displaced, while preserving classroom spots for the most experienced employees. The CTU's defense of these so-called "supernumeraries" was resolute, and Madigan would not move on a bill that the union opposed.

With the clock running down on the legislative session, Madigan decided to call for a vote on the Democrats' version of the bill.

Democrats had a comfortable majority in the House and a slim three-person advantage in the Senate, but then illness forced two Democratic senators from the floor, and with no Republicans backing the measure, it failed. The bill's stunned supporters were left with two options. If they wanted the measure to go into effect immediately they could try passing a modified bill but would now need a three-fifths majority vote. Their other option was to find a few more votes to pass the bill with a simple majority but delay the law from going into effect for one year. On July 2, Madigan chose to move the legislation right away and brought the Democratic bill back for a second vote. With every Democratic senator present in Springfield, including one who was dying, the state legislature approved the 127-page Chicago School Reform Act.[58]

The bill passed on strict party-line votes. Approving the bill without Republican votes created one big final hurdle: Republican Governor James Thompson threatened to block the legislation. Under the Illinois Constitution, the governor has the authority to make substantive changes to a bill through a process known as an "amendatory veto." As a check against the governor's power, the General Assembly, consisting of the Illinois House and Senate, meets for two weeks in November to consider any bills that have been either vetoed or subject to amendatory veto during the spring legislative session. The legislature would need a 60 percent majority vote to override a governor's veto.

While Republicans furiously condemned the bill, no one wanted to walk away from a Chicago school reform bill. In a standoff with Speaker Madigan, Thompson delivered an eighteen-page amendatory veto and pointedly declared that he would not allow a bill to be "shoved down my throat."[59] Chicago senator Arthur Berman, the sponsor of the bill, warned that without Republican votes for the changes, the legislation would fall victim to "the opponents of reform who will then prevail."[60] With only a few days of the veto session remaining, compromise on a bill looked unlikely, but then the CTU agreed to allow principals to fill school vacancies without regard to seniority, in exchange for a guarantee of employment, if declining enrollment or a change in course offerings dislocated teachers.

The union's concession broke the deadlock, but the act's primary focus was a decentralization plan that moved control of schools and resources away from the central administration and relocated it to the local school level. The mechanism for expanding school-based management was the creation of elected Local School Councils (LSCs) with broad powers to hire and evaluate principals, determine school budgets, and approve school spending and improvement plans. Embedding hiring and budgetary authority in a council made up of six parents, a principal, two teachers, and one community representative pushed Chicago into the forefront of the national school reform movement.

The new bill (Senate Bill 1840) won nearly unanimous approval in the assembly, and on December 12, 1988, it was signed into law by Governor Thompson. One year later Chicago's school system had risen from the ash heap of failure to become a national model of reform. Nebraska senator Robert Kerrey stood in Congress "to celebrate a great political victory in Chicago, a triumph of grassroots democratic political action," and "a triumph born of faith that parents, teachers, neighborhood leaders can run our public schools better than a top-down school board."[61]

Kerrey's accolades seemed well deserved when, in the first LSC elections held in October of 1989, an astonishing 17,256 parent and community candidates competed to serve a two-year term. The LSCs attracted 312,000 voters and filled 6,000 seats in 550 neighborhood schools. A radical form of grassroots democracy was giving parents, long disenfranchised by CPS officials, a chance to shape their children's schools. Education historian Michael Katz declared that the 1988 reform law "represents the most radical attempt to restructure an urban school system in the last hundred years." Katz noted that, in the past, reform efforts had simply "rearranged the furniture in big city school systems," but Chicago's plan "moved the walls." Most crucial, it altered the "relations of schools to their various communities."[62] It is precisely the deterioration of that new relationship that by 2012 helped to fuel a community response to a teachers strike different from what occurred at the dawn of school reform in 1987.

Chicago's LSCs not only dramatically transformed the site of school authority but, according to local activists, became "the largest body of elected, low-income people of color (especially women) in the United States."[63] In 2002, 1,800 African American parents and community residents and 700 Latino parents served on LSCs. By comparison, there were only 4,500 black and 1,400 Latino members on all the school boards in the country. The historical significance of the LSCs was not lost on the union but it generated mixed feelings. The LSCs gave teachers, for the first time, some authority over governance of the schools they labored in, but CTU objected to the composition of the councils. "We had only two votes and everybody's vote counted equally whether you represented ten people or ten thousand," complained union representative John Kotsakis.[64] In truth, the union was uncomfortable sharing power with parents.

In addition to establishing the school-level authority of the LSCs, the 1988 reform reduced the mayor's control over the Chicago school board by giving the City Council representation on a nominating board that chose board candidates. The Chicago School Reform Act revoked the mayor's unilateral authority to nominate school board members, and in its place created a Nominating Commission, made up mostly of LSC members, who were appointed to recommend three candidates for each of the fifteen seats on a new, permanent Board of Education. Unlike most of the country's other large urban school districts, Chicago had never had an elected school board. "Schools in Chicago," education reporter Linda Lenz points out, "have always been run top-down."[65]

Less than a year after Harold Washington's death and following the City Council's appointment of an interim chief executive, Chicago chose, in a spring 1988 special election, a new mayor with a familiar name and an old pedigree. Richard M. Daley, the son of a long-term mayor, Richard J. "Boss" Daley, was elected to run the city. Upon taking office he inherited the sweeping school reform plan that shifted significant power and responsibility from the system's central administration to parent-dominated LSCs.

Despite the preservation of much of the mayor's power, Daley chafed at having to adhere to the decisions of a grassroots body. He expressed more genuine interest in the operation and performance of the schools than his father ever had but did not like the shift in authority to parent councils. He astutely saw the schools as a political issue that would attract interest from middle-class voters and the business community. Despite a budget shortfall in 1990, but with an eye on his reelection campaign, Daley agreed, in 1991, to a three-year contract that gave teachers a 21 percent raise and avoided a strike.

A major deficit in the schools' 1993 budget caused an embarrassing ten-day delay in the opening of school that year.[66] Adding complexity to the situation, the school board and CTU were struggling to negotiate a new contract. Vaughn dismissed the board's opening offer as a "bitter disappointment," but after a sixteen-hour marathon session in mid-October, the parties settled on a two-year deal. It eventually took a federal court order, spurred by a class-action lawsuit of parents of minority children, to pry open the school doors.[67]

Labor peace and classrooms full of children were notable accomplishments, but if Daley were going to build a political platform around public education, he needed control over the school system. To get the authority he wanted, the mayor would once more need the state legislature to act. He turned to his new labor negotiator.

During the midsummer of 1995, CPS's lead labor negotiator, Jim Franczek, had just wrapped up negotiations on the city's first four-year contract with the teachers union. Daley expressed considerable pleasure with the contract's terms and duration. The agreement mostly paid teachers more in exchange for removing some of their control over school operations. As union leadership promoted its wage-setting success, it remained indifferent to a new reform consensus strengthening in Springfield. While the latest labor deal seemed acceptable to labor and management, what really enamored Daley was the law Franczek brought back from the state capital.

2

THE ERA OF MAYORAL
CONTROL BEGINS

In November 1994, the Republicans gained a majority in the Illinois General Assembly. The change in chamber majorities placed many suburban and downstate lawmakers who had long been critical of the Chicago school system in key legislative positions. The consolidation of political control in the hands of the GOP created an opportunity for radical school reform to unfold.[1]

As the political landscape became more hostile to CTU, education reform became a more popular and viable policy option. Unlike in the past, when an indifferent city hall embraced the educational status quo, the union faced a situation in which state and local political power would be used against them. Lacking community partners and having failed to mobilize its members, CTU could do little but acquiesce to an altered legal environment.

Daley Centralizes Power over Schools

As 1995 opened, the new legislative session created a frenzy of anti–Chicago teacher ideas. Republicans offered draconian proposals to ban teachers strikes, eliminate tenure, and inaugurate periodic teacher testing in the Chicago public schools. After Mayor Daley's reelection to a third term in April, Republican leaders urged him to present a plan for school reform. If the mayor did not come up with something soon, Republican Senate President James "Pate" Philip warned, the Republicans would enact a plan without him.[2] Daley and the Republicans promptly negotiated a broader takeover of the Chicago school system. The plan gave the mayor a large measure of control over the system, which he had long sought, while also containing "significant anti-union elements."[3]

The new law did away with the School Board Nominating Commission, permitting Daley to handpick his own five-person school board. The position of superintendent was also eliminated, and Daley now had the sole power to appoint a school "chief executive officer." Further weakening the influence of the CTU and its role in reform, at the mayor's insistence the law also amended the Illinois Educational Labor Relations Act (IELRA) by banning teachers strikes for eighteen months; prohibiting bargaining over class size, layoffs, staffing, and teacher assignments; eliminating seniority as a factor in filling teacher vacancies; and limiting teacher rights to file grievances.[4]

The targeting of Chicago teachers provoked a furious reply during the legislative debate from African American Chicago Democratic representative Monique Davis, who detected a racial undercurrent in the bill: "If you are a school teacher in Chicago and you don't like some of the collective bargaining that has taken place—around the rest of the state you can strike . . . but this legislation said 'oh no, you teach for that system.' You teach where those black kids go to school. You teach where those Latinos go to school. You can't strike. Who do you think you are? For 18 months you are going to be treated like a slave."[5]

Chicago Democratic Representative and union supporter Miguel Santiago had a different, more fundamental problem with the bill. In a protracted exchange with the legislative sponsor, Naperville Republican Mary Lou Cowlishaw, Santiago futilely searched within the legislation to find a single provision that improved student learning: "We are not reforming education, we are not improving education. What we are doing here is putting the school system into a receivership. This is what you are doing, you are putting the school system into the hands of individuals that are going to be corporate executives that do not have any idea of the educational system. . . . There is nothing in here that improves the educational system."[6]

The bill also had strong supporters who lapsed into derogatory and even apocalyptic imagery in defending the need for action. A prime example was Republican Representative Larry Wennlund's description of the school bureaucracy as a "sewer" and the legislative reforms as a "rod"; he then exhorted Mayor Daley to "take the rod" and "clean out the sewer." Not certain whether hygiene metaphors were strong enough to win over her colleagues, Republican Maureen Murphy declared, "We can not let this obscenity continue." She declared that there was a need for "cataclysmic change."[7]

The legislative debate focused mostly on the school system's structural issues and the lack of additional funding to close an expected school deficit. Surprisingly, the various limitations on union bargaining rights, except for the strike moratorium, did not elicit debate. Inexplicably, the CTU leadership was not only quiescent about its own hobbling but never mobilized against the law's passing and actually applauded parts of the legislation. CTU president Thomas Reece, who had assumed office in 1994 when incumbent president Jacqueline Vaughn died of breast cancer, pledged that the union would eventually repeal the law. He failed, however, even to criticize the Chicago-area Democrats, including Mayor Daley, who lobbied for the bill.

The 1995 law was a dramatic intervention into school operations and a crude wrenching of the bargaining relationship, and the mayor's chief labor negotiator, Jim Franczek, was there at its creation. Franczek asserted that he "literally drafted the statute."[8] Nebulously titled the Amendatory Act of 1995, the law launched the country's mayoral school-control movement and took direct aim at the CTU. As a sign of the legislation's intended effect on collective bargaining, *Education Week* pointed out that "the 141-page law restricts the power of the Chicago Teachers Union and gives principals new authority to fire employees and set their schools' schedules."[9]

The plan, according to Franczek, was "all but cooked" in less than three months.[10] It was a potent recipe. Prior to the 1995 law, CPS was obliged to negotiate over a wide array of subjects and, if needed, find areas of compromise with its teachers to reach agreement. Failing to do so would subject the school district to a possible strike. After 1995, the newly unfettered mayor-appointed school board needed to negotiate and compromise less. Among the items that no longer required compromise were many that the union had always previously negotiated, like class size, layoff procedures, and school closures.

The school takeover and its concomitant weakening of worker rights were enthusiastically supported by an organization of Chicago business leaders called the Civic Committee of the Commercial Club of Chicago. The committee's sixty-five members consisted of the chief executive officers of some of the city's largest employers, including the Amoco Corporation, the Commonwealth Edison Company, and the First National Bank of Chicago. Daley's school takeover plans depended on support from the business community, which had actively supported the coalition that demanded statutory changes from Springfield and had been critical of the teachers union. The Civic Committee made clear that its assistance would be secured by "a change in the size of the Chicago school board from 15 members appointed by an elected body of parents and community leaders to 'five or seven' board members directly appointed by the mayor."[11] The Amendatory Act of 1995 replaced the larger board and thereafter directed the mayor to appoint a seven-member board with staggered four-year terms.

Nearly all the board members appointed by Daley after 1995 were wealthy Chicago business executives or residents.[12] Critics of the mayor, including teachers, complained that too few members of the board had any experience in K–12 education and that, more revealingly, all had "been fierce partisans of privatization and other policies furthering the agendas of business groups."[13]

While critical voices offered divergent viewpoints about the law's impact, what was not in dispute was that restricting union rights was a real coup for the Democratic mayor who was widely supported by organized labor. Linda Lenz, an education reporter with nearly thirty years of experience, pointed out that Richard M. Daley was the first mayor "who said he needed some union givebacks."[14] The diminution of teachers' contractual rights by legislative fiat first compelled the CTU to challenge, unsuccessfully, the action in court; induced by a large infusion of state aid, however, in 1995 the two parties agreed to their first four-year contract.

While the law and increased funding forged a settlement, the agreement also began a process that would shape future negotiations. To ensure that they could act without union resistance, CPS and the mayor essentially bought labor peace. "Basically," Franczek candidly admits, "we paid to control the schools."[15] Throughout the 1990s, while the economy was roaring, union leadership had been largely willing to accept improvements in pay in exchange for ignoring the effects of education reforms dictated by the mayor and his chosen school CEO.

Putting aside the accumulating effects of politically imposed reforms on teachers, the 1995 teacher labor agreement appeared to be the end point of a confrontational past, which featured six strikes in nine years. With a labor agreement in place and mayoral control of the school secured, attention quickly shifted back to the classroom. Armed with the ability to shutter operations without union opposition, CPS and the mayor acted forcefully. In the 1996 school year, twenty-one schools were placed into remediation and thirty-nine nonprofit organizations opened alternative schools. Remediation was a designation applied to schools placed on the state's Academic Watch List due to low student test scores. Schools identified as in need of remediation were required to draft school improvement plans.[16] In a move that raised considerable alarm for the teachers union, powerful lobbying by Chicago's business community persuaded state lawmakers to approve a bill creating fifteen Chicago-area charter schools.

The charter law had a number of special conditions. Knowing the CTU's strong opposition to siphoning public dollars away from neighborhood schools for privately operated for-profit charters, legislators, at Franczek's urging, inserted protective qualifying language into the bill. Not only could CPS adopt new charter schools, but also, as Franczek pointed out, the charters "were a prohibited subject of bargaining, and CPS was not obligated to bargain over the effects of creating them."[17] There was one additional aspect of the law that incensed the union. Charter school teachers had to be organized school by school, as opposed to system-wide, and could not be organized under a CTU contract. (Charter school teachers could be unionized and belong to the CTU, but they had to negotiate separate collective bargaining agreements.)[18]

The ProActive Caucus Emerges

The years immediately following the Amendatory Act of 1995 saw 109 schools placed on academic probation. CPS also introduced another reorganizational wrinkle. The law allowed them to "reconstitute" schools that failed to make adequate progress after being placed on probation by closing the schools, firing the teachers and principals, and then reopening the facilities with new staff. The board reconstituted seven probationary high schools and removed 188 teachers in the process.[19]

In 1999, the fortunes of teachers took an unprecedented turn that deepened their suspicions about the course of educational reform and the role their union was playing. In a highly unusual move, CTU president Tom Reece negotiated a new four-year agreement with CPS school chief Paul Vallas nearly ten months prior to the expiration of the existing contract. With the tentative deal in hand, Reece quickly called for a union ratification vote. Opponents to the CTU leadership complained that the negotiations lacked input from the membership and that it was premature to rush into a contract vote. Their pleas, however, were met by a lobbying offensive by CPS and CTU officials, who convinced teachers to approve the deal. By a 13,501-to-9,942 margin, teachers ratified a deal few of them had even known was being negotiated.

The contract provided most teachers annual raises of 3 percent the first year and 2 percent in each of the next three years. Annual pay raises were also accompanied by enhanced longevity provisions designed to reward teachers for the increased value they brought to the classroom with each additional year of experience. In exchange for a fatter purse, CTU officials agreed to keep looking the other way as school reform continued unabated. Once again, CPS and the mayor had paid for the freedom to reorganize and close schools, subject students to increased high-stakes testing, increase high school class size, and further marginalize the control a teacher had over the school day.

One major problem that the agreement seemed only to aggravate was class size. While the 1995 law stripped from the union the ability to negotiate class size, the new contract did include a provision that permitted disputes over class size to be submitted to a joint union–school board Monitoring Panel. Class size was an escalating problem for the school system. A report from the Neighborhood Capital Budget Group (NCBG) identified twenty-nine of seventy-two high schools as overcrowded and claimed that 57 percent of all high school students attended overcrowded schools.[20]

Armed with what they thought was a tool for addressing this problem, teachers submitted complaints to the Monitoring Panel, but the panel's authority to compel correction proved to be an illusion. The panel rarely met and, when it did, it was more obstructionist than corrective. Franczek acknowledged the importance of denying the union the ability to compel CPS to bargain over class size. "Prior to 1995, class size was a huge deal that drove the whole budget process."[21] With each overcrowding complaint ignored, teachers' mistrust in their union leadership and anxiety over top-down reform methods percolated upward.

In addition to growing class sizes, CPS had rolled out a new initiative, labeled "reengineering," which ostensibly provided teachers with the opportunity to identify problems at a school and then develop their own improvement plans. Only if the school failed to show improvement would the school's teachers and principal decide what corrective actions should be taken, including the possible dismissal of poorly performing teachers.

The reengineering scheme was negotiated in the 1999 contract to provide an intermediate step that CPS could take before deciding to implement more drastic action against a school. CTU head Reece applauded the program as giving teachers "in the school (a role) to assess themselves and plan to improve themselves."[22] Teachers were less sanguine about the initiative, and one of them, Deborah Lynch, offered a critique of the plan. Lynch had formed the ProActive Chicago Teachers & School Employees (PACT) caucus to oppose the union's passive approach to CPS-imposed changes. She argued that teacher performance was not the issue and that "the problem in these low performing schools is a lack of resources and a lack of management and that they are in severely economically depressed areas."[23]

With power over the schools recentralized under the mayor's direction, CPS attention turned to the district's labor-management relations. Expecting a typical bargaining round in 2003, school CEO Vallas, Mayor Daley, and CPS lead negotiator Franczek were surprised when, in 2001, Reece lost his union reelection bid to Lynch. She had first run in 1996, collecting a modest 27 percent of the votes.[24] Lynch ran again in 1998, winning 42 percent of the votes; especially important, PACT secured all six of the high school union executive board seats.

Lynch's 2001 victory may have surprised CPS, but her campaign caught the anxious attention of others. She had relentlessly pounded Reece's United Progressive Caucus (UPC) alliance with Vallas, whose policies she constantly derided. As a measure of how compromised the union leadership had become, Vallas had taken the extraordinary step of publicly endorsing Reece in the 2001 union election by calling him "a great union president" who "took union relations out of the stone age."[25] Business leaders chimed in, warning that Lynch's election would be "a destabilizing force," and the day before the election the *Chicago Sun-Times* recommended a vote against the challenger. Despite the forces arrayed against her, in Lynch's third try for the union presidency she won 57 percent of the vote. PACT claimed all citywide positions on the union's executive board and more than two-thirds of the delegate seats in the union's legislative body.

Lynch presented CPS with a starkly different kind of union leader. Where Reece had easily accommodated the school governance wishes of the network populated by CPS officials and political appointees at city hall, Lynch had forged relationships with teachers frustrated by union indifference to their classroom realities. Where Reece was viewed as largely disinterested in nonmonetary aspects of a teacher's work life, Lynch had a reputation for being equally passionate about school structure, professional development, and curriculum, as well as pay and benefits.[26] Local education reporters were impressed with the new CTU executive. Kate Grossman, covering CPS for the *Sun-Times*, found Lynch to "be a real thinker" who "had an exceptional command of contract issues, was media savvy, and brought a broader agenda around income inequality and social justice" to discussions about the school system.[27] Lynch sent a strong message that her election would represent a sharp break from the past nine years. "People will see a much more dynamic, much more interactive union. It's my goal to make CTU members proud of their organization and more involved in it."[28]

Teachers were ready for a change. They had grown weary of being the scapegoats for the failures of the Chicago Public Schools. School reform had been imposed on them, and CPS officials, school board members, union leaders, and city hall had repeatedly showed teachers too little respect. Jon Hawkins, an English teacher and union delegate who voted for Lynch, complained that under Reece's leadership "most people felt we didn't have a union anymore. . . . [Now] we'll finally have a voice. I'm not sure any of us can put into words exactly what that voice will be, but we're tired of a union that just agreed with whatever the board put out there."[29] Lynch summed up the change in union leadership by noting that "this was an election on Tom Reece's silence . . . in the face of teachers having problems."[30] *Catalyst Chicago* magazine editorialized that "nearly everyone assumes Lynch will be noisier than her predecessor."[31]

Despite being recognized for achievements by President Bill Clinton in his 1999 State of the Union Address, CPS's various repackaged reform plans had produced little success, and speculation had arisen that Daley would be making multiple changes in the system's management team. The mayor had begun to grouse about the lack of substantive positive change and "scolded his team by suggesting publicly that they 'think outside the box.'"[32] The hard-driving leaders who had initially dictated standards to schools, principals, and teachers seemed at a loss about what to do next. Test score improvements appeared to have stalled, the financial condition of the schools was less healthy than in 1999, and the CTU had new leadership promising to be more confrontational. Uncertain of what proposals to make, CPS and the board "merely offered more of the same."[33] Changes to personnel were inevitable.

The first change came with the announcement that Michael Scott, a Daley political ally and an executive with AT&T, would replace Gery Chico as president of the Chicago Board of Education.[34] Chico's ouster was quickly followed by Vallas's forced resignation.[35] A few weeks later the school leadership got a complete makeover, and Lynch got a new bargaining partner. Roughly two months before the start of the 2001 school year, Daley appointed Arne Duncan, who was deputy chief of staff to Vallas, to succeed his boss as CPS CEO.[36] Duncan, like his predecessor, was not an educator, but he had a reputation for solving problems without antagonizing people. On the news of Lynch's victory, Duncan called the new CTU head "super-smart," and made clear that "there are huge areas where we can work together."[37] Coming so quickly after Lynch's upset victory in the union election, the addition of new top management personnel presented Chicago with an unprecedented situation. Both CPS and CTU would have new, untested leadership at the next bargaining table in 2003.

As the new CTU leader, Lynch saw the 2003 contract as a way to solidify her reputation. In a foreshadowing of her bargaining stance, in 1997 she had formulated her thoughts in an open letter to Vallas. No section of the letter spoke more poignantly to what was agitating a rank-and-file teacher rebellion than the following:

> From the outside, teaching looks like a profession and people blame the teachers if their schools are failing. From the inside, however, it isn't a profession at all. We Chicago teachers work in a huge bureaucracy with tens of thousands of employees. It has traditionally been a command and control bureaucracy that needs bureaucrats more than it wants professionals. It wants workers who will do what they are told to do, when they are told to do it and how they are told to do it. Professionals, on the other hand, lay claim to a body of knowledge.[38]

It was not just Lynch's leadership that prefigured a tougher negotiation process for CPS. A state school budget crisis was barely averted by a property tax increase and roughly $25 million in federal funds allocated as part of President Bush's NCLB law.[39] Escaping the fiscal cliff was helpful this time, but Franczek projected a more austere mind-set for the upcoming negotiations: "Expenses are going up. Revenues are going to be down. It's going to be a bear."[40]

Section 4.5 Subjects

The 2003 bargaining season appeared to be evolving into a difficult one. Even so, Lynch had pushed hard to adjust the framework for negotiations. She had made a campaign promise to restore bargaining rights and told the school board that negotiations would not even start until there was an agreement to revise the Amendatory Act of 1995, which limited the ability of the union to negotiate. Her administration initiated a campaign to win back full bargaining rights.

The effort was unveiled at the union's fall 2001 Legislators and Educators Appreciation annual dinner, where more than one thousand attendees wore buttons that read "4.5: Restore Our Bargaining Rights."[41] The "4.5" was in reference to a section of the 1995 law that prohibited the union and the school board from negotiating contract language that covered class size, layoff procedures, seniority protections, and teacher evaluations.

Lynch also met with the school board and business leaders to overcome their opposition to any liberalization of union rights. Discussions revealed that CPS would support restoration of some bargaining rights, if CTU dropped its opposition to a Civic Committee–endorsed proposal to double the number of charters permitted in Chicago. Lynch agreed. With an agreement worked out, state legislators approved a bill that at least partially restored the union's bargaining rights.[42]

The revision shifted some subjects from the prohibited into the permitted category. The CTU could for the first time request that CPS negotiate issues like class size and school closings, but CPS was under no legal obligation to agree to do so. Since 1976 the contract had included negotiated mandatory class size for both elementary and high schools. However, under the revision, CPS was required to bargain the effect of any changes implemented by the school district. The amended law further required the parties to submit any disputes about how the permitted subjects were to be implemented to a nonbinding arbitration process. The school board retained the final authority to impose its will on 4.5 issues, because the union could not strike over those quality-of-work-life issues. The two parties spent much of the summer hammering out an agreement and, on April 16, 2003, Governor Rod Blagojevich signed into law a bill restoring some bargaining rights to the CTU.[43]

With bargaining rights no longer a point of contention, the threat of a strike at first appeared unlikely. It had been sixteen years since the last teacher walkout, and the schools had experienced nearly ten years of labor peace. According to Franczek, the era during which CPS head Vallas and CTU president Reece had been in charge of their respective institutions was a "shining moment of labor relations within CPS."[44] He likely drew his nostalgia, in part, from the 1999 contract that Reece had gushed was "made in heaven."[45] The caucus that mobilized behind Lynch saw the times differently. According to the pro-PACT newspaper *Substance News*, the Reece-Vallas collaboration resulted in "the most concerted attacks on unions in the history of the city's school system," and culminated with the controversial 1999–2003 contract, which the paper condemned as "the worst in the history of Chicago Teachers Union's collective bargaining."[46]

Bargaining in 2003

Although fear of a possible strike in 2003 was low, it was undoubtedly part of CPS's prenegotiation preparations. *Catalyst Chicago* commented that a walkout that delayed the opening of schools would badly undermine Daley's "longtime dream of keeping middle-class families in the city and its public schools."[47] Franczek publicly attempted to ease concerns by stating, "The good news is, you've got people who are optimistic and positive and want to see it work . . . so, chances are, it'll work."[48]

Constrained by the law and confronting a mayor with muscular control over the schools, the union relied on its bargaining capacity to improve school working conditions. While its power to negotiate had been circumscribed, the union still had a potent strike threat. Reaching a deal in 2003 would require improving on a number of serious deficiencies in the previous contract. Salary data released by the Illinois State Board of Education (ISBE) revealed that veteran Chicago teachers earned less than their suburban counterparts.[49] While starting pay was better than that of most competitors, once a teacher was in the system the compensation advantage disappeared. The comparative disadvantage was a disincentive for experienced teachers to remain with CPS, but there were other forces that pushed teachers out of the city as well.

In 2003, the University of Illinois at Urbana-Champaign analyzed why teachers left the school district and concluded, "CPS has lost a large group of experienced, mature, very well educated, and career-oriented teaching professionals across disciplines and grades." Foremost among the reasons cited for the teacher turnover were the "behavioral problems of students," "school principals' lack of support and appreciation of teachers," "social and economic problems of students," "class size too large," and "poor physical condition of the school facilities."[50] A 1999 analysis of school board data found that "30 percent of teachers new to the Chicago Public Schools (CPS) leave within the first five years."[51]

After agreeing in the early summer of 2003 to a three-month contract extension, CTU negotiated a tentative four-year deal that offered teachers a 4 percent annual pay increase. The deal immediately ran into trouble. First, the union's House of Delegates issued an "advisory" vote to reject the deal. Some teachers thought the deal was inadequate because of proposed increases in health care costs; they wanted the union to engage in a more robust campaign to win an agreement. Delegate Jesse Sharkey recommended voting no and called for the union to "conduct the kind of contract campaign that we so far failed to do—with member involvement and education, rallies, and pickets."[52]

When it got to the membership, the deal fared worse than it had with the delegates. Union leadership was stunned when 60 percent of the members who cast a ballot rejected the contract. The no vote was sobering, and Lynch responded assertively: "The bargaining team will unconditionally support the members' decision and will fight to return to the table to fight for a better deal."[53] Fearing that a harder line would trigger a walkout, the editors of the Chicago Tribune, in an editorial titled "Earth to Chicago Teachers," implored the CTU not to send Chicago "back to the bad ol' days where teacher strikes were as regular as the falling of the leaves."[54]

The reasons for the vote on the failed tentative deal included genuine unhappiness with contract terms covering health care costs and the length of the school day. However, the contract also became ensnared in a form of union political retribution. Many no votes were preordained by the continuous warfare within the union between PACT members and delegates still committed to the UPC. Lynch and her supporters had won the right to govern the union, but a sizable opposition within the House of Delegates remained active and committed to returning to power in the 2004 union election.

Lynch's election had overturned thirty years of one-party rule. It also flipped the dynamics of a divided House of Delegates. Union representatives aligned with a newly minority but still sizable UPC had raised one objection after another to PACT-proposed actions. Loyalists to UPC had "mustered themselves to be as disruptive as possible."[55] The obstructionist strategy used by opponents to the new leadership was so transparent that it appeared to PACT followers that the UPC faction was "determined to destroy the union they once led."[56]

When the CTU and CPS went back to the bargaining table, three items remained unsettled. Along with health care, the two sides disagreed over the length of the contract (CPS wanted five years, CTU three) and a CPS proposal to lengthen the school day by twenty minutes. Until 1995, contracts had never been longer than three years. The two subsequent four-year terms were criticized by PACT as giving away too much leverage to the school system because it delayed the time when teachers could legally strike. CPS had an unstated reason for wanting to add years to the contract duration. By extending the deal its termination date would happen after the city's mayoral election. Not surprisingly, Daley placed a very high value on not having to face a possibly angry teachers union that might shut down schools just when he was trying to convince city voters that he was worthy of their continued support.

While it was the health care proposals that most roiled union members, changes in school time duration were not easy to produce. Despite the 1995 law and 2003 revisions, school duration remained one of the few noncompensation mandatory subjects of bargaining. If CPS wanted to extend the school calendar, it would, in Franczek's blunt language, "have to be paid for."[57] Under the law the school system could not unilaterally impose an increase in teachers' working time. In contract talks stretching back to the 1950s, CPS had asked teachers to work either more days or longer hours, and each time CTU countered by inquiring how much a teacher's time was valued. The school district had repeatedly claimed that Chicago teachers worked the shortest school days in the country. The union saw the charge as a mean-spirited rhetorical device meant to demonize teachers working under some of the toughest conditions in the state. Further, the parties disagreed on how to measure the length of the teachers' school day, and neither school board nor union had ever tried to determine how many hours a teacher actually worked in a day or a year.

After two weeks of considering alternative proposals on all three issues, the negotiations stalled. Duncan was reduced to issuing scripted optimistic comments about CPS's being "at the table" and "willing to compromise," while Lynch sounded more threatening in demanding "significant movement on the three major issues that remain on the table."[58] On October 29, the House of Delegates authorized by a 543-to-98 vote the first strike since the ill-fated 1987 walkout, setting a December 4 deadline. One week later, CPS made a second contract offer. Following a six-hour mediation session, a new set of proposals was finalized. Lynch expressed disappointment with the proposal and claimed that members are "not optimistic at all" that a strike could be avoided.[59]

"We were ready to take people out," Lynch admitted, but then the teachers were given a third proposal to consider.[60] The Chicago Board of Education dropped its demand for a five-year deal and offered four years instead. The school year would be seven days shorter, and the school day would be lengthened by fifteen minutes instead of 20. Health-care coverage would freeze "teacher contributions to two of five health plans and cut co-payments and deductibles," and teachers would get "four percent annual raises." Lynch called the new offer "worthy of consideration," but it was not obvious that the board concessions would be good enough.[61] The first test was passed on November 18 when the delegates recommended that the membership approve the contract.

During the day of the second contract ratification vote, union delegate Karen Lewis handed out ballots at Lane Tech College Prep High School. She was planning to vote for the deal but had her doubts about the outcome. "The biggest problem is that people are still concerned about the health care." Lewis expected the vote to be a "squeaker."[62] Union members had two ballot choices. They could vote yes for the contract, or vote no and agree to go on strike. As the day's voting neared its end, CTU Communications Director Jay Rehak cautioned that, "It looks like it's going to be a long night."[63] With uncertainty running high, a large number of union members cast ballots, approving the contract by a slim majority. There would be no strike. CPS and the union looked forward to four more years of labor peace.

The Old Guard Returns and Renaissance 2010

Although Lynch had negotiated her first contact, she had had very little time to reflect on the work. Many union members had judged her deal harshly, and the agreement hung like an albatross around her neck as she faced a new political challenge from the UPC in 2004. After two rounds of union voting, on May 21 and June 11, the membership returned the previous leadership to power. More than 22,000 ballots were casts for four slates of candidates. Under CTU rules, if one candidate did not receive at least 51 percent of the votes, a second election was held between the two leading candidates. In a runoff election, Lynch fell 560 votes short of victory, but in a surreal turn of events worthy of Chicago's reputation for political intrigue, she refused to leave office.

Claiming that election improprieties had occurred, she changed the locks at the union headquarters barring her victorious opponent, Marilyn Stewart, from entering. It was not until a final decision by the CTU's parent union, the AFT, legitimated the election results that Lynch turned the keys over to Stewart. In the end, the ability of the UPC to frame the contract as deficient had turned Lynch into the union's first one-term president. Stewart's election signaled a withdrawal of union attention from reform-like measures. During her campaign she had derisively referred to the union under Lynch's direction as acting like a "graduate college." She promised to return the union's focus to "better working conditions, benefits, and job security."[64]

Chicago's next big reform chapter occurred even before Stewart had been installed as CTU's next president. At a Commercial Club event in June of 2004, Duncan and Daley announced their latest school initiative, which carried the New Age–sounding title Renaissance 2010. The plan was to close nearly sixty neighborhood schools and replace them with at least one hundred new schools. These schools would be either small, charter, or contract schools (i.e., schools operated by private entities under contract with CPS). In some cases, schools would remain open but be "turned around" by replacing the principal and a majority of staff members in an effort to raise student test scores. Unlike closing the schools, which would displace children, teachers would be fired but students stayed put. Over the next two years, ten neighborhood schools would be closed or turned around.

School restructuring or closing under Renaissance 2010 was only one aspect of the debilitating process of privatizing education. With every closing or reconfiguration of a neighborhood school came the opening of another alternative school. In January 2008, Chicago caused a national stir when it announced that it would replace teachers at three high schools and the elementary schools that fed them. The private group leading the turnaround effort was the Bill & Melinda Gates Foundation. Gates pledged $10.3 million to place control of these schools under the auspices of the Academy for Urban School Leadership (AUSL). Founded in 2001 by venture capitalist Martin Koldyke, AUSL had previously run a one-year training and residency program for Chicago teachers. While AUSL's workforce would remain unionized, dismissed teachers at the neighborhood schools were notified that they would "need to reapply for their jobs."[65]

Moreover, as unionized public schools closed, nonunion charters seeded with taxpayer dollars opened. Private hedge fund firms invested millions in charters to create a corporate education model; teacher contractual protections like tenure and class size were viewed as inconvenient restraints on business. Teachers unions and their "contracts [that] don't budge" were anathema to running a profitable education business.[66] The annual ritual of uprooting students and teachers and phasing out community schools had a decisive impact on the workforce. Between 2001 and 2010 CPS shuttered seventy schools, and six thousand union jobs evaporated.[67]

Many of those displaced teachers were black men and women. Most African-American teachers were employed in low-performing schools that had more than 70 percent minority enrollment. These schools were also in some of the poorest neighborhoods in the city and happened to be the schools typically targeted for turning around or closing. Schools closed or put under private management had, on average, at least 90 percent low-income enrollment. With every closing came a permanent loss of African-American teachers. An assessment covering the period 2000–2010 found that turnaround schools saw their African-American teaching staff decline from 70 to less than 50 percent.[68] Charters were hiring two white teachers for every black instructor; between 2002 and 2011, the number of black teachers fell by 39 percent.[69] At least two thousand black teachers had been driven out of the school district. Equally disquieting, the share of Latino teachers had stagnated for years at around 15 percent, even though, by 2012, Latino student enrollment had skyrocketed to 44 percent.[70]

Daley touted "Ren 10's" success, but nobody else did. The *Chicago Tribune* did its own analysis and lamented that the "moribund test scores follow other less than enthusiastic findings about Renaissance 2010."[71] Assessments done by the University of Chicago Consortium on School Research, *Catalyst Chicago*, and DFC were equally discouraging. None of the bad findings deterred ex-transit authority president Ron Huberman, who was the new school head (Duncan had moved to Washington in 2009 as Secretary of Education). He inherited twenty-two schools targeted for closing and decided to shut down sixteen. Renaissance 2010 opponents like DePaul education professor and Small Schools Workshop Executive Director Mike Klonsky viewed the closings as a misguided application of performance management to learning. "You end up missing, devaluing the role of teachers," he warned. "You're turning teachers into delivery clerks."[72]

What most angered teachers and community activists who had fought for nearly two decades for genuine school improvements was that Renaissance 2010 did not include a clear strategy for improving neighborhood schools. As described by the parent advocacy group PURE, Renaissance 2010 was nothing more than CPS's maintenance of a "two-tiered school system."[73] Chicago's reform mania resembled a panicked medical response to a health epidemic. Charters, turnarounds, closings, and phaseouts were all treatments for schools diagnosed as ailing. In this case the patient showed only minor improvement, so the medicine was increased. By the time Duncan headed for Washington, the dosage had become dangerously high, and CPS had become addicted to a bad brew.

Chicago parent activist groups led by DFC rejected the notion of "failing schools" and instead put forward the concept of "effective schools." The "effective schools" movement began in the late 1970s and early 1980s with a group of educators and policy advocates who came together to work on public school reform. Proponents operated from the premise that educating primarily inner-city, poor students did not depend on any particular school organization plan. While always cognizant of socioeconomic inequities among students, the effective schools advocates made the claim that schools "control the factors necessary to assure student mastery of the core curriculum."[74] The skill level of the classroom teacher was unquestionably important, but students and teachers alike were only as effective as the support and leadership they received from school management.[75]

However, whereas groups like DFC continued to embrace the effective schools process for improving public schools, by 1995 the center of reform gravity had moved decidedly away from providing neighborhood schools with the support they needed to improve. Backed by the Civic Committee of the Commercial Club, CPS and the mayor's office grasped the "failing schools" narrative to justify privatizing public education. Suzanne Davenport was on the management team at DFC from 1983 to 2002 and was present at and contributed to the formulation of the school improvement elements of the 1988 reform law. "With the rise of corporate school reform," Davenport explains, research on Chicago reform "emphasized more the value of charter schools."[76]

Ignoring the systemic conditions that most determined how effective the schools were prolonged Chicago's misguided efforts at reform. But in 2007 the Board of Education and the union had a systemwide opportunity to address educational concerns by negotiating a new teachers contract. Unfortunately, that only made things worse.

The 2007 Contract

After a one-term hiatus, the UPC had returned to govern the union. In a 2007 rematch of their 2004 contest, Stewart decisively defeated Lynch. The CTU then faced a corporate onslaught to fix "failing" schools, just when its leadership was bereft of ideas and ill equipped to fight back. As reform accelerated, the UPC prepared to negotiate a new contact. Lynch had been forced to run a reelection campaign after negotiating a highly disliked contract. Stewart would avoid that sequence but was well aware that, as had happened for Lynch, a perceived bad 2007 contract would likely make her vulnerable to a challenge in 2010.

After an early-August House of Delegates meeting to discuss contract demands, a new tentative labor deal was announced at the end of the month. In an agreement negotiated early and with no rank-and-file involvement and little transparency, teachers would get a 4 percent pay increase every year for the next five years, along with incremental boosts in salary for added educational achievements and years of service.[77] In terms of real money the agreement was financially good for teachers, and it did not come with any extension of the school day, although not for lack of trying on the part of the school system. According to union notes from a bargaining session, CPS "asked for 45 more minutes and said no money was attached to it—and that was the end of that."[78] The board then offered teachers an additional one-time 2 percent hike in exchange for the extra minutes of teaching every day over the term of the contract. That offer was also rejected.

Despite the significant pay increases on offer, delegates were not unanimous in supporting the tentative pact. Like all other UPC-negotiated contracts, this one ignored quality-of-work-life issues like class size and school turnarounds. Recognizing that PACT and many teachers proposing a greater democratization of the union had opposed the agreement from the moment they had heard about the tentative deal, Stewart had given the delegates only three hours to comprehend the new contract. Consequently, after the August 31 House of Delegates meeting, roughly one hundred union delegates took up a "No No Vote" chant.[79]

"What happened," *Substance News* editor George Schmidt recounts, "was that Marilyn Stewart called for the 'Yes' votes on the proposed contract, then refused to call the 'No' votes and ran downstairs at Plumbers Hall [where the union held its meetings] to hold a press conference." Stewart had called for a division of the House, and those voting yes stood up. She then ruled that the deal had been approved. Opponents of the deal protested that they had a right to register their vote before the meeting was adjourned. They also believed that the delegates were divided and demanded an individual vote tally, but Stewart refused to take a head count. Inexplicably, in front of skeptical reporters, Stewart admitted that she had not actually conducted a standing vote count or roll call vote on the contract. Despite the irregular House proceedings, the membership approved the deal with 60 percent of the votes.

Stewart claimed the five-year labor agreement was the best ever negotiated.[80] PACT supporters thought differently and accused her of giving the "Daley administration the most favorable contract that management had seen in the 40 year history of teacher collective bargaining in Chicago."[81] From contrasting vantage points, they were both correct. Teachers would make more money and probationary teachers would benefit from some new job security provisions. But the unelected school board would also, in some instances, increase its control of public education and teacher work lives. While the contract offered no relief on overcrowded classrooms, preparation periods, school safety, or turnaround schools, the new deal included a pilot merit-pay plan, extra paperwork requirements, and the union's stated willingness to consider expanding the use of charters. Daley had wanted the school day lengthened but he backed off, fearing a strike.[82]

CTU at the Nadir

By the formal opening of contract talks in 2012, many Chicago school teachers had worked for nearly nineteen years under conditions dictated by CPS and aided and abetted by Jim Franczek. He, more than any other single person, was the architect of the labor agreements that roughly thirty thousand unionized CPS employees had built their working lives around. Even by his own accounting, few union teachers looked favorably on what he had wrought. At the dawn of the 2012 strike, Franczek recognized that "teachers had suffered the culmination of 19 years of dramatic change." Nearly two decades of having reform done to them triggered a desperate and dangerous sense of "fuck it!" He called the 2012 strike "the Great Expurgation."[83] The dramatic phrase seemed an apt one. Teachers in Chicago were in revolt over a badly misguided mission to remake public education on the principles that guided free-market institutions. Franczek helped apply the shackles they would try to throw off. Freedom to control their classrooms would not come without a fight, but a new union leadership was on the precipice of unleashing a raw, angry, and creative rank-and-file movement. CTU would mobilize its members and genuinely nurture community support. The bargaining process was about to be transformed into a fight for educational justice.

3

CHICAGO SCHOOL TEACHERS AND CORE

In 2008, a number of CTU members formed the Caucus of Rank-and-File Educators (CORE) in response to the growing anger teachers felt about being demonized as the cause of all problems in Chicago's public schools and about deteriorating classroom conditions, and in response to the board's policy of closing neighborhood public schools and replacing them with publicly funded, privately run, nonunion charter schools. Before describing how CORE organized, its fight against school closings, and its June 2010 election to CTU leadership, it is important to understand the sources of CPS teachers' immense anger and frustration.

A Teacher's Workday

In the late 2000s, Chicago public school teachers were angry about not having the resources to do their jobs. They were outraged at overcrowded classrooms. They were frustrated about being ordered to "teach to the test" rather than being allowed to focus on broader learning and dismayed at the enormous number of hours standardized tests stole from meaningful instruction. They were irate about dilapidated schools.

They were infuriated that the word *reform* had been hijacked by billionaire-backed foundations that blamed teachers for all the problems facing public education. They were resentful that teachers were being made scapegoats when the roots of problems in the schools were poverty, racism, and a skewed tax system. They were exhausted with the demonizing of teachers practiced by the mainstream media, both liberal and conservative commentators, and Democratic and Republican elected officials.

"When did teachers become the evildoers of our society?" wrote CTU member Maria Guerrero in a letter to the *Chicago Tribune* that captured public school teachers' pain:

> For 31 years, I have taught in two Chicago schools, and it never occurred to me that all along I was contributing to the demise of our city. I was giving my best every day to teach children to read, write, do math, and think for themselves. I thought I was working in an inner-city school because I wanted those children to have an enthusiastic, positive teacher who expected the highest standards from them and would not limit them because of where they lived. But not only is my city blaming me for its failures, but now even the state of Illinois is blaming me for the sad state of education in Illinois and is pushing more legislation against me and my fellow teachers. Instead of actually trying to fix our educational mess by listening to teachers and parents and doing the things that would actually make a difference, they are listening to out-of-towners with their own agenda for education and buying into their "solutions." They are willing to experiment with our children and further demoralize teachers because they have been sold a magic pill for education.[1]

In interviews with Chicago teachers done for the University of Illinois study *Beyond the Classroom: An Analysis of a Public School Teacher's Actual Workday*, teachers poured forth stories about their jobs that they felt the media were not covering and that most people did not know about. In words that reverberated across the district, one Chicago elementary school teacher noted that "I love working with the kids—being able to help them to learn new things, and develop skills. I like when they finally figure something out. It's never boring. I love what I do," but, she notes, Board of Education policies made her job much, much harder.[2]

In the debate in Chicago, said teachers, the challenges of teaching in a school district where the vast majority of children come from families living in poverty is brushed aside as "making excuses." CPS students' parents are far more likely than not to work a low-wage job or two jobs, work afternoon or night shifts, or have erratic shifts, be unemployed, or be absent from their children's lives altogether. Eighty-seven percent of Chicago public school students come from households with incomes low enough to qualify for free or reduced school lunches; nationally the figure is 45 percent. Child poverty in Chicago—using the artificially low government threshold—was 36 percent in 2011 compared to 22 percent nationally, and in Chicago it increased by nearly 20 percent between 2008 and 2011.[3] Sixteen thousand students—4 percent of the student population—are homeless.[4]

Studies have shown that family income is the most significant predictor of academic success among students in the United States.[5] Chicago independent journalist Stephen Franklin rightly noted that "Chicago's teachers work in schools marked by economic and racial isolation, schools where more than four out of five students are minorities as well as low income. Chicago teachers deal with students and communities marked and traumatized by violence. Schools in Chicago and countless other places are asked to come up with solutions to problems that others long ago gave up on."[6] Alex Kotlowitz, a producer of the powerful Chicago anti–gang violence documentary *The Interrupters*, wrote in the *New York Times* that the educational crisis is really a society-wide crisis:

> I've been spending time at Harper High, a neighborhood school in Englewood that started classes in mid-August. Over the past year, the school lost eight current and former students to violence; nineteen others were wounded by gunfire. The school itself, though, is a safe haven. It's as dedicated a group of administrators and faculty members as I've seen anywhere. They've transformed the school into a place where kids want to be. And yet each day I spend there I witness one heartbreaking scene after another. A girl who yells at one of the school's social workers, 'This is no way to live,' and then breaks down in tears. Because of problems at home, she's had to move in with a friend's family and there's not enough food to go around. A young man, having witnessed a murder in his neighborhood over the summer, has retreated into a shell. Just within the last month, another girl has gotten into two altercations; the school is naturally asking, what's going on at home? The stories are all too familiar, and yet somehow we've come to believe that with really good teachers and longer school days and rigorous testing we can transform children's lives. We've imagined teachers as lazy, excuse-making quasi-professionals—or, alternately, as lifesavers. But the truth, of course, is more complicated.[7]

Said one elementary school teacher, "My kids come to me and tell me, 'My dad came over and beat my mom and I spent the night in Cook County Hospital,' or 'My house burned down,' or there's a terminal illness in the family. What do you say to that?"[8] Added a CPS high school teacher:

> One of the most stressful things about my job is that I'm more than a teacher. Students come up to tell me about serious things in their lives.

About a friend whose boyfriend beat her up. About bullying. About sexual abuse. About being stalked. About being homeless—we've fifty homeless kids in our school. As their teacher, you're the only adult outside the immediate family that the child deals with. You are the normal for them. You are their teacher, counselor, and therapist; you are so much more than a teacher. Teaching is a very nurturing job. The school is understaffed—there aren't enough social workers to handle all the problems the kids have."[9]

Children living in poor households often lack access to health care, and so have undiagnosed medical or vision problems. They often do not get three meals a day, let alone healthy meals. They are far less likely than middle-class children to have computers at home with Internet access. They are far more likely than middle-class kids to experience frequent and sudden residential moves and therefore go to multiple schools. Studies show that poverty is associated with emotional problems such as depression, anxiety, and peer conflict.[10] They are less likely to see a way out or consider college as an option; only one in twenty Americans aged twenty-five to thirty-four whose parents did not finish high school has a college degree.[11]

"Why are teachers blamed for the problems of public schools?" asked one elementary school teacher in a refrain that thousands of other Chicago public school teachers would echo. "Why are police officers not fired for all of the crime we have? Why are politicians not terminated when budgets are not balanced? By the same token, should not doctors be held accountable because they have patients who die?"[12]

Chicago public school teachers were also fed up with the huge number of days they spent forcing students to take state-mandated standardized tests. CTU estimated seventeen teaching days a year were lost to standardized tests. And if the teacher had not taught the material on the test—for example, it was scheduled for a future lesson—many students felt demoralized when they had no clue how to answer those questions. Teachers spent enormous time helping students with special needs or who had fallen behind feel good about themselves, telling them that they were smart and capable. But forcing them to take the standardized tests, teachers felt, undid all those hours spent lifting up their students' morale.[13]

"I really worry about kids who are already on the margins when they take tests like that," said elementary school teacher Hen Kennedy. "I've seen so many kids cry before tests, throw up before tests. The stress is very, very real to them. They absorb the stress around them. I don't want my kids to feel like failures." Science teacher Monty Adams added, "The at-risk kids come in with so much baggage and such a feeling of failure. I spend probably about half the year trying to build their self-esteem when I first get them. These tests don't build self-esteem. . . . Everyone is trying to come up with a 'one-size-fits-all' in education, and it doesn't exist."[14] Said one elementary school teacher:

> What is upsetting is that you're being told you're a bad teacher because you have students who aren't meeting test requirements. But when you have a student with special needs, it stands to reason that they won't reach the level of expectations. That's why you have special classes so you can give them the special attention they need. But if you have a student with a learning disability, for example, that means that child learns in perhaps a different way; that child may need more time to grasp a concept. Consequently, that child may or may not meet the standards that are being required of the student. If you have several children with learning challenges, it becomes unrealistic if a teacher is going to be held accountable for them—especially when you do not have the kind of support that is needed.[15]

And the federal government has only made the situation worse for teachers. As one teacher noted, "As I reflect about my school, we had more, before the No Child Left Behind law was passed, than after. Our school offered a foreign language, we had a science lab, and we had a school counselor working with children on social issues. After No Child Left Behind, *we* were left behind. We have less of everything. We don't even have supplies. I spend about $1,000 every year out of my own pocket because CPS doesn't provide adequate supplies for the children."[16]

Teachers' jobs are made much harder when they are not allowed to teach the same classes each year, and when different courses are piled onto their workload each semester. Teaching a new subject takes long hours of preparation—"prep time," as teachers call it. A Chicago high school teacher noted, "I've taught six different courses over the past nine years. The schedule changes every two or three years. Right now I'm teaching three different classes each day, which is typical at my school. If I've taught a class recently, then there's less prep time. I might create a new homework, assign a new film to watch in class, find current events articles that tie in, or create a new project. If I'm teaching a new class, that adds at least another three or four hours a week to my workload."[17]

When you're a Chicago public school teacher you may face large classes that can contain 30, 35, 40, or even 45 students. No teacher can give her students the individual attention they deserve under those conditions. Chicago's average class sizes in early childhood grades (K–1) are larger than 95 percent, and Chicago's high school class sizes are larger than 99 percent, of all Illinois school districts.[18] The private University of Chicago Lab School, where President Obama and Mayor Rahm Emanuel sent their children, caps all classes at twenty-four students.[19] A Chicago kindergarten teacher vividly described why class size matters and the immense challenges of being the lone teacher in a class of young children:

> Imagine having 26 to 30 kindergarten children in your living room and you're trying to entertain them—I'm not talking about educating them—just entertain them, making sure they're safe, making sure they're emotionally secure, making sure you're providing the nurturing environment that you know they need. Now imagine all that but you're teaching them, and doing it alone, without an aide. And when you're differentiating instruction, it's exceedingly helpful for the aide to provide additional support for those children who need it. And, we do not have a bathroom in our classroom. When a child needs to go to the bathroom, we have to stop our class session and I have to take all of the children, because I do not have an aide to take that child, and the children cannot be left unattended. And aides are needed to assist in the lunchroom, particularly in the first portion of the school year. The children need help opening milk, getting trays, and those kinds of things."[20]

As a result of all this, the demoralization that Chicago teachers—and the vast majority of public school teachers in United States—felt was deep and growing. A 2012 study showed that teacher job satisfaction dropped fifteen percentage points in the previous two years, falling to the lowest level in more than two decades.[21] There were large increases in the number of teachers who said they were likely to leave teaching. And that was on top of the already astounding statistic that half of all teachers, after studying four to six years to fulfill their vocational dream, quit the profession in the first five years of teaching.[22] *Catalyst Chicago* magazine, which covers education issues in Chicago, has reported that the annual turnover rate in Chicago public schools is 18 percent. And in 132 Chicago public schools where the students are overwhelmingly people of color, a third of schools lost more than half their teachers between 2008 and 2012.[23]

Furthermore, CPS administration regularly determined that "failing" schools were in need of a "turnaround" and fired the entire staff. *Catalyst Chicago* noted that "at sixteen of the seventeen schools that underwent a turnaround between 2007 and 2011, more than half of teachers hired in the first year of the turnaround left by the third year. In the ten schools that were turned around in 2013, a third of the faculty left by the start of the current school year." The school board–appointed director of the turnaround schools strikingly remarked that he had no interest in having continuity of teachers: "It has never been our model that staff stay for three to five years," said Jarvis Sanford.[24] It would be impossible to find any city chief of police, fire department chief, or hospital director who would welcome a constant churning of police, firefighters, and doctors.

Many CPS teachers felt, moreover, that the board pressured veteran teachers to quit in order to save costs. "I have friends who are principals," said one teacher, "and they have been told, 'Target your veteran teachers. Get them out of there. They cost too much.' The more education you have, the more targeted you're going to be. Most of the teachers at my school have master's degrees. Many of them have two master's degrees. Yet they're being targeted." "Last year my principal moved me from special education," said Amy Rosenwasser, "where I'm a National Board Certified Teacher and I had always received superior ratings, to a fifth grade general education position, for no real reason other than I think she wants me to leave."[25] A Chicago high school teacher shared her deep frustration:

> The only thing that keeps me going during this really stressful, demoralizing year is the students. When students come to you with questions, when they ask for letters of recommendation, they keep you motivated. We're here for the kids, ultimately. So many teachers this year told me that they're thinking of quitting. It's sad. Every day teachers talk to me about the teacher-bashing in the media. People here work so hard. To hear they're retiring early and wanting to leave is really, really awful. Our kids deserve teachers who are happy to come to work every day and who feel supported.[26]

The Length of the School Day

Campaigning in late 2010 and early 2011, mayoral candidate Rahm Emanuel (whose election is discussed later in this chapter) denounced Chicago public school teachers for "having the shortest school day in the country." CTU leaders responded that what should be counted is the time students spend in the classroom, and in comparison Chicago public schools were average. They cited data that Chicago's 946 instructional hours a year was comparable to Los Angeles' 954 teaching hours and New York City's 930.[27] And the union argued that they welcomed discussion of a longer school day but insisted that teachers and parents be partners in determining what that school day would look like and what resources would be needed to implement it.

Nationally, most public and private school students have a lunch period in the middle of the day. This was the case in Chicago until the 1970s, as well; most schools had a 45-minute lunch period and two 10-minute recesses. But, in the

1970s, the CPS administration, in response to gang activity and to protect children's safety, enacted "closed campus" policies at most elementary schools, which ended recess, shortened students' lunch to twenty minutes, and moved teachers' lunch period to the end of the day after instruction ended. Seven of ten CPS schools do not offer outdoor recess. But those changes made the school day in CPS elementary schools 5 hours and 45 minutes, in contrast to the average Illinois public school day of 6 hours and 30 minutes.[28]

A longer school day, without addressing all the other problems in the underresourced schools, would not solve anything, said parents and educators. "Funding is not there for a quality day, period, no matter the length," said Wendy Katten of the parent group Raise Your Hand for Illinois Public Education.[29] "If there were resources, if there was more funding," a longer school day could benefit children, said parent Nellie Cotton. But "as it stands [at my kids' elementary school] we don't have a gym that's adequate for a recess period, we don't have a playground where we can have our kids out. It's just ridiculous. There is nothing. There is no library, no art."[30] CPS librarian Leslie Travis remarked that with "43 children in each of our kindergarten classes, with one teacher and no aide, the idea that we were going to have more kindergarten time with 43 bodies in one room and the one teacher, it just made your mouth hang open."[31]

A 2012 study showed that for the top ten Chicago-area suburban elementary schools the average school day lasted 6 hours and 28 minutes—but suburban schools achieved higher grades, test results, and graduation rates because they drew from middle-class students and the schools were far better resourced than most CPS schools. The study showed that the experience in Houston much touted by Rahm Emanuel in 2011 did not show that a longer school day was a panacea, but rather that students needed more resources like specialized tutoring:

> Chicago would do well to pay attention to the extended day experience of Houston, a city commonly cited by Mayor Emanuel and CPS leadership. An extended day and year were implemented in a 20 school pilot program along with other strategies, and in less than a year the extended day and year were dropped from the program while the other strategies were continued, based on detailed evaluation results. . . .
>
> In the first year of the program, the school district hired 254 full-time Math Fellows (tutors) for the 9 schools, at a cost of more than $2,500 per 6th and 9th grade student. Even before the first year of the program was completed, it was clear that the tutoring portion was a success: 6th and 9th grade math scores soared, and math scores in other grades increased as well. Reading scores remained largely flat. It was clear that the tutoring, and not the longer day, drove the results. In fact,

when the program was expanded to eleven elementary schools in the second year, the newly added schools included all of the program elements except the longer school day!

The mid-year evaluation report observed that "students and teachers have expressed some weariness because of the extended school day." There were also concerns raised about how the additional time was being used in the classrooms: "Teachers need additional support and training to increase instructional quality, academic rigor, and student engagement. In many classrooms, students are either engaged in low-level worksheets and activities or sit listening to teacher-centered instruction."[32]

A major part of the "longer school day" campaign, embraced by the *Chicago Sun-Times* and *Chicago Tribune* and nearly all pundits, was the implication that teachers worked far fewer than the eight hours of the average worker. What Rahm Emanuel and the media left out of the discussion was that teachers worked as many or more hours *outside* the classroom as they did *in* it.

The *Beyond the Classroom* study surveyed nearly a thousand Chicago teachers and found that their average workweek was fifty-eight hours. A Chicago public school teacher's average workday is almost eleven hours—nine hours at school and two hours working at home—and most teachers worked on weekends as well. A Chicago high school teacher noted that "during my lunch period rarely do I just eat lunch—I'm usually doing two or three things while I'm eating. I never feel like I'm done, I never feel like I'm caught up. We work very hard. Sometimes after school when I'm trying to enter grades I can hardly keep my eyes open." Added another teacher,

> When you're teaching, your day is never complete. You're always thinking, "What do I need to finish today, what did I forget to do, what do I need to do for tomorrow?" I often wake up in the middle of the night thinking about something I need to do the next day. That's a real normal thing for teachers. I cannot tell you how often teachers tell me, "I woke up at 4:00 a.m. and I couldn't go back to sleep, because I was still working through school problems." I'm thinking about school when I'm doing the dishes, when I'm doing house chores.[33]

The job of a teacher is so much more than just being in a classroom, teaching. There's all the prep work to teach a class. There's getting handouts ready, writing on the chalkboard and covering the wall with posters or paintings on classroom topics, and setting up the classroom for the next day's classes. There's grading homework and tests. There's meeting with students who are doing poorly. There's e-mailing and calling parents at home, and meeting with those parents who show up for parent-teacher conferences. And a hundred other things. A special education teacher notes, for example, that: "Once a year I have to write the Individualized Education Program (IEP) for each special education student. This takes at least a minimum of 6 hours. Sometimes they take as long as 12 hours. None of this is in the contract. This is expected work, and our job evaluations with the principal include our completing this work. There are 500 students with IEPs at my high school. Multiply that by 6 hours and that is a lot of work that is not on the books."[34]

On top of that, there are the long hours spent on data input and analysis required by the Board of Education. The *Beyond the Classroom* study found that teachers spend an average of three hours a day on nonteaching activities. "We're so inundated with polices and mandates and initiatives" from the board, noted one teacher. "We have to do all these mandates or we get written up," said another teacher. "But then in a couple of years they might not be there anymore. What's expected of us is so inconsistent, so unrealistic. That's one of the big things for teachers—the craziness with the board." Another teacher noted:

> The principal wants us to document everything we do and submit the paperwork. When we talk to parents on the phone, we have to document it. When I meet with colleagues about a class, we have to write up minutes. Of course there is always paperwork; that's part of being a teacher. But this is more than we've ever had to do before. Lesson plans have to be much more detailed than in the past. Course outlines for each semester have to be very, very detailed. All this additional paperwork takes two or three hours per week to fill out. It's not helping students achieve academically, and it's not helping the discipline problems in the school. Nearly all the faculty in my school feel worn out and burnt out, and they don't feel all the documentation we're doing is accomplishing much of anything.[35]

Charter Schools

Another issue that affects a Chicago public school teacher's work day is the competition with charter schools and magnet schools for students. Charter schools are privately run businesses that are publicly funded. Under Mayors Daley (1989–2011) and Emanuel (2011–), the CPS administration steadily closed traditional public schools and opened charter schools. Magnet schools are well-resourced "selective enrollment" schools; only students who win a lottery may enroll.

CPS teachers see some of their best students leaving for charter schools, while the charter administrators are free to expel students they do not want, who have discipline problems, or who have uninvolved parents, and send them back to the public schools. A *Reuters* report found that "charters aggressively screen student applicants, assessing their academic records, parental support, disciplinary history, motivation, special needs and even their citizenship, sometimes in violation of state and federal law."[36] In 2013, Chicago charters expelled students at a rate twelve times that of CPS-run schools.[37] Chicago Noble Charter schools served 35 percent fewer English language learners and 22 percent fewer special education students than Chicago public schools.[38]

And magnet schools, which have the most resources and are the hardest to get into, do not have to accept special education kids, who are disproportionately found in the schools where CTU members teach. "I teach in a neighborhood school," said one teacher in 2012. "It's really changed over the past eight or ten years. What has happened is that the magnet school and the charter schools are draining off some of our better students. There are always kids that will be really, really motivated, and now their parents send them to the magnet and charter schools. What do we do with the kids that aren't motivated? It takes more than me to solve this."[39]

From 1997 to 2012 the CPS administration closed 87 schools and fired the entire staff in twenty-four other "turnaround" schools; every year between 2002 and 2016, CPS announced more so-called school actions.[40] In the same time period CPS funded the opening of 112 charter schools, while every year claiming there was a financial crisis. The bulk of CPS teachers, unless they teach at a sought-after magnet school, lived in constant fear that their school would be added to the list and they would lose their jobs. In 2012, rumors came from CPS headquarters that another hundred schools would be closed, fueling anger that led to the strike.[41] When schools are shuttered, said special education teacher Rhonda McLeod, "We're done. We're terrified. We don't need to be dumped to the wayside. We're not trash, we're teachers."[42]

Educators complained that CPS seemed to be implementing a long-term plan to eliminate all traditional public schools in favor of charters—which in fact happened in New Orleans after Hurricane Katrina. As one teacher noted, "CPS would underfund a school and put charters around that school so that school could fail. The City of Chicago was purposely trying to destroy these schools, with the intent of bringing in nonunion labor and the expansion of charters."[43] CPS Chief Operating Officer Tim Cawley verified in 2011 the experience educators had seen countless times at their schools over the previous decade. "If we think there's a chance that a building is going to be closed in the next five to ten years," said Cawley, "if we think it's unlikely it's going to continue to be a school, we're not going to invest in that building." Cawley's admission also confirmed what parent advocacy groups had always believed. "I think [CPS] is deliberately starving these schools so that they become weaker and weaker before they're killed off," said Julie Westerhoff, executive director of Parents United for Responsible Education (PURE). "It shows that they feel absolutely no responsibility toward schools that are struggling. They're deliberately undermining them."[44]

Union activists raised the issue that the school closings, and the opening of charter schools, happened predominately in black and Latino neighborhoods; 88 percent of students affected by school closings or turnarounds between 2001 and 2012 were African American.[45] "You don't see charter schools in the affluent suburbs," said one teacher. "They won't allow that. So why are we testing our kids with the charter schools, our inner city kids who are so vulnerable. Why are we guinea pigging our students who are more at risk?"[46] And teachers argued that CPS seemed impervious to the fact that closing neighborhood schools meant that children in many neighborhoods had to walk through dangerous gang territory to go to school. At board hearings on school closings, teachers and parents repeatedly made this point but were ignored. At a 2008 hearing a teacher explained, "In your CPS maps you do not see all the gang signs and all the gang boundaries that our kids are going to have to walk through. Our kids are going to be walking through very, very dangerous areas just to be able to get to the new school."[47]

Educators were angry that, as *Chicago Reader* investigative journalist Ben Joravsky noted in 2011, "it's virtually impossible to determine how the charters spend the roughly $300 million in public funds they get each year. None of their budgets or payrolls are on the Internet for public view, and it's not clear how—or if—the city or Chicago Public Schools tracks the way charters spend tax dollars."[48] CTU educators took issue with the fact that wealthy investors and hedge fund managers were investing heavily in charters, and that they saw public education and teachers unions as deterrents to turning education into a for-profit business.

CTU members were also angry that most charters abused their employees. A primary reason politicians and billionaire-funded education reform groups pushed for more charter schools was that most charters were nonunion and their teachers had no rights. If Chicago charter teachers were members of the CTU or the charter school teachers union, teachers believed, elite support for charter expansion would sharply diminish. While CTU members were angry at charter schools, their anger was not directed at charter school teachers and staff. In fact, in 2011 the CTU loaned an organizer on its staff to the Chicago Alliance of Charter Teachers and Staff (ACTS), a sister union in the American Federation of Teachers.[49]

At many Chicago charter schools, educators faced the same problems that neighborhood public school teachers faced. "My charter school and most of the ones I have seen," Monty Adams said, "don't have libraries, science labs, all the textbooks."[50] "The head of my school says teachers don't need textbooks to teach students, that they're too expensive," said Rob Heise, "so we make a lot of copies." At UNO charter schools, where Heise teaches, "the elementary schools have 32 kids in every class; I have 174 students I teach every day. To charter operators it's a straight numbers game—'how can we bring in more money?'" Heise concluded, "Charters create teaching conditions that are unlivable for teachers. I just don't know how you can do this job and have a life and a family."[51]

Pay was significantly lower at charter schools. At Noble Charter's eleven Chicago schools in 2012, for example, the lowest paid teacher earned just $28,494—a little over half of a new CTU teacher's salary—and the average salary of $56,154 a year was far below that of CPS teachers. In 2012, the Illinois Network of Charter Schools reported an average teacher salary of $51,000 in all Chicago charters.[52] Charters often linked pay to test scores. According to a Noble Charter teacher, "There is a lot of individual pressure by the teachers since it's tied to pay, which I think makes a significant difference in the mentality for the teachers. I must teach these kids how to do X, Y and Z or else I won't get my bonus. It's a much more corporate style atmosphere in general."[53]

As a result of poor treatment and pay, charter school administrators expected a constant churning of teachers. Three-quarters of Chicago charter teachers had less than six years' experience, and 40 percent had three years on the job or less—while Chicago public school teachers averaged fourteen years' experience.[54] *Catalyst Chicago* reported an average 50 percent turnover at charters from 2008 to 2010.[55] "There is superhigh turnover in charter schools," said Heise. "Last year we lost almost 40 percent of our staff at my school. Our most senior teachers have been there six years; ten out of forty-eight staff at my school have worked there five or six years. Charters are also heavily reliant on Teach for America instructors [new college graduates who temporarily try teaching before moving on to other careers] and those teachers don't stay."[56] "I've heard charter teachers talk about what they call the 'suicide option,'" said Chris Baehrend, an English teacher at the Chicago charter school Latino Youth High School and vice president of the Chicago ACTS union. "You work for a charter for two years, then get a job teaching for the Chicago Public Schools, where they set your pay and seniority as if you're a third-year CPS teacher."[57]

Turnover was high because unionized neighborhood CPS schools paid more; those teachers also received raises based on years of experience and the number of university classes they took[58]; charter teachers had no voice over their working conditions; and charter managers were rarely education experts and were often seen by teachers as tyrannical and incompetent. Indeed, charter companies often called them "directors" instead of "principals." "Charter schools are public schools," said Baehrend, "funded by public money. The problem is having a private business run it. That turns public schools into businesses. Running a business has its own considerations which can be at loggerheads with the interests of students." A business can choose higher administrator pay over students. A business can take a huge percentage of taxpayer dollars and assign those funds to the administration. A business can choose to expand the business rather than use funds to meet the needs of its existing students. As a UNO charter school teacher told *Chicago* magazine, "We were told it is not a school; it is a business, and the children are your customers."[59]

Since most charter school educators were nonunion, they had no ability to resist unfair administration decisions. Nonunion charter teachers were employees with no due process, no seniority rights, and no right to advocate for their students when they saw charter administrators doing bad things. Teachers waited every May or June for a letter from the charter operator telling them whether they would still have a teaching position in the fall. As stated by the UNO employment contract, before the staff unionized, an employee could be fired "at any time for any legal reason or for no reason, with or without prior notice."[60] Baehrend noted that "at non-union charters, teachers are at-will employees, wildly afraid for their jobs, afraid to speak up for students, so there's huge teacher turnover. That is destabilizing for children, especially for children who already live in destabilizing environments."[61]

One of the most scandalous cases of CPS abuse of a charter school teacher was the firing of Meg Sullivan. A teacher at the Early College High School (AEC) operated by the ASPIRA charter chain, Sullivan was so distressed by what she witnessed at the school that she became a notorious whistle-blower. In 2008, after her concerns were repeatedly rebuffed by school administrators, she wrote a letter to Josh Edelman, director of the CPS Office of New Schools (the department overseeing charter schools). Nothing happened.

Sullivan's letter outlined flagrant examples of how ASPIRA was violating CPS policies and harming children, including strip-searching two female students, changing grades indiscriminately to make it appear that fewer students were failing, falsifying student attendance records, and ignoring student misconduct reports. Sullivan also used the letter to pull away the facade that charter schools were incubators for teacher development and student growth. "Taking young teachers without a safety net of a union or robust employment opportunities, denying them any support such as special ed., ELL (English Language Learners) or a coherent discipline policy, denying them resources such as books and basic supplies, miring them in a blatantly hostile working environment, and watching them put their heart and soul into teaching freshmen while challenging those who impeded their students' rights was downright amazing."[62] Five days after Sullivan wrote the letter she was fired. She subsequently went before a Chicago Board of Education meeting, an event that finally triggered an investigation. Sullivan told the *Chicago Sun-Times*, "If I wasn't willing to risk my job, nothing would have happened."[63] Her accusations were supported by other ASPIRA teachers, and she sued CPS for retaliatory discharge. She ultimately reached an out-of-court settlement with the school district.[64]

Additionally, charter administrators in Chicago, with the support of CPS administrators who fund the charters, use every means, illegal and legal, to prevent their employees from exercising their democratic right to form a union. "At Chicago Math and Science Academy," wrote Brian Harris, ACTS union president, "a teacher who went to deliver the news that the teachers had unionized was fired on the spot (she was eight months pregnant). At Youth Connections Leadership Academy, every teacher was fired within 36 hours of their unanimous decision to join Chicago ACTS. At other charter schools, union leaders have been intimidated, threatened, and harassed. Most often, teachers have had to face years of legal challenges despite obvious majority support for a union (and let's not forget those legal challenges are funded by public education dollars)."[65]

CTU President Marilyn Stewart

Meanwhile, amid CTU members' growing resentment and despondency over school closings, poor teaching conditions, the rush to open charters, and CPS policies, educators grew increasingly disenchanted with union president Marilyn Stewart. The bulk of the members felt that none of their concerns mattered to Stewart.

The United Progressive Caucus (UPC) led the CTU from 1972 to 2001. The CTU had been a militant union in the 1970s and 1980s, going on strike five times in eight years in the 1980s alone, to radically improve teachers' pay and working conditions. Jackie Vaughn, the CTU president from 1984 to 1994, was revered by the membership for her courage and combativeness.[66] She was the first African American and first woman to head the CTU.[67] The *Chicago Tribune*—no friend during Vaughn's life—said upon her death that "her unyielding tenacity drew cult-like adoration from union members." But under Vaughn's successors, Tom Reece (1994–2001) and Marilyn Stewart (2004–10), the union morphed into a top-down, bureaucratic organization with no trace of militancy. The UPC under Reece and Stewart represented the philosophy of *business unionism*: that union leaders should run the union with little or no member involvement, having as goals merely the bargaining and defending of a contract for its members, and with little or no outreach to the public or alliances with community groups.

Reformer Deborah Lynch and her PACT caucus won the CTU presidency in 2001, but, as discussed in chapter 2, in 2003 she brought back a concessionary contract that the members voted down. She went back to the bargaining table, and the members approved a revised contract, but there was deep frustration that she had exaggerated gains in the contract, boasting how great it was when it contained concessions in health care and other areas. Lynch lost a close election to Marilyn Stewart and her UPC slate in 2004. Lynch ran again in 2007 but lost badly to Stewart.[68]

By 2009, there was a widespread sense among CTU members that Stewart had no strategy to respond to the growing attacks on teachers. "I remember seeing Marilyn Stewart being interviewed on TV about school closings," recalled one teacher. "The reporter asked her, 'what do you propose?' and she answered 'no comment.' And she just kept saying 'no comment,' 'no comment,' 'no comment.' I had no idea what the leadership was doing. They didn't seem to have a coherent message and they weren't well-spoken."[69] Added another teacher, "When Marilyn Stewart would speak at House of Delegates meetings she would go like a pinball machine. The pinball would go here, then it would go there, and then here—and she'd talk for like forty minutes and just keep ping, ping, pinging all over the place. She'd be done and I didn't learn anything."[70] Delegates used descriptions like "constant arguing," "bickering," "fiasco," and "chaos" to characterize the monthly House of Delegates meetings under Marilyn Stewart. Microphones would be shut off so people could not ask questions. Nothing was getting accomplished. Many delegates gave up attending, or quit being delegates, in disgust.[71]

Under Marilyn Stewart's presidency, delegate conferences were perks given to her supporters rather than true educational and organizing events. "You'd get a room for the night on the union's dime at the Holiday Inn," recalled teacher Jackson Potter. "You'd go into a big room and have a fancy dinner, you'd have a keynote address by the president, and then you get top shelf liquor at an open bar. The following morning you'd go through this litany of trainings that essentially amounted to the field staff walking through the banal points of the contract. So you'd see plenty of people disappear or leave early. People found those trainings to be boring and a waste of their time."[72]

Under Stewart the union was not taking any action on school closings. The union had no outreach to the community or alliances with neighborhood groups. "It was actually worse than just no response," said Jackson Potter, "because the union was collaborating with management to allow these types of 'reforms' that were just devastating our ranks."[73] Stewart rarely called union actions, but when she did they were ineffectual. She ordered her staff to attend and sent an e-mail to the membership. In 2008 Stewart called a rally against the city's school closings, and a hundred members showed up. Stewart denounced the members' apathy. But, recalls Jackson Potter, "it was a Field of Dreams approach—you build it and they will come. You declare it is important, and it will be important. But the reality was that members had a nagging suspicion that the leadership did not have an effective strategy" to fight school closings. "Rather than trying to get to that root cause that was depressing turnout, rather than engaging members in a legitimate, honest way, they swept it under the rug and ignored it."[74]

The Caucus of Rank and File Educators

In response to members' anger at school board policies and their frustration with Stewart's inept leadership, a group of activists came together to try to push their union to change. CORE began in 2007 as a study group initiated by Jackson Potter, who, along with half a dozen educators including Jesse Sharkey, Norine Gutekanst, and Karen Lewis, would, in June 2010, take over the reins of running the union. Karen Lewis recalled, "We were concerned about the massive effort to close schools, to turn them into charters, basically giving away public institutions to private organizations. So we got together, teachers and a couple of paraprofessionals, to try to figure out what was going on. We started reading articles, but the big book that we read was *The Shock Doctrine* by Naomi Klein. It put so much in perspective."[75] The group also read books and articles, such as those by Professor Pauline Lipman at the University of Illinois at Chicago, critiquing the corporate education reformers' attacks on public education and teachers.[76] Jackson Potter, Jesse Sharkey, and other CORE founders tried to push the union to challenge closings of their own schools, without results.

In 2008, these educators turned their study group into the Caucus of Rank and File Educators—a proud name for a group with big dreams but only a handful of members. In December 2008, CORE members started going to Board of Education hearings on school closings to ask questions and to testify against closing schools and in favor of fully funding them. CORE members never missed a board meeting or school closing hearing, and they worked tirelessly to get parents and community leaders to join them.[77]

What is most important to understand about CORE is that the way its members organized themselves between 2008 and 2010, the program they arrived at, and the strategy they chose were all exported to the union as a whole when CORE won the election in June 2010. The foundation of the CTU's success in the 2012 strike lay in CORE's origins.

Most union caucuses are a slate of candidates led by a charismatic presidential contender, organized a few months before a union election. But the CTU members who formed CORE—two years before the next union election—were not focused on union office. The group formed because the leadership was not acting to challenge school closings, and because there was a deep level of anger among educators about their teaching conditions and their students' learning environment. CORE's purpose was to try to spark a social movement—to work with parents, parent groups, and neighborhood groups to challenge school board policies. "Our goal was really to push the existing leadership in the right direction," said Jen Johnson, who had been in the study group. "It was not our expressed intent to take over leadership of the Chicago Teachers Union when we founded CORE. We had community forums. We reached out to community organizations and we really just tried to build a framework for increasing rank-and-file participation and community participation in important fights in education."[78]

CORE's strategy was constantly to bring up at House of Delegates meetings the actions CORE was taking, and to push the union leadership to mobilize the members to join the fight. It was not a strategy of ignoring the union because the leadership was failing to act or of waiting for the union to act; rather, it was a strategy of doing the things the union should have been doing and pressuring the union's leaders to participate. "For two years we were a shadow union," said Karen Lewis.[79]

CORE activists met and learned from community activists who had experience protesting school closings, and built strong relationships that would serve them well during the 2012 strike. CORE worked with the Kenwood Oakland Community Organization (KOCO) based in the near South Side black community, the Pilsen Alliance based in a Near Southwest Side Latino community, Blocks Together based in the Humboldt Park Latino neighborhood, Teachers for Social Justice, the Grassroots Collaborative, and Action Now. After the June 2010 election all these groups would form the core of the CTU's Community Board, and building those ties to parents and the community in turn made CORE more attractive to teachers. In June 2008, CORE invited Canadian teachers union leader Jinny Sims to speak to a hundred educators about how teachers won an illegal 2005 strike by educating and organizing teachers and building strong parent and community relationships; her union's successful experience resonated with CORE members' own perspectives on how to organize.

CORE's outreach to the community was not a public relations effort, and it went far beyond just mentioning the importance of the community in speeches. Rather, it was a sincere long-term effort to build a coalition with community groups around shared goals and against common adversaries. "Nobody was in favor of the school closings, but groups were fragmented" when CORE began to organize, recalled teacher Xian Barrett. "We built a movement that started out as pushback versus school closings but turned into a rich conversation about what good, equitable education is. The key was to start by listening, rather than talking about what we want. We built relationships by listening. It is very important that we focus not only on what is wrong with corporate reform and school closures, but also on the positive side—what do parents and kids want out of their schools."[80]

The group held a two-day retreat in summer 2008. They asked themselves, said Karen Lewis, "If we could dream it, what would we want our union to look like? What would we want our union to offer? What would we want it to do?"[81] Part of the discussion was that CORE did not want to emulate the strategy of the PACT caucus, whose leader, Deborah Lynch, served as CTU president from 2001 to 2004. While Lynch and her caucus—in which several CORE activists had participated— had a progressive stance, PACT was formed as an electoral caucus. It did not seek to educate, organize, and mobilize members and parents to challenge CPS policy in the streets or to develop members into activists and leaders. And, once elected, Lynch ran the union in a top-down, reform-from-above manner.

CORE also developed a critique of how most unions relate to politics. The activists embraced the idea that politics was defined too narrowly by most union officials to mean only campaigning for candidates and lobbying elected officials, as opposed to daily citizen involvement in building social movements to pressure officials to do the right thing for working people. Several of the groups' founders were socialists with an established critique of the Democratic Party. Part of that critique was directed at a Democratic president who chose as his Secretary of Education the former CPS chief, Arne Duncan, who had sought to underfund and close neighborhood schools in Chicago while opening antiunion charter schools. Karen Lewis explained CORE's position on politics:

> It all comes down to how you teach people to fight with the tools they have. We have been fighting with the bosses' tools. We can spend a lot of time doing legislation. I think that's fine—have a legislative approach. But understand that you don't control that process. We can talk about electing the right people, but ultimately, unless we have a state house full of teachers, paraprofessionals, and clinicians, I don't think we'll get what we want out of state legislatures. You need to have good relationships with legislators; you need to have members get in touch and let them know what's important to you. That's one tool. But it's not the only tool. Our best tool is our ability to put people in the street. The tool that we have is a mass movement. We have the pressure of mass mobilization and organizing.[82]

As CORE grew, it continued to hold study groups and educational conferences. "I was part of another caucus, but then I joined a CORE study group," said one teacher, because "I was fascinated by the idea that I needed to study this, I needed to understand this. [CORE members said,] 'Let's get together and talk about what is a union, what's the purpose of a union, why is it that we're doing this, what is the law behind education, the idea of education, and the relationship of the union to the board and the mayor.'"[83]

When Karen Lewis and the CORE slate were elected to run the CTU in June 2010, their mantra was that CTU must be transformed into a member-driven, truly democratic union. That philosophy had its origins in how CORE functioned from its beginnings as a small group. "The union is pretty much modeled after CORE and CORE's democratic" process, recalled an early activist.[84] "The way other organizations are run," recalled Lewis, "there is somebody at the top. They make decisions and they tell their caucus what they're going to do. The difference with CORE is we really looked at a rank-and-file model. Anything that comes up, we discuss it, we debate it, we have good vigorous conversations, and then we vote on what to do. Then we task things out. It isn't like a lot of meetings that end up being a lecture from the leadership to the membership."[85]

CORE set about training members to become activists and training activists to be leaders. "We ended up building quite an activist base," recalled Jen Johnson. "People became leaders that didn't see themselves as leaders. I would consider myself one of those people. When people keep asking you to do something, you start to feel like you have to step up and you can't say no. And I think we just really grew that, person by person."[86] From its inception, CORE members created a culture of mutual support and camaraderie and often held social events to grow their membership and build friendships.

CORE steadily grew while its reputation as an organization of committed union activists spread in the union and in the community. In school after school, CORE activists held conversations with union members about the need to organize a fight back against school closings and the privatization of the CPS system through charters. "We met all the time," recalled Jen Johnson. "There were weeks we had three meetings after work just to talk about the next action. So it was just constant activity. I haven't been a part of something ever in my life [in which] the people have been so dedicated and hardworking. It's a calendar full of CORE. It's the way we built this organization."[87]

In 2009, after packing school board meetings and organizing demonstrations and press conferences, CORE achieved its first partial victory when six schools were taken off the initial list of thirty CPS wanted to close. The caucus and community groups, calling themselves the Grassroots Education Movement, mobilized a thousand people to protest. "The CTU finally joined the protest and then released a flyer to delegates saying they organized it," said CORE activist Kenzo Shibata. "Either way, we got them out, and won a big victory."[88] In 2010, CORE had six more schools removed from the list of sixteen CPS wanted to close.

A turning point came in January 2009 when CORE turned out—in the midst of a Chicago blizzard—five hundred parents, teachers, and community leaders from eighty-one schools to a conference at Malcolm X College to educate themselves and strategize against school closings. "That's when the union's leaders began to take us seriously," recalled Potter. "They were sitting around being smug until they saw how many people were showing up. It was an amazing experience. Teachers started listening to the message and they started coming to our meetings, asking questions and watching how we worked. Once they knew how we were approaching things and saw how inclusive we were, they just started joining, so our membership grew." That's when CORE members knew, said Jen Johnson, "when five hundred people showed up in the middle of a blizzard, that we were tapping into something real."[89]

Karen Lewis

By fall 2009, CORE had decided that pressuring the union to take action would not work. It was necessary to challenge the UPC slate for leadership of the union in the May 2010 election. The odds looked good. In addition to the deep discontent with CTU President Marilyn Stewart, the UPC was in disarray. Stewart had broken with two of her top officers. CTU Treasurer Linda Porter announced she was running for president with her new Caucus for a Strong Democratic Union (CSDU) slate; she had the support of former CTU Vice President Ted Dallas. CTU Field Staff Representative Ted Hajiharis put together a fourth slate with the new School Employee Alliance (SEA) caucus. A fifth slate was led by Deborah Lynch and her PACT caucus.

In January 2010, CORE members nominated Karen Lewis as their candidate for CTU president, Jesse Sharkey for vice president, Kristine Mayle for financial secretary, and Michael Brunson for recording secretary. Jackson Potter was first slated for the vice presidency, but CPS challenged his eligibility due to a leave of absence, and he decided not to protest the unfair decision.[90] As noted, CORE was not founded as an electoral slate, and it was a truly democratic organization where one leader did not dominate decisions. Nevertheless, any caucus's choice of a presidential candidate is an important one. People vote for the top candidate on a slate. The media focuses on that candidate. And even in the most democratic unions the president wields far more power and carries much more authority than any other officer or staff member. So the selection of Lewis to lead the slate was a critical one.

Karen Lewis was born to two Chicago public school teachers in the Kenwood/Hyde Park South Side Chicago neighborhood and went to Kenwood Academy High School in the tumultuous 1960s as the Vietnam War and the antiwar movement were raging. Martin Luther King Jr. was assassinated when Lewis was fourteen; when she was sixteen, Black Panther leader Fred Hampton was assassinated by Chicago police in his home. Lewis participated in civil rights walkouts by high school students, and conversations around the dinner table were frequently about social justice.

"My parents never placed limitations on me," said Lewis. "As far as they were concerned, I could be the president of the United States."[91] She first went to the progressive, all-women Mount Holyoke College in Massachusetts, then transferred in 1972 to Dartmouth College shortly after it began to admit women, graduating in 1974 with a degree in sociology and music. But she hated her experience there, because the male students opposed the Trustees' decision to open up the school to women, and she was the sole African-American female student. After some travel, she entered medical school but soon determined it was not for her. She had resisted following her parents' career path, but fell "madly, passionately in love with teaching" chemistry and soon became a high school chemistry teacher.[92]

Prominent people can get pigeonholed by the career they are known for, but Karen Lewis defies narrow definition. She is a gourmet cook, an opera fan, plays the piano and the flute, tried her hand at stand-up comedy, and is fluent in Italian and French. To improve her teaching skills, she took film classes at Columbia College in Chicago. Even her opponents in the mayor's office have praised her as a Renaissance woman. Lewis converted to Judaism twenty years ago and is active in her temple. "I was looking for something spiritual, and something in it just spoke to me," she said.[93]

In 1988, she got a teaching job at Lane Tech College Prep High School, a selective enrollment school on Chicago's North Side. She loved teaching chemistry at Lane, but, she recalled, "my work as a CTU delegate brought me into deep conflict with the principal, who I felt was a bully, unethical, and hypocritical. While he was never able to retaliate against me, he went after my closest friends and colleagues. My sense of fair play and defense of fellow union members had taken its toll." She took a job at a predominately African American South Side high school, Dr. Martin Luther King Jr. College Preparatory High School.[94]

She served as a delegate and was a leader of the PACT caucus. When Deborah Lynch lost to Marilyn Stewart in the 2004 union election, Lewis was nevertheless elected to the union's large executive board. "My time there was, to say the least, depressing," recalled Lewis. "PACT members were isolated and not allowed to participate in real union governance. The union's executive board meetings were dry-run rehearsals for carrying out the UPC leadership's will at forthcoming House of Delegate meetings and were a complete waste of time. There was no strategy for moving the union forward or for fighting against closing schools and opening charters."[95]

"I thought I was done with the union," said Lewis. "I was disappointed that neither the old guard UPC nor the supposed reformers in PACT were able to clearly articulate the nature of corporate school reform and build resistance among the membership. I had planned to retire in 2008, but my transfer to King made teaching joyous again, so I decided to postpone the decision."[96] Then teacher Debby Pope invited Lewis to a meeting, in April 2008, to talk about the future of the union with a dozen activists, which launched the fifty-two-year-old Lewis into renewed activism and the leadership of CORE.

By the time of the May 2010 election, CORE had grown to nearly four hundred members. They drew upon the relationships and organizing experience they had gained while building a movement to challenge school closings; they now directed their energy to running an election campaign in nearly six hundred schools. They flyered every school, developed a huge e-mail list, and talked to many hundreds of teachers and staff.[97] In the May 21 election, CORE came in a close second in a five-way race. Marilyn Stewart and her UPC slate won 35.6 percent of the vote, and Karen Lewis and her CORE slate won 32.9 percent, ensuring a runoff vote a month later.

Four days after the election, CORE was able to turn out 5,000 educators and supporters for a march downtown, the largest CTU action in more than twenty years. Acting on CORE's motion, the House of Delegates endorsed the march as an official union protest. The "Save Our Schools" action demanded that CPS not increase class sizes, fully fund schools, and stop school closures. CORE activist Nate Goldbaum wrote in *Substance News* that he "came away from the protest exhilarated . . . by a sense of power and unity one could scarcely guess had lain dormant in this union of 30,000 educators." The success of the action further demonstrated to CTU members that CORE was capable of transforming the union into the leader of a social movement fighting to defend and fully fund public education.[98]

In early June, as CORE activists again spread out across the city to campaign, they knew they could beat Stewart in a runoff because the other three opposition slates, which together with CORE took nearly 65 percent of the vote in the first round, endorsed CORE in the runoff. On June 11, CORE decisively beat the UPC with 59 percent of the vote, winning about 12,000 out of 20,400 votes cast.[99]

At the caucus's victory celebration on election night, president-elect Karen Lewis declared: "CORE's success is [that] we are a big-tent, grass-roots group led democratically from the bottom up. That was why CORE began in the first place—to activate and energize all members in running the union. It also turned out to be a winning campaign strategy."[100] As Jackson Potter, who would be the union's new staff coordinator, said, "Our message isn't that we're going to fight for you, but with you. . . . We've broken apart this mantra of reform that charter schools and firing so-called bad teachers is the solution to our education woes. I think this whole thing is coming off the rails, and this [election result] is a sign of that."[101]

CORE won, said high school teacher Bill Lamme, because "when the election came they didn't say 'Elect me and I'll do this.' They said, 'This is what we've been doing and we'll keep doing it.'"[102] According to another teacher, CORE won "because they had gained the members' respect. Five years ago, there wasn't a base in the union for a fight back, and there wasn't a base in the community for a fight back, but through CORE's work that base was built up. CORE went to the school-closing hearings, they went to the Board of Education meetings, they organized rallies, and they went to the schools that were closing."[103]

Lewis delivered a powerful indictment of the state of Chicago public schools and the legacy of administration "reform" efforts at her June 12, 2010, victory press conference:

> Today marks the beginning of the end of scapegoating educators for the social ills that all of our children, families, and schools struggle against every day. Today marks the beginning of a fight for true transparency in our education policy—how to accurately measure teaching and learning, and how to *truly* improve our schools and how to evaluate the wisdom behind our spending priorities. This election shows the unity of *30,000* educators standing strong to put business in its place— *out* of our schools. Corporate America sees K–12 public education as a $380 billion trust that, up until the last 15 years, they haven't had a sizable piece of it. So this so-called 'school reform' is not an education plan. It's a business plan, and mayoral control of our schools and our Board of Education is the linchpin of their operation.
>
> Fifteen years ago, this city purposely began starving our lowest-income neighborhood schools of greatly needed resources and personnel. Class sizes rose and schools were closed. Then standardized tests, which in this town alone [are] a $60 million business, measured that slow death by starvation. These tests labeled our students, families, and educators failures, because standardized tests reveal more about a student's zip code than [they do] about academic growth. And that, in turn—that *perceived* school failure—fed parent demand for charters,

turnarounds, and contract schools. People thought, "it must be true, I read it in the papers. It must be the teachers' fault." Because they read about it, every single week. And our union, which has been controlled by the same faction for about 40 years—37 out of 40—didn't point out this simple reality: What drives school reform is a singular focus on profit. Profit. Not teaching, not learning—profit.[104]

A New Mayor

The new CTU officers took office on July 1 but had only a few months to get settled when a political earthquake hit the city. On September 7, 2010, Richard M. Daley, mayor of Chicago for twenty-two years, surprised the city by announcing he would not run again. Rahm Emanuel defeated five candidates in the February 21, 2011, election, avoiding a runoff contest by taking 55 percent of the 575,000 votes cast.

A former three-term Chicago congressman and endorsed by both major local newspapers, Emanuel won in his former district, the wealthy North Shore, and drew the majority of the black vote due to the blessing bestowed by the country's first black president on his former White House chief of staff.[105] Due to his connections with the wealthy—he had been paid $18 million in two years as a Chicago investment banker, and his brother Ari had many affluent connections in Hollywood due to his work as a successful agent—Emanuel raised $13 million from mostly rich donors, far exceeding the combined spending of the other candidates. During the campaign he came across as smart, accomplished, and zealous to be the city's mayor.[106]

But the new CTU leadership had no such illusions. There was a reason that only one large union, the Teamsters Joint Council 25, had endorsed Emanuel's candidacy.[107] The old idiom "Hope for the best, expect the worst" characterized the CTU leaders' attitude toward the new Emanuel administration. Emanuel was known as a corporate Democrat—someone who endorsed the party's stances on racial and gender justice but was attentive to corporate interests and wanted to distance the party from its long-standing alliance with labor unions. As an adviser in the Clinton White House, Emanuel had pushed the president to gut welfare, embrace the North American Free Trade Agreement (NAFTA), and escalate trade with and the export of US manufacturing jobs to China through that country's admission to the World Trade Organization (WTO). In the Obama administration, he advocated that Wall Street banks receive the bulk of the federal bailout during the ongoing financial crisis, instead of home owners whose mortgages had ended up being higher than the depressed worth of their homes.

When the United Auto Workers (UAW) objected to huge wage cuts Washington demanded in exchange for rescuing Chrysler and General Motors from imminent bankruptcy, Emanuel famously declared "Fuck the UAW."

On December 13, roughly one month after announcing his candidacy, Emanuel delivered a major policy address on education that made it clear that he intended to wage war on the teachers and their union. Some parts of the speech sent cold shivers down the spines of the CTU leadership. Beginning with proudly taking credit for working "closely with Education Secretary Arne Duncan to implement the Race to the Top program," he acknowledged, "It's a program I'd like to replicate right here in Chicago. . . . The next mayor must lead an era of reform here at home." He advocated charter schools and called for a new teacher evaluation system. Without using the phrase *merit pay*, he advocated that teachers receive bonuses based on student performance. He claimed that Chicago had the shortest instructional hours of any big city in the country—which was not true—and blamed the CTU contract.[108]

CTU leaders knew Emanuel had a reputation as a bully. "The caricature of Rahm Emanuel," said the *New York Times* in 2009 about the then chief of staff to the president, is a "profanity-spewing operative with a keen understanding of how to employ power. . . . He believed the more someone used power, the more power that person had."[109] Journalist Kari Lydersen, who authored a book on Emanuel, added that "Chicagoans are used to profanity, but he shows profound impatience and even contempt for regular people and very little desire to listen to and learn from them."[110]

Once in office on May 15, 2011, Emanuel appointed as CPS head Jean-Claude Brizard. Brizard had been a teacher and administrator in the New York school system for many years, then, in 2008, the superintendent of the Rochester City School District. But although the new mayor had found someone with education experience to run Chicago's schools, the choice was the equivalent of a slap in the union's face. In New York Brizard had promoted charter schools and merit pay and had so infuriated the teachers union that it overwhelmingly gave him a vote of no confidence two months before he left for Chicago.[111]

In Chicago, the mayor could appoint the entire school board—the only board of education in the entire state that was not elected. The mayor appointed David Vitale to serve as school board president. Vitale came from the financial district—he had been CEO of the Chicago Board of Trade and vice chairman and director of Bank One Corporation—and had served as CPS chief administrative officer under Arne Duncan. Among the many wealthy individuals that were handpicked for the school board with an eye to future unanimous votes in support of Emanuel's policies was an heir to the Hyatt Hotels Corporation, billionaire businesswoman Penny Pritzker, whose family business was decidedly antiunion.

As CTU leaders surveyed the lineup of school district decision-makers who would have an authoritative hand in shaping the working lives of Chicago educators, they feared that their most alarming expectations had come true. To make matters worse, the mayor, school system, and Board of Education would have powerful legislative hammers to swing. The first blow would be aimed at teacher evaluations.

4

EVALUATING TEACHERS AND POLITICAL OPPORTUNISM

Emanuel's idea for raising performance standards for Chicago teachers and principals was not novel. It was quietly hatched six years before his election, over a number of Saturdays in 2005, by a group of business, education, and political leaders who met to discuss a plan for the state's education system. Referring to themselves as the Education Policy Dialogue Group, and invoking the visionary elements of Chicago's legendary landscape architect Daniel Burnham, the group produced a report they called *The Burnham Plan for a World-Class Education: Reforming School Quality and Accountability in Illinois*. Along with a three-billion-dollar price tag for improving schools, the plan proposed a "better system to determine teacher and principal effectiveness."[1] Under the subheading "Removal or Dismissal of Teachers," the plan "streamlines the tenured teacher dismissal process."[2] The plan also advocated increasing the number of charter schools permitted in Illinois.

Four years later, with federal stimulus money provided to the states and the grant application for Race to the Top heating up, the authors of the plan released a set of policy recommendations under the heading "Burnham 2.0—Plan for Education." Included among the authors of the original and follow-up plans were Robin Steans, director of Advance Illinois, a group focused on educational performance, CPS CEO Ron Huberman, the presidents of the IEA and Illinois Federation of Teachers (IFT), and Jim Franczek. Just as a good deal of Burnham's design for Chicago landscape actually came to be built, much of the education plan that borrowed his name was also implemented. Controversy met some of the architect's plans in 1909, and, similarly, one hundred years later, everything adopted from the education plan triggered fierce condemnation and resistance from the CORE-led CTU. Two major sources of tension were the report's call for a new teacher evaluation system based on student academic performance and its call for the expansion of charter schools.

Despite their opposition and decades of successful policy-making, on this occasion the state teachers unions lacked the political power to defeat a law ripe for misuse. Despite the unions' heavy financial contributions to Democratic and Republican legislators, three conditions reduced the union's lobbying influence. First, Obama's Race to the Top offered school districts badly needed funding and provided an incentive for state leaders to comply with the requirement to tie student testing outcomes to teacher job security to win federal grants. Second, the national trend of using standardized student scores to evaluate teachers was too strong for the unions to block implementation in Illinois. Finally, public-sector unions decided to conduct electoral politics independently of the conventional state Democratic Party leadership, which created a legislative opportunity to seriously threaten the professional standing of education employees. Unable to prevent changes to teacher evaluation systems, the IFT and IEA sought to influence the shape policy would take by participating in talks to write a new teacher evaluation law. But unlike the state-wide teacher organizations, CTU, under Marilyn Stewart, largely abstained from the bill writing and legislative process.

The Performance Evaluation Reform Act

In 2010, the Performance Evaluation Reform Act, commonly known as PERA, passed nearly unanimously in both the state House and Senate. It required all Illinois school districts by September 1, 2016, to design and implement performance evaluation systems to assess teachers' and principals' professional skills. Chicago was expected to have its plan in place for roughly half of its schools by 2012 and the remaining half the following year. The IFT and the IEA embraced the idea of improving notoriously subjective and unhelpful teaching evaluations. Though the purpose of the law was laudable, PERA did something deeply questionable, similar to what was being done in school districts across the country.

PERA mandated that teacher evaluations incorporate measures of student growth. At least three dozen other states had adopted similar evaluation systems in response to Race to the Top federal grants. Most likely, standardized test results would be used to determine in part the "value" a single teacher added to the cognitive development of an individual student. According to PERA, in the first two years that an Illinois teacher was evaluated, a minimum of 25 percent of his or her rating would be based on student test scores. The student achievement measure would grow to at least 30 percent of the total rating over time. The weight of the student growth factor could be negotiated between the teachers union and school district, but, if no agreement was reached, the employer was authorized to implement its final offer.

In addition to the student achievement element, PERA also reclassified and standardized the categories of teaching proficiency. Prior to the new law, school districts were not required to use a specific rating system for non-tenured teachers or a distinct rubric to evaluate the professional practice of teachers. Beginning with the 2012 school year, teachers would be judged "excellent," "proficient," "needs improvement," or "unsatisfactory." Teachers who were given two "unsatisfactory" ratings during a seven-year period were subject to termination. Any teacher with consecutive "excellent" reviews could be fast-tracked to earn tenure within three years instead of four. Contrary to past practice, nontenured teachers would henceforth have to be evaluated every year. It was commonly acknowledged that although evaluations for nontenured teachers were required, in some past cases they were not done. Tenured teachers would be evaluated every other year, unless they earned an "unsatisfactory" rating. In discussing a revised statewide evaluation regime, teachers union representatives agreed that the existing system was flawed. Teachers thought very little of how they were evaluated, and the reviews rarely offered any constructive guide for professional improvement.

Despite the broadly disliked evaluation process, it was not the dissatisfaction itself that produced change. The motivation for PERA was Obama's Race to the Top incentive or, more precisely, the millions of dollars dangled in front of states, like Illinois, suffering shrinking budgets. The 2008 recession had caused state tax revenues to plummet. Congress did pass a stimulus program that allocated funds to the states to retain public employees like teachers, but by fiscal year 2010 the money would be completely disbursed. School districts would then either have to raise local property taxes in a stagnant economy or lay off teachers. In many school districts the latter had never been done. To the teachers that made up the CORE caucus, this scenario was the consequence of the banking industry's crashing the economy and handing policy-makers a justification for undoing public education. It was the "shock doctrine" described by Naomi Klein applied to the $800 billion education industry in order to manufacture a crisis.[3]

To the state's education officials, Obama's educational pot of gold represented a lifeline. Unlike federal education support that had always flowed to the states on the basis of need, Race to the Top required states to compete for grants awarded by the Department of Education. Illinois initially thought highly of its chances. The president was a Chicago native, and Education Secretary Arne Duncan had very recently headed CPS. While Illinois appeared to have advantages in the contest for money, as Darren Reisberg recalled, the state also had "areas of vulnerability."[4]

Since 2005, Reisberg had worked for the Illinois State Board of Education (ISBE) as deputy superintendent of education and general counsel. In the summer and fall of 2009, he was tasked with chairing a group to develop a new state education law so that it would meet the criteria for winning up to $400 million in Race to the Top grants. The group was initially made up of school management representatives (e.g., the Association of School Boards and Association of School Administrations), the IEA, and Advance Illinois. According to Reisberg, "the state board became a locus to broker deals on education policy." He added that ISBE "had never been used that way before," but that it had "relationships with union, school management, and education reform groups." Under Reisberg's facilitation, all the appropriate stakeholders would be "around the table" ensuring that no one entity would "hijack the operations." While the IEA was involved in the process from the beginning, the IFT would eventually join the talks. The CTU, Reisberg pointed out, "was nowhere on scene."[5] Marilyn Stewart was invited to attend, but Reisberg recalled that a union representative participated in only one developmental meeting.

Illinois's grant application included expanding charters and allowing the state to take control of poorly performing school districts, but it needed a piece that would be responsive to Race to the Top's strong requirement to link student achievement with teacher and principal performance. To score at the highest level, a state had to demonstrate how evaluations would contribute to improved teacher effectiveness and school leadership.

The grant competition's focus on teacher evaluations was inspired in significant part by a 2009 report issued by The New Teacher Project (TNTP). Formed in 1997, TNTP claimed to be committed to developing excellent teachers for poor minority school children. For its first ten years, charter school advocate and anti–teachers union maven Michelle Rhee directed the organization. Titled *The Widget Effect*, the report claimed to show that teacher evaluations were "generally meaningless because almost all teachers received positive evaluations regardless of how their students performed academically."[6] The "widget effect" was the "tendency of school districts to assume classroom effectiveness is the same from teacher to teacher" or that teachers were interchangeable.[7] A study of a very small sample of participants from twelve school districts, including Chicago, found that only 2 percent of teachers did not earn at least "satisfactory" ratings and were subsequently dismissed.

The report speculated that the number of "unsatisfactory" and dismissed teachers was implausibly low. As problematic as was the infrequency of dismissal, the "larger, more fundamental crisis" was the "inability of our schools to assess instructional performance accurately or to act on this information in meaningful ways."[8] To put it bluntly, too many bad teachers were getting tenure. The report recommended that teacher job security be tied to measurable student outcomes; for those teachers who then were determined to be "unsatisfactory" and had to be dismissed, "an expedited, one-day hearing should be sufficient for an arbitrator to determine if the evaluation and development process was followed and judgments made in good faith."[9]

The report was provocative and raised a number of troubling questions. How many teachers are really ineffective? What percentage of "unsatisfactory" ratings should there be? What if 5 percent had been judged underperforming? Would that be high enough for a school district to feel confident in the quality of the teaching workforce? If not 5, would a 10 or 20 percent dismissal rate be sufficient? What would be a statistically expected percentage of teachers annually dismissed? The report offered no answers to such questions.

The 2 percent figure cited in the report may have been a fairly accurate estimate of ineffective teachers. In an effort to update the Schools and Staffing Survey (SASS) administered by the National Center for Education Statistics (NCES), the US Census Bureau sponsored a single telephone focus group with thirteen public elementary, intermediate, and high school principals. The focus group was designed in part to identify what formal processes school districts were using to dismiss underperforming teachers. Results indicated that the median and mean responses to the question of how many tenured teachers were considered "unsatisfactory" were only 5 percent. Principals who responded to the question about untenured teachers judged 2 percent "unsatisfactory." This is the reported number dismissed in *The Widget Effect*. Most of the participants in the same focus group also "did not feel that it was too difficult to dismiss nontenured teachers; they felt the current system worked well for these cases."[10]

There is substantial disagreement about whether inadequate teachers represent a relatively small number of school districts' workforces or amount to a crisis in US education. Reisberg's group was both responding and contributing to what education consultant Michael Long recognized as "a common perception among practitioners, policymakers, academics, and the public" that there were a significant number of "incompetent teachers in the United States K–12 schools who, for whatever reason, retain their jobs." Long referred to this dynamic as the "dismissal gap." It was a perception easy enough to feed because "much of this debate is not based on hard data, but on anecdotes or suppositions about what is going on in schools." [11] Nor, he claimed, is it evident that tenure is the most likely reason for the continued presence of underperforming teachers in the classroom. Instead of proving that ineffective teachers were working in classrooms all across the United States, what *The Widget Effect* likely exposed was how poorly prepared school administrators were to assess their teachers as good, bad, or something in between.

The report's findings about teacher effectiveness generated criticism from a union representative appointed to serve on the project's Illinois advisory panel.[12] In a postreport commentary, Rockford Education Association President Molly Phalen harshly condemned the study's very premise. "The discussion about teacher quality absent the discussion of administrator quality is irresponsible and short-sighted. Quality comes in many forms: quality of preparation, of the evaluation tool, of the teaching, of the evaluator, of the feedback, and the quality of assistance." Phalen further stated, "This study neither implicates nor supports the supposition that unions intentionally assisted in the perpetuation of ineffective teaching in schools."[13] In fact, unionization may have increased a teacher's probability of being dismissed for poor performance. According to the NCES, in states like Massachusetts, where nearly every public school teacher was in a union, the firing rate for teachers was approximately double what it was in North Carolina, where only 2.3 percent of the teaching force was unionized.[14]

While teacher quality was important, student achievement was not the sole product of a single input. Teacher skills mattered, but so did a host of other school and socioeconomic elements. In a post hoc response to the report, Illinois advisory panel member and Advance Illinois director Robin Steans articulated the study's unwarranted premise. "If there's one thing researchers, policy experts, and practitioners agree on, it's this: the push to improve student performance depends, almost entirely, on the skills, drive, and ingenuity of the teacher at the front of the classroom."[15] In fact, not only was there no consensus that student achievement was "almost entirely" the responsibility of the teacher, there was substantial evidence of other, stronger predictors of student learning, like a child's class status.

Ironically, *The Widget Effect* made an equally implausible assumption about good teachers. Following the authors' logic, a genuinely highly rated teacher would inevitably only have high-performing students. For those teachers the report had a special reward: "Modify teacher compensation systems, most of which are exclusively based on years of service and attainment of educational credits, so that they also reward high-performing teachers and withhold step increases for low-performing teachers."[16] Once again, the report jumped from a faulty premise to a speculative conclusion. There was no evidence that paying teachers on a piecework basis, as if they were churning out widgets on an assembly line, would generate higher-performing students.

Research would have revealed one other major problem with the report's recommendations. Testing entrepreneurs claimed that helping students improve on standardized tests would be a good predictor of achievement in higher education. The research, however, indicates that the best predictor of how a student will perform in college is her high school grades. Research conducted on the validity of standardized tests at individual institutions reveals the weak predictive ability of the Scholastic Aptitude Test (SAT). Studies at the University of Pennsylvania, University of California, and Bates College, for example, found that the Scholastic Aptitude Tests (SATs) I and II "were by far the weakest predictor[s]" of cumulative college grade point averages (GPAs) and that socioeconomic class was more correlated with first-year college performance.[17] It turns out that the iconic yellow report card still holds the most reliable school information about a student's likely college readiness. Also important, those grades are determined by the classroom subject-matter test that teachers design. Except for references to *The Widget Effect*, however, "research didn't matter" to Reisberg's ISBE group.[18] Illinois needed a Race to the Top grant, and to get it a new evaluation system had to be passed into law.

To fill a hole in the grant chase, PERA was born. From November 2009 until early 2010, an expanded group that grew to twenty or twenty-five people met once a week to work on legislation and the Race to the Top application. While reaching an agreement on performance evaluations was difficult, each group had its own reasons for wanting a new process. The IEA advocated for a more meaningful evaluation system and greater support for professional development. Mitchell "Mitch" Roth, general counsel for the IEA, was a prominent and well-respected participant in the PERA talks. Roth had a devastating critique of the way teachers were being evaluated.

> The evaluation system for teachers was poor. [Evaluations] were inconsistently administered across districts, were subjective, [addressed] the wrong goals, did not provide a fair assessment, [and] were done haphazardly by administrators who weren't prepared [to do them]. The evaluations led to unfair outcomes for teachers and didn't provide formative suggestions on how to improve skills.[19]

Roth also acknowledged that there was an increasing segment of IEA's membership that was uncomfortable with using seniority as "a sole determinant of a reduction in force." The union, he pointed out, had held focus groups, administered surveys, and appointed task forces to address teacher evaluations. Internal polling revealed that 70 percent of IEA's membership "supported a faster process to remove underperforming teachers."[20] The union's position on removing poor teachers, however, was leavened with "big doses of due process rights."

Along with Roth, IEA Executive Director Audrey Soglin was adamant that "evaluations were broken and no one paid any attention to what they [the evaluators] were doing."[21] Soglin had a special vantage point for thinking about PERA. She had served on an advisory panel formed by TNTP to oversee the work that went into *The Widget Effect*.[22] "Professionals need feedback," Soglin stressed, and they welcomed being a part of "reflective conversations." She explained that the IEA had wanted to make changes in the evaluation system "for a long time," but that the substance of the process was not a mandatory subject of bargaining. PERA would create a joint union–school district Performance Evaluation Advisory Committee that was empowered to design and implement the new evaluation system. Soglin saw this provision as being "better than making the process a mandatory subject of bargaining" because it gave the union, for the first time, an "equal voice in setting the terms of the evaluation."[23] Roth acknowledged that the teacher evaluation process was a "big pain in the ass," but "if done right could be very beneficial."[24]

CPS was no less eager to have a new system. Huberman was infatuated with metrics and wanted immediately to include student achievement in evaluating teachers. Steans advocated for a change because she wanted student achievement to be tied to employment decisions. "Performance should matter," she argued, and it was "too hard to fire teachers; the system was not set up to do that." In Steans's interpretation, collective bargaining agreements and teachers union political influence had given ineffective teachers a license to remain in the classroom. She viewed CTU as a major impediment to change because "they are committed to organizing and not what's best for students."[25] Roth acknowledged that IEA's relationship with Advance Illinois had been largely positive and that their interest in quality teachers overlapped, but he added that Advance was "wrong about who they represent." Despite public efforts to characterize themselves as also acting on behalf of teachers, Roth was adamant that Advance "mostly [represents] business interests."[26]

Steans, a mother of three children who were educated in Chicago public schools, had been a CPS teacher and served on two different LSCs. Her family started a foundation in 1986 to address the needs of thirty-five sixth graders living in public housing. By 2010, the foundation had amassed more than $22 million in assets. Along with her two sisters, one who would hold office in the state assembly, the family realized that the quality of schools was essential to lifting families out of poverty. "Schools," she believed, "can level the playing field."[27]

Convinced that education in the state was not making suitable progress and with a grant from the Steans Foundation, Advance Illinois was formed in 2008 to create a state policy body that would be an "objective voice in supporting a healthy public education system."[28] While viewing the CTU as an obstructionist entity, Steans pointed to a larger systemic problem plaguing the Chicago school system. To her, self-interested parties had conspired to preserve an ossifying bureaucratic system that protected ineffective school administrators and teachers, and that was "just fucked up."[29] She criticized CPS and Mayor Richard J. Daley for avoiding tough issues, like teacher evaluations, tenure, and the length of the school day. Change could never happen from within the system; it would require muscular intervention from outside.

In a remarkably short time, Advance had become an influential player in the state's educational politics. With ex-governor and founding member Jim Edgar and former US Secretary of Commerce William Daley serving as the organization's co-chairs, and significant financial support from corporate and philanthropic foundations, the organization had become a high-profile bipartisan presence in Springfield. Advance's board members also included prominent individuals, like James Franczek, who were familiar with CPS and education policy. Despite Advance's influence, however, the idea of tying a teacher's employment fortunes to student performance was dropped during the PERA and Race to the Top negotiations because of union opposition and the need to submit a grant proposal acceptable to all the parties.

With no disagreement on the principle of including student measures in teacher evaluations, the group rushed to complete a draft plan that would be adopted by the legislature. The group was also aware that Governor Quinn was anxious to sign a bill. Unfortunately, problems kept cropping up. With the deadline for submitting Race applications fast approaching, Reisberg stressed that "no one wanted to blow this up."[30] The group eventually endorsed a bill and held a final meeting with all the stakeholders present to announce the details of the plan. On this occasion, Stewart showed up at the meeting and kicked up a storm of opposition over inclusion of the student achievement items, but her complaints were ignored and raised much too late to affect the bill's outcome. The General Assembly approved the legislation and, on January 15, 2010, Governor Quinn signed the new evaluation system into law. Three days later, Illinois sent its Race application, PERA included, to Washington.

Illinois, surprisingly, did not receive funding. The state had come in fifth out of forty applicants, but only two states had been selected. As Reisberg and the group pondered the reasons for their disappointment, the Department of Education announced a second round of grants, to be awarded in the summer of 2010. After scoring very well in the initial round, Illinois eagerly entered again. This time, eight more states were funded. Illinois again was not one of them. "People here were furious," Reisberg explained. "We were back to square zero with no money but a major performance evaluation law to implement."[31] What had gone wrong? Washington signaled that it was PERA.

While PERA did incorporate student achievement scores into teacher evaluations, Reisberg pointed out that it "did not address what happened with these evaluations."[32] What, for example, would a school district do with student test results that were low, and how were teachers to be assessed? As Steans had wanted but could not get, the new law provided no employment consequence. The IEA and IFT could accept the modest use of test scores to partially assess a teacher, but they drew the line at allowing the test results to be used to threaten a teacher's employment. Standardized tests, they argued, were not designed for the purpose of evaluating teacher performance.

Both the IEA and IFT, as well as CTU, once CORE assumed the leadership, had raised serious questions about the underlying principle of using student test scores to evaluate teachers. The unions were not persuaded that one could accurately measure the "value" that a single teacher added to a student's learning in a given year. Reisberg admitted that if PERA had included a link to employment decisions, Illinois's Race to the Top submission "would have been a stronger application."[33] However, because of union objections that test scores were not a credible way to determine a teacher's job security, the state board had not been willing to go that far.

The machinations surrounding PERA and the two rounds of failed Race to the Top proposals affirmed CORE's belief that the true intention of alleged reform groups and their political allies was to act punitively toward the educational labor force. CTU's new leadership did not view Advance as having a legitimate claim on the future of public education. To them, the organization was a fraudulent shill for school-privatization interests and had to be driven back. Advance and its financial backers were portrayed by CTU in a memorable YouTube video as "fat cats" interested in a corporate-style takeover of public education.[34] Steans hated the video and considered it unfair to her organization. But for CTU's new leadership, compromise with groups like Advance Illinois, which were founded by business leaders and supported by financiers like the Bill & Melinda Gates Foundation as well as the local Joyce Foundation, was akin to surrender.

Pension Trouble and Stand for Children

As Illinois prepared a third and final try for a Race to the Top grant, the state was gearing up for a fall legislative session and election. Despite the reform laws, the teachers unions remained a formidable presence in Springfield. Their employees made up a powerful bloc of voters who found influence with Chicago-based Democrats as well as downstate Republicans. Jessica Handy knew all about the politics of education policy in Illinois. As Democratic State Senator Kimberly Lightford's legislative staffer on education policy, she participated in activities related to schools. In 2010, she left Lightford's office and took a new position as policy director with an organization unfamiliar to people in Illinois, the Oregon-based school reform group Stand for Children (SFC). It was a dramatic change for Handy, because SFC had a well-deserved reputation for being anti-teacher and overtly anti–teachers union.[35]

The organization's presence in Illinois signaled a profound change in the alignment of education interests swirling around Springfield. SFC believed that Illinois was ripe for a politically imposed transformation that would curb undue teacher collective-bargaining rights and legal protections. The group's optimism arose from an electoral opportunity that presented itself in the fall of 2010, resulting from a series of events set in motion by an action taken by the Illinois legislature just a few months earlier.

As the Illinois General Assembly opened its spring 2010 session, the biggest issue on its agenda was the state's worst-in-the-nation underfunded pension system. At the end of the 2009 fiscal year, Illinois' retirement systems had an estimated unfunded liability of $77.8 billion.[36] Severe market losses stemming from the 2008 recession had aggravated the funds' liabilities, but the state's problems had been developing for many years. While public employees had never missed a payment into the system, the state actually "passed legislation that provided for several years of pension holidays, allowing it to avoid making even the full payment [to retirees] that would have been required under the pension reform law."[37] Unable to act in a fiscally responsible manner to prevent chronic underfunding, in 1995 the state passed a law mandating an annual state contribution schedule that would fund the system at up to a 90 percent level by 2045.

Despite the law, by spring 2010 at least three-quarters of the system's unfunded liabilities were caused by delinquent state contributions. To address the mountain of owed contributions that threatened the state's bond rating, House Speaker Michael Madigan successfully sponsored a bill to shore up the funds. The new law, it was estimated, would save $119 billion over the next thirty-five years, by creating a two-tiered pension system. While current employees would keep their existing pension plans, new hires would be enrolled into a costlier and less beneficial system. Workers paying the required 4 to 12 percent of their paychecks into the new lower tier would lose thousands of postemployment dollars. Workers would also have to work longer and have their pensionable income capped. What the law did not include was any additional state contributions into the plan or a legal obligation to make any of the previously required payments by the state. Instead, the state chose to fix its pension affliction by punishing its future public employees.

Public-sector unions were furious. Henry Bayer, executive director of the state's largest public employee union, Council 31 of the American Federation of State, County, and Municipal Employees (AFSCME), explained that the "problem of our pensions is that we have not funded them year in and year out." Bayer recommended that the state act responsibly and meet its obligations. "The solution to the crisis," he said, "is to come up with the revenue to pay the $80 billion we already owe." Senate President John Cullerton agreed with Bayer but lamented that "we are where we are."[38] The answer triggered particular outrage from the teachers unions. While active teachers would not be adversely affected by the law, raising the retirement age and lowering benefits for future employees would make it more difficult to attract highly qualified people to the profession. The IEA expressed concern that increasing the retirement age could drive talented teachers out of Illinois and into neighboring states.

Ed Geppert, president of the IFT, noted, "If this bill becomes law, Illinois will have the highest teacher retirement age in the country." The bill not only became law over the objections of the IFT, but did so in a hurry. After passing out of committee around midday on Wednesday, March 24, it "won a 92–17 vote in the House at 5 p.m., and was ratified by the Senate 48–6 at 8:30 p.m. later that day." Governor Quinn signaled his eagerness to sign the bill by praising the legislature's action: "The General Assembly tonight took an important and vital step toward rescuing Illinois from fiscal calamity by passing public pension reform."[39]

The new pension law was the opening act in a drama that would ultimately lead in 2012 to the closing of streets in Chicago's financial district by thousands of teachers. Act II was hatched out of the teachers unions' anger at the Springfield officials who voted to slash retirement incomes for future teachers. The Springfield-based IEA and the Oakbrook-based IFT decided that they needed to do more than express their collective dissatisfaction. For many years Democrats as well as Republicans had been recipients of teachers unions' financial support, campaign volunteers, and votes. During the 2008 election cycle, the IEA and the IFT contributed $1,864,768 and $1,183,868, respectively, to candidates running for state office. Taken together, the IFT and its parent national organization, the AFT, gave $2,092,920 to Illinois politicians either holding statewide elected offices or representing state assembly districts. The IEA gave 58 percent of its contributions to Democrats and 35 percent to Republicans, while the proportion of IFT's total donations that went to Republicans was 14 percent. In 2008, contributions from CTU amounted to $400,000, nearly all of which went to Democrats. Both statewide teacher organizations backed many of the same officials and had similar electoral success. Nearly 75 percent of the candidates IEA and IFT backed won in 2008, and 85 percent of those unions' political money went to incumbents.[40] Political spending in 2008 mirrored previous electoral seasons. Unionized teachers were in every assembly district in the state; they voted in high numbers and in both political primaries. Their unions were perhaps the most politically active organizations in Illinois and, except for party committees, were the largest organizational financial contributors.

Despite IEA and IFT political influence, Illinois elected leaders summarily brushed aside their objections to the 2010 pension bill and voted to disadvantage the next cohort of classroom teachers. The insult was grievously felt. Determined not to be so lightly disregarded, the IFT and IEA made the choice to use their political capacity differently in the fall 2010 elections. In doing so they unwittingly attracted a deep-pocketed new enemy to Illinois.

Angry about the pension vote, the unions diverged from the customary practice of having organized labor make large contributions to the political action committee (PAC) controlled by House Speaker and state Democratic Party Chair Michael Madigan.[41] Teachers unions collectively had been among the Speaker's most generous benefactors, contributing nearly $700,000 between 1996 and 2010. The relationship between Madigan and organized labor had proved mutually beneficial. A member of the Illinois House since 1971, representing the Twenty-Second House District on the Southwest Side of Chicago, Madigan was considered a strong friend of labor leaders and for nearly forty years had earned unwavering union support. In four decades, Madigan cast votes on hundreds of bills that were important to organized labor, and his 85 percent lifetime prounion voting record was stellar.

While Madigan's aggregate prolabor record was excellent, his leadership had occasionally been crucial to the teachers. It was Madigan who, as House Speaker, insisted that no education reform bill would pass in 1988 without the teachers unions' endorsement. When the more stringent amended reform law passed in 1995, Madigan had been temporarily deposed as Speaker. Unions in Illinois knew that their fortunes were linked to the state's political establishment in the same way that labor movements in neighboring states were impacted by less friendly political parties. Electoral politics mattered—all things considered, Madigan, the one-time Chicago Thirteenth Ward committeeman, was an invaluable friend.

Yet, in the spring of 2010, it was this trusted ally of labor who led the drive against public-sector employee unions to amend the pension law. In response, the teachers unions recalibrated how they would contribute to candidates in the November legislative races. Instead of falling into line and offering their historical level of assistance to Madigan's prestigious PAC, they would hold back their contributions. While the IFT and IEA spent nearly $5 million on individual candidates, party committees, and ballot measures, their contributions to the Madigan PAC fell to nothing.

Fatefully, however, the absence of IEA and IFT money opened the third act of the drama that would produce new legislation, described by CTU as anti–teachers union. When the teachers unions refused to bank their money with Madigan, SFC noticed and rushed in to fill the void. Introduced to Illinois by venture capitalist, charter school advocate, and future governor Bruce Rauner, SFC formed a PAC and brazenly jumped into the fall elections. Funded by some of Chicago's highest-flying elites, like *Chicago Tribune* owner Sam Zell, Madison Dearborn Partners CEO Paul Finnegan, Citadel hedge fund chief executive Ken Griffin ("the richest man in the state") and the Pritzker and Henry Crown families, the group quickly raised approximately $6 million.[42] Roughly $285,000 of the money was funneled to half a dozen Madigan-backed candidates.

Another $50,000 was deposited with the state's Democratic Party, while Republican candidates shared $275,000 in donations. Rich Miller, the author of the widely read *Capitol Fax*, a daily political newsletter, called SFC's endeavor "the largest legislative campaign contribution in Illinois history by a political action committee."[43] SFC's executive director, Jonah Edelman, boasted that funding the "individual candidates" was "essentially a vehicle to execute a political objective."[44] After interviewing thirty-six candidates, the group endorsed six Democrats and three Republicans and, as Edelman explained, "tilted our money toward Madigan." The purpose was to show the Speaker that "we could be a new partner to take the place of the Illinois Federation of Teachers."[45]

The dispute over the pension funds, according to Edelman, created an opening for the Oregon-based organization. SFC's stealth thrust into state politics was highly unusual for an outside entity. "Huge contributions have been the norm in Illinois for decades," Rich Miller mused. "Usually, though, when we see big checks run through the system we have a general idea what the group wants." SFC's ability to quietly raise so much money so rapidly and to become a sizable donor to candidates was extraordinary. The influx of money did get the unions' attention. "Certainly, any time you see a new group not from Illinois dropping significant dollar amounts into legislative races, it does raise some red flags," said an IFT spokesperson.[46]

When the election results were in, SFC's political shopping spree appeared to have produced ambiguous results. Six of the SFC-bankrolled candidates won, but the five Democrats and one Republican all had been considered favorites. Each of the Democrats was a recipient not only of funds from Madigan's PAC but also of sizable amounts from organized labor. Each of the Democrats was also an incumbent who, with one exception, won comfortably. SFC's biggest beneficiary was a House Republican who lost: Ryan Higgins got $175,000 from the group and fell about seven hundred votes short of capturing an open seat. The Higgins donation was, however, "the single largest non-leadership contribution in modern Illinois times."[47]

The only SFC Democratic candidate to lose, incumbent Representative Bob Flider, had also received significant union donations. Flider was odd for a recipient of SFC money. He had sponsored bills making it easier for teachers to earn tenure more quickly. Next to the Democratic Party, labor organizations made up

Flider's largest benefactor. It is therefore highly questionable that SFC filled any funding hole left by the teachers unions. Rich Miller drew the same conclusion. "The thinking is that Stand for Children is now filling a unique void created by the relative lack of teacher contributions. But that theory doesn't totally hold up."[48] Nor does it seem likely that SFC's superrich Chicago funders provided the resources that determined the outcome of any race. Whatever the Speaker's feelings about the teachers unions, SFC's impact was not realized in the 2010 election outcomes. Its impact did come immediately after.

In December 2011, Illinois's third application was awarded a $42.8 million Race to the Top grant. But for the intervening passage of a new education law, motivated by the Obama administration's educational sweepstakes, and driven by SFC, the Land of Lincoln would never have won a penny. The bill was innocuously referred to as "SB 7," and it was about to change everything.

5

SENATE BILL 7

Maywood, Illinois, is located fifteen miles west of downtown Chicago. Founded in 1869, the village of roughly twenty-four thousand residents has retained a hold on the past. A person walking along its main streets would be impressed by the many properties listed on the National Register of Historic Places. A village memorial recounts the loss of eighty-one local men who died in the infamous Bataan Death March during World War II. To honor those soldiers, the US Congress designated the community the Village of Eternal Light.[1]

Maywood unexpectedly took its place in history again on June 13, 2011. In front of a large crowd jammed into Livingston Elementary School gymnasium, Governor Pat Quinn signed into law Senate Bill 7 (SB 7). The legislation was the state's latest education reform plan. As reported by *Substance News*, "The site of the signing was chosen because Livingston was the elementary school of State Senator Kimberly Lightford, who is credited with overseeing the contentious meetings that eventually hammered out the legislation."[2]

Along with the governor and Lightford, Mayor Emanuel addressed the crowd and repeated his demand that Chicago students have a longer school day and year. Everyone who spoke, including the heads of the two statewide teachers unions, praised the bill for moving Illinois to the forefront of cooperative education reform. Unlike in Indiana, New Jersey, and Wisconsin, where teachers unions were excluded from discussions about changes to education law, in Illinois teachers unions were part of the legislative development process. Not every key union leader showed up for the bill's signing. CTU's President Karen Lewis was conspicuously absent; Quinn said she was out of town.

Unlike the relatively substantive and benign discussions that were held prior to PERA, the prologue to SB 7 featured a new out-of-state interloper that threatened to shake the very foundation of collective bargaining in public education and sent shock waves through the teachers unions. Where the unions and other groups had worked collaboratively to craft the PERA bill to improve teacher and principal evaluation, the process used to arrive at SB 7 was fraught with adversarial behavior. To Robin Steans, who spoke at the ceremony, however, passage of the law was "exquisite timing."[3] But for CTU the law was a consequence of a political perspective on the part of both local and state Republican and Democrat lawmakers antagonistic to teachers unions and public education. Teachers would rely heavily on a few well-placed political friends to tamp down the worst aspects of the bill, but even with Democrats in control of state government, the legal context for labor relations in education was about to shrink yet again. When it did, this time the law made it harder for teachers to negotiate a deal and, paradoxically, easier for the union to justify to its members and the community a more militant approach to CPS.

The Performance Counts Coalition Emerges

By December 31, 2010, SFC had raised $3 million. Such a large sum was impossible for political officials, teachers unions, and education groups to ignore. That much money had to be destined for some large purpose. "It's not that legislators and their leaders slavishly bow deeply to anybody with a fat wallet," Rich Miller commented in his *Capitol Fax* newsletter. "But they most certainly take lots of notice when somebody comes out of nowhere and antes up with $2.9 million." Over a very short period, SFC had "gone from nowhere to one of the biggest and potentially one of the more successful players" in state politics. To the detriment of public school teachers, this evolution had happened "without attracting significant media attention."[4] The group's initial anonymity, however, was about to disappear.

Less than a month after the November 7 election, Madigan announced the creation of a bipartisan eight-member Special House Committee on Education Reform. The committee was charged with holding two days of hearings about an education reform bill. Senate President John Cullerton followed by naming a second committee to be chaired by Senator Kimberly Lightford. First elected to the Fourth District of the Illinois Senate in 1998, Lightford had risen to become the Senate's assistant majority leader. She chaired or vice chaired the Senate Education Committee for more than a decade and had been involved in numerous education policy debates. Among the entire General Assembly, there was no one who was more respected as an honest broker by education advocates, school officials, education lobbyists, and unions.

Shortly after the House committee was formed, a coalition of groups antagonistic to the teachers unions, headed by SFC and Advance Illinois, and including the Illinois Business Roundtable and the Civic Committee of the Commercial Club of Chicago, released a draft of an education bill.[5] Titled the Performance Counts (PC) Act of 2010, the measure was essentially a revocation of teachers' collective bargaining rights. Among other things, it would alter the state's teacher-certification, hiring, and dismissal process. Two elements were directed at the heart of the CTU. One would convert many mandatory and permissive subjects of bargaining into prohibited subjects. The other would place severe limitations on Chicago teachers' right to strike. While SFC received most of the attention, years earlier the Civic Committee of the Commercial Club had provided the ideational heft for weakening teachers unions. "The entire collective-bargaining apparatus has been designed less to improve teaching or student learning than to protect the interests of teachers," summed up the organization's enmity for teachers unions.[6]

Media reports of the Performance Counts (PC) proposal were glowing. "Some version of this school reform package should and must pass," editorialized the *Chicago Sun-Times.*[7] While the bill was popular with editors, it stunned the unions. Their concern increased when they became aware that the bill was on a fast track to be rammed through the legislature before it adjourned on January 11, 2011. In a frank public recitation of SFC's strategy delivered at an Aspen Institute talk, the SFC executive director, Jonah Edelman, gloated about what had happened; there was a "palpable sense of concern, if not shock among teacher unions in Illinois that Speaker Madigan had changed his allegiance. . . . We had the ability, potentially, to jam this proposal down their throat."[8] The IEA, IFT, and CTU testified against the bill at a mid-December House hearing in Aurora, Illinois. IEA's Mitch Roth explained, "We heard from our friends in the House and Senate that we needed to act quickly to counter the proposal."[9] One of those friends the teachers reached out to was the Westchester-based Senator Lightford. She had a 90 percent prolabor lifetime voting record. Lightford responded quickly by announcing a hearing to address the PC proposal.

With Lightford's forceful intervention, the "legislation ran into a brick wall."[10] Her capacity to block the fast tracking of the bill was reinforced by the sizeable opposition that CTU raised against the proposal. The union argued that its member mobilization was a major factor in stopping the bill. "The CTU and teachers unions across the state mobilized members and community supporters to lobby legislators, publicize the attack, and rally the public," said Karen Lewis. "Because of CTU's actions, Performance Counts went nowhere in January 2011. We won the first round."[11] For the moment, there would be no new education law.

On January 3, the unions released their own education bill, known as Accountability for All. While the union proposal addressed teacher performance, layoffs, and tenure, it strongly reaffirmed the teacher due-process rights that had been negotiated in collective bargaining contracts and provided by state law. The day the unions introduced their plan, Lightford's committee held its first hearing in the Thompson Center in downtown Chicago. The sixteenth-floor conference room was packed. Lightford took particular displeasure at all the lobbyists in attendance and decided to limit future meeting participation to a smaller group of representatives. From that point forward Lightford controlled the destiny of any education reform proposal.

Lightford's Table Takes Charge

Her first big decision was to inform all the parties that no bill would pass during the veto session. She also had to fight off efforts by SFC to surreptitiously pass piecemeal legislation diluting teachers union power. She was incensed at an attempt by Edelman to persuade a rookie senator to push a bill during the veto session that would remove the right of teachers to strike. In a Chicago meeting over tea with the first-term senator and a lobbyist hired by SFC, Lightford counseled against the idea and learned that Edelman had dangled a political contribution of $100,000 as an incentive. The meeting was not Lightford's first encounter with an SFC lobbyist. SFC had hired eleven experienced and prominent lobbyists to, as the senator put it, "work the legislature." Lightford had deep reservations about the characters camping near her Springfield office door. SFC's lobbying stable included some of the biggest contract lobbyists at the statehouse with ties to both parties and the Black and Latino caucuses. "These people knew nothing about education," the senator dismissively commented. "I never had a single policy talk with any of them."[12] Lightford concluded that SFC was not in Springfield because it cared about the quality of education children received.

Stretching into the early spring, Lightford's special committee would meet at least ten times. The major education groups, including the unions, spent hundreds of hours discussing proposals that would amend sections of the Illinois School Code. Lightford repeatedly reinforced the message that everyone's "commitment to children was paramount."[13] Borrowing a phrase from television personality Oprah Winfrey, each group would have to come up with a "big give" if legislation was going to pass. Lightford had no illusions that she could prevent a bill of some kind from passing. Madigan, Cullerton, Quinn, and Chicago Mayor-elect Rahm Emanuel supported a new education measure. She was also receiving daily phone calls from unelected prominent Chicagoans who pressured her to produce a bill that weakened the union's ability to strike.

Lightford, however, refused to allow a no-strike provision to be included in any bill. Despite demands that Chicago teachers be prohibited from striking, Senate President Cullerton had given her a "free hand" to produce a bill. While the political maneuvering was intense, Lightford had a promise from Governor Quinn that he would veto any bill that removed the right to strike.[14] She therefore insisted that the teachers unions had to be involved in the negotiations. Similar to Madigan's bottom line during negotiations in 1988, Lightford wanted a bill ready for a floor vote, but it had to have union support.

In addition to the special committee meetings regularly attended by, among others, IFT President Dan Montgomery, IEA Executive Director Audrey Soglin, and at times a representative from the governor's office, a smaller attorneys-only group was meeting with the Illinois State Board of Education (ISBE) General Counsel Darren Reisberg. Roth represented the teachers unions, while Jon Furr, a former ISBE general counsel, negotiated for the PC coalition. Sara Boucek, from the Illinois Association of School Administrators, spoke for the interests of school management. It was this group that assumed the primary responsibility for drafting legislative language. The meetings that Lightford chaired included her one-time education staffer, SFC's Illinois policy director, Jessica Handy.

Handy had been active in education policy for years, and she genuinely believed that the measure's elements dealing with teacher job performance and tenure were needed. So, too, was the call for a longer school day. Handy disagreed with CTU's insistence that extending the school day should be determined through bargaining. To SFC's new policy director, subjecting the longer school day to negotiations would "derail the talks" because CPS "would have to pay for it, pay for it minute by minute."[15]

Handy claimed that she was not ideologically opposed to unions or collective bargaining. Forcing the union's hand, she confessed, was a tough "moral dilemma," but "each time, change bumped up against the union."[16] Handy resolved her quandary by accepting that legislation was the only way to strip the CTU of its ability to block the changes she believed were needed to improve schools. In this regard there was no policy daylight between SFC and Advance. She explained that much of what SFC pushed in the PC bill began with Advance. In fact, it was often Advance's Steans who spoke out publicly against CTU's right to strike. In a *Wall Street Journal* story, she warned, "The threat of a strike is so significant, it casts a very long shadow over the negotiation process."[17]

CTU officials simply saw both organizations as dangerous enemies to public schools. Lewis had come to refer regularly to SFC as "Stand *on* Children" in private conversations and public comments. There was hardly a moment when she failed to frame the organization as using mostly minority students to promote the interests of rich white men. The union had no clever play on words for Advance but never missed an opportunity to lampoon Steans as a "fat cat" devouring public school children.

Despite the seemingly irreconcilable differences between CTU and the PC coalition, by mid-April a tentative agreement had been reached on a range of issues. Prior to handling items that directly threatened job security, Lightford's committee had dealt with relatively low-hanging fruit. Negotiations on teacher layoffs, the acquisition of tenure, tenured-teacher dismissal protocols, bargaining impasse procedures, and the incendiary right to strike were going to confront embedded and contradictory interests. Fortunately, the PC coalition and the teachers unions viewed Lightford as fair-minded. Her ability to keep the parties focused on the diverse pieces of the unfolding bill was aided by an organizing device she implemented for tracking the debate. After her initial meeting, Lightford created an elaborate chart that included each faction's ideas. Spanning eleven legal-size pages, the "Analysis and Comparison of Education Reform Proposals" helped Lightford direct and follow the negotiations.

The first element that generated tension was the question of how school districts would fill vacant teaching positions and decide layoffs. The original PC bill minimized the value of a teacher's experience in both filling vacancies and reducing staff. If Advance and SFC had their way, principals would have nearly unfettered authority over who should be hired and who should be fired. Teachers, by contrast, were fiercely protective of seniority. They feared that absent an objective standard for determining qualifications and performance, teaching assignments would be subject to bias, political considerations, and personal favoritism. Roth explained that after much debate, seniority was reduced to a "relevant" factor in filling vacancies only where the teaching candidates were "determined by the school district to have equivalent qualifications and merit."[18] The parties also agreed to a process whereby layoffs would be determined by performance levels, based in part on student test scores, while honoring teaching experience. The law, in effect, made earning tenure tougher. The multilayered arrangement appealed to Lightford. In her notes, she wrote the word "Excellent."[19]

The flip side to the procedure and disposition of laid-off teachers was the process for awarding tenure to teachers.[20] Tenure was designed to protect teachers' free speech rights and to ensure that children have access to varied points of view. Since 1998, teachers in Illinois needed to complete four consecutive school terms and be reemployed for an additional term to acquire tenure. In Illinois, the probation period for K–12 teachers was longer than those of 86 percent of the other states. On this issue, the PC coalition proposed an open-ended, unlimited probationary period for districts other than Chicago.

Union objection was swift. Without a bounded time frame, Roth argued, school districts could "keep teachers in a perpetual probationary period." They could do this by interjecting a negative evaluation in order to break a "string of positive evaluations."[21] In the final wording of the bill, the four-year probationary period was retained, but the unions did agree that a "proficient" or higher evaluation was required in either the second or third year of teaching, and a similar evaluation in the fourth, for a teacher to be eligible for tenure. The bill also created an accelerated path to tenure that permitted a teacher to be tenured in three years instead of four. Tenure portability was added, allowing a tenured teacher who moved from one school district to another to be awarded tenure in the new district in two years.

The "table," as participants came to refer to the special committee facilitated by Lightford, met for two to three hours a session from January 27 until April 7. Whereas most of the issues addressed were part of the state school code, items in one section of the IELRA attracted significant attention. They were known collectively as "Section 4.5 items," for the part of the law in which they were found. Here the PC coalition proposed a number of dramatic legal changes that would apply only to Chicago. When these labor relations items were discussed in Lightford's committee, her Senate and committee colleagues, Republicans David Luechtefeld and Matt Murphy and Democrats Ed Maloney and James Meeks, were in attendance. Unlike the committee chair, some of the other members were not considered friendly to labor. Luechtefeld, who had once worked as a teacher, and Murphy had only 32 and 29 percent lifetime ratings, respectively, from the Illinois AFL-CIO. Meeks was a leading advocate of charter schools. Their presence at the talks when the focus shifted to labor relations restrictions on Chicago teachers suggests that they were less interested in education reform than in encouraging new ways to handicap CTU.

Steans and Handy introduced the primary amendments to Section 4.5 of the labor act. Emanuel had made public promises to substantially lengthen Chicago's school day and year. In his campaign education address, the mayor declared, "It's difficult for Chicago teachers to impart the knowledge and skills their students require when our children spend less time in the classroom than just about anywhere else in the nation."[22] According to Beth Swanson, the city's deputy chief of staff for education, "the longer school day and year were viewed as an inequity" that had to be adjusted.[23] She described increasing instructional time as an essential element in the mayor's plans to make substantive structural changes in the city schools. Emanuel initially wanted the elementary and high school days lengthened by 90 minutes, but to get what he wanted he needed the law to change.

It was a staple of past labor negotiations that the mayor and the school board would proffer, then withdraw, a proposal to add time to the school day. Section 4.5 of the IELRA rendered certain items "permissive" rather than "prohibited" subjects of bargaining and outlawed the union's right to strike over them. However, prior to the PC-driven discussions, Section 4.5 was silent on the subject of the length of the school year and day. Nonetheless, the two subjects had always been negotiated. Small time adjustments had been injected into past agreements but failed to survive successive bargaining rounds. Knowing the bargaining history, the mayor decided to use his political prowess to obtain definitively from Springfield what he could not from the bargaining process. The PC coalition, guided by Franczek, proposed defining the academic year and school hours as prohibited subjects of bargaining. By doing so the subjects could no longer be negotiated and could instead be unilaterally set by the mayor's handpicked school board.

In addition to prohibiting bargaining over the length of the school day, the PC proposal would also deny the CTU the right to negotiate how such changes affected the teachers. The mayor, in effect, could unilaterally increase the time that teachers worked, and at the same time refuse even to discuss whether they should be paid more for doing the extra labor. If a bill passed with this language, it would be a solution to the school-time expansion issue that had escaped past mayors and school boards. In effect, the issue would no longer be open to negotiations. Despite making a fruitful living from the practice, Franczek argued that "collective bargaining was a roadblock to changing the system." He was unapologetic about using the political process to fulfill the mayor's wishes. Instructional time and school year length were items embedded in an "argument over the direction of the city schools" and, consequently, should not be addressed thorough bargaining but instead by policy-makers.[24]

CTU's response to the PC proposal was swift and unconditional. Lightford's notes said it all: "CTU = 4.5 to be repealed. . . . CTU wants to maintain what they have." What the Chicago union had was the right to demand bargaining over workday changes, to reject any changes in the workday without corresponding compensation, and to strike over both matters. CTU interpreted any restrictions on what had to be bargained as an unwarranted intrusion into the right of professionals to control their profession.

Adding the longer school day to the list of prohibited subjects would prevent the CTU from striking over the issue, and the PC language would block a work stoppage related to any dispute over the impact of the change. Despite the union's objections, the final disposition of the bill added the items to Section 4.5. The union could neither demand bargaining nor strike over the impact of these changes, although it could demand to negotiate about the effects of working longer hours. However, CTU could not strike over the outcomes of the bargaining. If the parties could not reach agreement on, for example, pay for additional work time, the issue could be deferred to a mediation process, referenced under Section 12(b) of the IELRA. But the optional step was illusory.

The mediation process was created as part of the 2003 amendments to the IELRA negotiated between the CTU and the Chicago school board. At the time the law was amended, it was considered an accomplishment for the union because the changes partially restored its bargaining rights. As part of the deal, the Board of Education and CTU also negotiated a separate agreement authorizing a panel of two CPS, two CTU representatives, and a third-party neutral to handle disputed 4.5 issues. If the panel failed to successfully mediate the differences, it could issue advisory recommendations, but neither the employer nor the union had to honor the recommendations. The agreement read, "Any such recommendations shall not be binding on the parties."[25] In effect, it was a dispute panel that could not resolve a dispute. Since 2003, the panel had never been called into service. Franczek claimed that he "regretted agreeing to the 2003 changes," suggesting that they had strengthened the union's bargaining capacity.[26] CTU attorney Robert Bloch, for his part, referred to the process as a "toothless, meaningless mediation panel whose advice went off into the ether."[27]

Along with the school day and impasse procedures, Advance and SFC also proposed amending Section 4.5 to include a merit pay plan that could be unilaterally implemented. As if to be sure that she understood the idea, Lightford handwrote on her chart, "reduce to merit pay." She also added and drew an arrow from the merit pay plan to the following caveat: "the school district can do all these things w/o bargaining."

The merit pay proposal was dead on arrival. It was likely put forward because Advance was incredulous that CTU had blocked a federally funded merit pay scheme. Upon taking office Lewis had been presented with a US Department of Education grant application to provide federal subsidies for a "CPS Teacher Incentive Fund."[28] The plan was designed to integrate a performance-based compensation system valued at roughly $8 million over five years into what CPS called its "Human Capital Framework."[29] Teachers would be awarded extra pay by applying a "value-added metric based on the Illinois Standards Achievement Test."[30] The application had been written while Stewart was president, and the submission deadline was approaching. To complete the grant, the union would have to add its signature to a letter of commitment.

Lewis had no intention of signing on. The union was resolutely opposed to any merit pay plan. As a way of expressing her disfavor with the incentive plan, Lewis wrote comments in a number of places throughout the application. For example, after reading "This framework combines base pay and variable pay to properly incentivize optimal performance," she wrote "WOW." In this case she explained that WOW meant, "I can't believe they [CPS] think teachers need to have a carrot dangled in front of their noses to do their best."[31] Lewis spared no disdain for the narrative's assertion that the incentive plan would aid CPS in a campaign to attract "top teacher and principal talent" by writing in her copy of the application, next to that claim, "A system so dysfunctional, we have to bribe." Lewis claimed that CPS submitted the grant application without her signature and somehow acquired the money illegally.[32] Within the committee, little actual discussion on merit pay occurred and the idea was dropped.

While the merit pay idea was ignored, the parties spent a considerable amount of time talking about the process for dismissing tenured Chicago teachers for poor performance. All the committee participants agreed that the existing process was too long and cost too much, but the reformer coalition's approach was, in Roth's terms, "immensely tilted toward school districts."[33] It would remove the role of an independent hearing officer in determining whether a teacher should be removed or retained. Instead, a panel of two local school district representatives and one union official would decide the teachers' fate. Teachers would also carry the burden of showing that the evaluation on which the dismissal was based was not valid.

The unions countered with preserving the hearing officer but introducing a time frame for issuing a final determination. The burden of proof would remain on the school district to justify the termination. "The unions' goal," according to Roth, "was to streamline the process, while maintaining fairness and objectivity." In the end, the committee agreed to a hybrid system that under PERA would incorporate a second neutral evaluator and the independent hearing officer as a fact finder who would make a recommendation to the school district.[34]

Further restricting the union's ability to bargain, the PC group also proposed binding arbitration to resolve all disputes. Edelman saw this approach as part of a Machiavellian strategy to box CTU into a corner. In his Aspen tell-all, he explained how binding arbitration fit into the PC coalition's antistrike scheme: "Jim [Franczek] and the other supporters had approved fallbacks from our initial proposal, essentially isolating Chicago and calling for binding arbitration or a fact-finding process that wasn't binding but would have a high threshold for unions to approve."[35]

According to Handy, CPS also favored the arbitration idea, but the non-Chicago school districts and CTU were strongly opposed. The idea was fraught with unintended consequences. Binding CPS and CTU to a neutral party's interpretation of what the terms of a labor agreement should be would certainly prevent a legal strike. That feature would come, however, with real risks. Relying on an arbitrator to select which proposal—labor's or management's—was the most appropriate was a crapshoot. You might win big, but you might lose equally big, and by deferring to the arbitrator's judgment, the parties were surrendering their own authority to negotiate a deal. Collective bargaining could be maddeningly tedious, but, unless the goal was to terminate the bargaining relationship, a deal would ultimately be reached.[36]

There is another complication with arbitration. Research suggests that the application of differing forms of contract arbitration on the bargaining process is not benign. For example, interest arbitration statutes can specify factors for the arbitrator to consider that limit the arbitrator's discretion or prioritize certain factors over others. Procedures can also expressly authorize the arbitrator to consider factors in addition to those expressly listed. The factors used to reach an award can predetermine the outcome.

Contract arbitration has been found to have a "chilling" or "narcotic" effect on the parties' willingness to bargain. Furthermore, as Chicago-Kent College of Law Professor Martin Malin has written, under certain models "the approach exacerbates the tendency of unions and employers to use interest arbitration as a means of avoiding accountability to their constituents."[37] Binding or "interest" arbitration is a very common and required practice for federal employees as well as municipal police and fire departments but is hardly ever used outside these sectors. It is the very rare employer or union who would prefer outsourcing the final authority over an entire contractual work arrangement, not just pay items, to a neutral party. Labor peace was much desired, but not at the cost of losing control over the ability to shape an institution's destiny.

The IEA was not opposed to third-party intervention but countered with a nonmandatory fact-finding option. CTU viewed the fact-finding option as just a blocking device meant to prevent or delay a strike. The union would accommodate submitting proposals to a fact finder but never agree to any provision that would permit the school board to dictate contract terms. The committee settled on different plans for Chicago and the rest of Illinois. School districts other than Chicago would not have mandatory fact-finding but would have to follow a mediation process that, according to Roth, "decreased the likelihood of a strike, without tipping the bargaining scale toward one party or the other." No such concern for equivalency was shown for schools organized under Article 34 of the school code, which addressed only cities with a population exceeding 500,000. There was only one such jurisdiction, Chicago. Advance and SFC, along with their allies in the Civic Committee, Business Roundtable, and Illinois Chamber of Commerce, desperately wanted language that would prohibit teacher strikes in Chicago. The PC coalition demanded that the IELRA be amended in such a way as to "effectively eliminate the legal strike."[38]

The Strike Threat

State legislators and Mayor Emanuel believed that Chicago should be treated differently because of the disruption a strike could have on the city's nearly four hundred thousand students. Lightford certainly recognized the concern. She not only wrote, "The Threat of a Strike!" on her notes, but then underlined the words and for further emphasis drew a box around the statement. The CTU countered by noting that there had not been a citywide school strike in a quarter of a century. But the teachers knew that nothing worried Emanuel more than the possibility of a strike. They also were convinced that the former presidential chief of staff wanted to push forward on plans to further privatize the school system, and that the only force likely to stand in his way was the CTU.

Whatever the mayor's real intentions were, the threat of a strike was no idle posturing. The final committee bill thus required both CPS and CTU to submit bargaining disputes to a fact finder. While the fact finder's recommendations were not binding unless approved by the school board and the union, the procedure would effectively delay CTU's ability to "strike for four months from the date the fact-finding panel is appointed."[39] Edelman, for one, believed that the committee's bill had eliminated the union's ability to strike. In his public talk at Aspen, he flat out declared that CTU had been tricked into effectively giving up the capacity to strike legally. Certainly the teachers unions feared that a blanket prohibition was possible. In the last couple of days of the committee's work, the PC coalition representatives made a proposal that Chicago teachers could strike only if they obtained a two-thirds vote of their membership. The proposal was a radical legal departure from how union strike votes are usually taken. Under private and public sector bargaining law, the process by which a union determines that it has received the approval of its membership to strike is dictated by the union's constitution and bylaws. Unless the right to strike is prohibited by law, how a union arrives at a strike authorization is entirely an internal matter. But the PC proposal would strip that right from the CTU, and only the CTU. Additionally, the bill would require that a super-majority authorization vote (rather than a simple majority) come from a percentage of the entire membership and not from a percentage of those members who voted, as is the common practice. Surprisingly, despite the obvious intrusion into internal union governance, the measure did not kick up any opposition from the teachers unions participating in the negotiation. Genuinely afraid that, if they did not indicate a willingness to at least make striking more difficult, an outright ban or binding arbitration was possible, CTU reluctantly agreed.

Lewis then left the negotiations, and Lightford called Emanuel with the news. She was happy to have the last piece of the puzzle in place. Only she was mistaken. Handy infuriated Lightford by opposing the strike terms. The senator accused Handy of "not caring about kids."[40] At that point Handy phoned Edelman. He directed her to up the ante. Handy was then called into Lightford's office, where she proposed that CTU should be required to obtain a 75 percent prostrike vote. The senator returned to the committee and asked the participants to consider a three-quarter union strike endorsement. The lawyers were still working separately on the bill's language and they were angered at the last-minute maneuvering. Lightford, however, had a bigger problem.

Lewis was in a car in Springfield driving to a restaurant under the impression that she had agreed to a two-thirds strike vote. Lightford, intending to draft a bill that very night, called Lewis and notified her of the 75 percent proposal. Dan Montgomery, president of the IFT, was in the car with Lewis when she took the call. Incredulously, she informed him about SFC's last-minute insistence on a 75 percent strike vote. Montgomery answered his colleague by assuring her that the "Mayor would get the teachers to the bar [i.e., the needed strike votes]."[41] To Lightford's relief and surprise, Lewis gave her consent. Unfortunately, the explanation of what Lewis had been asked to approve was inexact. At the time, no one involved in Lightford's committee realized there was a misunderstanding about the "75 percent," and the bill was finalized. Lewis believed that the 75 percent was only of union members. Handy, on the other hand, believed it included the nonunion members that CTU was required to represent.

Edelman claimed in his Aspen talk that when a serious divergence in views emerged over actions to address a bargaining impasse and the right to strike, "the IEA pressured CTU to take the deal." The IEA did have a pragmatic view of the negotiations and realized that some type of agreement had to be reached. Roth acknowledged that, given the politics of the moment, unrealistically holding onto "intractable positions would likely lead to legislation which would be harder" for the unions to accept.[42] Montgomery spent time negotiating SB 7 and concurred that it was the flexibility and general cooperation of the teachers unions that led to achieving a crucial worker protection. "Here's a big one: They wanted to end collective bargaining and the right to strike," Montgomery said publicly. If "we got rid of that," he stated, it "would have grotesquely ended negotiations, effectively ending teachers' ability to advocate for kids."[43] Lightford was blunt in her directions to the unions. If "you all can't agree, the legislature will make the decision."[44]

Edelman's analysis that IEA allied with the reformers against CTU to pressure Lewis to accept the provisions of SB 7 triggered tension between the unions. Some of those feelings played out on a popular blog site. Fred Klonsky is an education blogger as well as an ex–school teacher and former local IEA union president. He wrote an incendiary post about IEA Executive Director Audrey Soglin and former President Ken Swanson's role in the SB 7 negotiations: "These two sad excuses for union leadership were sent to pressure the CTU into accepting the Edelman language. They treated the newly elected reform president of the CTU like the new kid at school. They acted like bullies, plain and simple."[45] In reply, Roth wrote the following defense:

"As you know, Audrey and I were the primary IEA representatives who directly participated in the discussions which led to SB 7. In particular, I was present for the discussion regarding the CTU strike authorization vote. At no time did Audrey, Ken (who wasn't there for the discussion), me or anyone from IFT bully or otherwise pressure CTU President Karen Lewis to accept the strike authorization vote language. She, along with the other CTU representatives present, as well as its legal counsel, weighed the plusses and minuses regarding the issue and decided to accept it. Both the IEA and IFT supported whatever the CTU believed was in its best interest. Anyone who knows Karen clearly understands she is not a person who is susceptible to bullying."[46]

Lewis never acknowledged being strong-armed by anyone at the IEA. In the end, CTU's initial concurrence with the bill's changes to the state labor law had more to do with the threats that Lewis faced. The inexperienced CTU president was buffeted by pressure from Springfield officials and Emanuel, who cast a big shadow throughout the negotiations. One observer colorfully described the mayor's razor-like attention to the bill's development as being "on it like shit on a stick." Nonetheless, the CTU had preserved its right to strike, but just barely. Lightford's committee finished its work on April 7, and one week later the full Senate passed the legislation by a unanimous 59-to-0 vote.

CTU Reaction to the Bill

Although Lewis had consented to the bill, she still needed to win the approval of the union's House of Delegates. Expecting to have the support of her caucus and union members, Lewis planned her travel back to Chicago. Before leaving Springfield, she appeared on April 13 in an evening videoconference broadcast to a meeting of the union delegates. Inexplicably, Lewis did not report that she had signed off on the legislation. To make matters worse, the union's other elected officers and membership only realized that SB 7 had passed a short time later, when according to *Substance News*, "Sen. Lightford entered it into the legislative record."[47] Lewis's first public statement on the bill came the following morning via a CTU press release that advocated for the deal, which, she said, was littered with "bitter pills" but worthy of support.[48]

But when Lewis arrived back in Chicago, she confronted hard questions about why she had acted without the input of her executive board and the schools' union representatives. She was criticized for an act of "presidential fiat" instead of defending her "commitment to union democracy."[49] At the next regularly scheduled House meeting on May 4, the delegates effectively condemned their president's actions. They voted to withdraw the union's support for SB 7 and directed their leaders to "lobby state legislators to remove the anti-union bargaining restrictions of the bill."[50] In defense of her actions, Lewis used her regular column in the union newsletter, the *Chicago Union Teacher*, to inform the membership of the hostile context in which the 75 percent strike authorization proposal was made. "Let's be crystal clear about our recent negotiations with the state legislature. The alternative was NO STRIKE, with the de-certification of the union if we did take that job action."[51] Along with her explanation, however, Lewis also demonstrated genuine respect for her membership's demand that the bill be revised. "Our members have spoken clearly and decisively—they do not like this bill and demand changes to the language inserted during last-minute midnight maneuvers that restricted their collective bargaining rights."[52]

In her comments Lewis also accused the bill's writers of altering what she believed was in the legislation. Recall that she had left the last meeting before the bill was drafted. CTU's counsel Robert Bloch specifically drew attention to how the "meaningless" new provision in Section 12(b) of the IELRA had been dangerously modified. The new, unapproved language, inserted by CPS, offensive to the union, stated: "A dispute or impasse over any Section 4.5 subject shall not be resolved through the procedures set forth in this Act, and the Board, mediator, or fact-finder has no jurisdiction over any Section 4.5 subject. The changes made to this subsection (b) by this amendatory Act of the ninety-seventh General Assembly are declarative of existing law." Bloch called the Section 12(b) amendment a "two-sentence atomic bomb that was slipped into the 110-page bill at the last minute." What the first sentence meant was that the law would essentially prevent the CTU from using the IELRA and the collective bargaining process to address disputes over 4.5 issues. But what most worried Bloch was the last four words of the second sentence. By stating that the amended law would be "declarative of existing law," the parties would be acknowledging that the previous law would undermine pending charges against CPS by retroactively rendering the conduct legal. According to Bloch, the language sabotaged union bargaining rights and permitted CPS "to tear up labor contracts it made [previously] on school issues found in Section 4.5 which pertain only to Chicago, such as class size, class schedules, pupil assessment policies and now the length of the work and school day and length of the work and school year."[53]

In addition to the Section 12(b) revision, CTU delegates raised a concern that the union would have needed a three-quarters "vote of all bargaining unit members to strike [both workers who were union members and those who were not union members] instead of bargaining unit members who were also members of the union."[54] When Lewis conceded to the unpopular, higher three-quarters threshold, she assumed it was a vote of 75 percent of *union members*. Roughly one thousand employees were covered by the CTU contract but were not full dues-paying members. The former requirement would have increased the difficulty of passing the legal threshold. Emboldened by the delegates' resistance, Lewis took the opportunity to fire a final salvo at SB 7: "Bargaining in good faith appears to be a bar set too high for these so-called education reformers— Advance Illinois, Stand for Children, Illinois Business Roundtable and their millionaire funders—who joined forces with the mayor-elect to steer the conversation, and the legislation, away from school improvement to an attack on unions and the children and families they serve."[55]

Upon hearing the news that CTU was rescinding its support for SB 7, leaders of the PC coalition expressed outrage. Steans claimed that Lewis had been largely a passive observer during the talks but knew precisely what had been agreed upon. The PC group issued a joint statement that read, in part:

> SB 7 is the same legislation that the Chicago Teachers Union assisted in crafting and openly supported in the Illinois Senate. For more than three months, state senators, school management groups, the State Board of Education, education reform organizations and teachers' unions—including the Chicago Teachers Union—sat at the same negotiating table and hammered out the specifics of SB 7. . . . The Chicago Teachers Union has now removed its support from SB 7 and in doing so, has undermined the good faith in which it was negotiated.[56]

Following the delegates' meeting, Lewis traveled back to Springfield, this time with attorney Robert Bloch at her side. Bloch had not been part of the initial negotiations over the bill. Bloch and Lewis's purpose was to negotiate a "trailer bill" to clean up the language in SB 7 to which CTU objected. Illinois's legislative process provides a mechanism for making technical adjustments to recently passed bills in order to ensure that the legislation aligns with what the parties intended. Lightford then sponsored an amendment to the House bill (known as Senate Amendment 1) that dropped the two sentences that Bloch claimed would blow up the bargaining relationship, permitted either side to declare a bargaining impasse once the fifteen-day mediation process began, and left no uncertainty that a three-quarters vote of only CTU union members was needed to commence a strike.[57]

While the trailer bill was being negotiated, and roughly one month after the Senate voted, the House passed SB 7 by a vote of 112 to 1. A trailer bill was subsequently passed.[58] Now acting with the backing of CTU's activist school leaders,

Lewis gave a final blessing to the bill. "I am satisfied with the outcome" of the negotiations producing the new language," she stated.[59] Surrounded by representatives from the large network of committee participants, but minus Lewis, Governor Quinn enthusiastically signed the measure into law on June 13, 2011, in Lightford's elementary school gymnasium. The senator's notes revealed that she believed her committee's work had produced a "game changer." In one way, it had.

Relishing the power he expected to get from the legislature, Emanuel proclaimed from the safety of a press conference at a charter school, "We're not going to negotiate or discuss whether children get more instruction—we will work together so that gets done. I'm not deviating from that. I was clear about it."[60] Lewis had stumbled in Springfield, but by respecting the collective voice of the delegates, she regained her footing. She also, crucially, advanced her democratic credentials as a union leader. Lewis could have ignored the criticism she heard from other union leaders and asserted executive authority. Instead, her willingness to acknowledge a mistake and adhere to the directives of the school-based leaders signaled that the union really was acting as though it belonged to the membership. At a time of great uncertainty for Chicago teachers, and long before CORE had established its governing credibility, Lewis fatefully acted consistently with her stated values. In doing so she turned what, at the time, was perceived by outsiders as a sign of weakness, into an evolving strength of leadership.

When asked about the law's passage, Lewis simply referred to it as "a beautiful organizing tool."[61] But no matter how offensive the law was, the legislation would not organize the CTU members by itself. For that, the union would have to construct an elaborate and unprecedented internal and external mobilization campaign that used the collective bargaining process as an opportunity to invigorate a school-based social movement. While the campaign was consistent with CORE's ideological identity, the result of a diminished political capacity highlighted the need for rank-and-file education and street-level clout.

6

THE CONTRACT CAMPAIGN

From the moment they took office in June 2010, the new CTU leadership and staff, together with CORE activists, began the process of transforming the CTU by educating, organizing, and mobilizing the members. By September 2012, hundreds of inactive members had been transformed into activists and leaders, who then energized and united a membership capable of waging a successful nine-day strike. For most local unions in the United States, the core strategy for collective bargaining is to reply on experienced, skilled union staff to negotiate an acceptable contract, whereas rank-and-file members have a negligible role to play. Negotiations are held behind closed doors, with little or nothing reported to the members by mutual agreement between the management and the union bargaining teams. The role of the members is to wait passively and then vote to accept or reject the contract. Rarely, in an era when most striking members can lose their jobs, do they vote to strike. As one teacher put it, "A lot of what people felt was [that] this malaise hit, not just the Chicago Teachers Union, but unions in general. Unions are known for having their bigwigs and the lawyers go into the [bargaining] room, come out with a contract, [and tell the members] 'Here's what we came up with, accept it or reject it.' And everybody goes, 'Ah, well, it's probably the best we're gonna do' and members accept costly cutbacks and concessions with quiet resignation."[1]

But since the 1990s an increasing number—albeit still a minority—of local unions have begun to educate, organize, and mobilize the members in the months leading up to a contract's expiration in what is labeled a "contract campaign." In a contract campaign, the union's leadership does not see the union's power as existing only at the bargaining table, but also in a united, mobilized membership prepared to strike.

In most local unions, it is challenging to organize a successful contract campaign, because many members and leaders define the role of union leaders as representatives solving problems *for* the members rather than as organizing members to come together to win justice on the job. So when some members are asked to become activists, their initial response, as one CTU teacher stated about her attitude before the contract campaign, is "I pay $1,000 a year in union dues and they are supposed to do certain things for me. Because I don't want to be a union organizer."[2] As staff coordinator Jackson Potter said, the immense challenge was "to transform a moribund union" into a bottom-up, member-driven, organizing union.[3] Especially daunting was the size of the task—26,500 union employees were spread across 580 schools in a city of 228 square miles.

Their greatest obstacle to mobilizing CTU members—both when CORE led the fight to keep schools open, and in 2011–12 with the contract campaign—was not, as many unions lament, member apathy. As organizing coordinator Norine Gutekanst put it, "Our people care about the mayor taking back their negotiated 4 percent raise, they care about their working conditions, they care about their students' learning conditions, and they care about job security. It's not apathy. Member hesitance is not apathy. Our goal is convincing them that by fighting together we can be effective and we can win."[4] Through the course of the contract campaign, union staff and activists undertook tens of thousands of conversations to overcome this sense of hopelessness and to convince educators that the union had a winning strategy to defeat Mayor Rahm Emanuel, his appointed school board, and the huge array of forces aligned against them.

A National Upswing in Activism

A positive national and international context made it easier for CTU to convince members that tens of thousands could be mobilized and achieve success. In Wisconsin, in February 2011, mass marches were held every day to protest proposed legislation that would cripple public-sector unions. Saturday mobilizations reached 150,000, and hundreds of protesters occupied the capitol building for two weeks. The CTU sent buses of members, who came back enthralled by the size and energy of the movement and by the commitment to mass nonviolent civil disobedience. As teacher Sarah Chambers recalled, joining the mass protest in Wisconsin was "one of the greatest days of my life. They shut down their capitol. So we thought after that, 'OK, why can't we shut down our city with twenty thousand marchers?'"[5] On April 9, 2011, the CTU turned out hundreds of members to join ten thousand unionists at the Chicago Federation of Labor's "We Are One" rally in solidarity with Wisconsin workers.

Then in fall 2011, the Occupy Wall Street movement rapidly spread from New York City to scores of cities across the country. In Chicago, daily protests began in the financial district, drawing in hundreds of mostly young people who had never been part of a social movement. An Occupy Chicago labor working group drew dozens of union activists, including CTU representatives, to its meetings; participated in numerous labor actions in 2011 and 2012; and sought to educate unions on why they should support the Occupy movement. All this activity culminated in a successful January 2012 conference attended by 250 unionists and young Occupy Chicago activists.[6]

The Occupy Wall Street movement coincided with the actions of a new labor-community coalition initiated by the Service Employees International Union (SEIU), Stand Up! Chicago, which called demonstrations in downtown Chicago, attended by thousands, to "fight for a fair economy." Stand Up!'s biggest effort came in October 2011, after a week-long series of actions. Five feeder marches, each taking up a theme of schools, jobs, or housing, culminated in a seven-thousand-person rally at the site where American Mortgage Bankers Association bankers were holding a convention in downtown Chicago. The CTU had a major presence in all the actions, and CTU leaders were arrested while carrying out nonviolent civil disobedience.

The Arab Spring began in December 10, 2011, and engulfed Tunisia, Egypt, Libya, Yemen, Bahrain, and Syria. Those historic protest movements showed that change was possible—dictator after dictator fell as millions took to the streets demanding democracy. And the protests, especially in Tunisia and Egypt, took on a new tactic soon replicated by the Wisconsin and Occupy protesters and later by the CTU for the first four days of the 2012 strike: daily mass protests.

In May 2012, 150 CTU members, their registration paid by the union, joined 1,350 union activists from cities across the country at the biannual Labor Notes conference in Chicago to discuss and debate tactics and strategies to move the labor movement forward as a democratic, member-driven social movement. CTU activist Jen Johnson was a keynote speaker, and teachers from across the country met in a workshop to share experiences and debate strategy.[7] High school teacher Cynthia Smith recalled, "It was phenomenal. It really opened my eyes to the labor movement. Just talking with people, finding out that the issues that exist are not just for the Chicago Teachers Union, but it's a much broader spectrum. It's a nationwide, worldwide issue."[8]

First Steps

In June 2010, the newly elected CTU leaders took strategic steps to launch an intensive internal organizing drive. The officers cut their own salaries by an average of 35 percent and eliminated or reduced staff members' exorbitant perks in order to raise funds to hire organizers.[9] A new Organizing Department was created, led by veteran elementary school teacher and CORE activist Norine Gutekanst. The department brought in a group of teachers as part-time summer organizing interns, then, in September, hired six of them as full-time organizers. All were energetic, talented organizers in their twenties or thirties; five were teachers, and a sixth was an experienced health-care sector union organizer, Matt Luskin, who had led contract campaigns. Each organizer was assigned one hundred schools. Their first task was to make sure each school had an active delegate, and that the delegate was educated about and in agreement with the union's organizing program.[10]

That summer, the organizing department held contract campaign trainings for delegates. By October, there had been organizing meetings at 200 of the 580 schools, and the union held eight regional meetings to garner feedback on what members wanted in the next contract. That month's lead article in the *Chicago Union Teacher*, "Let's Unleash the Power of 30,000: Join the CTU Contract Campaign and Get in the Fight!," officially launched the campaign.

In fall 2010, CTU asked the Labor Education Program (LEP) at the University of Illinois to provide training about the contract campaigns. The CTU-LEP relationship had begun in early 2010 with classes on union leadership, organizing, and history that were attended by CORE activists who would, a few months later, become the union's officers and staff. In the fall, LEP was asked to collaborate with the CTU's education arm, the Quest Center, led by veteran teacher Carol Caref, to produce a video on the attacks assailing teachers, CTU history, the issues facing the CTU, and the need for all CTU members to get involved in the campaign. The 11-minute video, called *Meeting Challenges, Past and Present*, was completed in March 2011. Copies were distributed to all delegates to show in their after-school union meetings, and the video was available on the union's website. President Lewis narrated the video and concluded with a call to arms:

> We need you to: Attend after-school union meetings. Join a union committee. Go to union rallies. Talk to your neighbors, family members, friends, and your kids' parents. Help build a parent-teacher-community coalition to defend quality education in your school. Help educate, organize, and mobilize as part of the union's campaign leading up to our June 2012 contract. . . . Now, in order to do our jobs, in order to guarantee that our students get the education they deserve, we have to fight.

We are the ones who care about our students and our communities. It is time to bring back the joy of teaching and learning. We can do this together. Because the union makes us strong![11]

The union's strategy was focused on having tens of thousands of conversations with the members about the challenges they faced and the strategy that was necessary to win. As organizer Matt Luskin put it, "Our work really did become about winning the membership over to a strategy, deeply discussing with our members an analysis of what was happening in the world, and building confidence that there was a strategy that might beat it. That was the heart of the organizing."[12]

In July 2011, LEP held a week-long class on messaging and contract campaigns for CTU activists. Then on October 12, 2011, LEP led a workshop for forty CTU district supervisors who were appointed by the officers. The district supervisors—an unusual name for union leaders—functioned as intermediate leaders between the CTU's officers and staff on the one hand, and the eight hundred delegates who meet monthly at the House of Delegates meetings on the other. Each elementary school had one delegate, and high schools with a larger staff might have two or three delegates.[13] A more descriptive title for the district supervisors might be "delegate coordinators." In the 1980s, they had served as strike captains during five strikes, but, in the 1990s, under a business unionist leadership, they had evolved into a body with minimal duties: they met monthly to hear the CTU Executive Committee minutes and they oversaw delegate elections. The new CTU leaders moved the monthly meetings to the week before the House of Delegates meeting, instead of the night before, so they would have time to organize their delegates.[14]

By 2011, there had been a huge turnover of district supervisors; most were thanked for their service and let go, and delegates who saw themselves as organizers were brought in as district supervisors. The union organizers recruited new people, who were told, as CTU Financial-Secretary Kristine Mayle, who oversaw the district supervisors, recalled:

You are going to be a wing of our organizing model. There are only six full-time organizers, so you are going to be the union's eyes and the ears in the schools. You're going to tell us who the good people are that are willing to work. You are going to help us get problems solved and troubleshoot for those who are having issues in their building. Your main task is to build relationships with people. Your delegates should know you, they should know your phone number, they should know your e-mail, and they should expect a call from you at least every month.[15]

Each district supervisor was assigned to oversee membership involvement and delegates in roughly fifteen schools. It was their job to make sure a contract action committee was formed in each of their schools. Recalled CTU organizing coordinator Gutekanst, "We insisted that there be regular conversations, not just on e-mail, with the delegates and their schools. Every month we would have a set of 'asks' that the district supervisors would ask the delegates to do. It was a way to turn the district supervisors into organizers and also give delegates the message that this union is really reaching into your school and trying to get your people informed and active."[16]

The October 12 LEP workshop at CTU headquarters outlined the goals of a contract campaign, how contract action committees would function, and work-site activities and community outreach that each committee could undertake. Prior to the meeting, the district supervisors had been mailed a letter explaining the campaign and asking them to watch the *Power at Work* contract campaign video produced in the late 1990s by the Teamsters.[17] Together with the video, handouts distributed at the October 12 meeting outlined the structure of the contract action committees. The organizing work could not be done by just one or two people—each school's union delegate would need to recruit people to the committee. The committee needed to be as racially diverse as the membership and include teachers who taught different grades, clinicians, and paraprofessional staff.

The heart of the program was that each member of the committee would be responsible for regularly talking to ten CTU members to answer questions about the union's goals and strategy, address mistruths in the mainstream media or rumors, update members on the progress of the contract campaign and of bargaining, and organize members to participate in union actions. One teacher recalled, "As soon as we would get information, we would spread it out. We kept the members very, very engaged. They knew what was going on."[18] Members were also urged to sign up to receive regular CTU e-mails with updates on bargaining and contract campaign actions.

In the fall, as well, the union set up a biweekly organizers' meeting to plan and assess the strengths and weaknesses of the contract campaign. Three organizing conferences for delegates were a key part of implementing the contract campaign. The first was held on November 5, 2011, and was attended by two hundred activists. Delegates listened to CTU Vice President Jesse Sharkey outline the campaign and watched the *Power at Work* video. Then teams of two district supervisors assisted by the organizing staff led twenty workshops on how to implement the campaign. Attendees also participated in union skills-building workshops.

Organizing in the Schools

Just as the contract campaign was beginning in September 2011, Chicago Mayor Rahm Emanuel pushed an issue that forced the union to rapidly gear up. The mayor had campaigned on the need for a longer school day and helped pass SB 7, which allowed him, starting with the 2012–13 school year, to lengthen the school day. But he surprised the union by going to individual schools, a year before the law was to take effect, to offer monetary rewards to individual teachers if they would vote to immediately implement the longer school day.[19]

It was clear to the union that the mayor's plan was to target schools with newer or younger staffs, or with staffs that were all new because everyone had been fired in a "turnaround" administered by a private organization, the Academy for Urban School Leadership. CTU contended that CPS illegally "threatened to close schools if teachers did not approve contract modifications; interrogated teachers about their union activities; directed teachers to report their communications with the union; and banned CTU representatives from consulting with teachers before they were coerced into waiving parts of their labor contract."[20]

The "waiver vote"—teachers at a school waiving their right not to have a longer school day imposed until the law allowed it a year later—presented the union with its first big organizing challenge. CTU's school-by-school battle against the waiver began a constant assessment process that quickly became integral to all the union's organizing. "It forced us to look at every school," recalled Jackson Potter, to look at what actions the members were taking, to assess union strength in each school. "Did the delegates circulate a petition to the Local School Council around why a better day is a critical aspect of a longer day, if there is going to be a longer day, and why we have objections to the longer day? Will they vote up or down on the waiver? What was the vote total? Every day we were updating and it got us into some good habits around doing assessment." And it forced the union to move quickly to get a new delegate in every school that did not have one or that had an inactive one.[21]

"And the entire time," said Karen Lewis, "we were having conversations with our parents about what would make schools better. We always had a different vision of what schools should look like. We said to the board, 'You have the right to a longer day, but let's make it a better day, because if you're only elongating the day we have, everyone's just going to get tired. There's no evidence that a longer day in itself is better.' Parents wanted art, music, PE [physical education], world languages. They wanted classes that were not just reading and math all day long. The parents understood that the mayor was bullying us."[22]

In 185 schools, teacher activists organized mock votes in which teachers voted down the mayor's effort to by-pass the union by immediately implementing the longer school day. On November 4, the IELRB found the mayor's action to be illegal. "The narrative in the press was that it was the Illinois Education[al] Labor Relations Board that stopped the mayor," noted Jackson Potter. "That wasn't true. It was helpful but it was the organizing campaign that stopped him."

When school resumed following the winter break, the organizing staff and district supervisors escalated the contract campaign. They distributed an Open Letter petition against the implementation of the longer school day, with a goal of having it signed by thousands of members and parents.[23] And they publicized a drive for CTU members to wear the union's red shirt, or any red shirt, every Friday, to signal their solidarity to the CPS administration and the mayor.

Momentum steadily built so that, by April 2012, CTU members were regularly wearing red on Fridays at 90 percent of the schools. Schools took group photos of red-shirted members and posted them proudly on the CTU website. One CTU member recalled,

> En masse, we started running red, we took red as our color. Red's a great color. It looks good on a lot of people. It's the color of labor. But it was a grudging process for some people [who would say], "Oh, I don't believe in the union, what has the union done for me, or whatever." [And we'd say,] "Just wear red every Friday." And I think that that symbolism started transferring into other things. [We'd say,] "Well now that you're wearing the red, can you come out to this rally and wear your red?" And it was a gradual building.[24]

Special education teacher Sarah Chambers related how organizing the campaign evolved at her school:

> Organizing took a lot of time and a lot of work. [To form] the contract action team, I chose one member from each grade level. We made it diverse in terms of age, in terms of race, and also subject area. And these [activists] eventually turned into the strike lieutenants during the strike. And with our CAT [Contract Action Team] members spread throughout the building, we were able to disseminate information about upcoming union events and other union news. So our teachers were really informed, which was really, really important because of all the misinformation in the news. And these teams also planned actions to grow our unity and power. We started small. Just getting everyone to wear red was a start. And from there we grew. We had informational pickets, we made flyers, speaking out to the parents, speaking out to the community. We wrote a letter to our Local School Council asking them to

support us with our contract demands. All these actions helped us become more organized and prepared for the strike. It took a lot of work. It wasn't a cakewalk. For the last three years every morning, every lunch, all the preps [i.e., prep time], [we] were basically speaking one on one to teachers. [In the beginning] a lot of our teachers were even antiunion. But by June 2012 almost all the teachers were on board. There were teachers that were antiunion before, who hated the union, who now were preaching to other teachers that "You better vote yes for that strike authorization vote!"[25]

Across the system, the process was, naturally, uneven. By spring 2012, hundreds of schools had active contract action committees. And in some schools, the idea of one contract action committee member's being in regular touch with ten members deepened to the point that the ten members saw themselves as a close-knit team with responsibility to be in touch with one another. But in other schools organizing was harder. One teacher recalled that organizing at her school was uphill, so that "everybody who showed up at the union meeting was the contract action committee."[26] And in some schools the delegate and one or two other activists did all the work of informing and rallying the members.

As the contract action committees organized, they drew on the experience and passion of scores of CORE activists. As one of these activists noted, "CORE had a big influence on all of this because the CORE members are really strong—I think some of the strongest leaders in the whole union. We were leaders in building up to the strike. We kind of modeled how to [organize], where other schools learned from us and heard our stories." In March, CORE members began distributing a flyer at hundreds of schools headlined, "Is Your School Prepared to Strike?"[27]

On March 10, 2012, the union held its third delegates' conference, attended by more than five hundred delegates and contract action committee members. The union's staff led small-group discussions to assess the strengths and weaknesses of the campaign. Each participant received a list of the teachers and staff at her or his school so delegates could note each member's participation in specific actions. Participants shared their results with the group and discussed ideas for expanding the campaign and ways to organize in schools with hostile principals. As Luskin summarized, "We focused on mapping and assessing your entire building, with the message that . . . the job of the delegate was to have a plan on how to move people. We offered them skills about how to overcome obstacles. It was empowering."[28]

In the workshops, delegates at some schools reported that many of their members were afraid to show their support for the union because principals would yell at, intimidate, and threaten teachers and staff. (At one school the principal went so far as to call the police when CTU organizer Gutekanst entered the building. The police officer, when shown the union contract allowing access, refused to do anything.) Activists discussed how schools in which the union was strong, as well as high schools with far more members than elementary schools, could assist unionists at nearby schools with bullying principals. As one activist noted, the delegate trainings focused on "how to get people [active] who aren't on board, [how to talk to] people who were afraid, what can you do to get the people who were really scared to kind of take a step forward and another step forward, and then how to network out to your parents and what to say and how to say it in a positive way."[29]

As the contract campaign unfolded in April and May, the committees began to initiate their own actions. Some schools met with their aldermen to explain their issues. Others knocked on doors in the school's neighborhood to talk to parents. Some spoke with local small business people and clergy. Others leafleted parents on report card pickup day. And many held their own mock strike votes. As Luskin related,

> We spent a lot of energy giving members the skills and tools they needed to reach out to unorganized parents and community members. This was really important. We said to our members, "Do it. You don't need our permission. You don't need to go through us. Here's some training on how to do it." So our members built the parent support themselves through the Local School Council meetings, calling for meetings with parents, leafleting parents after school, and petitions. There were an amazing number of parent meetings popping up all over the city.[30]

During the contract campaign CTU leaders and organizers also began to educate members about approaching the grievance procedure differently. This procedure, though a victory for unions when it was established in the 1930s and 1940s, and one reason workers join unions, had serious flaws. It could take a lot of time. It could create a culture of passivity in which the members, when they filed a grievance, were often told by the union representative or steward that they did not need to do anything but wait for "the union," defined as the staff and not the members, to handle the negotiation of the grievance for them. Under previous CTU administrations, the union's full-time field staff handled nearly all grievances; delegates were not trained to be union stewards and handle grievances themselves. The new leadership and CORE activists pushed members to view the grievance process more aggressively. They told members that sometimes grievances that affected numerous employees could be opportunities to educate, organize, and mobilize the members, in the process empowering them with the knowledge that if they came together they had the ability to stand up to principals who disregarded the contract.

Jackson Potter recalled that, at one elementary school, the principal tried to bully teachers, telling them "You're going to work an after-school program, but I'm not paying you for it. And I'm not taking input on what it will look like." In response, the members decided to circulate a petition among the teachers and staff and confronted the principal at his office. Within two hours the principal sent out an e-mail that the program was voluntary, people who participated would be paid, and he wanted their feedback on what it would look like. "So at delegate conferences when we had stories like this," said Potter, "we would bring these people out to talk about what they did and share their experiences, and it was infectious. We were really deliberate about doing that."[31]

Thousands of the members went through a steady evolution from being uninvolved, to wearing red T-shirts on Fridays, to attending union actions, to becoming organizers at their schools, to giving speeches about their cause. As one teacher recalled, "I started out small—just participating in a march. Then at a small demonstration, somebody handed me a megaphone and said, 'Can you say a little something?' So then it went from megaphone to megaphone, to being a marshal at union actions, to really feeling like I was a complete, absolute part of the movement."[32]

A rank-and-file teacher who served on the CTU Executive Board recalled seeing a radical shift in how a co-worker viewed herself and the union: "The principal made some statement about 'Your union should have told you this . . .' and someone responded, '*We* are the union. We tell them; they don't tell us!' I never heard that from her before, and she was never really active before. She never would have said that before, but she finally got it. It is *we* who enforce change. And whether or not CPS says something, if we as a union get together on an issue, we don't have to take what CPS says."[33] Such stories happened thousands of times across the city. As a new teacher recounted, "A CTU organizer came to our school and she said something that really stayed with me. She was a teacher for many years and she said she used to see the union as 'They are there to fight for my rights.' But then she came to realize, 'No, *I* am there to fight for my rights. You can't leave it up to other people to fight for your rights.'"[34]

Especially as the possibility of a strike loomed closer, activists across the city gave special attention to speaking with younger teachers who had little experience with the union; had not fully experienced the travails of working in a Chicago public school; and were nervous, as new employees, about the idea of striking. The union also organized phone banks targeting new teachers to answer questions and engage in conversations about the union's issues and strategy.

Polling the Members

In order to assess the strength of the contract campaign and prepare for the official strike authorization vote in June, the union planned to hold a practice strike vote in May. But in the meantime, in early April, some schools took the initiative of surveying members about their willingness to strike, and when other schools heard about it they did the same. Lewis called a press conference on April 5 to announce that her members had voted "overwhelmingly" in 150 schools to support strike action. In a May 9 *Chicago Sun-Times* opinion piece, she declared that the vote came because her members were furious "at the district's bullying behavior that has created a hostile and volatile work climate for our members."[35]

The union set May 10 for a citywide poll about contract issues. This was not a strike authorization vote, but a practice vote—a survey of the members' feelings about the mayor's and the school board's actions. Survey questions were designed to exclude mention of a strike, although the implication was clear. The four questions were:

1. Do you believe the Board of Education's proposals are disrespectful to teachers, clinicians, and paraprofessionals?
2. Do you believe that the Board's proposals would harm students and lower the educational quality of your school?
3. Do you believe the Board's proposals should be rejected by the Union?
4. Do you think CEO (Jean-Claude) Brizard should resign?[36]

The poll showed more than 90 percent voted yes on the first three questions and a lower figure for the fourth. But the real goal was to note the turnout at every school so that the union could send more organizers to weak schools. With SB 7's mandate that 75 percent of all members must authorize a strike, the union did not want holes in its organizing drive.

Union officials announced at a May 22 news conference that the polling showed that 21,000 members had opposed the district's contract offer. Reporting the results, Lewis declared:

> This exercise was not only a way for us to gauge what our members think about the board's current contract proposals, but to show the public that CPS is trying to mislead taxpayers and destroy quality public schools. We are being very transparent as we all prepare for the worst. None of us want a strike—it isn't good for anyone, not our members and certainly not our students. However, if the board insists on destroying the love and joy of teaching and learning, our members will be left

with no other option; they will take a stand against this escalating disrespect and school sabotage.[37]

The May 10 poll and each subsequent union action had four goals. First, the union aimed to show Mayor Emanuel and the Board of Education that the members were unified, that the leadership at the bargaining table spoke for 26,500 angry members. Second, the union sought to show the public—and in particular parents with kids in CPS schools—that the union was fighting for them and their children. Third, the actions were designed to increase the rank-and-file CTU members' self-confidence and belief in the power of a member-driven union to win justice. And fourth, union leadership used each action to assess where the organizing department needed to shift resources to more effectively educate and organize members. This was a lesson, learned from union organizing campaigns, that proved to be vital to the union's success.[38] Every action, said Potter, "was a test we created ourselves" to assess strengths and weaknesses.[39] And each successive action drew in more members as activists, raised union consciousness, and increased morale.

The May 23 Rally and March

The May 23 rally proved to be a turning point that electrified the membership. The union called the weekday rally for its members at the Roosevelt University Auditorium Theatre, which seated four thousand, in downtown Chicago. It was the largest venue available, so the union organized a rally at a nearby park for the hoped-for overflow crowd. The park at Congress and Michigan had a symbolic significance; twice, several thousand Occupy Chicago protesters had marched to the site in October 2011 intent on setting up a tent encampment, and twice Mayor Emanuel had ordered hundreds arrested.

The May 23 date was set to precede the June 6 strike authorization vote, and to coincide with a rally called by the Stand Up! Chicago labor-community coalition initiated by the SEIU the previous summer. Several thousand Stand Up! protesters were a half mile away protesting the city's corporate welfare tax giveaways to the Chicago Mercantile Exchange. The CTU had, from its inception, been a key player in the Stand Up! Chicago coalition. And the CTU was also fighting corporate welfare as tens of millions of dollars each year were diverted from the schools to highly profitable corporations through the city's Tax Increment Financing (TIF) program.

In the weeks leading up to the rally, the union knew the contract campaign was working. They knew that the bulk of their members at hundreds of schools were wearing red union T-shirts every Friday, and that the turnout for the May 10 practice strike vote had been high. They knew that more than a hundred buses had been rented by the contract action committees for the rally. The union would never have called the rally if it had not set up the contract action committees. Calling an action and having a low turnout would have demoralized the entire union and set back bargaining. As one teacher noted,

> With the action teams [i.e., contract action committees] we were able to reach out to members and organize them and get them to go to the May 23 action and other rallies. There were people in my staff that went who had never been to a protest in their entire lives. We had a member from each grade-level team to reach out to their people. Before, it was just the delegate and me saying, 'Come on, come to this rally,' but now you had your friends [on the committee], and people felt accountable to bring people from their team to these rallies.[40]

But there was no guarantee that overworked teachers would leave school and take a bus or a train downtown, knowing that they would not arrive home until nine o'clock and still have hours of grading and prep work for the next day's classes. "Can we really fill this place?" Kristine Mayle asked a fellow teacher on the stage.[41]

As teachers poured off buses and trains, the auditorium's main hall began steadily to fill. The noise level grew as teachers cheered, chanted, and sang along to prounion songs played over the sound system. As the second and then the third tier of the balcony filled with red-shirted teachers, they could feel the crowd's electricity rise. "I never thought so many teachers would come out there that day," said one teacher, echoing many members' sentiments. "That changed everything; that was the beginning of the whole movement."[42]

A May 25 *Chicago Sun-Times* editorial called it a "thunderous, revival-style rally." Rank-and-file teachers, community supporters, City Council members, and a high school student all spoke. Mayle laid out the indictment against the Board of Education's antiteacher, antistudent policies. Lewis was the last speaker. No one on the stage had mentioned the word strike, but as Lewis denounced the board's policies and then asked the crowd, "Why are we here?" the entire crowd began to chant "Strike! Strike! Strike!"

As they poured out of the auditorium, members grabbed union signs reading "Yes to Respect," "Yes to Dignity," "Yes to Student Needs," and "Yes to Smaller Class Sizes." Activists handed out a thousand CORE buttons; they "went like hotcakes" recalled Jen Johnson.[43] Teachers interviewed during the one-mile march echoed the same theme: "I can't believe we did it!" "I've been in the union for decades and we've never done anything like this before!" and "It's amazing, it's exhilarating."[44]

High school teacher John Thuet expressed the feelings of the mass of teachers when he told the *Chicago Tribune*, "I feel like we're getting walked on. If we don't stop it now, I don't know when it will stop."[45] From that rally and march through the others that were to come, the phrase "a sea of red" became the most common description protesters used to portray the throngs of red-shirted activists at CTU actions.

CTU member Jay Rehak, who called the day "historic," aptly expressed the emotions among CTU members at the May 23 action. "It was one of the best events of its kind I have ever attended. [We] were fired up, with a great spirit and energy." "This is the proudest moment of my twenty-six-year teaching career," said high school teacher Anthony Smith. "It was a glorious moment [of] inspiration and a message of hope."[46]

People on the street gave the thumbs-up sign, onlookers waved from high-rise windows, and travelers in cars and buses who were delayed as the marchers flooded the streets surprised the teachers by honking and waving their support.

There were chants—"CTU, CTU, CTU" was the most popular, followed by "Hey hey, ho ho, Rahm Emanuel has got to go!" and "We need teachers, we need books; we need the money that Rahm took!" But the dominant sound was a loud cacophony of screams and cheers expressing both the teachers' deep frustration with the mayor and his appointed Board of Education and their exhilaration at the march's massive numbers and unity. As the marchers merged with the Stand Up! Chicago protest already underway blocks from the auditorium, they saw a huge banner proclaiming "We Support the Teachers." Television news reported that the crowd grew to ten thousand.

Teachers were also struck that, as they gave passersby stickers reading "Yes to smaller classrooms" to put on their shirts, none of the scores of police officers present turned one down or took it off his or her shirt. In the rallies and picket lines over the next months, police, firefighters, sanitation workers, bus drivers, and other public workers showed strong support for the teachers, because they also faced demands for weaker contracts and diminished working conditions.

Before the rally, Mayor Emanuel did his best to deflect media attention to himself by suddenly praising Chicago's teachers and claiming that there was no need for a strike. "Chicago teachers deserve a pay raise," Emanuel said, for the first time since his election. "They work very hard. They deserve a pay raise. Chicago school children do not deserve a strike. We are working with an independent arbitrator to ensure that we achieve both of those goals, and we're committed to that process." Then the mayor took off for a Chicago White Sox baseball game, with the unsubtle message that the teachers' demonstration was unworthy of his attention.[47]

Leadership

The new CTU leadership set out to change the relationship between the union's members and its leaders. As one member put it, "Before the strike I saw the union as an entity up there, some far-out office away [from my school]."[48] A common feeling among CTU members during Stewart's tenure as president from 2004 to 2010 was: "I'm paying my dues, but what the hell are they doing for me?"[49] Or as one member put it, in the past "there was no room for the membership to do anything, because the leadership's attitude was 'We'll take care of it.' I just paid my dues. There wasn't any education about trying to get the community involved. There was no fight against the damage that was being done by the City of Chicago's policy of closing schools."[50]

The new leadership embraced the philosophy that victories came only from a democratic, grassroots, member-driven union. As Lewis put it:

> I trust our membership, totally. And when you trust your membership, good things happen. The key is that people need to decide what they want their union to be, and I'm talking about members as opposed to leaders. Every union needs to do some soul searching about what its purpose is. . . . The union leadership does not tell the members what to do. To me, having those discussions in the rank and file is so important. We do take democracy seriously. And I know that's frustrating for people, but in the end it is ultimately a better way to govern a union because it is not top-down leadership. We have encouraged healthy debate and we have encouraged analysis. It was something that was never encouraged by union leadership before. It's a better way to move the union.[51]

The leadership repeatedly told the members: This is your union. You run the union. You are the union. Step up. Take initiatives in your building to organize the members. Don't call union headquarters to ask permission—just do it.

As CTU organizer Matt Luskin recalled, the union began by saying to the eight hundred delegates, "Your role no longer is to go to the monthly House of Delegates meeting and then have a meeting at your school and present the information. Your role isn't to be an information conduit. Your role is to become an organizer." He added that, initially, "some people embraced it, and some thought it was crazy talk."[52] Those unwilling to take on the new role often resigned as delegates and were replaced by members eager to organize.

As a twenty-seven-year veteran teacher put it, the union's leaders "went into it with a sense that things need to change. [Their attitude was] 'We are not the decision-making body here.' It doesn't happen in the offices. It happens with the people, so how are we going to strategically do this so that the people will say 'Yes, I feel this, I want to be a part of it.' The leadership encouraged us to do anything by any means possible to build the contract campaign."[53]

An indication of the leadership's democratic approach was the formation of a "big bargaining committee" of thirty rank-and-file members in addition to the ten CTU officers and staff sitting at the bargaining table. In contrast to the secretive nature of traditional union-management collective bargaining, there would be complete transparency. The rank-and-file members' role was to participate in committees to discuss specific areas of the contract and to share information with the members on the progress of negotiations. As Lewis explained, "We had members from all over the city in different areas—high school, grammar school, our paraprofessionals, our clinicians—all on our big bargaining team, so that they could actually see the process of negotiations. They could see that it wasn't like a little room with just two or three people in it just haggling [it] out. So that made a difference, too, because people felt involved."[54]

As one member of the big bargaining team remarked, "[Management] wasn't ready for all of us to be part of the negotiating team. They thought that we were some sort of audience thing, some sort of gimmick. . . . The mayor thought of the union as the way a lot of unions have become lately where it's some sort of top-down thing where 'We're negotiating with Karen Lewis' really is the way they look at [it]. . . . They were exceptionally disrespectful to us and to Karen Lewis in particular," until the union leaders made it clear that "this isn't the audience, this is part of our team, they help us, and they're part of this thing. . . . The tone changed as we went along, they kind of figured out that we're not going away." And, she added, "We kept members so well informed. Very few people felt like anybody was hiding anything. Everything was very transparent."[55]

The Schools Chicago's Students Deserve

The new leadership redirected the work and increased the number of staff of the union's Quest Center, which had focused on professional-development trainings. In 2010, led by veteran CORE activist Carol Caref, it would also become the Research Department. Throughout the contract negotiations the Research Department "costed out" the contract (i.e., determined what items would cost over the length of the deal), checked the school board's figures, compared other contracts and health-care plans, and did critical research legwork for the bargaining team.

They also generated research reports, which were to play a critical role in the union's struggle, to provide important information for members, parents, and the public. In February 2012, shortly before bargaining began, the department released the forty-six-page report *The Schools Chicago's Students Deserve*, which put forward CTU's own analysis of what was wrong with Chicago's schools and its perspective on what was needed to improve the schools. The union sought to change the conversation from what the union was fighting *against* to what the union was fighting *for*. The report would also help educate the members about the issues so that they could better talk to the press and have conversations with their schools' parents and community leaders.

The report had sections outlining the need for smaller class sizes; for a full curriculum that included art, music, physical education, and languages; nurses, social workers, and counselors in every school; prekindergarten education; quality school facilities ("no more leaky roofs, asbestos-lined bathrooms, or windows that refuse to shut"); and fully fundied public education. The report boldly asserted that every CPS student "deserves to have the same quality education as the children of the wealthy"; that "the education children receive should not depend on zip code, family income, or racial background." At the union's press conference announcing the report's publication, Lewis asserted that "for far too long our students have been short-changed, their teachers have been undermined, and their schools have been financially starved of the resources they need. Today we release our vision of what a CPS education should look like for every student, not just those from higher income brackets. We need fresh and innovative ideas, not the same status quo and failed policies of the past seventeen years."[56]

The report called the Chicago public school system "educational apartheid" and Lewis and other CTU leaders began regularly to use that phrase. It highlighted the fact that CPS schools were heavily segregated. It pointed out that CPS denied resources to the neediest schools, which were usually in black and Latino neighborhoods, and linked poverty to poor student outcomes. It noted that Chicago teachers struggled to meet the needs of fifteen thousand homeless students who were largely black and Latino, and that discipline policies had largely harmed students of color.

It reported that while 43 percent of CPS students were black, teacher layoffs had disproportionately impacted black teachers. In 1995, African-Americans were 45 percent of CPS teachers, but by 2012, they had dropped to 20 percent. When the union talked about 160 schools that did not have a library or librarian, the issue was both about every student's needs *and* about race, as most of those schools were in predominantly African-American neighborhoods. "I think that making a decision to talk about race in a really serious way wound up really mattering for us," said Luskin. "The support that came from black and Latino communities was huge, and that was opened up much further by us talking about racism and taking on the demands of those communities around schools and their needs in public education."[57]

As Gutekanst noted, "This report was pivotal in building support, both within our ranks and among parents. We circulated it everywhere, among parents, politicians, education experts, and the press. We also distilled the report into a ten-point one-pager in English and Spanish and took it to every meeting."[58]

Union activists embraced the document, and contract action committees discussed how the facts and arguments in the report could be used to unify the members and reach out to parents. It gave us "the ammo for taking on the media," said CTU activist Michelle Gunderson.[59]

Clinicians and Paraprofessional Staff

Roughly 5.5 percent of CTU members were clinicians—social workers, nurses, speech pathologists, psychologists, and occupational or physical therapists. Another 13 percent were Paraprofessional and School-Related Personnel (PSRPs): teacher assistants, school clerks, and other support staff.

During the 2010 union election campaign, social worker Susan Hickey began calling meetings of CPS social workers, which were then expanded to include all clinicians. CORE activists established a temporary group called Clinicians on the Move, which sponsored a lively "Meet the Candidates" forum. In late 2010, Hickey was appointed by the new leadership to chair a Clinicians Steering Committee, which adopted the goal of making sure clinicians were part of all CTU committees and that clinicians' issues were acknowledged and highlighted. "The clinicians themselves embarked on a project to educate the union leadership," recalled social worker Carol Hayse, "that our issues in some ways are very different than the teachers. It took a somewhat vigorous effort to do so. Fortunately, this dovetailed perfectly with the leadership's insight that poverty, family stress, and so on have huge impacts on children's learning."[60]

The new leadership team made a determined effort to make the union more inclusive to the clinicians and support staff, who had felt excluded in the past. It was more difficult to involve clinicians, since most worked at several schools. And language was an additional obstacle—clinicians and paraprofessionals felt excluded when union leaders used the word "teachers" to refer to all CTU members. "Karen Lewis and the leadership started adding the words *clinician* and *paraprofessionals* every time she spoke," said one social worker, "which was huge" to us.[61] The change in language was like a breath of fresh air to the clinicians and support staff.

"We injected ourselves into activities that would previously have been for teachers only," said Hayse. "For example, we suggested that at an event the clinicians would need their own workshop as our issues from an organizing standpoint were quite different. CTU staff would say things like 'When you are organizing at your school . . .' and we would pipe up, 'Yeah, but clinicians have two to five schools each. How does that work for clinicians?'"[62]

The union also broadened its message to include children's learning conditions and the defense of public education. It embraced clinicians and support staff by calling for a nurse in every school, a social worker in every school, and a library and a librarian in every school. The union emphasized the value of the clinicians' work by talking about the impact on CPS students of poverty, racism, gang wars, drugs, teenage pregnancy, homes with no electricity or heat, children coming to school hungry, and homelessness, and the effects of those problems on the ability of a teacher to teach children who were suffering.

As a social worker noted, the union emphasized what the clinicians knew so well, "that these family issues that are coming to the school, the kids are bringing them and the teachers can't do it all, because they're trying to teach—that the schools can't work without more clinicians."[63] The CTU's *The Schools Chicago's Students Deserve* report emphasized, "CPS is far behind recommended staffing levels suggested by national professional associations. The number of counselors, nurses, social workers, and psychologists must increase dramatically to serve Chicago's population of low-income students." One of the most repeated facts in CTU officers' speeches was that there were only 350 social workers for 400,000 students.

The union commissioned an internal poll of union members that found that the PSRPs expressed less support for a strike than teachers. But one of the questions asked about the issues that concerned them, and more than 80 percent of PSRPs were willing to strike to stop the school closings in black neighborhoods. The CTU felt, said Luskin, "that the problem was that in the past the union didn't talk to the PSRPs, so they were less organized, so they were less willing to believe there was a winning strategy. So the union organized phone banking targeting PSRPs to hear what their issues were and to communicate to them" about the union's issues, the school board's intransigence in bargaining, and the contract campaign.[64]

Reaching Out to Parents and the Community

The union knew that, if it came to a strike, it could not rely only on the unity of its members but would also need the solidarity of parents. The media and the mayor were putting forth a narrative that the teachers were greedy, concerned only about a big raise for themselves, and did not care about how a strike would impact the students. From day one the union made outreach to parents a cornerstone of its contract campaign.

The union built on the fact that teachers have personal relationships with parents. "I think parents trust us," said one CTU teacher, and they know "that we would not do anything that wasn't in the best interests of their kids."[65] Many teachers had taught several children in a family. And teachers had regular contact with parents, either at parent-teacher conferences or when chatting with parents after dismissal as they picked up their kids.

The bulk of adults in the United States attended public schools as children and had at least some great experiences with a teacher. There are nearly five million teachers nationwide, and nearly everyone has a relative or neighbor who is a teacher. National polls in 2011 showed that 73 percent held a favorable view of public school teachers. The union funded a September 2011 poll of Chicagoans that likewise found that 74 percent felt favorably about all public school teachers, and 60 percent favorably rated the job done by Chicago public school teachers. Only 8 percent said the teachers were overpaid; 49 percent said they were not paid enough.[66]

At each of the union's three contract-campaign delegates' conferences, members attended workshops to discuss how to have conversations with parents to counteract the antiunion narrative, and contract campaign committees organized outreach efforts. Although many teachers were told by their principals not to discuss bargaining or a possible strike during parent-teacher conferences, many teachers did so anyway—and certainly were not shy when parents themselves brought up the issue. Teachers sought parent signatures to the Open Letter petition that outlined what a better school day, not just a longer one, would mean for students.

Teachers talked to parents about the massive amount of standardized testing that the students had to endure. They shared how teachers received only one hundred dollars from CPS administration each year to buy supplies, so they spent hundreds of their own dollars to buy what their students needed. They discussed how every school deserved what wealthy suburban schools had—a social worker and nurse in every school, libraries and librarians, air conditioning, and school buildings that were not falling apart.

Through the contract campaign and strike, said one teacher, "parents felt more empowered. They want to know about conditions, why do some schools have art and music and those kinds of programs, but my child's school does not. They're starting to be more aware that there is a disparity." And we "told them that's what we want for every school. We want everyone to have access to arts, to physical education, to all those programs, not just certain schools or certain districts."[67] As one teacher put it, "We're educating our parents about what their role is, and that we have a role together to make this work. We said to the parents, 'Teachers can't do it without you and you can't do it without us. We need a partnership.'"[68]

The union also reached out to the community in other ways. "In the weeks leading up to the strike all I was doing was going to community meetings" at schools, recalled Luskin. To involve churches, the CTU took advantage of its relationship with the faith-based workers' rights group Arise Chicago. Every Labor Day weekend, Arise worked with clergy to bring rank-and-file workers to speak from the heart about the meaning of Labor Day. On the 2011 Labor Day weekend, and again in spring 2012, Arise and the union brought CTU members to speak at fifty religious congregations across the city.

In the midst of the intensifying contract campaign in late 2011 and early 2012, the CTU, parent groups, and community allies repeatedly mobilized in protest of CPS school closings. CTU and community activists packed every Board of Education meeting to speak out against the board's planned school closings. At a December 2011 protest by more than three hundred parents and teachers at a CPS board meeting, the activists, feeling they were being ignored by the board, used the Occupy Wall Street tactic of "mic checking" the meeting to shout out their concerns. Sometimes referred to as "the people's microphone," the technique is a way to amplify a message within a large crowd of people, by having the words of a designated speaker in the crowd repeated by others in the group. The board promptly adjourned the meeting, and the activists held their own community "town hall" discussion.

In January 2012, two hundred parents, teachers, and community activists held a three-day sit-in, outside the mayor's office at City Hall, initiated by the South Side Kenwood Oakland Community Organization (KOCO). Roughly one month later, on February 17 and 18, a twenty-four-hour occupation of Piccolo Elementary School by parents and the community group Blocks Together protested a school turnaround, after parents had voted overwhelmingly against the board's plans for their school. More than a hundred parents, teachers, and community supporters—including members of Occupy Chicago, who put up tents in front of the school—came on short notice and stayed late into the night to support the parents.

A week after the Piccolo School occupation, on February 23, more than five hundred mostly African-American and Latino parents, joined by CTU members, held a silent candlelight march past Mayor Emanuel's house to protest the board's plans for school closures. Columnist Mary Schmich of the usually anti-union *Chicago Tribune* penned a supportive column:

> By going out of bounds, the protesters are telling the power brokers in a palpable way: Your decisions about our schools affect us in our neighborhoods, in the privacy of our homes. See how it feels to have us in your neighborhoods, at your homes. . . . The protesters are rightfully frustrated that (Mayor Emanuel) hasn't talked directly with parents

about their ideas and fears. They're within bounds to do what they can, peacefully, to take their views directly to him. . . . They came, they lit candles, they prayed. They left. They made themselves heard.[69]

On February 25, two days after the march, more than four hundred mostly African-American and Latino parents, joined by CTU members, filled two rooms and the lobby of the CPS building to testify against the Chicago Board of Education's plans to close or turn around seventeen schools. Civil rights leader Rev. Jesse Jackson Sr. was the first speaker, declaring:

> Poverty matters. Racial equality matters. Inadequate distribution of educational resources matters. . . . We cannot have a two-tier system, where we have the very best for a few and the very worst for the rest. We deserve equal protection under the law. Schools located on the West and South Sides of the City of Chicago are placed on a different tier from those schools located on the North Side of town. There are 160 schools without a library; 140 of them are located in schools south of North Avenue. . . . This is educational apartheid.[70]

And on March 8, two hundred parents, teachers, and community members from Chicago's Nineteenth Ward packed a meeting at the Morgan Park High School auditorium to challenge CPS administrators on their plans for a longer school day.[71]

The union's hard work seemed to be paying off—a poll reported in the May 15, 2012, *Chicago Tribune* was a big morale booster for CTU members. More than two-thirds of those with an opinion sided with the union over the mayor in the debate about improving the city's public schools, and among public school parents support rose to 73 percent. Additionally, when asked if teachers should be paid more for working longer hours, 92 percent of public school parents agreed.[72]

The Strike Authorization Vote

When negotiations bog down, unions routinely ask their members to vote to give the leadership the authority to call a strike if necessary. The hope is that the vote will persuade employers that a strike could happen unless there is rapid progress at the bargaining table. Unions always want a high member turnout and a high yes vote, but the traditional legal standard is that 50 percent, plus one, of the members who vote must authorize a strike. The passage of SB 7 in April 2011, however, ratcheted that number up to 75 percent of the entire union membership, making the teachers' strike authorization vote of paramount importance.

Without 75 percent of the membership authorizing a strike, the union could not strike and so had no leverage with management. If, for example, 83 percent of the members turned out to vote—a very high figure in union votes—and if 90 percent of those voting authorized a strike, the result would be 74.7 percent authorizing a strike, an insufficient number. In CTU strike authorizations votes in 1991 and 2003, only 60 percent of the members turned out to vote yes. "The people who framed this law intended it to be an insurmountable obstacle," said CTU Vice President Jesse Sharkey.

What Mayor Emanuel and the CPS administration did not anticipate was that passing SB 7 would backfire by energizing CTU members. The mayor's rhetoric and actions since the law's passage had further inflamed the membership, as had the district's meager offer of a 2 percent raise over five years (i.e., a 0.4 percent raise per year) and its concomitant demand that teachers work a 20 percent longer school day, and the board's refusal to negotiate on improving classroom conditions and reducing class size.

When Karen Lewis announced plans for a strike authorization vote at a June 1, 2012, press conference, it was not hyperbole but an accurate reflection of her members' emotions when she said, "We are tired of being bullied, belittled, and betrayed by this district."[73] Said one CTU and CORE activist, "We understood that if we didn't have more than a 75 percent vote we weren't going to have a strong strike anyway. So we said, 'Let's use this as a motivating tool. Let's make sure it's 90 percent.'"[74]

Additionally, although the contract expired on June 30, the mayor expected that the union would wait until a mediator issued a nonbinding fact-finding report in July, as SB 7 established. Because this would have meant that the union would call a vote in the summer when school was not in session and turnout would be low, the union set the vote for the week before classes ended.[75] The mayor and the CPS administration bemoaned the union's "rush to vote" in the press. They went to the Illinois Educational Labor Relations Board to try to block the vote, but in early June the board refused to act.[76]

Finally, the mayor was completely unprepared for the union to set not one but three full voting days in order to maximize turnout. Union leaders had researched the law and had found that nothing prevented them from taking as many days as they wanted for a strike authorization vote. They kept this knowledge secret until they announced the vote dates. In fact, if the union had voted on only one day, the yes tally would have come close but failed to reach the 75 percent threshold; in the first day's balloting, 72.5 percent of the union's members voted to authorize a strike.

Sarah Chambers recalls the extensive efforts that went into achieving a 100 percent turnout at her school: "We had six teachers who were out with babies or illnesses. We drove around to their houses. We drove out to the suburbs, we drove all over the city, to get that vote so we would have 100 percent voting yes for the strike authorization."[77] Daniel C. Beard Elementary School teachers posted a YouTube video showing that six members fulfilled a promise to CTU activist Jean Luchini by driving downtown to the Rehabilitation Institute, where she was recovering from surgery, to bring her a ballot.[78]

High school teacher Victor Harbison told the *Sun-Times* that the vote represented "the failed leadership of Mayor Rahm Emanuel and his staff. They took up the mantle of leadership, said 'Follow me,' and 90 percent of our people said, 'No thanks.' We're not agitators. We're moms and dads and members of the community. I think we deserve a good contract. We feel threatened at every turn. We're blamed for things that are way beyond our control."[79]

Meanwhile, both the *Tribune* and *Sun-Times* editorial pages denounced the union for calling the vote. CPS head Brizard sent an e-mail to CTU members insisting it would be "disrespectful" to vote before the independent fact finder issued a report in mid-July. The antiunion group Democrats for Education Reform (DFER) flooded the radio airwaves with ads attacking the union for calling the vote and made thousands of robocalls asking people to call CPS opposing the vote. DFER head Rebeca Nieves Huffman had called Lewis a "thug" in a May 4, 2012, *Sun-Times* opinion piece. The radio ads were, said *Sun-Times* columnist Mark Brown, "designed by Mayor Emanuel's media strategist."[80]

On the first day of the vote on Wednesday June 6, as the first ballots were delivered from across the city to the union's downtown offices, the district supervisors—all working teachers, clinicians, and paraprofessionals—sat at tables in a huge conference room counting the ballots. The mood combined an intense camaraderie with great somberness. "We've been pushed, and pushed, and pushed—and finally we get a chance to push back," said a CTU activist as she counted strike authorization ballots."[81] They were all tired from getting up early to talk to teachers about voting before the school day began, then working all day, only to drive downtown to count ballots late into the night, knowing they'd get only a few hours' sleep before doing it all again the next day.

The union was aware that the mayor might well proclaim the vote counting a fraud; the two newspapers had already hinted that something was shady when the union, to save several hundred thousand dollars, did not hire an outside company to count the ballots. So, at the union's invitation, Arise Chicago brought clergy to witness the ballot counting and to sit in on discussions about ballots that were hard to decipher. Each night around midnight clergy taped up boxes of ballots and signed their names over the tape; the next afternoon clergy brought the boxes out of a locked closet, verified that they had been untouched, and reopened the boxes of ballots so that counting could continue.

It was immediately clear how the vote would go, as each district supervisor began to stack the ballots in tall "yes" and tiny "no" piles. What was not clear was the size of the turnout. So as the boxes of ballots arrived at union headquarters, a quick notation of the total number of votes at each school was made before the boxes were moved to the large room for counting, a process also overseen by the clergy. Those notations were taken to a small room in the depths of the union's offices. The walls were covered with white flip-chart pads listing each of the 580 CPS schools. As the tallies arrived, the sheets filled with numbers, and the organizers noted where turnout was low.

Calls were made to delegates and leaders of the contract action committees at those schools to analyze why their teachers and staff were not voting in large numbers. And the union made plans to send fifty organizers—CTU staffers and thirty organizers borrowed from SEIU Healthcare Illinois—early the next morning to schools with low turnout to encourage people to vote. That exceptional level of planning and organization enabled the union to increase turnout at schools where numbers had been low on the first day.

The final tally was announced on Sunday, June 10. Surprising no one among the union activists and leaders, it showed that 98 percent of the members who voted had authorized the leadership to call a strike. The overwhelming vote was, in Lewis's word, a powerful "indictment" of CPS management.[82]

A whopping 93.4 percent of members turned out to vote, 24,756 of 26,502. Only 1,746 did not vote. The vote showed that 89.7 percent, or 23,780 of 26,502 CTU members, approved a strike, with only 482 members or 1.8 percent voting no—thus blowing past the 75 percent threshold set by SB 7. In addition, 494 ballots were marked as "spoiled" as the ballot counters bent over backward to ensure there wouldn't be the slightest hint of irregular counting; nearly all those discarded ballots were yes votes.[83]

"Teachers Roar"

On June 12, the *Chicago Tribune* headline declared "Teachers Crank Up the Heat," an accompanying editorial was headlined "Teachers Roar," and the *Sun-Times* declared "It's a Landslide."

At a time when the *Tribune* and *Sun-Times* editorial stances were decidedly hostile to the union, a June 12 *Sun-Times* guest column by veteran Chicago reporter Carol Marin came as a breath of fresh air to CPS teachers and staff. "If I had been a Chicago public school teacher last week," wrote Marin, "I would have done as 90 percent of them did and voted 'yes' for a strike authorization. Teachers in this town have been demonized, demoralized, and disrespected. Taking a sledgehammer approach to CPS teachers and their union has backfired on the Emanuel administration." She concluded, "In a city where we don't have a handle on the intractable violence that plagues neighborhoods and seeps into many of our schools, teachers are often on the front line of kindness and caring in a really harsh world. We used to treat their profession with respect. They know that. And said so in their vote."

As the news media reported the voting results, across the city thousands of teachers had wide smiles on their faces. They had either seen or heard about the comment by Stand for Children founder Jonah Edelman that the CTU was incapable of achieving a 75 percent strike-authorization turnout, so when the members heard they'd received a 90 percent yes vote it filled them with pride. As one teacher put it, "When people have had enough, when they believe enough in something, then we're going to overcome. Seeing that video and then we got 90 percent—it was very empowering. It makes you feel powerful as an individual and as an organization."[84]

The CTU was able to garner 93 percent of their members to vote as a result of their two years of grassroots educating and organizing in the schools. "The strike vote could not have happened a year or even six months earlier," said Luskin. "We had to build the contract campaign infrastructure and build the organization. And also, we had to build individual leaders and to build a real debate and conversation within the union."[85]

But the overpowering reason that 98 percent of the voting members authorized the leadership to call a strike (and this was no bluff; the 26,500 members knew that a strike was extremely likely) was a result of the actions of both Emanuel and Lewis.

As discussed in chap. 5, teachers across the country were bewildered and angry at the rising tide of teacher bashing both in the media and by politicians in both political parties. In Chicago, teachers grew even angrier at their treatment by Emanuel. In March 2011, days after winning the February 22 election, Emanuel had lobbied heavily in Springfield to pass SB 7—essentially, he thought, taking away the teachers' right to strike. In June 2011, just weeks after being sworn into office, he said teachers had given "students the shaft" in their 2007 contract and ordered his newly appointed school board to rescind the teachers' 4 percent raise at its first meeting—while simultaneously giving huge raises to his newly appointed CPS administrators.[86]

In August 2011, he went to schools, particularly those with a large number of newer teachers, and tried to bribe them into accepting the longer school day until the union convinced the labor board to stop his illegal action. In spring 2012, he returned to Springfield to unsuccessfully lobby for legislation to stop teachers from taking a strike vote. In 2011–12, fourteen schools were closed and nine turnaround schools had their entire staffs fired, while fifteen nonunion charter schools were opened. In more than a year of bargaining, the mayor had ordered the management bargaining team to demand massive changes in the existing contract and a minuscule raise over a proposed five-year contract. "With Rahm Emanuel," said a high school history teacher, "it was him laying the gauntlet down [against the teachers] when he's elected, the back stabbing, the threats, the intimidation, the fear—it was overwhelming." As another union activist put it, "I am so appreciative of Rahm Emanuel. He united the union, he united the teachers. I mean he is such a persona non grata" with the teachers, he "made it easy to do."[87]

The strike authorization, as one district supervisor put it, "was long overdue. The time was now." They knew, as the leadership told them, that "the strike would be just the beginning" of a long struggle for "the soul of public education," but it was a step that had to be taken.[88]

The leadership had never wanted to appear to the members as though they were pushing for a strike. In the May 10 practice vote, the survey questions did not ask about a strike. At the May 23 union rally, no speaker said the word *strike*; instead the chant arose from the floor. As Mayle reflected, "We had to wait until our members were there. And doing it the way we did it, it was actually better because it was coming from members. I would go to school meetings and they would say, 'When are we going to go on strike?' And it was like, 'Whoa, we were waiting for you guys to be ready. I guess you are.' Coming from the members, it was way more powerful than from union leaders. The members were saying it. It empowered them."[89]

The members also overwhelmingly voted to authorize a strike because they believed in Lewis as their leader. The overwhelming sentiment of the membership in September 2012, as one teacher expressed it, was that "Karen Lewis is a powerhouse. She's mighty and she stands her ground on everything and she doesn't mince words."[90] Said another teacher, "The membership had confidence in the leadership, and they were willing to go out and stay out."[91]

Members recognized that Lewis was human and that she made errors—such as in a speech making fun of Secretary of Education Arne Duncan's lisp, joking about smoking marijuana while at Dartmouth College, or being pressured into initially endorsing SB 7.[92] But the things the media criticized about her the most—her toughness, her forcefulness, her strong ego, her sometimes acerbic edge, and her steadfastness when cursed at to her face by Mayor Emanuel—were the things that endeared her to the members.[93] They felt that to confront the larger-than-life personality of Emanuel, who was widely seen as a bully even by his admirers, it took an equally large personality like Lewis's. Only a person with her confidence could stand up to him and lead the union into battle.

CTU members believed that Lewis, the organizing staff, and CORE activists had laid the groundwork for uniting the membership. They believed—as turned out to be the case—that in the event of a strike only a handful of their 26,500 members would cross the union's picket line. They believed that, due to the union's extensive campaign against school closings and outreach during the contract campaign, CPS parents would stand by the teachers. They believed that under Lewis's leadership the union would win a strike, even against a powerful Democratic mayor who had the first African-American president's blessing. If, as CTU expected, CPS forced a strike, the union would be ready for one the likes of which the city had never seen before.

7

EMANUEL PROVOKES, TEACHERS PREPARE TO BARGAIN

The calendar said June 2010, but strategic positioning for the Chicago schools' 2012 bargaining had already begun. Teachers felt it: an unavoidable battle over school policy was coming. Franczek called it "a surge that begins in 2010," like two armies, the mayor's and the teacher's, advancing into attack formation.[1] Unlike previous contract negotiations, this one featured a union strategy backed by member involvement and community activism. The employer did not frame the issues. Instead of accepting its one-dimensional portrayal as a labor-market institution, CTU self-identified as a robust defender of public schools. The union also pursued a strategy in the court system that brought temporary relief but ultimately proved unsuccessful and helped persuade its leaders to eschew further civil action for mass mobilization tactics. A different kind of fight was coming and it would unfold on multiple terrains. The employer fired first.

The School Board Announces Layoffs

A mere two weeks after the new union leadership was installed in June, the school board sent a hostile message. It threatened the "honorable terminations," or layoffs, of more than a thousand teachers, many of them tenured, unless the union made $100 million in contract concessions.[2] It was actually Lewis's second day on the job when she was notified of the board's ultimatum. The union leadership promptly rejected the equivalent of a gun to its head. Despite the unexpected receipt in late August of $105 million in federal education funds sent to the state as part of the American Recovery and Reinvestment Act (ARRA) to stem cuts in school staffing, the employer made good on its threat. Lewis was furious and released a statement defending the role of tenured teachers in protecting student interests: "Parents and students should be outraged that CPS clearly targeted tenured teachers. Without tenured teachers, students are at increased risk."[3]

The ARRA infusion of money alleviated the board's need for the labor cost concessions, but it fired people anyway, although, under withering union criticism, it subsequently recalled approximately 715 teachers. Robert Bloch pointed out, however, that these teachers were not recalled pursuant to an official recall policy, because Chicago had none. A recall policy stipulates the rights and procedures that teachers who are laid-off due to financial reasons have to be returned to their jobs. Rachel Resnick, at the time the board's chief labor relations officer, explained, "A teacher who is laid off may be rehired, but we [the school board] have no recall policy."[4] In response, CTU filed a lawsuit claiming a violation of federal due process under the Fourteenth Amendment.[5]

The union achieved an initial legal win over the school board when US District Judge David H. Coar found that CPS had violated the rights of more than one thousand fired tenured Chicago teachers.[6] Coar's decision directed the board to "rescind the discharges of tenured teachers . . . [and] promulgate, in consultation with the Teachers Union and after good-faith negotiation, a set of recall rules that complies" with the Illinois School Code.[7] The union had protected tenured teachers for the moment, but this was only round one of the legal fight, and CPS planned to appeal.

The dismissals were a hostile opening salvo directed at public school teachers from a lame-duck school board that would be reformed by a new mayor nine months later. On May 16, 2011, Rahm Emanuel was sworn in as mayor of Chicago. Elizabeth "Beth" Swanson, the mayor's deputy chief of staff for education, stressed that Emanuel intended to make his first term in office all about "safe streets, strong schools, and stable finances."[8] There was an undeniable connection between each of those objectives because strong schools were essential to safe neighborhoods and they required adequate levels of public spending. Emanuel, however, would not be like his predecessor. Where Richard M. Daley wanted control of the schools but never tied his electoral identity to education reform, Emanuel was staking a larger claim to fixing a broken system. To observers like the *Sun-Times'* deputy editorial page editor, Kate Grossman, it appeared that "Rahm intended to be much more involved in running the schools."[9] By his own subjective construction, Emanuel's political fortunes would be intricately bound up with how his policies affected the public schools. While the issues he committed to addressing were not easy to handle, nothing about Emanuel's agenda required confrontation with the school teachers. Unfortunately, the relationship between CTU and CPS was about to get worse.

No to 4 Percent Pay Raises

At its very first meeting, the new school board voted to cancel 4 percent annual raises for school employees during the final year of the labor agreement. An obscure, hitherto unused contract clause gave the mayor the option of canceling a pay increase during a fiscal emergency. Declaring fiscal emergencies had been routine in Chicago, but the money to pay contractually negotiated raises had always been found. Emanuel said that the money was needed because the school district was facing a $712 million deficit, but the union believed Emanuel had an ulterior motive. Lewis explained that Emanuel "took the 4 percent back to bait the union into reopening the contract" negotiations.[10] His reason, she believed, was born of his impatience. The passage of SB 7 allowed the mayor to set the length of the school day, but not during the life of the reigning collective bargaining agreement, which would not expire until August 2012.

When the board canceled the pay hikes, the union had the option of terminating the contract in the final year. Doing so would compel the board to negotiate a new contract and also permit it to implement the longer school day. Terminating the contract would give the union a chance to reverse the pay cut, and, because compensation was a mandatory subject of bargaining, the teachers could strike over a failure to reach agreement. Bloch saw the pay cancellation as an opportunity. "I was urging the union to terminate [the] contract and strike," he recalled. He reasoned that the board and CEO were new and barely organized and could be "push[ed] back on their heels."[11] His recommendation touched a nerve. "We seriously considered doing it," CTU Vice President Jesse Sharkey acknowledged.[12] Enticing as it was, the mayor's opening gambit failed. The union decided, in Lewis' words, not to "overreact."[13]

Sharkey said that, when the mayor cut teacher pay, the union confronted two strategic choices that had diametrically opposed implications for the organization. CTU's ultimate choice signaled the union's fateful commitment to confront the political assaults on public education by using the bargaining process as a platform for developing an activist rank and file and linking it to the building of community coalitions committed to neighborhood schools. Sharkey explained the leadership's theorizing about the 2012 bargaining process:

> If we negotiated the pay, we may have got all or some of it restored, and the longer school day was inevitable anyway. We likely then would not

have struck. But what kind of a union would that make us? If, how-ever, we refused the opportunity to make some kind of a deal, we could instead build the union from the bottom up and confront education reform head on. Our issues were privatization of schools, poverty, the lack of school libraries and inadequate paraprofessionals, class size, and school closures. Pay was never our compelling issue. It became an issue when CPS wanted us to work longer for nothing and demanded we accept a merit plan. But, in the past, teachers got more money to accept less school control and respect. And truthfully, at that time we weren't certain our members were ready to win a strike. We hadn't had an opportunity to fully educate and mobilize them. That was ongoing, and the layoffs and holding back their pay became powerful grievances to rally them around. But timing was important. And we weren't interested in a trans-actional exchange with the board where we simply rearranged things. We knew the members were fed up and wanted something more decent. We wanted a bigger, fuller debate over how the schools were organized. That meant living with the pay loss and building a rank-and-file union that could do more than negotiate a deal. We wanted a union that would become an essential, powerful voice in protecting public education. Not sure we could have gotten that if we had reopened the contract.[14]

Sharkey's deconstruction of the union's approach to bargaining corresponded to Franczek's interpretation of what was unfolding. "This CTU was ideologically driven and less 'meat and potatoes' focused."[15] In the past, bargaining with the union had taken place over the terms and conditions of jobs, not over school governance. In 2010, the elected leaders were not indifferent to the insult of withholding pay, but their bargaining agenda transcended that offense. The school board then added insult to injury by awarding the new CEO and four other CPS executives very generous salary increases. *Sun-Times* education beat reporter Rosalind Rossi wrote, "The vote on whether to boost executive Chicago Public School salaries comes only a week after the same board members, in their first official action, found the deficit-ridden system did not have enough money to pay for 4 percent raises to teachers. . . ."[16] In the words of Robert Bloch, was there "anything more Rahm Emanuel could do to piss off teachers?"[17] It turned out that there was.

The Pioneer Schools

As the final school year under the agreement got under away, but still a few months before bargaining would begin, CPS took another premature run at implementing the longer school day.[18] The union was not opposed to a longer school day, but argued that a longer day without additional resources would not help students. An obscure part of the Illinois School Code allowed any provision of a labor contract to be waived with a 51 percent vote of teachers in a school. CPS decided to apply that waiver to the longer school day. Without consulting the union, CPS introduced the "Pioneer Program," whereby teachers in all 472 elementary schools were asked to vote on adding ninety minutes of instructional time to each day. In exchange for accepting the longer school day, teachers would receive a one-time 2 percent bonus (an average of $1,250 before taxes) and an iPod, and each of their schools would receive an additional $150,000 in their budgets. According to Swanson, the school-by-school option was a way to seed "pilot" programs that would spur "innovations about what to do with the added time." Schools that adopted the changes would be providing the system with invaluable information about how to "roll [innovations] into planning taking place on the ground in anticipation of full intervention."[19] The CTU leadership had a different name for the Pioneer Program: a bribe.

Although the Pioneer Program was deeply unpopular with teachers, principals, according to Bloch, "pounced on it and immediately started pressuring their teachers to vote for the waivers, in some cases raising the specter of layoffs if their school didn't get the $150K."[20] The pressure on the teachers to abandon their collective bargaining agreements came from multiple fronts and was well orchestrated. New school CEO Jean-Claude Brizard announced at a Board of Education meeting that CPS had "made a proposal to the CTU to look at ways to increase the elementary school day beginning this year, because we know that every day we wait, our kids are losing." Lewis, on the other hand, was suspicious of the board's plan and offer. "I'm not bargaining anything right now. We're not having that discussion," she said.[21]

Within the first week of the district's bonus offer, thirteen elementary schools voted to accept the longer school day. Emanuel and Brizard trumpeted the early votes as signs that the teachers really wanted to work longer hours. The Chicago press added its praise for both the mayor and the schools and framed the votes as antiunion: "As of Tuesday, teachers at four additional schools had voted for the extended schedule, bringing the total to 13 schools whose teachers are willing to defy the Chicago Teachers Union, securing bonuses for themselves and financial incentives for their schools."[22]

CTU Financial Secretary Kristine Mayle pointed out, however, that the schools that adopted the change were those "with young staff, with Teach For America staff, or schools without CTU delegates."[23] The mayor could then cause the media to trumpet the narrative "The teachers want this," and he could force the longer day upon every school in the district. Reports came into the union office of "intimidation, coercion, and threats of layoffs or school closures if edu-cators did not vote in favor of a longer school day."[24] Feeling ambushed by the maneuver, CTU relied on its new organizing infrastructure to engage members on the dangers of the school-by-school votes. In what would serve as a dry run for mobilizing the members before and during the strike, the union organized hundreds of school, LSC, and parent meetings. They also began to work with the elementary school teachers on how to speak directly to parents about school issues and a "better school day, not simply a longer" one.[25] The school-by-school battle against the waivers began the constant assessment process that became in-tegral to all the union's organizing. "It forced us to look at every school," recalled Jackson Potter, "to look at what actions the members were taking, to assess union strength in each school."[26]

Acknowledging the impact CTU's organizing was having in raising questions about the waiver vote, Brizard issued a letter to the teachers explaining that a revised ballot would address any misconceptions. "CPS is willing to spell out, in as much detail as teachers need, exactly which rights will NOT be waived in each vote. We've lengthened the ballot for two schools already to help allay your con-cerns and are perfectly happy to spell out as much details [sic] as teachers need to be comfortable in their support."[27] The school CEO's communication and CPS's expanded ballot did nothing to assuage teacher concerns.

After a full-court press in the schools the union came up with the first of what would be many clever tactics. The schools' delegates organized teachers to conduct advance mock votes on extending the workday. In all of the 185 schools that participated in the exercise, teachers pretended to vote down what they were derogatorily calling "ransom money." CPS was stunned by the organiza-tional strength exhibited by the union in the schools. It quickly got the word to principals: do not have your school vote if you expect to lose. The Pioneer Program abruptly lost its momentum, but it formally continued until the CTU filed an unfair labor practice with the IELRB. The union alleged that while the school code permitted individual waivers, CPS could not use the waivers to affect district-wide policy in violation of the labor agreement. In oral testimony before the IELRB, Bloch argued that if the school board were allowed to pursue the waiver votes "it would emasculate the CTU as a bargaining representative. . . ."[28]

Concurring with the union's position, the IELRB ruled on November 4 that it would hold a hearing to consider seeking a preliminary court injunction pro-hibiting any further schools from voting on the longer school day. Teachers were further encouraged by the labor board's issuance of a multicount complaint accusing CPS of "coercing longer school day votes in 13 CPS schools."[29] Lewis stated that the school district "engaged in illegal, immoral behavior that threat-ened the future of collective bargaining and of our union."[30] It was a big win for the union. Except for the elementary schools that had already voted, every other elementary school would be covered by any future injunction. Unwilling to face the likelihood of a court-ordered injunction, CPS ultimately capitulated, but not without a rather undignified final push.

In a meeting room one floor below the mayor's office, the union and the school board met to negotiate a settlement of the unfair labor practice. Chicago Federation of Labor (CFL) President Jorge Ramirez had arranged the meeting. Months earlier, when the Pioneer Program was launched, Emanuel had requested that Ramirez join him in a press conference to extol the longer school day. Ramirez agreed in principle with the need for added instructional time but warned the mayor that the school waiver votes would backfire. "I told him that CTU would file at the board and that he should reach out to Karen to negotiate a settlement."[31] Emanuel emphatically refused even to talk to the union, but, after CTU had gone to the IELRB, the mayor relented, though he wanted the CFL president to be part of the discussion.

Ramirez called Lewis, who was opposed to a meeting. In a reference to the advantage she believed the regulatory panel's possible injunction request gave the union, she yelled into the phone "We got him!" After further discussion, however, she agreed to try to negotiate a settlement of the dispute. She also asked Ramirez to attend the meeting. Emanuel was at city hall the day of the meeting but did not join the talks. Nor, at first, did the one person both sides had asked to be present. The morning of the meeting, Ramirez was stuck in traffic behind an accident on Interstate 55. When he finally arrived at the meeting, Chicago school board President David Vitale was justifying the school waiver votes. Brizard, Franczek, and CPS attorney Joseph Moriarty joined Vitale in presenting the Board of Education's case. Lewis, Sharkey, and Bloch attended for CTU. Despite what, to Ramirez, seemed like differences between Lewis and Sharkey over whether to settle, progress was being made. He noticed that Lewis's cell phone was sounding constantly and reasoned that she was getting texts from people advising her about what to do.[32]

The sides had been talking for hours, and Lewis and Sharkey had grown more agitated. Lewis was really angry about the explanatory letters Brizard had sent to the teachers. The union considered the communication a subtle form of direct dealing with the membership over a subject of bargaining. "We wanted a pound of flesh," Sharkey admitted later.[33] Realizing that the issue was a sticking point, Ramirez suggested that Lewis demand that Brizard sign a statement apologizing for the letters. The idea appealed to the union president but the school CEO refused to sign such a note.

When Brizard was shown the letter that Bloch and Sharkey had drafted, he sat impassively in his chair, arms folded across his chest. Talks dragged on. It was clear to Ramirez that the letter had become the main issue. As the day grew late, the CFL leader stepped out of the meeting to take a phone call. He ran into the mayor in the hall. Ramirez let Emanuel know that settlement talks were continuing, but that the school CEO was balking at signing a union requested letter of apology. Ramirez added that the mayor could either be hauled into court and found guilty or compel Brizard to swallow his pride and sign the letter. He told Emanuel, "Get this signed and we're done."[34] Ramirez shared his conversation with the CTU delegation, and a few minutes later Brizard signed. Teachers had actually fought city hall and emerged victorious.

While the win over city hall was important in halting CPS's plans to undermine the union's authority to negotiate the longer school day, the fight itself had proven liberating. Prior to the Pioneer Program, CTU leaders had been girding for a fight with the Board of Education and the mayor but had not yet formulated a strategy for tapping into teachers' anger about the pay freeze. The union needed to find a way to create an action that would allow teachers collectively to express their resentment about losing control of their workday. Unlike the withholding of pay, which had happened in the summer, before the vast majority of teachers had returned to their classrooms, attempts to make teachers agree to work longer hours were unfolding in the schools during the academic year. Teachers could come together in the schools to share their common grievances about CPS and the mayor, and with each story told they built a collective consciousness of resistance.

Energized by the audacity of CPS's heavy-handed approach, CTU leaders seized the opportunity to transform elementary school teachers into union activists. By the end of the school year the Pioneer experience became a primer for CTU to understand when and how it could most effectively confront the school board and city hall.

On other fronts the union had less success. In March 2011, CTU won a second round in its court fight to restore the jobs lost by tenured teachers. The school board had appealed the fall district court ruling in favor of CTU and suffered another setback when a divided panel of the Seventh Circuit affirmed the earlier ruling. In June, however, the full appeals court vacated the March decision and directed the Illinois Supreme Court to determine whether tenured teachers had any recall rights under state law.

Acknowledging the value of protecting tenured teachers, education advocacy groups like Parents United for Responsible Education (PURE) and Designs For Change submitted amici curiae briefs in support of the union. The question the court of appeals put before the state's top court was whether the school code created "a property interest in employment," and therefore granted laid-off tenured teachers any statutory rights to their jobs. In February 2012, three months after bargaining had commenced, the Supreme Court answered the question. "In a series of questions, the court of appeals first asks whether section 34–18(31) or 34–84 of the School Code, individually or in combination, give laid-off tenured teachers the substantive right to be rehired after an economic layoff. We conclude they do not."[35] By a 5-to-2 vote, the state's top legal tribunal handed the teachers a painful loss. Bloch admitted that the eight-month expensive roller coaster ride through the courts "left a bitter taste in the mouths of the CTU leadership."[36] The outcome left the union reluctant to employ further strategies in the courts for fighting CPS.

Lewis and Emanuel Meet

The IELRB and Supreme Court adventures were legal skirmishes in which the union and the school board expressed their bargaining differences. As Franczek framed it, "it was just one part of the crucible" that CPS, CTU, and, eventually, the whole city would be thrown into as bargaining for a new school contract approached.[37] The contextual elements of the unfolding conflict were on a Shakespearian scale. First, there was a new cast of characters, beginning with a first-term, uncompromising mayor who, unlike any of his predecessors, tied his political identity to education policy. Next was a passionate, novice union president, who promised to lead her membership in a radically different direction. These two individuals had in common a desire to make major changes, and neither had any collective bargaining experience. To add some personal flavor to the drama, the leading protagonists had apparently, in private company, slung obscenities at each other.

Sometime between early March and early April 2011, Lewis had accepted a gracious invitation from Emanuel to accompany him to a ballet at the Harris Theater. Emanuel had not yet been sworn in as mayor and felt that a get-acquainted gathering with the new union head would be a friendly way to socialize. Lewis playfully suggested that he up the offer to include a dinner. It was their first negotiation, and it went very well; the mayor kindly complied and they went to Henri on Michigan Avenue. Both ordered lamb and the same wine. During an otherwise pleasant social evening, at some point the conversation drifted to the school district's obligation to all the city's children. Here their accounts diverge. According to Lewis, Emanuel told her that 25 percent of the city's school kids "are never going to amount to anything and I'm not going to throw resources at them."[38] Lewis said she was stunned by the comment. The night ended on a sour note, and the relationship between the two further hardened when, nearly a year later, Lewis publicly recounted the statement. Emanuel strongly denied saying any such thing. "One, it's totally false. Two, or furthermore, any sentiments around that statement do not reflect, or square, with the actions I've taken to make sure every child has access to a quality education."[39]

The two later met for a second and, as it turned out, last time before the strike, in the mayor's office. Immediately the mayor's interest in a longer school day consumed the conversation. Emanuel expressed dissatisfaction with "having kids on the street at 1:30 or 2:15" every afternoon.[40] Lewis accused the mayor of not being honest about the school day. "So this is not about education. This is about safety.... This is babysitting and warehousing."[41] In reply, according to Lewis, the mayor then stood up and yelled, "Fuck you Lewis!"[42] She said, "Then it got nasty," but that she "stood [her] ground."[43] Most observers took that as an admission that Lewis responded with her own profanity. Emanuel was evasive when asked about the meeting. "I'm not going to get into a he-said, she-said. We had a good meeting. It was not a long meeting. We talked about a longer school day and we talked about focusing on elementary kids," the mayor said. He then added impishly, "To tell the truth, she hugged me at the end of the meeting."[44]

Also gathering just outside the perimeter of negotiations were the avowed enemies of CTU. Advocates of school privatization lined up alongside philanthropic foundations and hedge fund billionaires to push a corporate education agenda. Even Chicago's favorite son and expected champion of public school teachers, Barack Obama, was instead singing from the charter school hymnal. And across the border in Wisconsin, a Koch brothers–backed governor had stripped bargaining rights from teachers. Peacefully reaching an agreement was further handicapped because bargaining for a new contract would take place in a bad economic climate. And there were plenty of media outlets to report all the innuendo, drama, betrayal, insults, punches, and counterpunches that were set to take place.

The School Board Negotiators

One harbinger of how this bargaining would be different from previous ones was the fact that the CTU and the Board of Education were at odds over the rules and procedures for negotiating. Emanuel's preemptive belligerent actions and the unelected nature of the school board persuaded CTU that the employer was unlikely to be a cooperative bargaining partner. But at least the union knew who would sit across from it at the negotiating table. Franczek was experienced and well known. In 1994, he was hired as CPS's new chief labor negotiator. Labor relations in the schools were complex, but it was the kind of work, he said, that "you lived for: the Olympics of negotiations."[45]

Lewis and the rest of the CTU leadership knew "he respected collective bargaining" and according to Bloch, "invested in relationships."[46] Union leaders held Franczek responsible for a good deal of the harm that education reform had done to teachers, but they recognized that the mayor's lawyer understood the art of deal-making.

On the face of it there was no one better to negotiate for the school board and city hall. Under Daley, Franczek had enjoyed a "silly degree of freedom" and signed two decades' worth of contracts without a strike.[47] Yet the union had reason to wonder about Emanuel's commitment to Franczek. Although Franczek was a formidable negotiator, he had also signed all the previous agreements that the mayor appeared to disparage. In nearly two decades of negotiating contracts with the teachers and other city unions, he had refrained from making inflammatory comments about his counterparts. The union speculated that, perhaps because Franczek had accumulated a record of bargaining successes, Emanuel saw him as a little too invested in compromise. The mayor, CTU believed, would need someone to represent him at the table who was not so interested in compromise—someone to signal Emanuel's defiance. The mayor, CTU believed, would accept an agreement, but only if he could dictate the terms. Union leaders, therefore, expected outrageousness from someone on the school board bargaining team serving as Emanuel's proxy.

Their suspicion seemed justified when Tim Cawley was named as a CPS bargaining representative. Cawley was CPS's new chief administrative officer. He had previously served as the managing director of finance and administration for CPS's favorite turnaround operator, the Academy for Urban School Leadership (AUSL). To CTU, he epitomized everything that was wrong with CPS. "He knew nothing about education," said Lewis.[48] Cawley's formal role in bargaining was to present the school district's financial data, but those contributions were summarily dismissed by CTU because of his comments on educational practices. According to CTU lawyer Robin Potter, at one point Sharkey insisted that bargaining had to address poverty. In response, Cawley incredulously proclaimed, "What! Education has nothing to do with poverty."[49] Lewis joked that "Cawley would say the craziest shit, just straight up crazy."[50]

If Cawley was a negative CPS presence, then Rachel Resnick would be an unfortunate absence. Resnick had been CPS's chief labor relations officer since Arne Duncan appointed her to the position in 2005, and she was stepping down with the start of the 2012–13 school year. "She was valuable to CPS because she knew where all the bodies were buried," Lewis noted admiringly.[51] Before resigning,

Resnick had been an unwitting participant in a bizarre case of union spying. On August 24, 2011, she received a fifty-bullet-point e-mail at 11:51 p.m. from a CTU delegate, Marc Wigler. The e-mail, according to the *Chicago Sun-Times*, "detailed what CTU officials told union delegates during a special meeting the evening before."[52] The House of Delegates meeting had been called to determine how the union would respond to CPS's "insistence that it could not afford a scheduled 4 percent raise." The *Sun-Times* story quoted Sharkey as explaining that one of the bullet points Wigler sent Resnick directed the delegates to "stop telling Franczek everything and stop running to the Board and telling your principals everything." While it's not clear what impact, if any, CPS's seeing the e-mail had on the actual bargaining, it did not help the labor-management relationship. Resnick's job and bargaining slot were both filled by Joseph Moriarty, who had been part of the 2007 bargaining and, since 2005, had defended the board in grievance and arbitration cases.

A third person contributing to CPS's bargaining effort, CPS Chief of Instruction Jennifer Cheatham, further disenchanted CTU. Cheatham, according to the mayor's education advisor Beth Swanson, had been the "driving force behind implementation of the longer school day."[53] She was also the chairwoman of a CPS steering committee organized to plan the content for the extended day. Karen Lewis was invited to serve on the committee but declined when she was informed that Robin Steans was also participating. Cheatham had also initially participated in a small CTU-CPS committee that discussed teacher evaluations. She had never participated in the bargaining, and, like Resnick, who also spent some time with the evaluations committee, was leaving the district.

No matter who made up the CPS team, the union knew that bargaining would occur in anticipation of a possible strike that Lewis said the mayor was "paranoid about."[54] Chicago, CTU declared, would not be Hartford or Newark or Baltimore or Cleveland or DC or Denver or any other place where teachers unions bargained as collaborators with the corporate education agenda. When Franczek heard that kind of message coming from the union, it made negotiating with CTU feel "like I was being waterboarded."[55]

CTU's Big Bargaining Team

The union further pushed Franczek's tolerance when it made a strategic choice about its own bargaining team. In the past, CTU had approached negotiations as a deliberation between a few highly placed select leaders. A bargaining team would consist principally of the local officers, an IFT representative with bargaining experience, and a lawyer. Just as CTU was familiar with the school board's representatives, Franczek always knew the union players. Familiarity bred stability in the bargaining process and a comfort level with the people involved.

This time none of the union's officers was familiar to Franczek, and one of the lead negotiators, Robert Bloch, had never imagined he would be bargaining for teachers. A self-described "old school labor guy," Bloch was an unlikely legal advisor to unionized teachers. His bargaining and legal experience had mainly taken the form of representing laborers and Teamsters in the private sector, but his labor law work was anything but conventional. Bloch's involvement in helping two Teamsters locals settle a nine-day Chicago city and suburban strike of sanitation workers earned him the street honorific "the garbagemen attorney."[56] When the CORE slate was elected, its officers asked Bloch to work for CTU. He knew nothing about the education sector and had never represented a teachers union but was comfortable with big dramatic assignments, and CTU's emerging fight with the mayor seemed as large as any labor dispute could be.

Although issues may be difficult to address, negotiations are also interactions between people with particular personalities, reputations, and skills. If negotiations are like a game, as many experts contend, then the players matter. In CTU's case, not only were the particular bargaining individuals important but the number "playing" would also be a factor. CTU insisted on a large bargaining team made up of teachers, clinicians, and paraprofessionals. Jesse Sharkey pointed out that the union's decision was an important symbolic break from the past. "In the past, CTU leadership promulgated a false separation between leaders and members." He added that "CPS took that separation for granted and used it against us." Sharkey, Lewis, Michael Brunson, and Kristine Mayle had all been elected to union office as rank-and-file CORE leaders. They held fast to the sentiments of their members, and, as Sharkey explained, "we carried their aspirations forward into bargaining."[57]

Including union members in the bargaining process certainly reflected a stronger bond between the CTU's leadership and the rank and file than anything CPS had faced before. The union's decision to expand the team to include members was also done for a genuine functional reason. Lewis explained that the new school administration "had no clue what was happening in the classroom." What the union wanted to do was to bring some of their members into special bargaining sessions to give testimony about the realities of working in a CPS school. "We wanted," Lewis explained, "to make the classroom real."[58] Despite their good intentions, the union's insistence on a big, member-driven negotiation team kicked off an equally big argument. The school board argued that the size of the union's team was detrimental to the nuanced and complex aspects of collective bargaining. Nonetheless, CTU prevailed, and, once a month, both sides met with thirty to forty rank and filers.[59]

Before determining the full contract package that the union's rank-and-file bargaining members would have to endorse, Sharkey revealed that the union leadership invested "lots of time thinking about our strategic goals." Over time they winnowed the list of goals down to those that "could be well articulated."[60] The final list was framed by their analysis of the corporate-led reform efforts rocking public education. The union was not so much bargaining a labor agreement as it was battling to preserve a teacher-centered view of public education. Achieving anything close to that goal would require that the union win a good contract; it would also necessitate building deep and lasting public partnerships with parent and community groups to ensure that what was good for teachers was also good for school children. The union was committed to becoming a forceful institutional and political voice for working-class Chicagoans on education policy. Pursuing that goal first required hearing from union members about what they wanted in their contract.

The union created a contract proposal form that members could fill out and turn in to their school delegate. More than 250 individual members submitted proposals that either introduced a new contract article or amended an existing article. The breadth of suggested items reflected both the membership's desire for better working conditions and their interest in having a voice in governing the school district. One proposal that was adopted by CTU was a request that "accurate and current information with respect [to] a teacher's tenure date and/or status must be available in a confidential online location and/or [available] upon request." Errors in teacher records were common, and CPS was often reluctant to confirm a person's employment status, fearing the false information would trigger a complaint from the union. Another proposal addressed the need to amend the evaluation plan for probationary appointed teachers (PATs) because the "non-renewal process is too often abused by principals."[61]

Not all rank-and-file proposals came from teachers. Clinicians put forth their own ideas. For example, "school psychologists, social workers, nurses, speech pathologists, vision and hearing technicians, occupational and physical therapists . . . shall be provided with appropriate workspace to include desks, chairs, testing tables, [and] computer[s]." Additionally, lending credence to the union's justifiably making air-conditioning in all the schools a bargaining issue, the clinicians demanded that the school board provide "adequate heating and ventilation which entails proper air-conditioning of all school units."[62] Perhaps no union demand was more lampooned by CPS and the media than air-conditioning the schools. But these proposals addressed an array of workplace health and safety problems that added up to a serious grievance related to working and learning conditions.

One additional clinician proposal that not only triggered a serious conversation at the bargaining table but that led ultimately to membership testimony and a new contract provision focused on the bullying of staff. The submission included the following complaint: "We have been given ultimatums in citywide meetings and threatened with disciplinary actions . . . 'Do this or you will be fired if you don't' or 'you're lucky to have a job!'" Teachers were also unanimous in their unhappiness about the district's requirements for submitting written daily lesson plans. "A reasonable lesson plan format," read a member contract suggestion "would be nice, not some seven page manifesto."[63]

Members also provided contract recommendations as constituency groups within CTU and as participants on one of twenty-eight special committees. Special education teachers jointly submitted a multipage series of contract revisions. Their suggestions included, for example, insisting on the availability of a sufficient number of "full-time counselors performing only counseling duties." The union's Women's Rights Committee submitted three proposals dealing with providing a "clean and sanitary location for lactating mothers to express breast milk during the school day," the ability of mothers to reserve "sick days for use following their return from FMLA [Family and Medical Leave Act]" leave, and expanding birth control options within the health plans to "cover devices that are prescribed such as IUD's [intrauterine devices] and diaphragms."[64]

Equity issues were often addressed in members' submissions. Roughly 10 percent of CPS teachers and paraprofessionals were not permanently assigned to one school and were forced to travel around the district. One proposal tried to rectify this bias by giving "a monthly allowance or mileage reimbursement to all citywide teachers for travel when extensive travel throughout the city is a requirement for work."[65]

In addition to equity and basic workplace issues, members submitted recommendations for lowering class size, increasing the ratio of counselors to students, and improving the retirement plan. Taken together, membership-submitted proposals were incorporated into the range of issues that CTU bargainers debated at the table and brought into the streets. Despite CPS's accusation that the union was fighting about illegitimate issues, CTU was rigorously responsive in mobilizing behind its members' interests. Union members had a vision of student-centered public education that they intended to inject into the bargaining process. Lewis explained that CTU's strategy was to have the bargaining "narrative focus on what teachers do."[66]

While the teachers consistently called for numerous changes, the Chicago media speculated that the union had overreached. The *Sun-Times* editorialized that "Lewis won't be able to deliver the moon for her members, and she owes it to them to prepare for that eventually."[67] However, unlike many of her contemporaries, Grossman was able to offer a more nuanced assessment. She recognized that, given all that was wrong with CPS, the teachers were being asked "to perform miracles."[68] Teachers were crying out to the public, "Do you people have any idea what we're dealing with?"[69] If CTU were going to meet its goal of producing a good contract it would need to address the large and the small of working for CPS.

CTU Goes to Washington

The new union leadership had never bargained a contract, and the first one would be a monumental undertaking. To prepare for the experience, in late September the CTU leadership attended a two-day collective bargaining workshop in Washington, DC, held by its parent organization the AFT. AFT President Randi Weingarten arranged the training, and Lewis found it "extremely helpful."[70] Fearing that the rookie leadership might be "in over their heads," Bloch noted that the national union offered a good amount of assistance.

The CTU leadership had initially been leery about working too closely with the AFT. During the 2011 local union election, CORE members suspected that AFT staff had inappropriately aided Marilyn Stewart's reelection bid. Mark Richard, a special consultant to the AFT, admitted that when Lewis won her election some AFT "voices were naysayers and wondered if they [CORE] were fringe elements."[71] CORE also assumed that the AFT would be opposed to a Chicago strike and might actually interfere to avoid one. An early fall strike date would mean that the third-largest teachers union could be walking picket lines in a Democratic stronghold—governed by an ex-aide to Obama—during a presidential election season. A strike, the AFT feared, might be harmful to the president's reelection bid, and the national union informed Lewis that it could be "terrible for the labor movement."[72]

To reassure the local leaders, Weingarten and Richard traveled to Chicago and met with Lewis at her home. "CTU was in control," Richard said, and the message from the national was that AFT "would be hands-off."[73] While the national union maintained a vigilant interest in the bargaining unfolding in Chicago, representatives from the AFT, including Richard and one-time chief of staff Al Davidoff, proved very helpful to the local by "bouncing ideas off [the local leadership], asking questions and serving as a resource."[74] Davidoff traveled to Chicago often, spending many long hours in intense strategy meetings. By his own account, he became enthusiastically committed to the CTU fight.

According to Richard, most of the discussions with CTU revolved around trying to construct a delicate balance among three dynamics: the interests and mobilization of the membership, the engagement of the community, and the need to resolve very practical contract issues. "Because CORE's DNA was direct contact with the membership and they wanted a dialogue in the street about public education," Richard explained, the organizational challenge was finding a "balance between creating a social movement and closing out a collective bargaining agreement."[75]

While the inexperienced CTU leaders went through a collective bargaining boot camp, the school board's representatives were conducting their own preparations for negotiations. Prior to developing contract proposals, Moriarty, Franczek, and Swanson held a number of sessions with the board members. In talking with the full board "we got a great deal of feedback" about labor costs, Moriarty noted.[76] The team also scheduled weekly meetings to hold strategic conversations on major contract items. Various CPS officials would join the sessions based on their expertise in areas like budgeting and curriculum. With the very occasional exception of board President David Vitale, school board members did not attend these sessions. The strategy behind the working groups, according to Swanson, was to have staff-level personnel involved who would insure that the school board's negotiations reflected "system knowledge of all school activities."[77]

It was also important that the employer's planning integrate three relevant institutions: the school board, CPS management, and the mayor's office. Each body had institutional knowledge to share and an investment in the details of a new labor agreement. The approach made intuitive sense, but the tripartite negotiation arrangement raised questions of coordination. Moriarty frankly pointed out that "our internal team sometimes struggled to be realistic about our proposals." A question that they continuously posed while drafting their bargaining agenda was whether the CTU would accept a proposal. Moriarty stressed that he wanted as much as possible to avoid making proposals that are "hard to accept [and] can poison the bargaining environment."[78]

As it turned out, as negotiations evolved, the employer's three-headed structure, plus Franczek, seemed to complicate the process. Lewis claimed that the school board representatives "were often a chaotic mess."[79] Union negotiators groused about occasions when the parties appeared to have reached consensus only to have someone working at CPS, but not present at the bargaining table, countermand the employer's agreement. CPS did appear handicapped in negotiations by the changing players on its side of the bargaining table. The proteacher paper *Substance News* referred to the churning as "playing musical chairs"; the paper had a point.[80] Except for Franczek and Moriarty, no one on the employer's team participated in negotiations from start to finish.

CTU president Karen Lewis speaking to 4,000 teachers and staff at Chicago's iconic Auditorium Theatre, with an overflow crowd of 2,000 at a nearby park, on May 23, 2012. Afterward, CTU members marched downtown to the financial district, where they joined another union rally, boosting their numbers to 10,000 protesters. Photo from Victor Powell Photography.

Chicago public school teachers rally outside the Chicago Board of Education headquarters, 125 S. Clark St., on the first day of the strike. Sun-Times photo.

CTU strikers often carried placards and banners asserting that the strike was not centered on compensation issues but was a fight to defend public education. Photo courtesy of the Chicago Teachers Union.

Throughout the strike, CTU leaders and members emphasized that their strike demands included compensation issues but that their central strike issues were a call "for better schools" and for "the schools our students deserve." Photo courtesy of the Chicago Teachers Union.

During the strike, CTU members often marched to the offices of local government officials who had attacked the teachers strike, as in this protest in front of State Representative Deborah Mell's office. September 13, 2012. Photo courtesy of Carole Ramsden.

Thousands of CTU members and supporters, including busloads of teachers from nearby states like Wisconsin, rallied at Chicago's Union Park and then marched through the Near West Side neighborhood. Saturday, September 15, 2012.
Full funding for special education was a key CTU demand. Photo courtesy of the Chicago Teachers Union.

Karen Lewis, president of the Chicago Teachers Union, and CTU executive
officers and core negotiating team meet with the media after Lewis's talk with
teachers and the House of Delegates, where she explained negotiations with
the Chicago school board. Friday, September 14, 2012. Left to right, Kristine
Mayle, Financial Secretary; Lewis; Robert Bloch, CTU attorney; Jesse Sharkey,
Vice President; and Michael Brunson, Recording Secretary. Sun-Times photo.

Chicago Public Schools CEO Jean-Claude Brizard listens as Chicago mayor
Rahm Emanuel speaks at A. O. Sexton Elementary School during the announcement that Chicago schools will start the year with a full school day: 7 hours
in elementary schools and 7.5 hours in high schools. July 25, 2012.
Sun-Times photo.

James Franczek, chief labor negotiator for City Hall, Chicago Public Schools, Chicago Park District, City Colleges, and Metropolitan Pier and Exposition Authority, in his Loop office. Wednesday, October 3, 2012. Sun-Times photo.

Chicago Board of Education President David Vitale states that teachers will get the respect they deserve. September 14, 2012. Sun-Times photo.

On the eighth and ninth days of the strike, CTU strikers gathered in front of their school buildings to discuss the tentative contract agreement in a profound exercise of union democracy. CTU members who work at the Maria Saucedo Elementary Scholastic Academy discussed the contract on September 17, 2012. Photo courtesy of Shaun Harkin.

8

THE START OF 2012 CONTRACT NEGOTIATIONS

In previous school negotiations, it was not uncommon to open contract talks eighteen months before the term date (i.e., before the contract expired). This time, however, negotiations started with only seven months left before the reigning agreement ended in June 2012. It was not until November 10, 2011, that CPS and CTU "met for the first successor [i.e., the next labor agreement] bargaining session."[1] As a result, Bloch lamented that "negotiations started very late" and never really kicked in until December 2011.[2]

When negotiations did begin, however, the union smartly navigated through a labyrinth that while legally restrictive and littered with minefields, was also surprisingly navigable and vulnerable to a seismic street-level campaign. CTU had no illusions about the advantages the Springfield political class had handed the board. Nonetheless, the employer's legislatively constructed process, meant to bind union members, was not without its vulnerabilities. The union found and exploited each ambiguity in SB 7. More instructive, they figured out how to use the law's proscriptions to their advantage.

Bargaining Away from the "Thin Contract"

Franczek hobbled into the first negotiation session in CTU's Merchandise Mart offices aided by a cane. The sixty-eight-year-old had had his right hip replaced, but before the start of bargaining, the metal ball and artificial socket had to be readjusted. The needed correction was minute, but the follow-up surgical procedure and the associated pain put Franczek into a foul mood. He proceeded to propose a contract that surprised and annoyed the union.

The employer opened the bargaining by offering CTU a streamlined "Framework for a Modern Successor Agreement," eliminating hundreds of pages of contract language that had protected the teachers.[3] Lewis scoffed at the proposal and accused CPS of trying to "gut the contract."[4] Pam Massarsky, who was retired but had served on many past CTU negotiation teams, was incensed at the offer and demanded that the board "come back with a new agreement."[5] CPS Chief Labor Relations Officer Joseph Moriarty, along with Stephanie Donovan from Franczek's office, had drafted the radically reframed contract. He introduced each item and painstakingly offered a rationale for the proposals. The presentation drew a distinctly harsh response. Bloch derisively spoke against the "thin contract," referring to it as a barely veiled request for CTU to waive years of protective contract language. CPS was relentless and kept insisting on seriously discussing the twenty-five-page contractual rewrite. The union, Lewis admits, was at first "thrown off" and it "took a long time to get CPS to drop" the "thin" offer.[6]

Finally, on February 1, the parties gathered around a mahogany table in a conference room adjacent to Lewis's office and exchanged comprehensive proposals, including wage offers. The school board proposed a four-year contract with a one-time 2 percent salary increase in the first year, while also eliminating step pay increases, which are customarily used in labor agreements to incentivize teachers to invest in long-term careers with a school district. Accompanying the board's wage offer was a request to develop a merit pay plan. If the opening proposal on February 1 was meant to poke the teachers in the eye, it worked.

Teachers were still agitated about the heavy-handed withdrawal of the 4 percent pay increase in June 2011, and Emanuel had professed his intention to increase their work by 20 percent without paying them a penny more. CPS now planned to wipe away the contractual step increases, which, though distinct from annual adjustments to a teacher's salary, nevertheless represent a real increase in a teacher's compensation. Eliminating them would be the equivalent of a reduction in pay. Under the circumstances, asking teachers also to adopt a merit pay plan was a provocative move. Lewis stressed "that when we asked our members about merit pay, they said 'Hell no!'"[7]

Board negotiators had expected the idea to be controversial, and, according to Moriarty, "we didn't have a model [of how to apply merit pay increases] to propose." He acknowledged that in preparations for bargaining, the employer was "struggling with a real model that works." Nonetheless, CPS negotiators told the union that "we think [merit pay is] a good idea," and they insisted on discussing a possible plan.[8] Franczek, however, regretted having it as a proposal and was later blunt in his feelings about the idea: "It was stupid," he said.[9]

Union bargainers were no less insulted by the school district's first-and-only-year offer of a 2 percent salary increase in a four-year contract. In response, the CTU, in Lewis's irreverent words, "answered their crazy with our crazy."[10] The union proposed a 29 percent salary increase over two years. Despite an agreement that the parties would keep their negotiations confidential, the cloak of secrecy was quickly ripped away. In an attention-grabbing headline, the *Chicago Tribune* announced "Chicago Teachers Asking for 30% Raises over Next 2 Years."[11]

But this apparently unreasonable initial wage offer was actually not what it seemed. The union arrived at the 29 percent total by restoring the 4 percent taken from the final year of the 2007–2012 contract and then adding 1 percent for every 1 percent increase in anticipated work time. That brought the wage demand to 24 percent. In CTU's view, the union was simply asking that its members be paid for the hours they worked and would be working. The union's actual wage increase demand was not 29 percent, but 5, spread equally over two years, or a very modest 2.5 percent per year. Rhetorical ploys aside, CTU had a serious reason for opening up with a headline-grabbing number.

It was true that CPS's nearly nonexistent wage offer invited the union's equally outsized response, but CTU counted on CPS's offering practically nothing. Despite what the union said in public, it was relieved when the employer made an offer that was easy to refuse. Sharkey explained that "we knew that we needed the process to be long, to allow time and cover to bargain over other 4.5 issues." The 4.5 issues were the permissive ones, like the hotly contested longer school day and year, class size, libraries, and staffing, which CPS had no legal obligation even to discuss. Union negotiators knew that pay was important, but it was not even listed among the union's top thirty issues. "What we needed to do was to preserve a wage claim—a real big one," Sharkey noted, to allow enough time to create bargaining leverage over the permissive subjects.[12] A very large wage demand would undoubtedly be rejected by CPS, and, given how low the school board's initial offer was, it would take many iterations of counteroffers to move the parties to a potential settlement point. In other words, CTU was going to use a mandatory subject of bargaining, wages, to extend negotiations over permissive subjects.

It was a bold and risky maneuver. The union could legally strike over mandatory subjects of bargaining like pay, but not over class size or the longer school day. If, however, the union could keep compensation alive as an issue, then CTU could look for bargaining leverage over 4.5 items and possibly initiate a strike ostensibly over legal items, including pay. Franczek recognized the strategy and countered by trying repeatedly to draw the union into impact negotiations over 4.5 items. *Impact bargaining* refers to the parties' obligation to negotiate over the *effects* of a particular change in working conditions. If CTU took the bait, then it would be trapped in the mediation black hole, because if the two sides couldn't agree, then the employer was free to unilaterally do what it wanted, which would end with the school board's implementing its final offer. Unfortunately for the employer, as CPS's own summary of the bargaining timeline revealed, the union "never demanded impact bargaining . . . over the longer day and school year."[13]

Understanding CTU's thinking requires realizing that timing was essential to the union's strategy. SB 7 mandated a rigid but not exact time frame for how unsettled bargaining issues were to be addressed. More important, the law's time restrictions influenced when a strike could legally occur. CTU took close notice of the calendar prescribed by SB 7. Bloch later revealed that the union's tactical objective was to "control the timing of bargaining so that, if needed, a strike would occur when the teachers wanted it."[14] He further pointed out that the negotiation protocols submitted by CPS did not specify when mediation or fact-finding, if necessary, had to start. Bloch subsequently persuaded Franczek to agree to set specific dates proposed by the union for when mediation and fact-finding could begin. It was a decision Franczek came to regret badly.

If the parties were at an impasse on an item, either side could request that a mediator be brought into bargaining any time on or after February 1. The bargaining protocols further prescribed that if the mediator was unsuccessful in breaking the impasse, either party could request that the fact-finding process begin on or after April 1.[15] Once fact-finding began, 75 days were allotted for it to conclude.

An important fact was that neither CPS nor CTU was obligated to accept the fact finder's report. If the report was not adopted as a way to overcome the impasse, then the teachers were free to issue a ten-day *Notice of Intent to Strike* with the IELRB and the school board. By accepting the union's prestrike hurdle dates, Franczek had unwittingly allowed CTU to set a preferred early September strike date. To avoid an unfair labor practice charge for violating the IELRA, CPS's attorney had to agree to some dates; these dates, however, happened to favor the union. CTU was now in charge of the bargaining calendar. Ironically, the public policy meant to cripple the union's ability to strike and hamstring its bargaining power became a tool for constructing a path to the first teacher work stoppage in Chicago in more than two decades. With a shadow strike date in mind, and having calculated the likely ebb and flow for the next seven months, CTU formally demanded mediation immediately following the February 1 bargaining session. The clock had begun ticking.

David Born, a mediator from the Federal Mediation and Conciliation Service, joined the talks. He was an experienced mediator, but his presence had little impact. According to Bloch, "negotiations progressed predictably, nowhere or slowly."[16] CTU believed that Emanuel felt confident that PERA and SB 7, or as the union referred to them, "his pair of aces," left him without a real incentive to bargain.[17] The sides were discussing many proposals, but negotiations were stalled on the longer school day, teacher recall rights, and how much of a teacher's evaluation would be linked to student test scores. Union requests to discuss class size, air-conditioning, and proper clinical staffing for schools also floundered on the employer's unwillingess to take up these items. Ever mindful of the calendar, on April 2 CTU "demanded fact-finding consistent with the impasse resolution procedure set forth in the IELRA."[18] Enter Edwin "Ed" Benn.

The Fact-Finding Process Begins

The parties jointly selected Ed Benn to serve as the fact finder. More precisely, according to the dispute resolution machinery created by the law, he would be the "neutral chair" of a three-person panel. One representative each from the union and the Board of Education would join the chair on the panel. Benn was a highly respected arbitrator who had resolved many public-sector contractual disputes over decades. There was no arbitrator in the state who had written more rulings than Benn, and he had gained a degree of public recognition unusual for the profession. As arbitrators go, he was the industry's equivalent of a rock star.

Benn was fearless and scrupulous in applying the principles of arbitration to the cases he was selected to hear. The CPS-CTU dispute, however, would not be an arbitration case. Benn would not have the authority to impose a decision on the parties. SB 7, furthermore, expressly prohibited the fact finder from having any jurisdiction over 4.5 bargaining or impact issues. Benn's authority covered only all mandatory non-4.5 subjects of bargaining. It was a sizable responsibility, but if fact-finding was supposed to help the parties resolve disputes there was a problem with Benn's charge: it explicitly left out one of the most contentious issue separating CTU and CPS, the longer school day.

Roughly three weeks after the fact-finding process began, the employer submitted counterproposals to the union on all outstanding items, including a 2 percent pay increase annually for four years. The union, however, was still interested in discussing what the board thought was a seemingly settled item. Negotiations over PERA had recently concluded, but CTU pivoted back to the law's requirement for incorporating student performance into teacher evaluations. The union's insistence on revisiting CPS's plan to comply with PERA, known as "REACH (Recognizing Educators Advancing Chicago) Students," was initially resisted by the employer.

The parties had already spent more than ninety hours in negotiations over nearly four months hammering out an evaluation system. The negotiations had begun before the actual start of full contract bargaining, in a small committee designated to discuss PERA. Under the law, Chicago had to adopt a new evaluation plan by the start of school in 2012, and because the subject was of extreme importance, the parties agreed to initiate the dialogue early. Committee discussions touched on all areas of the evaluation process, but there was a major disagreement over the committee's expected final product.

According to the board, the entire teacher evaluation plan was to be negotiated within the committee. The union, however, argued that only the size of the student growth factor to be used as part of the teacher assessment was an appropriate subject of the committee's charge. Robin Potter, the union's litigation counsel and a member of the small group, explained that "the board's plan was to first obtain a total agreement on evaluations" before the parties entered into full contract bargaining. But she pointed out that CTU had made a strategic choice "not to allow the small committee to determine the final contract language [on the whole evaluation plan]."[19] Under the contract then in force, a joint committee was established to discuss terms of an evaluation plan, but the union contended that final agreement on a plan was subject to the full bargaining process.

To the union, the employer's plan was grossly unfair to the teachers, and Lewis called the whole evaluation proposal a "hot mess."[20] Nonetheless, after ninety days, the board did submit a final offer to the union on a new evaluation plan and also threatened to implement the changes if the union refused to agree. CTU promptly rejected the offer, and while the board made clear that it had the authority to impose terms, bargaining continued on the student growth factor. Potter contends that the employer kept negotiating because it smartly realized that if it had bluntly wielded the force granted to it under the law, bargaining would have imploded before it ever really started. "Teachers would have gone crazy!" she noted. Despite the board's view that by late April REACH had been comprehensively developed, it was still a volatile subject of bargaining that "remained a critical issue of negotiations until the last day of the strike."[21]

One week after the employer's April 23 counterproposals were submitted, CTU and CPS agreed that Benn would issue his findings on July 16, 2012. News of an administrative deadline for the pending fact-finding report went largely unnoticed by the public because the union used the symbolism of the occasion of May 1—International Labor Day—to endorse a boisterous Occupy Chicago rally. The countdown to a possible school strike now had a new procedural threshold to cross. Another more threatening line, fertile with meaning, was about to be set.

CTU's Strike Authorization Vote and Fear of Reprisal

On May 31, the union and the Board of Education held their initial mediation session with Benn. The next day, CTU announced in a press release that in five days it intended to conduct a strike authorization vote.[22] Fact-finding had just begun, and there was no recommendation yet by Benn for ending the impasse or a final contract offer to reject or strike over. Leaders of the PC coalition were furious. "Robin [Steans] had a cow," over the announcement, according to Mitch Roth.[23] She excoriated the union for even daring to consider a strike.

Franczek contemplated seeking a court injunction to stop the vote but he was uncertain whether he could obtain it. The law was ambiguous. On June 6, the union began the strike authorization vote and, on June 11, it announced that 98 percent of those voting, or, astoundingly, 92 percent of the total membership, had authorized the strike. The union had blown past the three-quarters legal threshold. Mark Richard, chief of staff at the AFT, boasted with immodesty that "the world shook as the numbers came in."[24]

The union's audacious strike vote not only stunned observers; it also seemed to have come out of nowhere. Emanuel and the school board were apoplectic when they heard the news. The decision to take the authorization vote on the heels of beginning the fact-finding process was, like everything CTU did, related to the way SB 7 created a time frame for a strike. The union did not want to take a strike vote in the fall; furthermore, as Bloch explained, a vote after the fact finder issued his report might put "pressure on [union] members to accept a lesser contract."[25]

The idea to take the vote was Bloch's. He noted that while the law anticipated a strike ratification vote as the final act after fact-finding, "it didn't actually state that a strike vote must be taken at the end of the process."[26] Nor did the law state how the authorization vote was to be conducted. Franczek admitted that the language of SB 7 was ambiguous about when the strike vote could be taken. He also admired the tactical impact of the vote's timing, remarking, "It was a brilliant move."[27]

Voting after June 1 was not merely a matter of counting backward from early September. The CTU leadership knew that the strike vote would be controversial. They also knew that the mayor would use every political means at his disposal to stop a strike from happening. While the union had secretly settled on a June strike vote in May, it was careful not to announce the date until after June 1, one day following the closing of the Illinois legislative session. If the union had gone public with its vote plans before the General Assembly adjournment, the mayor could have gone back to Springfield and tried to amend SB 7 to force a later authorization vote or, even worse, a blanket prohibition against striking.

The union was right to worry about this scenario. A year to the day after SB 7 became law, a backdoor political drive attempted to make it even harder for CTU to strike. "Once SB 7 passed, the advocates had a victory party and boasted about the 75 percent threshold and time delays," State Senator Kimberly Lightford disdainfully explained. At that point the union had not indicated any intention of striking, but Lewis's confident acceptance of the challenge of meeting, if necessary, the three-quarter-vote bar had already begun to unnerve the Performance Counts crowd and the city's political establishment. When CTU revealed its intention to authorize a strike, "Rahm was livid," Lightford recalled.[28] The mayor believed that Lewis had promised not to strike. Lewis had made no such promise, but she traveled to Springfield sometime after the union strike vote to forestall another possible legislative assault on her union's right to strike.

At this point, CTU got a supportive hand from an unexpected source. House Speaker Michael Madigan received a phone call from Chicago Federation of Labor (CFL) President Jorge Ramirez informing him that Lewis was on her way to Springfield to fend off an effort by the education reformers to revoke the right to strike. Madigan was supportive of SB 7, and his quarrel with the teachers unions over the pension law had opened the door to Stand for Children in the 2010 assembly races. But the Speaker had no tolerance for any further legislative maneuvering. He entered a meeting with Lewis and promptly declared that he was not interested in passing another bill. The reformers had got what they asked for and now had to live with it. Madigan, according to Lightford, also accused the reform coalition of "acting like sore losers."[29] Lewis left Springfield relieved and called Ramirez to thank him for interceding.

Madigan's intervention was important, but CTU Staff Coordinator Jackson Potter believed that the union's mobilization activities in May had deterred state officials from taking further restrictive action. "I think once people saw thousands of people in the streets and this sea of red and they saw the overwhelming support for a strike, it rattled them and it made it real that we weren't just selling 'wolf tickets' [i.e., making improbable threats]."[30]

CTU needed political influence to ward off a complete strike prohibition, and its street-level activism conveyed a political threat. In the shadows of Republican assaults against public sector unions in Ohio, Wisconsin, Michigan, and Indiana, moves by a Democratic-controlled government to completely shackle the state's largest teachers union was a step beyond where the Democrats' electoral calculus could go. Street actions here in this case were not a mere adjunct to or substitute for political heft. On the contrary, building a social movement around public education helped CTU elicit political assistance and stymie any further erosion of its members' voices.

The Fact-Finding Hearings

With the union's accomplishment just forty-eight hours old, on June 13 the parties began a two-day fact-finding hearing. Meeting at Franczek's law offices on Wacker Drive, the union brought in a number of key staff members, including Carol Caref and Lynn Cherkasky-Davis from the Quest Center, to educate Benn about teacher evaluations. The union made its case first and, though fearing that SB 7 prohibited Benn from addressing the longer school day, it wanted desperately to convert the fact-finding process into a platform for debating how CPS would compensate teachers for forcing them to work longer hours. Its strategy was to present evidence about teachers' current heavy workload without formally asking Benn to rule on what he was allegedly barred from acting on, the question of added working hours and possible pay.

Although the parties would spend time talking about teaching workload and hours spent on the job, it would be done as if the new 4.5 items did not exist. The union's task was to present evidence to Benn that it believed was supportive of its pay proposal. Benn's job, the union and the board assumed, was to hear testimony and examine the facts without taking into consideration the longer school day and year. In reality, the union wanted the hearing to be all about what the law said it could not be about. If CTU could get Benn to address the hours that teachers worked, then it was likely he would see the longer school day as a compensatory issue that needed to be ruled on. Although the union expected the board to reject a recommendation to pay teachers for working 20 percent longer, the fact-finder's opinion would legitimize the union's claim that without resolution on the matter a labor deal was impossible.

Sharkey spoke at length about how a Chicago teacher's school day and compensation compared to teachers at other major urban K–12 school districts. His presentation was meant to counter directly one of SB 7's directives to the fact finder to use certain financial criteria to determine a recommendation. Under the law, the fact finder was supposed to consider a comparison of the wages, hours, and conditions of employment of educators in the ten largest US cities.[31] The union had been contesting flawed claims made by Emanuel that Chicago teachers worked the shortest hours in the nation. CTU submitted as evidence a report conducted by the University of Illinois that showed teachers working at least a 58-hour week.[32]

CPS produced data apparently revealing that "Chicago students receive the least instructional time of any students compared to the country's 10 largest cities." Emanuel was fond of a direct comparison with one southern city. "From kindergarten through high school, a Chicago child will receive nearly 3 years less instructional time than a peer student in Houston."[33] Sharkey's testimony drew directly from a union analysis comparing Chicago to New York, Los Angeles, and Houston. The comparison found that Chicago schools had more "instructional time per year than either New York or Los Angeles," and that the Houston school day was as long as the Chicago teachers work day.[34]

Emanuel's reflexive repetition of Houston as his shining example was further tarnished when observers looked more closely at the southern city's academic achievements and found very minimal differences with Chicago. Commenting on the value of adopting a school calendar that was more similar to Houston's, *Tribune* reporter Eric Zorn wrote, "The evidence is far from overwhelming that it would result in an uptick in student achievement."[35] During the fact-finding hearing, Sharkey took glee in noting that Houston also had smaller classes and a smaller percentage of poor students. He was letting Benn know that a comparison with other large school districts was not only fraught with complexities but also likely to favor the union's position. Sharkey was also baiting Franczek to assert CPS's stance on working hours. If he could get Franczek to respond to the union's argument that teachers were already working long hours, it would inject the longer school day into the fact-finding process and perhaps open up a chance for Benn to rule on the issue, despite the board's contention that he was legally barred from doing so.

In reply, on at least two occasions Franczek pointedly reminded the union and Benn that 4.5 issues were out of play. In the third slide of a fifty-two-slide PowerPoint presentation that he presented, Franczek read out loud the following admonition: "Fact-Finding Must Adhere to Provisions of Section 4.5." On a slide that drew scoffs and shaking of heads from CTU, Franczek recited, "Neither the [IELRB] nor any mediator or *fact-finder* [emphasis in original] . . . shall have jurisdiction over . . . a dispute or impasse" regarding a Section 4.5 subject."[36] Benn sat passively during this part of the employer's presentation. Franczek went on to remind his audience that along with the school day and year, class size, staffing, and hours of instruction were either prohibited or permissive subjects of bargaining and therefore explicitly inappropriate items to address in fact-finding.

Franczek never offered any comparable evidence on working hours but did call attention to differences between the compensation of Chicago teachers and teachers in other school districts. Teacher pay was a mandatory subject of bargaining rightly before the fact finder. Along with the city comparisons, Franczek's presentation also included revealing data about how total teacher income was determined. School contracts had provisions for giving teachers incremental pay boosts for years of service, referred to as "steps," and for acquiring additional education, called "lanes." While the value of teaching experience was at the heart of disputes between corporate education reformers and teachers unions, teachers were required to upgrade their knowledge and competencies constantly. The school board's initial contract proposal called for eliminating step increases. Franczek wanted Benn to see how lucrative these seniority pay adjustments were to teachers.

Under the 2007–2012 contract there were sixteen steps. After step 14, which occurred at thirteen years of employment, teachers would climb the final two rungs on the service ladder at twenty years (step 15) and twenty-five years (step 16) of teaching. According to CPS data, the average step increase added 3.41 percent to a teacher's base salary. Benn took note of these figures. He read intently from the PowerPoint handouts provided to everyone and quickly estimated the overall "new money" that teachers had received over the preceding four years. After writing the calculations out, he spoke up and declared that the annual pay raises and step increases that teachers earned demonstrated the power of compounding. It was clear that Benn believed that Chicago teachers had done very well over the previous four years, even with the mayor's cancellation of the 2012 pay hike.

CPS went on to claim that CTU's two-year 29 percent wage increase proposal would cost the district roughly $527 million. The union's additional demands to shrink class size, place libraries in all schools, and fully staff clinical positions would add another $516 million. It was the employer's contention that adding nearly a billion dollars more in expenses to a $5.4 billion budget was fiscally impossible. Franczek also warned of the pension "bomb" that was about to go off. In fiscal year 2014 (beginning on July 1, 2013), CPS was required to make a $600 million payment into the teachers' pension fund. The school district had been permitted by the state legislature to withhold contributions from 2011 to 2013; as a result, the bill coming due had grown exponentially. "We wish we could invest more in our teachers," stated the employer's budget summary, "but the funds are simply not there to do so."[37] It was a closing argument meant to shift responsibility for hard realities to others, like legislators in Springfield who, CPS charged, were underfunding the school district. No one on CTU's side of the table believed a word of it.

CTU pointed out that the employer's data-driven presentation was missing a lot of other data. CPS's ability to afford the "schools that students deserve" should also have included the half million dollars of TIF payments annually drained away from the schools to fund private development. It also should have included the nearly $500 million spent on charter schools backed by the same finance capitalists who were sucking tax dollars out of the public schools for private gain. CPS's ability to afford better schools also had to include the increased salaries for central office executives and the city's unwillingness to raise revenue by fairly taxing the same wealthy people who were benefiting from shifting tax dollars into profit-taking endeavors. And what about the millions of dollars the city and school district were spending on bank fees and investment payments from loan agreements misleadingly sold by Wall Street to help fund the school district?

From 2003 through 2007, the district issued $1 billion worth of auction-rate securities (bonds whose interest rates floated), coupled with contracts called interest-rate swaps. CPS contended that these financial arrangements would save the district money over traditional borrowing based on fixed-rate debt. The deals, however, were risky and depended on a complex alignment of interest rates. When the global economic crisis nearly brought down the banking industry, the district's gamble proved damaging to the schools. A 2014 *Chicago Tribune* analysis projected that the auction-rate deals were likely to cost CPS an estimated $100 million more in bank payments than the district would have paid on equivalent fixed-rate bonds. CTU claimed the costs would climb to at least $500 million. Each dollar paid to the banks was a dollar not invested into the classroom. The newspaper's analysis also found that dealmakers like Goldman Sachs and lenders like Bank of America had never adequately disclosed the risks.[38] Affording to do more for teachers should at least require that CPS renegotiate lower repayments from the same financial entities that were profiting handsomely at the expense of working-class Chicagoans.

The board's assessment should have also at least acknowledged that a "broken" pension system was not caused by excessive retirement expenditures but by the "tax maneuvers of Chicago's mayors."[39] Until 1995, the pension plan had been fully funded, but when Daley gained control of the schools the legislature also transferred to him dominion over the Chicago Teachers' Pension Fund (CTPF). This oversight came with his promise to make the payments necessary to keep the plan at least 90 percent funded. In 2010, however, Daley persuaded the state to grant CPS a three-year pension holiday. By skipping three years of payments, Daley could siphon off $1.2 billion from teacher pensions for other city expenditures. The city would then spend money borrowed from its school employees, who upon retirement receive, on average, a modest $41,000 annual pension, earned over nearly thirty years of service.

The school district's bargaining proposals were based on a severe austerity framework similar to what was being implemented across US cities and school districts. CTU rejected austerity as a manufactured problem, falsely pitting one worthwhile public need and group against another. For the union, the problem was not budget disparities but the loss of democratic control over the public square. City hall and the school board were now handmaidens of a well-off few instead of protectors of the common good. Franczek heard the analysis over and over again. He recognized that it was unlike anything that a CTU leadership had ever brought into the bargaining process. Nonetheless, in his opinion, the critique of CPS's proposals that CTU offered was political rhetoric meant to whip up the emotions of parents. Franczek was at the bargaining table to negotiate a new contract, not to defend capitalism. His task was conceptually and procedurally straightforward.

CTU's objective was a complex high-wire act without any precedent to serve as a safety net. In their proposals, the union was blurring the lines between what was and was not a legitimate bargaining issue. It was certain that what was damaging public education in Chicago and in other cities was racial and economic injustice. Conceptually, CTU was prepared to bargain an "education justice" agenda and to use the negotiations to improve city schools.

Benn could not have had more diametrically opposed sets of approaches and factors to weigh. He also had, by the parties' stated accounts, limited room to operate and the highly combustible issue of the longer school day shadowing the impasse. Over the next three weeks, Benn would spend the better part of five days with the parties taking testimony, examining evidence, questioning witnesses, and familiarizing himself with the case. On July 9, CTU and the board engaged in their final mediation session with the fact finder. With only one week remaining in the seventy-five-day period required before CTU could set a strike date, Benn did what he had always done when asked to arbitrate a labor dispute. He offered a solution.

The Fact Finders' Report

As prescribed by SB 7, on July 16 Benn submitted his findings and recommendations privately to the board and to the union. Both parties would now have an opportunity to review the report and, through their representatives on the fact-finding panel, accept or reject the recommendations. Benn's report declined to issue any rulings on pedagogical issues like evaluations or on union proposals dealing with job security, reassignment, and appointment of classes to teachers. He acknowledged not having enough content expertise to understand them fully and, more important, he did not believe that these items should be determined "through the impasse resolution process" but should be negotiated by the parties.[40] His report focused only on the monetary items; those items, explosively, included compensation for the longer school day. In Bloch's terms, the findings "went directly to the heart of [the] dispute."[41]

Benn first recognized that under the 2007–2012 agreement CPS employees "did extremely well."[42] By his estimates, during the previous five years employees had earned approximately, between 19 and 46 percent in wage increases. He then noted that the school board was exercising its statutory right to lengthen the school day and year, thereby increasing work time for the employees by 19.4 percent. And there it was: the longer school day. Benn made it clear that the employer's imposition of more work without additional pay could not stand. Given the additional time demands, "it is simply unrealistic for the Board to expect the employees to work the substantial additional hours and days imposed by the Board for free or without fair compensation. . . . With the offer it made, in this case (2 percent per year for four years), that is what the Board appears to be doing."[43] Despite the repeated reminders from Franczek about the fact finder's authority, Benn stated unconditionally that "compensation for the longer school day and year is the major flashpoint of this dispute." It was the "proverbial elephant in the room" and "that issue must be decided."[44]

To CTU's delight, Benn recommended that in order to fairly compensate employees for working 19.4 percent longer hours, they should be given between a 15 and 18 percent raise in the first year of the contract. His recommendation included a 2.5 percent cost-of-living adjustment. Anticipating CPS's objections, Benn was blunt and unsympathetic about the employer's options. "The Board is totally in control of this issue and can literally dictate the added compensation, if any, attributable to the longer school day and year. However, what the school district cannot do is increase the school day and year to the extent it has done and also expect the salaried employees to effectively work the additional hours for free or without fair compensation because the Board claims it cannot pay for the increase it imposed."[45]

During the fact-finding hearing, Franczek had made a special point to stress that the report's recommendations had to take into consideration certain "factors" as applicable under the law. Franczek certainly had in mind factor "F," which was taken from a list of financial factors identified in Section 12 of SB 7, which stated that "the employer's financial ability to fund the proposals based on existing available resources" had to be weighed. The school district had estimated a nearly $700 million deficit for 2013 and perhaps shortfalls in the $1 billion range in 2014 and 2015. Benn accepted the district's leaner budget projections for the next few fiscal years and found them relevant in determining a standard annual pay increase. He informed the board, however, that it could not rely on ability to pay for "determining the issue of compensation for the longer school day and year." After all, CPS had created the problem in the first place by unilaterally implementing the longer work hours. The employer could not "defeat additional compensation for those longer hours" by also arguing that it could not afford to pay employees for the time they were forced to work. Benn then drew an analogy that CTU repeated often: "The analogy raised by the Board's argument is to an individual who buys a car he cannot afford, and because he cannot make the payments argues that he should be able to keep the car even though he cannot make the payments. In such a case, 'I can't afford it' is not a defense—he simply should not have bought the car in the first place."[46]

Benn had emphatically touched the "third rail" of the bargaining dispute and issued a whopping verdict in favor of the union. He knew the implications of his decision and chose an evocative adjective to describe the dispute. "This is a volatile labor dispute in a *toxic* collective-bargaining relationship. The different approaches of the parties have resulted in a confrontation that has all the makings of a full-scale labor-management war."[47] Benn went on to further justify his decision by explaining that he had a duty not to ignore the "most important issue which, standing alone, may well be the issue which sets off a strike putting up to 25,000 teachers on the street and keeping 400,000 students out of school. . . ."[48] But did he have the authority to consider the issue, or had he simply usurped the right because the ends (i.e., trying to avoid a strike) justified the means (i.e., paying employees for the hours they worked)?

Franczek said Benn had no such authority. The union never said either way, but Bloch noted that the law was harmful because it kept the parties from discussing what they considered important. He did acknowledge that the law seemed to restrict the fact finder from taking action on the longer school day but, thankfully, Benn had "acted on it anyway."[49] Benn did address the question of his authority in his ruling. In a nearly two-page endnote, he argued that the full extent of the neutral chair's authority was not defined: "The short answer to the jurisdictional question raised by the Board is that I have not been informed with finality by any duly established entity that I do not have jurisdiction to consider the matter. . . . The Board has not shown with any degree of certainty that I cannot consider the issue of additional compensation for the longer school day and year."[50]

Benn's warrant to act did not rely solely on the lack of an interpretive ruling explicitly prohibiting him from taking up the longer school day. Whether the fact finder could act on the longer school day was, in Benn's analysis, an unsettled "technical dispute" over the law's implementation, but to ignore the extended work hours requirement was to be blind to the real, undeniable issue bringing the parties to the brink of a strike. "Keeping 400,000 students out of school on arguments that are, for all purposes technicalities, will be completely contrary to my directions" under the law.[51] In his view he wasn't acting without authority. He was doing precisely what he was hired to do.

Moriarty strenuously disagreed. As the Board of Education panel member, he expressed, in a written dissent, regret that "in his zeal to mediate a settlement," Benn had come "to a seriously flawed recommendation."[52] He accused Benn of acting on "issues explicitly beyond his legal purview" and for substituting "his judgment for the mandates and prohibitions of the General Assembly." Moriarty took aim at Benn's fear of a citywide school strike as a justification for issuing a salary recommendation. "The Neutral Chair is worried about the prospect of a CTU strike, a strike he appears to recognize is illegally motivated." In the first footnote in Moriarty's fourteen-page dissenting opinion, he chastised Benn for even suggesting that the longer school year and day might set off a strike "when the law clearly prohibits such a strike."[53]

Serving as a thinly veiled expression of the employer's growing anxiety about CTU's strike plans, Moriarty's argument could not have been clearer: a teacher walkout over the longer school day and year was illegal, so there was no pressing need for Benn to offer a salary recommendation to forestall a job action. It did not matter how angry employees were or how unjust it was to force people to work more hours for nothing. Nor did it matter how seriously the process offended Benn's professional integrity. The law was the law, and it favored the mayor. In closing, Moriarty claimed that the fact-finding process had not "produced a basis for further negotiation or a path forward to resolve this dispute."[54]

Under SB 7, the employer's rejection of the report was sufficient to render it null and void. Given how favorable the salary recommendation was to the union, however, casual readers of the news could be excused for being surprised to learn that CTU had also dismissed the recommendations. "The long-awaited fact-finder's recommendation on how to solve 'toxic' Chicago teacher contract talks was finally made public Wednesday—but nobody wanted it," read the *Chicago Sun-Times*.[55] The union countered by reminding the public that the board had repeatedly said that it was important to wait for the fact finder's report to substantiate the legitimacy of its position on the longer school day. But Kristine Mayle pointed out that once the "fact-finder said something they don't like," the employer dismissed the report's validity.[56] It was left to Jesse Sharkey, CTU's representative on the fact-finding panel, to file the union's official dissenting opinion. Sharkey concurred with the salary recommendation and noted, "If that were the sum total of the issues on the table the Union would accept the report." However, fair compensation did not "trump our concerns about class size, a better day, and job security."[57]

The union intended to continue bargaining over teacher evaluations and, because Benn's report was silent on this issue, Sharkey found the recommendations inadequate as a basis for agreement. He also disagreed with Benn's recommendation of a four-year labor deal. Sharkey's simple dissent was a tactical move and a signal to Emanuel. The school board's desire for a four-year deal would push the beginning of a new contract cycle beyond the mayor's reelection bid in the fall of 2014. If the contract were to instead run only three years, it would terminate in the summer of 2015. But that would mean that the union would likely be making loud threatening noises about bargaining right at the time the mayor was trying to win reelection. As it turned out, Emanuel wanted the extra contract year so badly that the duration issue would be one of the last items settled late in the strike week. Though Sharkey said nothing about the union's reasoning for rejecting the contract duration recommendation, he offered the union's strongest dissent over the issue of job security and reassignment:

> CPS in recent years has laid off thousands of teachers for reasons that have nothing to do with teaching abilities or job performance, but rather to balance its budget or to close schools. Unlike almost any other employees with collective bargaining rights, these teachers currently have no right to be recalled to employment. . . . The Board's stated policy of school closures combined with a stated goal of operating 60 more charter schools within 5 years ensures that layoffs will be a semi-permanent feature of life in the Chicago Public Schools for the foreseeable future.[58]

Sharkey's opinion addressed another of the major flashpoints fueling the strike, one that the union could not force the employer to discuss. Everyone in the city knew that CPS was planning to close an unprecedented number of schools before the 2013 school year began. The closures would displace thousands of mostly South Side black and Latino children, and likely many African-American teachers and paraprofessionals. During the bargaining, CTU tried to engage the board on its plans to shutter schools. Each time Franczek demurred that the subject was, according to union negotiators, "above his pay grade."

There were divergent views about Benn's actions on the longer school day and year. "Like it or not," *Chicago Sun-Times* columnist Mark Brown wrote, "nobody can fact-find their way out of the tough decisions."[59] With the fact finder's report rejected and a strike authorization vote attained, there were no longer any serious procedural barriers or time frames stopping CTU from setting a strike date. After the seventy-five-day fact-finding process had concluded, the Chicago school board realized that the principle of paying workers for the hours they worked was inviolable.

9

A BREAKTHROUGH AND PRELUDE TO A STRIKE

Although the rejection of the fact-finding recommendations by both the union and the school district appeared to scuttle the likelihood of avoiding a strike, its release had a dramatic impact on the bargaining. Bloch claimed that it "hit like a bombshell."[1] Local media began to question Emanuel's thinking. A *Chicago Sun-Times* story charged: "For a political chess player who never makes a move without thinking three moves ahead, Mayor Rahm Emanuel looks more like a high school clubber than a grand master when it comes to the teachers contract."[2]

Linda Lenz, publisher of *Catalyst Chicago*, a newsmagazine that covers CPS, reflected on Emanuel's inexperience by noting that he's "made some miscalculations, perhaps out of not knowing the lay of the land" at the sprawling school district.[3] The mayor's mistakes prompted reporters to ask union leaders if a teachers strike was now certain. "That will depend on the mayor," Lewis said. "He doesn't want a strike. But the question is, what will he do to avoid it? That's the question that needs to be asked of him—not me." Lewis then reminded the readers that "our members have already spoken on the issue."[4]

CTU's decisive strike vote was one of the influential strategic moves taken within the bargaining process and permitted by the law. Despite the board's and the mayor's efforts to nullify the effects of bargaining on the most critical issues, the union had mobilized its members to signal that no settlement would be possible without negotiations over the longer school day. With the fact-finding process concluded and a real strike looming, CTU would compel the board to do what the SB 7 law was principally intended to prevent: bargain an agreement on extending the school day.

The Sharkey Plan

The disavowed fact-finding report also compelled reporters to doubt that SB 7 had been effective. Senator Lightford slyly insisted, "It is working," but just "not yielding the results that CPS and the mayor wanted." The *Chicago Tribune* declared that the much-ballyhooed law had "been out-maneuvered by the Chicago Teachers Union." Lewis was equally dismissive of the law's intent. CPS and the mayor "just wanted to take away our ability to stop them from doing anything they want to do." As dismal as the situation seemed, however, the first-term union president suggested that a solution to the longer day and year was possible. If Emanuel was willing to back away from what the union viewed as an intransigent posture, then a deal could be reached. Lewis used a popular cultural advertising reference to make the point. "So let's get out of Burger King mode where they think they can have it their way and let's work together to actually put bones to this contract."[5]

The union demonstrated what was needed to obtain an agreement by creatively using its rank-and-file bargaining representatives. These "big table" workers told stories about what was happening in the schools. At first, the board representatives seemed uncertain about how to respond to the presence of rank-and-file members. Union members who attended many of the larger group negotiation sessions recalled the unsettling effect of being there. Lewis, however, genuinely believed that as workers poignantly spoke about the conditions of their work, the employer's side "became more amenable to being educated" and that it contributed to obtaining agreement on a number of lower-profile items that were important to employees, such as reducing teacher paperwork and bullying of teachers by principals.[6]

Susan Hickey, a social worker, found the inclusive approach very helpful. She was pleased to "see how much clinicians" were able to "speak at the meetings, because we are neither fish nor fowl—we're not teachers, we're not PSRPs [i.e., paraprofessionals]."[7] On several occasions the union invited a member to speak poignantly on behalf of a particular topic. But the absence of an educator on the employer's side created barriers to fully appreciating the vivid inside accounts of working in the school. One worker said, "We're telling [them] how things work, but they were totally ignorant on so many levels. It was astounding really."[8] Franczek concurred that the personal witnessing was an effective method of putting a human face on a contract item. He also thought, however, that the big table too often devolved into "CTU show time."[9]

The divergent opinions about the expanded team sessions aside, the parties diligently kept to a schedule of meetings between much smaller groups. Negotiations were conducted principally with three to seven members on each side.

These sessions allowed participants to ruminate about novel ideas as well as to barter the details of a proposal. One item raised intriguing possibilities. Early in the bargaining process, Sharkey put forward a staffing proposal that would require new hires but would permit CPS to lengthen the school day without extending a teacher's workday. Unfortunately, the employer ignored the plan. Lacking any board willingness to consider the idea, it seemed dead, but once again the inner workings of SB 7 unintentionally delivered the opportunity for reconsidering the notion and offered genuine hope that a strike could be averted.

The fact-finding hearings presented CTU with a different platform to discuss the staffing proposal. On Bloch's recommendation, during the first day of the hearing Sharkey explained the union's plan to Benn. The chair was very attentive. He took a lot of notes and asked a number of questions. At exactly 4 minutes and 58 seconds into his presentation, Sharkey unveiled the staffing plan with hard numbers attached and compared its overall cost to the union's demand that employees be awarded a 21 percent salary raise.

While the parties had agreed to rules that allowed testimony to be given without objections or questions raised, this was yet another occasion when Franczek pointed out that any negotiation over 4.5 issues was out of bounds. He may have been right about the boundaries, but the proposal was now before the fact finder. It turned out to be a fortunate occurrence. Faced now with the pressing fear of a work stoppage, the employer revisited what Franczek called the "Sharkey Plan." While Benn knew that CTU's proposal "can't be in the report," he did include a very oblique mention of it in his recommendations that only the parties could decipher. Under the suggestive heading "Alternatives Available to the Board," he wrote, "There may be other ways for the parties to resolve the compensation issue. . . . However, those other ways must come through collective bargaining and not through the impasse resolution process."[10]

While Emanuel had dismissed the fact finder's report as "not tethered to reality," the union recognized a deeper, more productive impact of Benn's work.[11] In an e-mail Bloch sent to Benn one day after the report was publicly issued, he suggested that the fact-finding process had indeed helped to break the impasse over the longer school day. "Ed: just wanted you to know that, despite all the public statements, your award [i.e., Benn's recommendation] is having the effect you intended [pushing the extended working hours into the bargaining process]. I'm hoping the parties will make an important announcement in a week or two. Robert."[12] Only twenty minutes later Benn replied by thanking Bloch, and stated "that really means a lot to me. I told you, I take heat." He also shared his confidence that "Jim [Franczek] will come through."[13]

One week after the fact-finding panel's recommendations were dismissed and speculation about a strike date was running wild, the parties announced a dramatic breakthrough. An "interim agreement" was negotiated that lengthened the school time for students by, in Sharkey's words, "staffing up."[14] The school board agreed to fund 477.5 new elementary school positions, later upped to 500. These new hires would provide extra student instructional minutes in noncore areas, which the district had slowly eroded over time, like art, music, world languages, technology skills, and physical education. Under the reigning collective bargaining agreement, the elementary school day could be lengthened if teachers were given a forty-five-minute duty-free time off during the middle of the day. The interim agreement also established sixty-four duty free minutes a day in which to plan and take care of other noninstructional requirements. As a result, the elementary school day for children would be seven hours long, instead of five and a half. An important element of the agreement was that elementary school teachers' instructional minutes would not be increased.

As positive as the accord's time components were, it was the way in which the new positions were to be filled that appeared to transform the outcome of the bargaining. Tenured teachers displaced since 2010 would be given first crack at the new positions. Principals would retain the authority to select the teachers, but if at least three displaced teachers applied for a slot, the school head was required to choose from among them.[15] The union was ecstatic about the interim agreement. Bedeviled by an imposed lengthening of the workday without additional pay, CTU not only had managed to avoid forcing teachers to work longer hours, but had also found a way to put hundreds of its members back to work.

Convincing the employer to accept the staffing plan was not easy. Lewis stressed, "It has taken a march of nearly 10,000 educators, a strike authorization vote, and a fact-finder's report to get CPS to move on this issue."[16] The deal also ensured that the employer would get what it most wanted. Emanuel simply called the agreement "a breakthrough" and, when asked during a news conference at Sexton Elementary School on the South Side if the school year would start on time, he offered a one-word answer: "Yes."[17]

Sharkey's proposal brought Emanuel's deputy chief of staff for education, Beth Swanson, into the bargaining. Before this pivotal point, the school board's team had been looking for an appropriate time for the city's chief executive to figuratively enter the bargaining. According to Swanson, the interim agreement was "a watershed moment" that justified having a "trusted advisor" at the bargaining table to make certain the mayor's "voice was heard." While extending the school day would not be cost free with an estimated price tag of $40 to 50 million, it ended the acrimony over the issue. Swanson added, "We thought the full school day was *the deal* and believed the trajectory was toward a final settlement."[18]

With the biggest issue settled, it now appeared that it was possible to negotiate a new contract without a strike. Bloch believed that the interim agreement created an opportunity to formulate a way to address the union's general job security concerns. He claimed, "CPS negotiators suggested this could be a model for the contract."[19] Optimism about a deal was very high. Franczek also believed that the "Sharkey deal" decreased the likelihood of a strike. The longer school day was described by the parties as if it were a transcendent issue until Benn's surprising ruling encouraged CPS to take seriously the union's staffing proposal. Franczek expected that agreeing to the deal would "take the wind out of the union" and would "relocate the key issues."[20] For the first time since Emanuel began campaigning for mayor, expectations of a strike had receded.

The media was elated. "Tuesday was a tremendous day for Chicago school children and their teachers," read the opening line in a *Sun-Times* editorial. Most important, "the deal means Chicago will likely avoid a devastating teacher strike."[21] The paper's assessment that the interim agreement was a "major win for Chicago teachers" was illustrated by the joy on Lewis's face as she spoke during a press conference announcing the deal. "Have you ever seen me smile like this?" she asked.[22] Franczek, whom Lewis teased mercilessly during bargaining in an attempt to make him laugh, was also pleased. The arrangement, he was certain, "should have settled it."[23] Public expectations were that the agreement foreshadowed a broader "successful labor deal."[24] The union and the board shared that optimism, but they were badly mistaken. What went wrong?

It was the union's position that the recall provisions used to add additional staff to extend the working day would further serve as a mechanism for handling all laid-off teachers. Bloch was certain that Franczek was considering the breakthrough as a roadmap to a bigger agreement. But David Vitale, president of the school board, who formally entered the bargaining just four days before the strike started, argued that the union had simply misinterpreted the board's intentions. He contended that despite CTU's claim, the formula for staffing the longer day was never meant to be used in the main agreement. Vitale believed that the union saw the "Sharkey Plan" as "the baseline" for a broader agreement.[25] But for CPS, it was the end line.

Vitale joined the negotiations because Emanuel asked him to get involved. "My entry signaled that it was time to get serious and move," and he believed the "union viewed it this way."[26] Vitale had a reputation for knowing the facts better than anybody in the district. He had assisted in the 2003 and 2007 school negotiations, and ex-interim Chicago school head Terry Mazany was optimistic that a deal would now be achieved. Mazany called Vitale's involvement a "game changer."[27] After his first day of negotiations, Vitale was very upbeat. "We've actually made a lot of progress," he said, and he expressed his belief that "absolutely a deal can be made."[28] The union recognized that Vitale's late appearance lent gravitas to the bargaining, but his presence mostly signified that the strike threat was having its intended effect of driving the mayor to make a deal on terms more favorable to CTU. The disagreement over the interim plan was not easily resolved. Vitale admitted, "We got hung up on this for some time."[29] Negotiations stalled as a result, and it took a while to convince CTU that the employer was not going to carry the interim agreement over into a general rehire provision.

In the immediate aftermath of the interim accord, it appeared that everyone involved achieved what they wanted. Unfortunately, nobody achieved an end to the employment dispute. Ironically, the deal may have actually increased the likelihood of a strike. The interim proposal was very popular with the union membership and raised expectations for a negotiated job-rehiring plan. CPS, however, received tremendous blowback from school principals who, Sharkey believed, bristled at the requirement that they "must hire from an approved list." Preserving the autonomy of principals to hire the staff they wanted was a bedrock principle of the employer's bargaining objectives. Emanuel insisted that his plan for school improvement relied on being able to hold the principals accountable for their staffing choices. The employer's willingness to compromise on that stance was narrowly tied to securing the mayor's signature school objective, the longer school day. Sharkey said that this only caused further confusion and antagonisms. "CPS never should have made a deal in July [when the interim arrangement was done] that they weren't willing to make in August" to avoid a strike.[30]

Job security was the critical issue. With layoffs looming and no formal way for the union to compel the board to negotiate the school closings, it appeared to Sharkey that "it was fair to assume that the interim [agreement] would be applied" universally. "Recall was a bitter issue because of a legacy of school closings and expected closings," Sharkey explained.[31] The experience of losing one's job through no fault of one's own, without a right to be recalled, had a visceral impact on school employees. When expectations about the interim deal were shattered, the warm feelings of rapprochement quickly disappeared.

The parties kept meeting and continued to slog through item after item. By Vitale's account, in mid-August CTU claimed to have sixty-three outstanding issues. After seven months of bargaining, that was an extraordinary number of contested proposals. The sheer number of issues, ranging from the length of lesson plans to the use of job performance in determining layoffs, placed an enormous burden on the parties to reach an agreement before school opened on September 4.[32]

As CTU and the employer struggled to regain the momentum that the longer school day agreement had fleetingly generated, the union exercised its right to set a strike date. On August 29, it served the required ten-day notice to the Board of Education that, absent an agreement, the union would strike on September 10. The deadline was set as "some 700 Chicago Teachers Union delegates thundered 'aye'" in response to a motion put forward by Lewis at a union meeting.[33] When she asked for any "nay" votes "the union hall fell silent." Afterward, Lewis summed up the union's sentiment by telling reporters, "Enough is enough. We're done."[34] The audacity of the union's actually exercising its legal right to strike outraged some commentators. An opinion piece in the *Chicago Tribune* blustered that the mayor should go as far as to try a destroy the union: "If the CTU goes on strike, Emanuel should act to decertify [i.e., abolish] the union. . . . Teachers would be asked to return to school, and those who refuse would be replaced. Mayor Emanuel, don't blink."[35]

With a strike countdown running, the bargaining pace would not only intensify; it would also take place in tandem with an unfolding union contract campaign that galvanized Chicagoans behind the teachers' cause. On a daily basis, newspaper, television, and radio news fixated on the labor-management hostilities associated with the mayor's education agenda. Bloch marveled at the way the "press [was] whipped up to a frenzy."[36] Coverage of the threatened strike was extensive, but the *Sun-Times'* Kate Grossman defended the media's attention. The "public doesn't care about contract talk," but "they did have an appetite to read about a strike threat."[37] While the media accounts had an overly dramatic quality to them, the bargaining process was generating little progress. The issues seemed intractable.

Whereas CPS wanted layoffs to be strictly based on teacher performance, CTU insisted on preserving seniority. The union wanted a universal right to recall for laid-off teachers. The school board objected. When schools were closed and students were reassigned, CTU wanted the right for teachers and staff to transfer alongside their students. The employer objected. When the board wanted a two-year limit on how long a teacher could remain at the "needs improvement" stage before they could be summarily discharged, it was the union's turn to object. The union also opposed CPS's demand that the high-stakes testing required under PERA be immediately implemented. It equally rejected the district's insistence that student growth scores account for 45 percent of a teacher evaluation, way above the 30 percent minimum set by the law. Even the issue of extended working time was not fully settled. The interim agreement had addressed the longer school day but not the longer year. The board was looking for seven extra workdays and the union was not. And the mayor was desperate to obtain a five- or four-year deal, while CTU was already contemplating the political impacts of a three-year pact. Money, according to Vitale, was "in the room," but CTU had largely accepted most of CPS's financial offer.[38] The school district, however, was still insisting on dropping steps, and the union was opposed to the employer's health insurance proposal, which, they estimated, would increase employee costs by as much as 25 percent.

Vitale respected the urgency of addressing the relationship between teacher evaluations and job security. He had less patience for the time taken on most of the "sixty-three items that CTU knew were going to get resolved without any difficulty" or without the need for a work stoppage.[39] Franczek recognized the sizable leverage a strike would give to the union. He had advocated for the higher strike threshold and impasse procedures because, as it applied to schools, the "power of the strike was disproportional."[40] A big-city mayor had no real authority to oppose a citywide shutdown that would keep children out of school. He contrasted the school board's capacity to resist a strike with a commercial work stoppage. "In the private sector we could wait for workers to come back."[41] This moment was a "ripening" point where both labor and the employer "felt a little pain." At such a juncture a settlement was possible. But when it involved the Chicago schools and four hundred thousand students "every day is a drama and you can't wait for the moment."[42]

Franczek needed to achieve a deal before CTU convulsed the institution that was central to his boss's political fortunes. Lewis accepted that the mayor did not want a strike, but in her mind, the question was always "What was he willing to do to avoid one?" Feeling as if the sand was draining within the hourglass, Franczek took measure of all the hours his team spent "mapping out strategy, preparing data and arguments, meeting in different groups, and making PowerPoint after PowerPoint."[43] They had come a long way. In previous bargaining rounds, with other CTU leaders, it would have been enough. But this CTU was different, and if a strike was going to be avoided, Franczek's team was going to have to go further.

Meeting predominantly at the union's offices in the city's massive art deco Merchandise Mart, between September 6 and 9, the employer offered a flurry of modified proposals to the union. By midweek, the board had dropped merit pay as a demand. After addressing a House of Delegates meeting, Lewis shared with reporters that this was "reasonable news," but warned that problems remained.[44] Nonetheless, new district proposals followed, which covered the major economic issues, including finally restoring the step system and retaining the lane schedule.[45] On the eve of the strike, CPS offered pay increases over three years of 3, 2, and 2 percent plus an enhanced payment for steps.

Franczek was also authorized to offer teachers and paraprofessionals a 3 percent pay hike for an additional fourth contract year without tying the increase, as the employer initially wanted, to the application of a merit pay–based plan. The employer's eleventh-hour offerings also removed the offensive contract language that had allowed Emanuel to revoke the final year's pay increase in the reigning contract.[46]

As a 4.5 item, class size was not an issue that generated formal proposals, but that did not prevent discussions from happening during bargaining. CTU was adamant that the current class size caps were too high for all grade levels. Under the contract, the "maximum number of students" for elementary schools was 27 to 29, and 30 to 32 for high schools. While CPS retorted that average class size did not exceed the contract ranges, the union pointed out that hundreds of classrooms exceeded the maximums and too many classrooms were overcrowded. While the school district had assiduously refused to bargain over class size, it did agree to provide $500,000 each year of the contract to a joint class size–monitoring panel.

The board also made a concession in the area of teacher evaluations. Instead of insisting that the new system be implemented right away, CPS agreed to delay its use for tenured teachers until the second year of the contract. The employer also modified proposals on tenured teacher layoff and recall rights, which under certain circumstances extended job protections during school closings. Failing to abide by the hiring requirements obligated the district to pay a financial penalty.[47] Tenured teachers displaced from schools for nonperformance would have a "right of recall to a position" from which they were honorably dismissed for ten months. Finally, recognizing the union's concerns that the district's minority workforce had shrunk, the board agreed to a "recruitment plan to attract racially diverse teacher candidate pools."[48]

The employer's proposals reflected a serious reality it had not expected. Teachers had given a robust indication that they were willing to strike. No further provocation was needed. With the consequences of a failed negotiation confronting the employer, it unmoored its proposals from their preferred piers. CPS was now ready to adjust its proposals to try to get CTU to agree to a deal. Bloch argued that finding creative ways to craft a compromise had been problematic because he felt that the board team had less room to maneuver. But, with the strike now hours away, the dynamic changed. "For a few moments," Franczek noted, "I was fully liberated." Franczek had what labor negotiators crudely refer to as a "'What the fuck' moment, let's do a deal." The city had experienced a violent summer of murders, and the mayor wanted to avoid the untenable scenario of hundreds of thousands of school children with no place to go. "We were at our weakest point," Franczek admitted, joking that he was "giving away more money than I was allowed to!"[49]

On Thursday, September 6, four days before the strike deadline, Lewis felt that CPS was finally serious about reaching an agreement. She said, "Franczek asked, 'What will it take to settle?'" He also suggested ideas by asking, "What if I did this or that?"[50] Typically he would then wait for the union to caucus. When the CTU team replied, he would recalibrate his options. The negotiations became so involved and fluid that the union suspected that Franczek was ignoring texts and phone calls that he was receiving from Emanuel.

At the close of each long day, the smaller CTU bargaining team would provide an update to its larger rank-and-file group, which held its own concurrent sessions in another union office. The board negotiators would likewise end the day by returning to Franczek's office to hold a conference call with the mayor. Following the daily roundups, CPS Chief Labor Relations Officer Joseph Moriarty and Swanson would share a ride home. They lived near each other in the Edgewater section on the North Side. Driving the roughly seven miles to the lakefront area provided the occupants with a few moments to decompress from the day's pressures. Some night rides, they admitted, were too short to serve as a suitable release from the intensity of the bargaining and threatened strike. But, feelings aside, progress was genuinely being made.

The union was pleased by the new exchange of offers. On Friday morning, Lewis appeared on WLS-TV in Chicago and stated that negotiations with the district had taken a "turn for the better." Lewis also added that she was "more heartened by recent talks."[51] Bloch agreed that a "framework" for a deal was in place and acknowledged that the "union felt good about what they had."[52] This was the first time that any of the negotiators publicly used the term "framework" to signal that a deal was at hand. Lewis's first positive words about the progress of bargaining, spoken so close to the strike date, raised expectations that a deal would be obtained. The expectation proved misplaced, however, because the sense of hope had decidedly diminished after Friday's session. "We were very much hoping that yesterday we would begin an offer that could really bridge that gap," Sharkey explained. But he complained that "the offer they came back with was disappointing, to say the least, and frankly, there [were] not enough pieces of the puzzle to make a picture."[53]

Vitale was more optimistic. "It's unpredictable, but I think it's close enough that it could breakthrough at any point."[54] He also hedged a bit and alerted parents to make alternative plans for Monday, just in case. Sharkey's comments were a coda for the current state of the bargaining. There were plenty of pieces of the contract puzzle lying on the table. An outline to an agreement existed. Every important issue had been addressed, but for CTU, it did not add up to a good enough whole. The school district had compromised on nearly every issue, but there remained serious problems with the terms on layoffs, recall, employee evaluations, and teacher ratings. The parties were no longer negotiating over transformational issues, like the longer school day, but the matters that lingered were nuanced and time consuming. Franczek had an evocative phrase for these items: "granular elements."[55]

An unprecedented number of changes were being made to the contract, and many involved school-level adjustments. Any one element was not in itself a deal breaker, but cumulatively they added up to a redefined working day for thousands of employees. Teachers had grown weary of seemingly random, unwarranted, and endless incursions into how they did their work. More than two decades of mayor-led school reform had worn away any level of trust that employees had for school administrators. Emanuel made the situation worse. He had provoked and insulted teachers. Lewis went so far as to charge that Emanuel was "carrying all the dirty water" for people, like Robin Steans and Bruce Rauner, who vilified teachers unions.[56]

With less than forty-eight hours to go before the strike deadline, the parties were still apart on how to stitch together each thin strand of a workday into a coherent, sturdy, and frictionless fabric. Unfortunately, Saturday's session, which Lewis predicted would be "intense," was a bust.[57] CPS consultant Barbara Byrd-Bennett, who had joined the bargaining, said a "strike seemed eminent" and it all "began to feel very eerie."[58]

Twenty-Four Hours to Strike Deadline

As dawn broke to a clear blue sky Sunday morning, union negotiators were deeply skeptical that a strike could be avoided. Bloch and Sharkey had spent long hours parsing employer counterproposals and they believed that the board needed to do better. If the "granular" pieces were not sufficiently improved now, when would they be? Lewis was in no mood to back off the union's demands. "Working conditions were paramount," she insisted.[59] More important, the union leadership had asked the membership to shape the contours of the new contract. Their school delegates had been transformed into activists and had taken votes on union governance. Democracy, Lewis explained, really influenced how the union reacted to CPS proposals. "We set out to develop a collective, collaborative approach with our members."[60] In the past CPS had perpetuated what Lewis said was a "reign of terror, and CTU would no longer be complicit."[61]

As Vitale made his way to the union's offices, he felt confident that the contract terms were good enough for both sides to agree on. He believed the parties were close to a settlement and insisted that the union had no justifiable reason for striking. Emanuel would spend Sunday marching in the Mexican Independence Parade on Twenty-Sixth Street and attending a street fair at the Misericordia home on the North Side before returning home to his family. Sensitive to re-porter questions about why the mayor was not attending the bargaining session, spokeswoman Sarah Hamilton said that although "he's not in the room . . . he's very well tuned into what's going on." She also noted that because Beth Swanson was part of the employer's team, it was "pretty clear that when she's talking, she's talking for him."[62]

The early autumn temperature outside the Merchandise Mart would slowly reach a very pleasant and cool seventy-two degrees. Enjoying the Sunday morn-ing weather, people had already begun to stroll along upper Wacker Drive, which wound in front of the Mart parallel to the Chicago River. It was a popular walk for residents and visitors, providing the visceral pleasures of the river as well as the omnipresent architecture of the historic commercial building. Inside CTU's twenty-second-floor offices, two groups also gathered. In one room, the union and the employer's core bargaining teams met, just as they had for nearly one hundred prior meetings. In a second larger room, in earshot of the main bargaining room, CTU's "big" team of school-level leaders congregated. Across from the larger room and connected to the primary room used for negotiations was Lewis's office. Un-like the people walking along the river unburdened by time constraints, the folks now holed up in union meeting rooms experienced a dire sense of urgency.

Speculation had begun about the curious absence from CPS's team of Emanu-el's new school CEO. As the strike deadline grew closer, rumors of Brizard's firing were rampant. According to a *Chicago Tribune* story, "Education and business leaders . . . told Chicago Public Schools CEO Jean-Claude Brizard that he'll be blamed by the mayor for the city ending up on the brink of a teachers strike and he may be on his way out."[63] City hall followers charged that Emanuel needed a scapegoat for negotiations that had gone terribly wrong. The threat of being re-placed was enhanced by a board performance review that, while praising Brizard on many fronts, also criticized his management style.[64]

Although Brizard had not attended any of the bargaining sessions, in mid-April, a key deputy, Arnaldo Rivera, began representing his office during nego-tiations. The union had expected the CEO to participate in at least one meeting. During an early morning Saturday "session at Franczek's office," Michael Brunson recalled, "we were waiting for Brizard to come, but he didn't show."[65] Instead, a large box of donuts was delivered to the negotiators courtesy of the CPS chief ex-ecutive. Franczek admitted that Brizard was told at the last minute by someone in the mayor's office not to attend. No reason was given for the decision. Although CTU made note of his absence, past school chiefs had rarely, if ever, participated in labor negotiations.

Negotiations began at roughly 10 a.m. By 5 p.m., the talks appeared dead. "It became clear late Sunday afternoon that we were not going to get over the goal line," Vitale recalled.[66] After hours of discussions about issues like teacher evaluations and job security, Sharkey believed that "we were miles apart."[67] The union had given a document to the employer on Thursday that detailed what CTU needed to reach a deal. It had been handwritten during a union caucus meeting. Lewis, who liked using multiple differently colored pens to take notes, insisted that each line of the proposed settlement pact be prepared in a different hue. Sharkey maintained that, except for employee pay increases, the colorful blueprint for a deal had been rejected by the board.

At this point most of the negotiations were between Franczek, Moriarty, and Swanson, representing the employer with Vitale also attending, and Bloch and Sharkey for CTU, along with Mayle and Brunson. A former union officer, Pam Massarsky, who brought a historical perspective to the evolution of the current 217-page labor contract, also aided the CTU team. Curiously, Lewis came and went from the main negotiating table without explanation. Franczek thought she looked ill. "Everyone was under a lot of pressure," he allowed and surmised that the union president was "suffering from some stomach issue."[68]

Whether because of stress or just bad luck, Lewis was feeling sick. She was suffering from a full bout of acid reflux; her symptoms were classic and debilitating. By midday, Lewis was experiencing bad heartburn, regurgitation, chest pains, and nausea. Each time she left the bargaining she escaped to the solace of her office. Sitting with the lights off, she was joined by her assistant Audrey May, who applied cold compresses to Lewis's forehead. It was not the first time May had seen her boss this way, but this time was the worst. Vitale had understandably grown frustrated by Lewis's mysterious absences. He was doubtful that the CTU leader was really too sick to stay at the bargaining table. Lewis kept the truth from the employer's team because she did not want them to think her illness was a sign of weakness. Vitale attempted repeatedly to schedule a one-on-one meeting with Lewis. Finally, a brief private discussion was arranged. "Karen used the meeting to ask if we could discuss school closings," Vitale revealed. "I said definitely not."[69] After that, there was no further conversation.

Lewis's absence, however, did not restrain the parties' ability to exchange proposals and argue positions. Swanson in particular seemed to perform an important interactive role. She was not only engaged in face-to-face discussions with the union but was almost simultaneously communicating with the mayor. Mayle explained that during the bargaining, "in front of her [Swanson] she has two phones," sitting on the table in plain view. Referencing an iconic prop from the 1960s *Batman* television program, Mayle and union negotiators jokingly referred to Swanson's multitasking by noting, "She had the Batphone." Swanson was aware of the joke and took it in good spirit. Mayle recognized that "He [Emanuel] was in the room with us as much as he could have been."[70]

Either by design or seeking the psychological comfort that comes from talking with a more friendly opponent, the negotiators began to pair up, and a number of little side meetings broke out. These micro–joint caucuses allowed two people who seemed to have a high level of rapport to talk perhaps more frankly and persuasively. "Everybody was trying to appeal to that one person they had a connection with," Mayle admitted.[71] As 8 p.m. approached with no agreement in sight, Vitale made an atypical move. He demanded that Lewis agree to extend the strike deadline. "It was the only time he tried to use force," said Bloch.[72] The union was put off by the board president's posture and found his demeanor condescending. Though the parties had not rounded off the sharp edges of the union's job security concerns, Vitale hung onto the belief that enough progress had been made in the bargaining to warrant delaying the Monday morning strike call.

According to Sharkey, the board president pushed back into his chair and in a very stern voice told Lewis that "she was going to go out there [to a press conference] and say we are close to an agreement."[73] "He just got bigger" in his chair, Mayle recounted.[74] For a moment, the union's negotiators held their collective breath. They were worried that Lewis would agree. She did not immediately respond. Instead she paused. She paused for what seemed an interminably long time. Bloch thought Lewis intentionally delayed her answer in order to "let the room die a little bit."[75] Then, in what Sharkey called a "testament of human endurance," Lewis mustered the strength to firmly reject the opportunity to delay the strike and promptly left the room for the comfort of her darkened office.[76]

On her way back to her office, Lewis detoured into the larger room to speak with the assembled rank-and-file members of the bargaining team. Under noticeable physical strain, Lewis marched into a cantankerous group of CTU activists. Her brief visit produced a loud cheer that was audible in every corner of the union's spacious offices. The board's negotiators were startled by the sound. Sharkey described Lewis's visit as a "a pep talk."[77] Swanson thought it was further proof that the CTU head was not really sick but was deliberately avoiding the negotiations. Vitale was now convinced that the union president was dodging him for strategic purposes. For the first time since he had joined the bargaining three days earlier, Vitale thought that schools were not likely to open on Monday.

Lewis's unexplained behavior had also come to the rapt attention of a very nervous mayor. Throughout the day, as breaks from the talks occurred, Swanson and Vitale had been on the phone with Emanuel.[78] Driven by the recognition, perhaps for the very first time, that a strike was going to happen, Emanuel or his aides made a bizarre, desperate move to backstop the board's position. Late in the day, following one of Lewis's departures, Bloch received a phone call. He excused himself to find a private place to talk. The caller informed him that Emanuel or "the mayor's people" had been calling political allies in Springfield suggesting that the union president was behaving irrationally and perhaps was unfit to lead the bargaining. Bloch replied incredulously that Lewis was feeling ill but, under the circumstances, was holding up pretty well. As he ended the call and started back toward the negotiations, he shook his head and thought to himself that it was "Rahm's people who are going nuts."[79]

After continuous talks throughout that pleasant Sunday, hopes for an agreement had largely faded, but the bargaining had not formally concluded. Franczek, Moriarty, and Swanson, along with Sharkey, Mayle, Brunson, and Bloch, returned to the negotiation table for one last-ditch effort. Despite earnestly trying to close the gap that separated the parties, the timeframe that SB 7 had set to resolve impasses had finally run out. As the hour grew very late, an awkward silence permeated the bargaining room. With Swanson and Franczek having run out of offers and room to move, Sharkey matter-of-factly turned to Bloch and said, "I think we're on strike."[80] For what was to be the last time for the next several days, the employer and the union were in complete agreement.

Despite Friday's budding promise of a deal, the parties continued to struggle over job security. Sharkey boiled it down to a blunt question: "What would get a teacher fired?"[81] His question referred to how the district's new, PERA-influenced REACH (Recognizing Educators Advancing Chicago) evaluation system would affect teacher ratings. The problem, as CTU saw it, was in where CPS was setting the cutoff scores for determining which of four performance categories a teacher fell into. The scores that made up the upper and lower boundaries of these categories were referred to as "bans" by the negotiators. Although PERA had mandated the use of student test scores in evaluating teachers, the negotiators did not know how to define quantitatively the difference between the "bans." Each teacher would be assigned a point score, but the place where that score fell between a "proficient" and "developing" rating, for example, would have a significant impact on a teacher's rating. "CPS's cutoffs," Sharkey warned, "appeared to subject teachers to an unreasonably high score in order to avoid being placed in the lowest two ratings."[82] The "ban" for "developing" preferred by CPS, according to Sharkey, was "just too big."[83] Bloch pointed out that how the upper and lower boundaries of teacher scores for each ban were determined contributed to a teacher's "ability to withstand a layoff."[84]

The union was resolute about mitigating the worst effects of what it knew would be a diminished level of job protection, despite recognizing that teacher evaluations and the process for shaping layoffs were nonstrikeable, 4.5 issues. Protecting teacher jobs while preserving the district's nearly unilateral authority to determine layoffs was the Gordian knot of the CTU-CPS bargaining struggle. Compensation was not the problem. Franczek raised the board's pay increase offer to 16 percent if the union would accept a four-year deal but, in contrast to previous bargaining rounds, this time there was no price that would move CTU to a settlement. Bloch summed up the dilemma by stating that "both sides were trying to get from each other what neither side could give."[85]

Vitale rejected the notion that the remaining disputed items necessitated a strike. He laid the problem at the feet of the union. "CTU," the board president claimed "didn't want to" reach a settlement. Vitale drew this conclusion from his analysis of the union's initial bargaining strategy. "The union," Vitale claimed, had "committed to a public negotiation where their authority would come from the masses of their teachers and the public." He reasoned, "If you're going to play it publicly, you have to take it to the brink."[86] His analysis was predicated on the belief that the union was obligated to provide its mobilized rank-and-file members and extensive community supporters with a means to act publicly. A settlement without a work stoppage would deny the union and community an opportunity to properly assert their ownership of a correction to nearly two decades of top-down corporate education reform. Vitale thought that "going public" was a dangerous strategy, and his critique had merit.

Against great odds, CTU had formed a vibrant nascent public out of people feeling powerless in the face of economic and political elites. Thousands of union members had participated in countless hours of training and school-based organizing. They had been primed to be more than passive benefactors of union decisions. Union leaders discussed the potential for community advocates and educators to be transformed by a call to the picket lines and to march in the streets. The experience would be empowering and, perhaps, create new possibilities for activism in the future. Sharkey explained, "People had to fight first, then realize what was possible."[87] What CTU was after was not only a better platform to represent workers, but a more permanent membership-led institution that could powerfully confront those groups pushing for destructive changes in public education.

A new school labor agreement was now a social compact with neighborhood groups who were fighting racism, poverty, and violence, as well as underresourced schools. In contrast to 1987, in the fall of 2012 the community appeared resolutely ready to stand with the union against the school board. Lots of people were involved in the dispute, and now they needed a place to act. Conference rooms in the Merchandise Mart were not a fitting location for a constituted public to exercise its will.

No School Tomorrow

Upon leaving the Mart, the board and union negotiators were accosted by a phalanx of reporters. "It was crazy," Bloch recalled: "people everywhere."[88] Still brooding over Lewis's vanishing act, Vitale rushed to get the employer's message out first. At approximately 10 p.m. he stepped before a bevy of microphones and waived a copy of the contract proposal that CTU had spurned high above his head, inviting the union to make a counterproposal. Union officers watched on television as he stressed that the employer had offered a generous 16 percent pay hike at a time when the district's "fiscal situation is really challenged."[89] Lewis had no choice but to let Vitale go first. While waiting for him to finish she and her assistant did their best with a makeup kit to help the CTU president look less sick. When her time came to face the cameras she said calmly but firmly, "No CTU members will be inside of our schools Monday."[90] She accused the school board of failing to address the remaining issues.

After successive press conferences, the employer's team piled into a cab and traveled to the mayor's office. They found Emanuel dressed casually in khaki pants and in a calm mood. His staff immediately began prepping the mayor for another news conference by tossing him possible questions. At approximately 11:30 p.m., the school district's negotiation team went over to the Harold Washington Library Center, where all CPS's department heads were waiting. During the press conference Emanuel used a line that had come up in preparation with his staff. "This strike is a strike of choice." It became a popular sound bite and a headline in the following day's papers.

Emanuel also stated that his bargaining team was willing to continue negotiating throughout the night. That was unwelcome news to his team. When Franczek heard the offer all he could think was, "We're so fucking tired." Thankfully, Vitale, also showing signs of exhaustion, told the mayor that nothing more could be accomplished tonight and refused to reconstitute the meeting. However, while preparing to drive home, Bloch heard Emanuel challenge CTU to keep talking. Not wanting the union to appear unwilling to negotiate, Bloch sent Franczek a text message indicating CTU was ready to meet. But what Bloch did not know was that his legal counterpart did not use text messaging. "Thank heaven I didn't see it," laughed Franczek."[91]

At 1:30 a.m. on Monday the parties finally went home. In a few hours they would be back at the bargaining table. Only this time, schools would be closed and large numbers of union members would be walking boisterous picket lines all across the city.

10

THE STRIKE

A few days after the overwhelming strike authorization vote was announced on June 10, classes came to an end. The union told members, before they left their schools at the close of the school year, not to take expensive vacations or make any big purchases. The message was, "Save your money, because we may have to strike and it could conceivably be a two- or three-week strike with no paycheck." As teachers went home for the summer, the intense organizing of the spring ended, although the union's Organizing Department, for the second summer in a row, hired CTU members to do summer organizing internships. After trainings, it sent them door-to-door across the city to talk to members and parents about the union's issues.

Informational Picket Lines

In 2012, CPS had a two-track calendar system: 243 Track E schools opened on August 13, whereas about 335 other schools did not start classes until September 5. During the week of August 20 to 24, the union called on members to organize informational picket lines at the Track E schools before or after school and asked teachers and staff who were not yet back at work to join the picket lines.

When a union holds an informational picket line, it is making management aware that a strike is imminent unless there is progress at the bargaining table. The union saw the picketing both as a show of force to the management bargaining team and a signal that time was running out. In addition, it was a practice run to work out any logistical kinks before teachers and staff picketed for real in a possible strike. The picket lines were also an opportunity to talk again to parents about the teachers' concerns about students' unacceptable learning conditions. They held signs highlighting their issues and handed out a CTU flyer asking parents to call the board and tell them to negotiate the resources teachers needed to make "a better school day" for CPS kids, not just the longer school day which was being implemented that fall. Over the course of the week, teachers and staff had thousands of conversations with parents, who were naturally startled to see their children's teachers walking picket lines at their schools.

A twenty-seven-year veteran teacher recalled, "At my school we did the mock or practice picket on Monday, Tuesday, and Wednesday. I was able to model the things I had learned, and the chants I had learned, for the younger teachers, and before they knew it, they had the megaphones and they were leading the chants. That was the beginning of us knowing that there are people behind us—people were tooting their car horns. The energy started building in a rapid momentum."[1]

At a number of schools, groups of teachers and staff waved signs at busy intersections, receiving in return a constant stream of supportive honks. Activists at some schools marched through the neighborhood. "People were coming out of stores to take literature," recalled Kimberly Bowsky. "People were putting up fists and waving and continuing to honk as they went down the street. Then we went through the neighborhood and chanted and talked with people we met."[2]

Labor Day

On August 30 the CTU gave CPS the legally required ten days' notice, which would allow a strike date of Monday, September 10, if a contract could not be settled. By this point, there were daily news articles in the *Chicago Tribune* and *Chicago Sun-Times* and daily coverage on the evening TV news about the progress of negotiations. CPS officials repeatedly emphasized that progress was being made and a strike would be averted, while CTU officials took a more cautious position.

CTU officers and staff debated whether they could let the symbolism of the September 3 Labor Day holiday pass without making another strong public showing. While one-third of the schools had been back since mid-August, teachers and staff in the remaining schools would return to their schools to do classroom setup only a few days before the holiday. Was that enough time to organize a big turnout? How many teachers would be in town on the three-day holiday weekend and not have family obligations that day?

CTU leaders knew that if a strike had to be called, they would not start it on the first day of class, Tuesday, September 4, for the roughly 335 remaining schools. Instead, they would wait until all teachers had been back at work a week, to give teachers and staff time to talk to parents. They therefore did not expect to be on strike by Labor Day. While Chicago is known as a strong union town, it does not usually host large rallies or parades on Labor Day. The Democratic Party convention was scheduled for September 4 through 6 in Charlotte, North Carolina, and most Chicago union leaders would not be in town to attend a rally. As a result, the CFL had not planned anything for Labor Day.

In the end, CTU leaders decided that, with a strike pending and after the great success of the May 23 action, it was time to hit the streets again. Despite the absence of many local labor leaders, CTU called for a Monday, September 3, noon rally at Daley Plaza across the street from city hall.

As with the May 23 rally, the first impression many teachers, staff, and supporters had of the Labor Day action was taking a train downtown and finding cars filled with red-shirted union supporters. A special education teacher remembered "getting on the 'L' train to go downtown to the Labor Day march, and the car was filled with teachers in red T-shirts. Every time somebody got on, it was great, people were whooping and hollering. There was just a sense that, 'Wow, we are really in this together.' I loved reading people's signs because I found out a lot about what was going on in other schools just from the signs, like one that read, 'Talk to me about my 43 kids!'" referencing the number of students that CPS had crammed into her classroom.[3]

As more and more people arrived, the plaza overflowed. Scores of teachers and staff brought handmade signs expressing their anger. Speaker after speaker— equal shares from the community and from the union—revved up the crowd. Attendance was so large, however—at least fifteen thousand people—that the insufficient speaker system left those in the back unable to hear most of the speeches.

Public-sector unions in particular turned out in large numbers. A teacher recalled, "It was so great, we had people from different unions, the firefighters, the police officers, the mail carriers, all these different organizations were showing that they supported us. It made you feel like part of a larger labor movement."[4]

Lewis stepped to the podium to thunderous applause after an effusive introduction by police union head Michael Shields. "CTU, CTU, CTU," roared the
crowd. "Brothers and sisters, we did not start this fight. But brothers and sisters,
enough is enough!" she declared in what many members would label her "Stand
Up to Bullies" speech, and the crowd took up the "Enough is enough" chant. She
continued:

> We did not start this fight. But I do want to correct something my
> brother Mike Shields said. Karen Lewis did not get a strike vote. Let's
> be clear. That was the hard work of every single member of the Chicago
> Teachers Union! [Huge cheers] This fight is not about Karen Lewis. Let's
> be clear. This fight is for the very soul of public education, not only in
> Chicago but everywhere. . . . A little over a year ago they wrote us off.
> They said, "We have a new law to stop you from doing anything other
> than what we tell you to do." They went on TV and bragged about it.
> And building by building, school by school, we all came together to stop
> the juggernaut that doesn't care about our children, doesn't know what
> we do, and that had written off 25 percent of our children. *Our* children.
> The mayor of the city of Chicago can stand up and say 25 percent of
> our children will never be anything, never amount to anything, and I'm
> not wasting money on them. [Boos] Then got in public and denied he
> said it. He's a liar. [Roars] And a bully. The only way to beat a bully is to
> stand up to a bully! [Cheers] I want you to know, we will continue to
> negotiate, to work as hard as we can to get a fair contract. And we know
> there is a finite amount of resources. But we also know we didn't create
> that problem. Our children are not a campaign promise. Our children
> are not numbers on a spreadsheet. When you come after our children,
> you come after us! [Roars] Brothers and sisters, we did not start this
> fight—but enough is enough![5]

The crowd again shouted the "Enough is enough" chant. After the rally, the
plan had been to circle the square block of city hall with two or three rows of
protesters linking arms, but the huge size of the crowd made that impossible.
The police initially tried to keep the crowd on the sidewalks but soon gave up,
and the crowd took to the streets, exuberantly marched several times around
city hall, and then took over Clark Street to march the three blocks south to CPS
headquarters.

The next morning's *Chicago Sun-Times* front page featured a nearly full-page
photo of thousands of red-shirted teachers and supporters with the powerful
headline, "Do You Hear Us, Rahm?"

Strike Preparation

The next week, with everyone back in the schools after the summer break, the teachers and staff were unified like they had not been in decades. Yet only a tiny number had walked picket lines in the last CTU strike in 1987 or in any other strike, so members had many conversations, reassuring themselves, telling each other that if they stood together they would win. As one teacher noted,

> The very thought of a strike is scary. "What? I'm not going to get paid? What? We don't know how long it's going to last? What? I have to pay a mortgage? What?!" So what we had to do was take the fear and, like Karen says, turn it into anger; and then take your anger and turn it into fight. And that was the process that everyone went through. And we would just reiterate what it was that we needed to do. We said, "Don't be afraid." And members would ask, "What do we do if . . . ?" And we would have an answer for them.[6]

During the first week of September the union held trainings for contract campaign leaders, who would become the strike captains at their schools, on the nuts and bolts of organizing picket lines, on the necessity of being in touch with every member every day, on the plans for afternoon rallies, and on talking to parents about the strike. Contract negotiations with CPS continued nearly nonstop over the September 8 weekend while the union made preparations for the strike. Teamsters Local 705 generously donated for use as CTU strike headquarters two rooms and the adjacent large auditorium on Van Buren Street just west of Ashland Avenue.[7]

On Friday and Saturday, dozens of members helped move to the Van Buren office thousands of picket signs along with microwaves, refrigerators, and other supplies they'd need if there were a long strike, and the union put up a large "Strike Headquarters" banner. Friday night and into the weekend, in the large auditorium, an assembly line staffed by teachers and Chicago Teachers Solidarity Campaign (CTSC) volunteers stapled thousands of picket signs to thin pine sticks; by the start of the strike, every Home Depot, Menards, and Lowe's in the city had sold out of the sticks. Other volunteers punched holes and tied string so that placards could be hung around striking unionists' necks.[8]

The Van Buren location turned out to be perfectly situated; it was a low-traffic street just west of downtown Chicago, with easy access off and on the Eisenhower Expressway, where members could quickly park by the curb and pick up supplies. Tables were set up on the sidewalk with the union's daily *On the Line* strike bulletins, picket signs, and union T-shirts. As one member recalled, "The delegates were told that they had to come in and pick up the strike materials early on Monday morning the first day of the strike, and all but six schools came in. It was so organized. A car pulls up, load 'em up. A car pulls up, load 'em up."[9]

Nearly twenty-four thousand members had voted to authorize a strike in early June. When the TV news reported from the CTU's 10:00 p.m. press conference on Sunday, September 10, that the strike was on, the dominant response among the members was complete support tempered by profound frustration. CTU members were deeply pained that they could not be in the schools doing what they loved to do, but they ardently believed that the mayor and the Board of Education had left them no choice but to strike for the children's needs and to assert their rights as educators. When they read the *Chicago Tribune's* September 9 article on the negotiations, which said, "Inside the mayor's camp, few thought a strike would become reality," their collective response was, "Rahm, what planet are you living on? You and your board have acted like it's your way or the highway for two years." They had the identical response when, the next day, the first day of the strike, the mayor told the media that it was an unnecessary strike, a "strike of choice."[10]

Some members also responded with a sigh of relief. They believed that the power the union had demonstrated during the contract campaign and repeated mobilizations had not done enough to show the mayor that he should respect teachers and parents and treat them as partners, not adversaries. A strike of at least a day or two was necessary, they felt, to drive that message home. It had long been a foregone conclusion among many CTU members that, given the mayor's bullying tactics, a strike was inevitable. "We know a strike is really going to be painful," said union delegate Jay Rehak. "People will be hurt on both sides. But in the end, it's like saying, 'I'll be bloodied and you'll be bloodied, but at least you'll know not to bully me again.'"[11]

A minority of teachers and staff, however, were shocked and initially somewhat demoralized that a contract could not be reached. How could the mayor have let it come to this? Hasn't he learned over the course of the past six months that his plan to steamroll over teachers' and parents' concerns wouldn't work?

Walking the Picket Line

As a result of months of organizing, the strike structure was in place. The district supervisors became strike coordinators, in constant touch with the strike captains at ten to fifteen schools, and the union added leading activists and staff to bring the number of strike coordinators to about eighty. Members of each school's contract action committee became strike lieutenants. The coordinators met each day at noon with the organizing staff in a large room off the Teamster auditorium to discuss how the morning's picketing had gone.

Teacher Sarah Chambers recalled that her school used the contract action committee to ensure picket line turnout:

> Every single day we had someone call every single member. Not text, they didn't just e-mail, they talked so they [could] hear their voice, and you could hear [if there was] wavering. The union did trainings on that, [telling us] "If you talk to them and they sound a bit hesitant, ask them questions. Ask them if they have concerns." It really kept people accountable. They really wanted to show up then. On the first day we got 100% attendance in a large school of eighty staff. And during those seven days we were on strike, there were only about two teachers that were out maybe once or twice with emergencies. We stayed strong the full seven days.[12]

During the five strikes in the 1980s, teachers and staff picketed for two or three hours in the morning, went out to have breakfast, then went home. The 2012 plan was different—picket lines would last about four hours each morning, then each day in the afternoon all members were asked to participate in a large action. The details were not all planned in advance, except for the first march that would take place in downtown Chicago on Monday afternoon. The daily *On the Line* strike bulletin outlined each day's agenda.

The informational picket lines and the Labor Day action had boosted the already high morale among members. As the picket lines went up, the overwhelming sense among the teachers was that the union would win a fair contract. The union estimated that at least 95 percent of its membership walked the picket lines during the strike.[13]

For thousands of teachers and staff, walking the picket line was a unique time that brought people closer together. Teaching can be an "isolating profession, you're in your own little bubble," noted one teacher. "If it hadn't been for the strike, I might not even know the names of people in my school."[14] Teachers are in the classroom all day. If they're not working during a meal break, they often eat with colleagues who teach the same grades. Chatting on the picket line created a deeper camaraderie.

The strike was "life altering," said one teacher. "Everyone was united like they had never been before. So many teachers came to me after the strike and said, 'Do you know how many people I met on the line, people I never even knew?!' You know, Joe whoever and Suzie whoever, they teach in the same school but haven't spoken, and now they're marching and chanting together, sharing life stories, and finding out how many things they had in common. It was a really enriching time."[15] Looking back, one teacher reflected, "It's a relationship that can never change, that will never be broken."[16]

The response from parents overcame any trepidation striking CTU members felt. "We had pancakes made for us by parents," recalled Sarah Chambers. "They were out there cooking enchiladas for lunch and serving hot coffee. Every single day we had breakfast and lunch provided for us. Parents joined us in marches. And our [school] band came out and played music for us every day." Echoed another teacher, "We had regular fiestas going on in some of the schools. The parents would bring food and feed the strikers. The parents wanted to be visible."[17]

"Every day we were on the picket line," a high school history teacher recalled, "there were city electricians coming by, city firemen, we had cops on the picket line, people that can't really voice their [views] because they are prohibited from striking."[18] Many picket lines were lively, with chanting, drumming, singing, and music. Teacher Gregory Michie noted,

> Based on three days of picketing with fellow teachers in the Back of the Yards neighborhood, I'd say the honks and hollers of support have outnumbered the thumbs-down gestures about five hundred to one. And the encouragement is coming from a wide cross-section of Chicago's working and middle classes: Latinos, African-Americans, whites, Asians, parents, former students, Chicago Transit Authority drivers, police officers, landscapers, plumbers, streets and sanitation crews, roofers, long haulers, and people who drive tortilla trucks, milk trucks, and beer trucks.[19]

The CTU picket lines had high visibility in the city because there was a school every several miles in any direction. Anyone driving for a half hour on city streets could easily pass half a dozen schools, each with dozens of red-shirted picketers.

By the second day, despite the excitement of the downtown mass marches, picketing at the schools started to feel uncreative to members at many schools, and they began marching around the neighborhood, talking to small businesses about putting CTU signs in store windows (and letting strikers use their bathrooms), handing out flyers at a train stop, or marching up and down busy boulevards. "We kind of expanded our horizons," said one member. "It was empowering."[20] Striking teachers at many schools marched to their alderman's office to demand a meeting; thirty-three aldermen had signed an open letter to Lewis the weekend before the strike urging the union not to strike, while only eight came out publicly in support of the teachers. The other nine were silent.[21]

Scores of creative actions took place across the city, and the union's *On the Line* strike bulletin shared stories from many of them, along with photos. On the Southwest Side members lined Archer Avenue with a red human chain. At Gage Park High School, strolling troubadours sang and greeted parents and children with a prostudent, proteacher message. At Goethe Elementary School, tree trunks were covered with red "yarn bombs." The Pilsen–Little Village cluster of schools held a well-attended picnic with parents.[22]

And while just about every member had a story to tell of someone who cursed at them or gave them the finger, overall the response was overwhelmingly positive. "We picketed on Western Boulevard and all the cars were really supportive," honking loudly, said one member. "There were like two drivers who were negative out of thousands in the whole strike."[23] Throughout the strike, CTU members proudly wore red every day and reported that when they were running errands, walking down the street, going into a store, or eating at a restaurant, people would frequently come up to them to express their support.

Pickets were also set up at CPS's "holding centers," where the mayor told parents to send their kids during the strike. Few parents did, and most of those who did quickly stopped doing so when striking teachers told them that there were no teachers or qualified personnel inside. CPS's instructions to holding-center supervisors sounded like a parody, in that they reinforced the very reasons the teachers were striking. They quickly went viral—including that supervisors should "wear a watch [as] your room may not have a functioning clock," "dress comfortably as many schools are NOT air conditioned," and bring your own personal supplies from home of "pens, pencils, notebook paper, and books" as none would be supplied by the district.[24]

During the strike some principals were barely seen; some took vacation time for the length of the strike. Some remained the same bullies they'd been before the strike and illegally threatened strikers that they would be disciplined or fired. Sarah Chambers related that her vice principal came to the picket line to "tell our teachers that they should sit like his dog, whom he'd brought with him, and be well mannered. Teachers were pretty mad. So at our daily end-of-the-day discussion, I told my teachers, 'You do not have a boss right now. You're not working. I don't care who your boss was last week, you do not have a boss right now.' So we were not intimidated. We all felt the unity and power."[25] Other principals confidentially told picketers they wished them well and even brought them coffee and donuts and allowed them access to the school's bathrooms. "Our principal," recalled one teaching assistant, came out and "told us to stick with it, don't back down, keep going, and that made a world of difference to me."[26]

Meanwhile, every day at noon at CTU strike headquarters at the Teamsters auditorium, the eighty strike coordinators met to discuss the morning picket lines and the previous afternoon's action. When organizing coordinator Norine Gutekanst asked for upbeat stories, dozens of hands excitedly shot in the air. At every meeting the union's rank-and-file leaders embodied confidence that the strike would be successful.

Throughout the strike, supporters and teachers also came to strike headquarters to paint signs and banners, tie strings around placards, eat, talk, and buy CTU and Chicago Teachers Solidarity Campaign T-shirts. The setup was based on the model of how graduate students in the Teaching Assistant Association had organized logistics during the February 2011 two-week occupation of the Wisconsin state capitol in opposition to a pending antiunion bill.

Downtown Marches

In contrast to the CTU strikes in the 1980s, the union decided that picketing at schools in the morning was insufficient. There was no disagreement among the staff that all the members needed to come together in late afternoon mass mobilizations downtown, which they did on Monday, Tuesday, and Thursday during the first few days of the strike.

The actions served several purposes. They would be a show of force to the mayor and his appointed board, a demonstration that the union members stood behind their bargaining committee. The mass marches would show the mayor that the union, not the mayor, had the support of the community. Most community and union supporters worked during the day and could not join morning picket lines, but the late afternoon marches gave them the opportunity to show their solidarity. The demonstrations were also planned to reinforce to the members and the public that this was no ordinary strike; rather, it was a mass social movement to defend public education.

The mass protests would attract significant media attention and would provide powerful images for TV news that hundreds of thousands of Chicagoans would see. Most members and supporters sensed that the media coverage shifted, after the first two marches on Monday, September 10, and Tuesday, September 11. Initially the coverage was somewhat antiunion and incorrectly represented the union's primary goal as winning a hefty raise. But, by the third day of the strike, coverage became more sympathetic, with a greater focus on the union's efforts to improve students' learning conditions.

Finally, the mobilizations were planned to be uplifting to CTU's 26,500 members. After all, unlike the case with other unions, the members never had a chance to come together in one place. Whereas a union with a few hundred or a few thousand members might have one or two huge meetings to discuss contract

negotiations, the CTU was much too large for that. And unless there were delegates who befriended other schools' delegates at the monthly House of Delegates
meetings, or unless they were members of a caucus like CORE, CPS elementary,
middle, and high school teachers and staff did not have opportunities to associate
with one another. As one marcher noted, as they marched "teachers were sharing stories and experiences [that we had] with our principals and it was really a
good time."[27]

In conversations with CTU members during the mass marches, and in later
interviews, participants used words like "amazing," "awesome," "unbelievable,"
"historic," "pride," "changed my life," and "empowering" to describe the mass
marches. As one teacher said, "I think if we had struck, just stayed at our schools,
and gone home at noon, then morale would've dropped. You could see, the next
morning at the picket line, the energy level of the people who had marched the
previous afternoon. They were pretty stoked."[28]

The unionists viewed the marches as a spectacular success.[29] At Monday's
late afternoon march, thirty-five thousand crowded the streets. In most political
marches, police insist that protesters stay on the sidewalk. At the most, in larger
marches, police give protesters one street lane in which to march. But during the
CTU marches, protesters covered four lanes and both sidewalks and surrounded
the Loop. Looking ahead or back while marching, all one could see was a sea of
red-shirted protesters chanting and singing. At every intersection, people could
look eastward and see masses of protesters marching, with the recognition that
somewhere up ahead, beyond their sight, the huge march had turned east and
then a block later headed south.

These were not somber protests, despite the seriousness of the strike and the
recognition that students were missing classes—the huge size of the protests created an exuberant spirit and solidified the teachers' sense that they would win this
battle. After Monday's march, recalled one teacher, "a large circle of teachers and
their supporters formed around a group of drummers and impromptu dancers,
all of us bouncing up and down and chanting to the beat, 'I believe we are gonna
win! I believe we are gonna win!'"[30]

Unlike the case at most labor protests, a large majority of the marchers were
women. A good number were mothers—and many were parents of kids in CPS
schools—with kids in tow or pushing strollers as they marched. In recognition
that the CTU strike combined a fight for workers' rights with the fight for wom-
en's rights, women's movement icon Gloria Steinem released a statement the day
before the strike declaring, "As an 87% female workforce, and one that is nearly
half African-American and Latino, the Chicago Teachers Union knows what their
students need. This is why this country needs unions, collective bargaining, and
mayors who recognize, honor, and fairly pay the people our children know—and

who know our children."[31] And it did not go unnoticed that among the flood of online comments beneath any news article about the CTU, many antiunion comments attacked Lewis with vicious sexist language.

One could hear the CTU members' changing consciousness in the chants. As with the May 23 and Labor Day marches, at Monday's march the predominant chants were "CTU, CTU, CTU" and "Hey hey, ho ho, Rahm Emanuel has got to go!" A new one, angrily responding to the mayor's Monday assertion, was "Rahm, hear our voice; the strike is not a choice!" But by Tuesday another chant was also commonly shouted; it reflected a broader understanding of the strike and its place in labor history: "Go up, Go down, Chicago is a union town!," with participants raising their hands then lowering them and leaning forward as they chanted.

Chicago, of course, is a historic union city. Key labor history events that happened there were Haymarket in downtown Chicago in 1886, the initiation of a national rail strike from the Pullman neighborhood in 1894, and the police massacre of unionists on the South Side during the Republic Steel strike of 1937. The city has more "Local 1's" than any other city, including, of course, the CTU, which is American Federation of Teachers (AFT) Local 1.

Some schools marched together and brought banners. Some teachers and supporters brought musical instruments or drums. One school's teachers marched arm in arm singing the civil rights ballad "We Shall Not Be Moved" in four-part harmony. Large numbers of high school students joined the marches, some bringing their school marching bands. Three hundred members in five schools in the Pilsen–Little Village neighborhoods joined together to march a mile and a half through their neighborhoods to the downtown march, calling their feeder march on a specially designed Facebook page "a day without a teacher." One feeder march participant said, "We wanted to make the first rally of the strike be great, and it was beautiful."[32]

Hundreds of striking teachers and staff brought beautifully drawn handmade signs declaring, for example: "CPS Students Deserve Art, Music, P.E."; "Hey, Rahm—Did You Forget CPS Is a No Bullying Zone?"; "Our Teaching Conditions Are Your Child's Learning Conditions"; "If You Think This is All About Teachers Wanting More Money—You Aren't Paying Attention!"; "My Textbooks Are Older Than My 9th Grade Students"; "Fighting for the Schools Our Students Deserve"; "We Do Not Like Our Classrooms Jammed—We Do Not Like It, Rahm-I-Am"; "'I Do This for the Money'— Said No Teacher Ever"; and "If You Can Read This Sign, Thank a Teacher."

On Tuesday afternoon during the march more than a dozen Chicago labor leaders plus AFT President Randi Weingarten held a sidewalk press conference to reinforce their support for the teachers' strike. At the start of the walkout, the AFT issued a statement supporting the action: "The American Federation of

Teachers and our members across the country stand firmly with the CTU, and we will support its members in their efforts to secure a fair contract that will enable them to give their students the best opportunities."[33] It was her second trip to the city to speak on behalf of the union. Weingarten had been in Chicago during the strike authorization vote but had not attended any public union events. This time, as she addressed the large crowd of union supporters, Weingarten used her remarks to ramp up the crowd by characterizing the strike, as Lewis had, as "a struggle for the heart and the soul of public education for the kids of Chicago."[34]

Chicago union leaders joined the AFT president in equating the teachers' fight with the defense of a broader national cause. The second day of the strike just happened to be September 11, the anniversary of the 2001 terrorists attacks on US soil. In an extraordinary appearance at the same downtown rally, Mike Shields, president of the Chicago-based Fraternal Order of Police, "blasted" Emanuel for being tone deaf to what a "hero is on this day of honoring heroes." The police union head reminded the throng of people in attendance that "Chicago teachers teach over 400,000 students in the city of Chicago. . . . To me those are heroes." He then used a personal comparison to embarrass the mayor. "I have a 4-year-old son that understands who heroes are. He understands that Chicago policemen are heroes, Chicago firemen are heroes, and Chicago teachers are heroes, but somehow our mayor cannot understand this and we need to send that message to him."[35] And Tom Balanoff, president of SEIU 1, had previously announced that thousands of Chicago school janitors represented by his union would wear red kerchiefs around their necks in support of teachers.[36]

On Wednesday, the union decided to move the mass mobilizations from downtown to three neighborhood high schools. They announced that in an expression of support for neighborhood public schools, strikers and supporters would march through the neighborhoods on the South, West, and North Sides of the city. Tens of thousands joined those marches at Dyett High on the South Side, Kelly High in the southwest Brighton Park neighborhood, and Marshall Metro High on the West Side. For many teachers, those neighborhood marches were a highlight of the strike because they directly connected them with their students' parents and neighbors.

Organizing with Social Media

Social media was also a potent weapon in the teachers' battle. WBEZ, the Chicago National Public Radio outlet, noted that "for the CTU, Facebook and Twitter are wielded like a battle-axe, [but] for CPS it's more like a billboard."[37] CTU's efforts were led by CTU Communications Department staffer Kenzo Shibata, one of many CORE activists who joined the union's staff after the June 2010 union election. Shibata had worked nearly a decade as a CPS English teacher. He quickly convinced the union leadership that he should take on the tasks and title of new media coordinator, in addition to editing the union's *Chicago Union Teacher* monthly magazine. Shibata's groundbreaking work made a tremendous impact on the union's ability to use social media to get its message out and organize its members and community supporters.

On August 16, as the union was expecting a strike, Shibata initiated a workshop for members on how to use social media to educate and organize. The workshop handout noted:

> As a union, our power is our numbers. We have 30,000 potential online activists (and their family and friends) waiting to be engaged. If all 30,000 members engage their circles of influence with the union's messages, we have the potential for millions to hear our stories, even if the *Tribune* and the *Sun-Times* print the Mayor's agenda word-for-word. Print is on the decline and more and more people are turning to Facebook and Twitter to stay in the know. Our ability to saturate social media and stay on message is how we measure our power.

Shibata told the CTU members at the workshop that social media was not just for teens and young adults. Its use had spread through all age groups, and the percentage of people who had accessed a link to a news story through social media was skyrocketing.[38] He shared the story of CTU activist Jen Johnson as an example of how social media could achieve results. Johnson was outraged that the antiunion, antiteacher, billionaire-funded front group Stand for Children was using the progressive petition website change.org to distribute an antiteacher petition. Shibata described how Johnson started a counterpetition on change.org; explained why people should sign and posted links to the petition on Facebook, Twitter, and progressive blogs; then made a YouTube video of herself reading the petition; and blogged on the popular Huffington Post website as the petition drive gained momentum—all of which was further shared on social media. A key social media organizing principle was: you do something on YouTube, you share it on other social media; you blog, you share it on other social media; you write a post on Facebook, you share it on other social media. Very quickly managers at change.org, worried about their reputation in the progressive community, ended Stand for Children's access.

Then Shibata explained to workshop participants how to set up Twitter and Facebook accounts and how to use them to educate and organize. After the workshop he followed up with an August 23 e-mail to all CTU members with links to a new twenty-three-minute video made by the Communications Department, "Chicago Teachers Union versus Astroturf Billionaires."[39] The e-mail asked members to spread the word by linking to the video on Facebook and Twitter. The video quickly got 21,000 Facebook hits, and Shibata received many replies asking how members could do more on social media. CTU social media organizing expanded rapidly from there.

In an interview, Shibata explained the union's social media strategy:

> We focused a lot of attention on social media through this strike. We knew that we could not rely completely on traditional media to tell the story.... Our members feel ownership of their message. They are able to talk about the issues that mean the most to them and watch them shared all over the world. We've been training members for months during the contract campaign. We know that the mainstream media would portray a skewed version of the campaign so we empowered members to become citizen journalists. They're finding each other and making connections from school to school.[40]

The CTU Facebook page garnered 35,000 likes by the first week of the strike, with 81,000 people talking about the issues introduced on the CTU Facebook page—compared to 2,000 likes on the CPS Facebook page and 3,000 people talking about it. Many schools' contract campaign committees created their own Facebook pages to supplement face-to-face organizing, and continued to use their Facebook pages during the strike.

As the strike began, the union was responsible for the two top trending topics on Twitter in the United States; number one was #CTUStrike and number two was #FairContractNow. The union promoted both hashtags through mass e-mails, electronic mailing lists, Facebook, and word of mouth. The union had 7,000 Twitter followers, and Kenzo Shibata and dozens of CTU members regularly tweeted about the strike.

Members and supporters uploaded hundreds of photos and videos of picket lines and the afternoon mass rallies to their Facebook pages, the union's Tumblr page and Flickr website, and the CTU channel on YouTube. Members shared photos of classroom thermometers to counter the mayor's dismissive comment that classroom air-conditioning was not important and shared photos of the most poignant handmade picket signs.[41] Members were encouraged to blog about the strike and to share their blogs on Facebook and at websites like AlterNet, Huffington Post, and Gapers Block. A September 9 blog post, "Why I'm Striking," by young teacher Xian Barrett, was widely shared on Facebook, and CTU supporter Fred Klonsky's blog provided strong support to the teachers.

Two YouTube videos were particularly popular. On September 12, the Chicago hip-hop band Rebel Diaz, whose members were CPS graduates, released "Chicago Teacher." The video showed the band singing, alternating with the mass teacher marches and picket signs. The song, which within days got 32,000 hits, begins:[42]

> "Homey, I was taught by a Chicago teacher!
> Chicago teacher, Chicago teacher!
> I learned to read and write from a Chicago teacher,
> So I'm inspired by the fight from our Chicago teachers!
> The teachers are tired, the students dumbfounded,
> the budgets get cut so classes are overcrowded.
> Streets full of violence, the blue code of silence
> so I'mma keep rhyming til salaries start rising!
> The unions uprising! Takin' to the streets!
> The workers are united so the Mayor's got beef!
> Rahm's a fake pretender with a corporate agenda
> Neoliberal offender, of course you offend us!
> This ain't about money! That's far from the truth,
> they want better work conditions to teach the youth."

And teachers at several schools came together to make a humorous jab at the mayor in a parody of the Carly Rae Jepsen hit song "Call Me Maybe." The video got 30,000 hits within days. The lyrics emphasized that the teachers did not want to strike but had no choice until the mayor produced a fair contract: "Hey we've been striking, and this is crazy. When there's a contact, then call us, maybe. We've been striking for so long we want to stop that, we want to stop that, we want to stop stop that. We've been teaching for so long we want to go back, we want to go back, we want to go go back."[43]

The Media and the Union's Message

Throughout 2011 and into the start of the September 2012 strike, there was a big discrepancy between, on the one hand, what the 26,500 Chicago educators were saying, and, on the other, what the mainstream media was reporting and the city's two papers were writing in their editorials. The schism signified that education was one of the few issues in the United States that united both political parties in an attack on teachers unions.

The *Chicago Sun-Times'* editorials regularly attacked the CTU and its "flame-throwing" and "rabble-rousing" leaders. The strike was "the union's bad call" and "an unwise strike of choice," as headlined in its September 6 and September 10 editorials. What was holding up an end to an "unnecessary strike," said the paper's September 11 editorial, was the union's "pie-in-the-sky demands" to improve children's learning conditions.[44]

The *Chicago Tribune* called the strike "unnecessary," declared that the union was on "the losing end of history's arc," and said the union was "abandoning children." The union was not, as it claimed, "fighting for the best way to educate children" but rather "fighting to protect the jobs of adults." The strike, the paper declared, was about "who controls schools and classrooms," the mayor or the union.[45]

Chicago Tribune columnist Eric Zorn's columns blamed the teachers for the strike and demanded they "stop asking for more money."[46] *Chicago Tribune* education reporter Noreen Ahmed-Ullah, when interviewing striking educators, was fixated on money issues but showed little interest when they wanted to talk about learning conditions. When, at a July 22 edition of the WTTW *Chicago Tonight* television show, host Joel Weisman asked panelist Ahmed-Ullah about the teachers' call for improvements in the schools, such as smaller class sizes, Ahmed-Ullah stunningly implied that union members were liars by claiming that, when the unionists talked about reducing class size to improve students' learning conditions, it was "a code word" for their sole real goal of stopping layoffs.[47]

The September 12 editorial of the liberal *New York Times* called the strike the "teachers' folly," "senseless," "unnecessary," and a power play by Lewis, and said the strike was driven by salary issues and evaluations. *New York Times* reporter Monica Davey wrote that the strike was essentially "a dispute over wages, job security, and teacher evaluations."[48] *Washington Post* columnist Charles Lane fixated on wage issues and denounced the CTU strike "against the aspiring poor."[49] Much of the analysis by pundits of both political parties echoed the argument of Wisconsin Governor Scott Walker, who, when pushing through an antiunion law in Wisconsin in early 2011, said that public sector unions were the enemy of private sector workers.[50] *USA Today*'s September 11 editorial was headlined "Striking Teachers Flunk Sympathy Test," and the paper argued that the central strike issues were wages and evaluations.

However, the union's message in the year-long contract campaign and then during the strike was clear. They did believe that teachers deserved a raise, because they believed that all workers deserve a raise every year, and because every year without a raise in reality meant a pay cut due to the rising costs of goods and services. They did not oppose being evaluated but thought an evaluation system and teacher firings tied to student test scores was not accurate or fair, and they wanted to be part of the process of figuring out a just, workable evaluation system and real mentoring of teachers. They wanted qualified teachers who lost their jobs due to school closings to be among the first hired when there were openings.

But their primary message was never about money. Lewis made it her mantra, from fall 2011 on, that the Chicago educators' fight was part of a national struggle "for the soul of public education."[51] There was no separation, said the teachers, between what their children needed and what the teachers needed. "Our teaching conditions are our students learning conditions," said CTU members.

The union leadership had to be very careful about how they chose their words. Legally, they could not strike over learning conditions. Every official CTU statement included the words "The union is not on strike over matters governed exclusively by IELRA Section 4.5 and 12(b)." The school board by law could not be compelled to negotiate learning conditions, and indeed they refused to do so, as Lewis noted in a June 12, 2012, letter to the *Sun-Times* responding to an antiunion editorial:

> The [board has] outright refused to negotiate about class size, even though Chicago has some of the highest class sizes in the county and the state. The district has refused to bargain about art, music, world language and physical education classes, even though 40 percent of our schools are without full-time art or music programs. The city has refused to discuss playground facilities or libraries, even though 98 schools have no playgrounds and 160 schools are without libraries. The board has also refused to negotiate staffing levels for nurses, counselors, school psychologists, and social workers even though the ratio is at levels set in the 1960s, one-third of the number of school specialists currently needed in our schools. Lastly, the district has refused to discuss ways to honor and develop experience in the classroom by making it more difficult for highly qualified and experienced educators to remain in a system that every year engages in massive layoffs, contributing to half of all teachers leaving the system every five years. Certainly CPS is not obligated to bargain the fact that out of the 10 largest cities, we have the third-highest student-to-nurse and student-to-counselor ratios. However, it is in the best interests of children for CPS to figure out these vitally important concerns with the experts who have to teach every day.

This was exactly what rank-and-file teachers repeatedly told reporters in the months leading up to, and then during, the nine-day strike. Those were the slogans on the CTU-printed signs that first appeared at the May 23 rally, and the slogans on the hundreds of handmade signs teachers carried on the picket lines and downtown marches during the strike. Those were the issues that drove the members' passion to picket and march. CTU leaders had to be careful what they said, lest they be charged with leading an illegal strike—but the members were under no such constraints.

A teacher interviewed by *Mother Jones* magazine explained her rationale for striking in words that any CTU member could have used:

> I am protesting for my students. I am striking because I don't want any child to be in a classroom with 40 other children and one adult. I want enough school nurses, social workers, speech pathologists, and occupational therapists to service my students. I want children to have art, music, and physical education. I want children to be taught foreign languages and to get to go to school buildings that are not falling apart, and are safe. I want all children in public schools to have adequate resources to be able to succeed in school. I want to be evaluated in a fair way, not primarily by tests scores. I am protesting because teachers have not been included in school reform talks, and sadly the only way to get our voices heard has been to strike. In the long run it will hurt our students more to give up this fight.[52]

In a much-shared blog post, Xian Barrett responded to Brizard's statement that "everyone knows that a strike would only hurt our kids," by writing in words that could have been written by any of thousands of CPS teachers:

> When you make me cram 30 to 50 kids in my classroom with no air conditioning so that temperatures hit 96 degrees, that hurts my kids. When you lock down our schools with metal detectors and arrest brothers for play-fighting in the halls, that hurts our kids. When you take 18 to 25 days out of the school year for high-stakes testing that is not even scientifically applicable for many of our students, that hurts our kids. When you spend millions on your pet programs but there's no money for school-level repairs, so the roof leaks on my students at their desks when it rains, that hurts our kids. When you unilaterally institute a longer school day, insult us by calling it a "full school day" and then provide no implementation support, throwing our schools into chaos, that hurts our kids. When you support Mayor Emanuel's Tax Increment Funding [sic] (TIF) program in diverting hundreds of millions of dollars of school funds into the pockets of wealthy developers like the billionaire member of your school board, Penny Pritzker, so she can build more hotels, that not only hurts kids, but somebody should be going to jail. When you close and "turnaround" schools, disrupting thousands of

kids' lives and educations and often plunging them into violence, and have no data to support your practice, that hurts our kids.[53]

As discussed in earlier chapters, for two years the union had engaged in a conversation about the role of race in the struggle. During the strike, a key part of the union's message was that CPS policies were racist. Rank-and-file teachers interviewed by the press frequently brought up the fact that the defunding of public schools and the school closings occurred overwhelmingly in neighborhoods of people of color, that black teachers were being eliminated from the schools, and that there were schools overwhelmingly filled with black students that had few or no black teachers. At the conclusion of the Tuesday, September 11, downtown march, organizers were standing on the stage in front of the CPS building, surrounded by thousands of people. Recalled organizer Brandon Johnson:

> Matthew Luskin looked at me, and says, "Brandon, we don't have an emcee, you're up." There's nothing more precious as a black man than for a white man to come to you and say, "You better bring it. This crap is racist and you better tell them." That's all the reassurance that I needed. Millions of people were paying attention to Chicago. To look into the cameras of the world and say that this movement that we're building is to take on sexism and racism. The [positive] response from the crowd, which was predominately white, was a moment that I think in this struggle finally allowed the exhale to happen.[54]

It can be granted, though, that the CTU made a rare messaging error when in February 2012 the press reported that the union had asked for a 30 percent raise at the bargaining table—and then Lewis said "no comment" when reporters asked about it. For the next seven months news reporting included that demand, and it was mentioned in most poststrike news articles.[55]

It was a messaging error because it was not true. The CTU did not ask for a 30 percent "raise" over two years. It asked for a 5 percent raise, or 2.5 percent a year, and that the 4 percent raise negotiated for the 2011–12 school year that had been appropriated by the mayor be returned. In addition, it asked that, if the mayor insisted on teachers working 20 percent more hours with the longer school day plus added days, they be paid 20 percent more pay.

Brizard echoed the mayor when he wrote, in an early June letter to CTU members denouncing the strike authorization vote, that "teachers deserve a raise and will receive one that is fair. How much that raise should be is in the hands of an independent fact finder."[56] In his July 16, 2012, report, the independent fact finder recognized the legitimacy of the union's position by recommending a

12.6 percent raise for the additional work hours.[57] But CPS and the mayor quickly dismissed and denounced the fact finder's recommendation when it came out. The *Chicago Sun-Times* reported that the report has "blown up in the mayor's face."[58] The union rejected the report's recommendations on other issues, but endorsed all the report's wage recommendations. The whole issue was dropped on July 24 when the mayor surprisingly agreed to hire more teachers to meet the demands of the longer school day.[59]

What virtually the entire mainstream media missed was that the 4 percent was not for a raise—it was a request to be paid previously promised money. The 20 percent was not for a raise—it was a request to be paid for additional work. The actual raise the CTU requested was 2.5 percent a year. And as noted by Franczek, who led the management bargaining team, "The strike really was not about money. Money was one of the less difficult issues" in the bargaining.[60]

Poll Numbers

CTU members' spirits were lifted when the *Chicago Sun-Times* reported on Tuesday, September 11, the second day of the strike, that a poll showed that Chicagoans supported the teachers' strike by 47 percent to 39 percent. Although 14 percent said they did not know whom they supported, among those who said they "knew," support for the union was actually 55 percent.[61]

An important moment in the strike came on its fourth day, Thursday, September 13, when a poll reported that two-thirds of parents stood with the teachers. The poll of voting Chicago households asked, "In general, do you approve or disapprove of the Chicago Teachers Union's decision to go on strike?" The percentage approving was 55.5; 40 percent disapproved, and 4 percent had no opinion.

CTU support jumped to 66 percent among parents of public school children, with 31 percent disapproving; 63 percent of African-Americans and 65 percent of Latinos expressed approval. It should be noted that African-Americans, Latinos, low-wage workers, and young people have low voter registration rates, so a poll of all Chicagoans including those not registered to vote likely would have shown even higher support for the teachers. Finally, the poll showed that 53 percent either blamed Mayor Emanuel or the school board for the strike, with just 29 percent blaming the CTU.[62]

As it turned out, the widespread media and political predictions were dead wrong in their forecast that Mayor Emanuel would win the support of CPS parents and so come out the winner of the strike. Republican politicians and think tanks, the city's two newspapers' editorial boards, and the billionaire-funded anti-union groups Democrats for Education Reform, Advance Illinois, and Stand for Children predictably blamed the CTU for the strike and claimed that parents would as well.

Many liberal media outlets also assigned responsibility for the strike to CTU. In a strongly antiunion editorial, the *New York Times* on September 11 warned the union that "if the strike goes on much longer, the union could pay a dear price in terms of public opinion." Hugo Lindgren, the liberal editor of the *New York Times Magazine*, argued that "the thing that will resolve this [is] the power of the Chicago parents association," an organization, it should be noted, that does not exist.

On the liberal television station MSNBC, host Alex Wagner organized panelists that uniformly opposed the CTU, and she declared, "I'm not betting against Rahm Emanuel on this one." "Rahm will win this battle," declared *New York* magazine's John Heileman. Melissa Harris-Perry wrote in her column in the liberal *Nation* magazine that not only school boards but equally so teachers "are supposed to have children's best interests at heart but seem willing to allow this generation to be lost." On her MSNBC show, Harris-Perry argued that children were the true victims and that parents would blame both the mayor and the union for the strike, an argument echoed by *New York Times* columnist Nicholas Kristof and most other liberal mainstream media commentators.[63]

Their predictions all proved wrong. Most CPS parents strongly supported their children's teachers for the duration of the strike.

Community Support

For the afternoon march on Thursday, September 13, the union turned to the community organizations, which for two years had partnered with the union in its Community Board to fight school closings. The march began at the downtown Hyatt Hotel to put the focus on CPS board member Penny Pritzker, whose family owned the Hyatt chain. Hyatt had received $5.2 million in Tax Increment Financing (TIF) funds from the city to build a hotel in the affluent Hyde Park neighborhood, while seven nearby schools lost $3.4 million from their budgets. The hotel workers' union, UNITE HERE, was also battling Hyatt's antiunion actions.[64]

The Thursday march was so successful that the *Chicago Tribune*, whose coverage had been decidedly antiunion, covered the role of community organizations supporting the teachers in a Sunday, September 16, article titled "Shadow Strikers Marched with CTU." The *Tribune* reporter wrote: "They are the shadow strikers. Behind the bullhorns and police lines, hundreds of community organizers and their compatriots strategized, marched, and danced in solidarity with the Chicago Teachers Union. Quiet as it's kept, the city's robust community-organizing movement has been a potent sister act for the CTU. The organizers mounted a full-court backup in the strike effort."[65]

The neighborhood-based Community Board organizations sent many hundreds of members to join school picket lines in their neighborhoods and to all the downtown marches. Especially high turnout came from the Albany Park Neighborhood Council; Action Now; the Kenwood Oakland Community Organization; the Logan Square Neighborhood Association; Blocks Together; Voices of Youth in Chicago Education; and the Grassroots Collaborative.[66]

The neighborhood group Blocks Together "supports the teachers striking," said leader Ana Mercado, who was interviewed during a march, "because we see them standing up for some of the basic things that students need—like not being in a classroom that's ninety degrees, and not overtesting the kids. We see this as a human rights issue, a civil rights issue." Parents 4 Teachers leader Erica Clark said, "Teachers want smaller classes. Parents will tell you—35, 40 kids in a class! That's just unacceptable. But you don't hear the president of the board, you don't hear [CPS head] Brizard talking about how they're going to use this contract to bring smaller classes to the schools."[67]

"Community, parents, young people, and students stand in solidarity with the teachers," said Grassroots Collaborative leader Amisha Patel, who was also interviewed at a march. "We've been fighting for years for a just educational system against a school district that is intent on privatizing schools, shutting down schools, and eliminating parent voice in the schools. We've been fighting really hard, and the teachers' fight is the climax of that effort. We know that what the teachers are fighting for is a broader educational vision that's grounded in justice."[68]

Mayor Emanuel made some efforts to organize community support for his position, but he was outgunned by the CTU's efforts. On August 25, 2011, the mayor called one hundred clergy to a breakfast to ask for their support for his longer school day agenda. But then the "rent-a-protester" story broke that Rev. Roosevelt Watkins III, who sat at the lead table during the mayor's breakfast and whose Helping Organizing People Everywhere (HOPE) Organization had won nearly $1.5 million in Chicago Public School contracts since 2010, paid people to be bused to Chicago Board of Education meetings to support school closings.

The deception was exposed when several of the protesters went public about the con. Thaddeus Scott told the *Chicago Sun-Times*: "I don't want the $25 he owes me. He can keep his dirty money. Why am I speaking out? Because I am in support of Crane [the high school whose closure Scott says he was paid to support]. . . . They thought for a few dollars they could get us to say whatever they want. We were preyed upon." There were, however, two African-American ministers who had long worked in coalition with the CTU through the group PEACE (Chicago Parents, Educators and Clergy for Education) to fight for neighborhood school funding and against school closings: Rev. Alvin Love of Lilydale First Baptist Church and Rev. Larry Roberts of Trinity All Nations Church. They spoke to the press to sharply criticize the hiring of fake protesters by the mayor's allies.[69]

The press subsequently revealed that the efforts were funded and directed by an Emanuel insider. "Greg Goldner, who ran Emanuel's successful 2002 bid for Congress," said the February 13, 2012, *Chicago Tribune*, "dedicated the skills of Resolute Consulting to write press releases for pastors, produce a video presentation, and help plan events."[70]

For those activists who did not have a neighborhood organization to join, on June 26, 2012, 110 people came together to form the Chicago Teachers Solidarity Campaign (CTSC). CTSC evolved out of the Labor Working Group of Occupy Chicago that had formed in late 2011. Some unions like the SEIU, government employees of AFSCME (the American Federation of State, County and Municipal Employees), National Nurses United, American Postal Workers Union, and CTU sent official representatives to the body. Individual union activists and nonunion progressive activists were also drawn to the group.

CTSC distributed educational material about the teachers' struggle throughout the city and to union members. It held a July 11 press conference outside CPS budget hearings at Malcolm X College, which forty CTSC members attended and where many spoke. The group also organized an August 8 press conference and more than a hundred picketers at the site of the proposed Hyde Park Hyatt Hotel that was receiving millions in tax subsidies. The support group further organized an August 29 town hall meeting with 250 participants at the downtown First United Methodist Church at the Chicago Temple.[71]

During the strike, thirty-one CTSC members took shifts to staff strike headquarters, and the CTU assigned CTSC member Steven Ashby to be the volunteer strike coordinator. The faith-based workers' rights group Arise Chicago also donated two staff to help out nearly full time during the strike. CTSC members did whatever tasks CTU organizing coordinator Norine Gutekanst needed, including making many trips to buy materials and driving across the city on the sixth and seventh days of the strike to distribute strike bulletins to schools.[72]

CTSC also initiated an online donation fund to pay for CTU members' lunches at strike headquarters, particularly the more than eighty strike coordinators and staff who met daily to assess strike activity. The idea was based on the donations that flooded into Ian's Pizza in Madison, Wisconsin, during the 2011 occupation of the state capitol. Hearing about the call for donations on Facebook, on blogs, or in tweets, people across the country called in $4,000 in donations to Primos

Pizza, ten blocks east of CTU strike headquarters, to deliver Italian lunches each day. Owners Gus and Daisy Selas were strong supporters of the teachers and sharp critics of Mayor Emanuel.

CTSC also designed and sold 3,600 "Stand with the Chicago Teachers Union" red T-shirts and 200 yard signs. The back of the shirts proclaimed "Fighting for the Schools Chicago's Students Deserve."

And under the direction of Stavroula Harissis and Bob Simpson, CTSC used social media aggressively. The group had 6,278 likes on Facebook, including 297 from outside the United States. During the strike week, 17,930 stories created from information on CTSC's Facebook page reached 435,475 unique people. CTSC had 434 followers on Twitter and 618 subscribers on its text messaging system, which it used to direct activists to schools that needed reinforcement on the picket line.

As teachers across the country logged onto the CTSC or CTU Facebook pages to obtain strike updates, many initiated campaigns to "wear red today in solidarity with the CTU" and sent photos of their schools' red-shirted teachers to the union. By the third day of the strike, 1,500 people from across the country had donated $80,000 to the CTU's Solidarity Fund, which was set up to help pay for strike materials, and many local unions also sent large donations.[73]

A Final Mass Rally

An emergency House of Delegates meeting was called for Friday afternoon, the fifth day of the strike. Many members anticipated that the leadership had reached an acceptable contract and that the delegates would vote to end the strike, but no resolution came, and another House of Delegates meeting was set for Sunday afternoon. A teacher recalled, "When we heard on the news it wasn't over, then we had to show up on our picket lines the next day. I was a picket captain and we had a 100 percent picket participation, but everybody was so low. They could barely drag themselves out of bed because we all had in our mind we could strike for five days and that our parents would be with us and the community groups with us, but we were quite fearful of the backlash that was going to happen if this went on for two or three weeks."[74]

Saturday's front-page *Sun-Times* headline blared "Close to a Deal." "We think we have found common ground," said CTU attorney Robert Bloch. "We have a framework of an agreement." Lewis acknowledged that, although there were still details to be hammered out, she was "very comfortable with the terms of the tentative deal." Vitale, looking more upbeat than he had in two weeks, encouraged parents to be "prepared to have their kids in school in Monday." Bloch added that the union's negotiations committee expected to recommend the deal to the delegates and, "if we have been listening to the membership well and have heard their concerns, then the agreement will be acceptable to our membership overall."[75]

As accurate as those statements turned out to be, it was a misstep by CTU leaders to publicly state that a deal was done the day before a major rally was planned. Saturday's rally, this time at Union Park on the Near West Side, had been announced in the union's *On the Line* strike bulletin on the third day of the strike, when negotiations were bogged down. A Saturday rally made it possible for teachers and supporters to drive in from nearby states, and for local supporters who had not been able to come to the afternoon weekday marches to attend.

The Thursday, September 13, *On the Line* promised that it would be "our biggest mobilization to date!" It was advertised as a "Wisconsin-style" rally; two Saturday rallies in Madison in February 2011 had exceeded one hundred thousand people. But with the headlines declaring that a contract was close, and with teachers having picketed for five straight mornings and attended four mass marches, most CTU members took the day off to rest. Still, fifteen thousand people attended the rally. Teachers unions organized buses from Madison; Milwaukee; Minneapolis; and Dearborn, Michigan. Numerous union and community leaders spoke, and Lewis declared, "The strike is not over. . . . I am tired of billionaires telling us what we need to do for our children, as if they love our children more than we do."

A notable banner at Saturday's rally read, "Democratic Party: Where Are You?" Through the week, CTU members and supporters recalled Barack Obama's declaration when he campaigned for office in 2007 that when workers were in struggle, "I'll put on a comfortable pair of shoes myself. I will walk on that picket line with you as president of the United States of America. Because workers deserve to know that somebody is standing in their corner."[76] But leading up to and during the strike he issued no statement in support of the teachers' issues; nor did he walk any picket line. His press office issued a tepid statement about wishing things could be quickly resolved so that students could return to classes.[77] Democratic Senator Dick Durbin reacted with a similarly lukewarm statement.[78]

As negotiators for CTU and CPS scheduled around-the-clock bargaining for the weekend, union leaders and board officials were indicating that the momentum was toward an end to the strike. In truth, putting into writing what the parties had in principle verbally committed to was fraught with difficulty. Just getting to the point where the union and the employer agreed to a deal was in itself a struggle. Before the strike could end, CTU would engage in an unprecedented act of democracy; the union's 26,500 members halted picketing for two days to analyze the contract proposal and debate whether to end the strike.

11

BARGAINING DURING THE STRIKE AND A DEAL REACHED

When the CTU and the board met at 11 a.m. on Monday, September 10, the first day of the strike, they were no longer at the Merchandise Mart. Vitale demanded that the teams meet on neutral territory. He was annoyed by the way the union had limited his team's access to certain rooms inside CTU's suite of offices. "We were being manipulated," Vitale claimed."[1]

The parties subsequently agreed to alternate sessions each day, as needed, between the offices of their legal counsels. On day one of the strike, bargaining restarted shortly before noon at Franczek's office in the 300 South Wacker building. The thirty-fourth-floor suite had served as the location for the two-day fact-finding hearing, and a smaller conference room had been set aside for the bargaining sessions. Participants had a bird's-eye view of the Willis Tower, the second tallest building in the country. Window gazing would serve as only an occasional distraction, though, because the parties had a lot to talk about.

While they talked, thousands of CTU members boisterously walked picket lines, and a large number of supporters marched in the city. A movement of disaffected parents and school activists had jelled around a union that chose to fight back against the deterioration of public education. School strikes were once ubiquitous, but, for nearly a quarter century, political deals had muted union collective action and left community activists to struggle against CPS alone. Unlike strikes in the 1970s and 1980s, however, this one was being waged with organized community partners.

Bolstered by broad public support and a labor relations law that was not working as the reformers had expected, CTU drove an invigorated bargaining position beyond what the economic model of labor unions would have predicted. Instead of school employees' acting for purely self-interested pecuniary gains during a politically reactionary period and an austere fiscal climate, negotiations played out in a highly charged, public context that strengthened the relationships between parents, community, and workers. CPS, the board, and city hall had anticipated bargaining against a narrow school-level union agenda. To their surprise, they confronted an idea that had empowered their adversaries: CTU represented the interests of children and had a legitimate claim to how the Chicago Public Schools should function.

Days One and Two

As bargaining quickly restarted, Franczek stressed, "We continued to have a big fight over the threshold line" dividing the bans, mainly the ones that defined who was a "developing" teacher. He admitted that in CPS's prestrike position, the "developing" rating "covered a shitload of people."[2] Under the original proposal, the union estimated that six thousand teachers could lose their jobs within two years. Along with the rating bans issue, however, the union informed its members of other reasons why a strike had and had not been called. In its *On the Line* strike bulletin, the CTU made clear that there remained a basic question of "pay fairness"; equally important, union members were also reminded that "the Chicago Teachers Union is not striking over any matter governed under Sections 4.5 and 12(b) of the IELRA."[3]

Talks on day one of the work stoppage started early and ended approximately at 9:45 p.m. They had not produced any new offers and left Vitale feeling frustrated. Lewis, however, had a more generous interpretation of the session. "Today we made some progress," and, she added, "We got a lot of work done today."[4] The union had emphasized the importance of addressing evaluations and job security, but Vitale claimed that it mostly "danced around the issues."[5] Lewis countered by claiming that the district did not offer "anything new" on either item to discuss.[6]

The linguistic jousting playing out in the media was to be expected, but it took a surprising turn once the strike had begun. Emanuel's "strike of choice" quip angered the union and implied that teachers were self-serving. Vitale also found the implication unfair. He acknowledged that the CORE leaders "did more to engage on behalf of kids than every or any other union leadership."[7] Emanuel's latest media framing also seemed to be an overt signal to allied groups, like Democrats for Education Reform, Advance Illinois, and Stand for Children to publicly bash CTU. However, each time the mayor's surrogates said something offensive about the union, it further hardened CTU's position.

The board president was feeling his own irritation about the Performance Count groups' media behavior. He and the rest of the school board negotiators had been targets of public and private criticism that they were "caving" into CTU demands.[8] Responding to news reports that CPS had "softened" its earlier stance on teacher evaluations, Robin Steans commented, "It's a shame the changes being discussed now are happening under" pressure from the union.[9] Vitale incredulously recalled that, "We were taking heat from the reformers," who, with no understanding of the collective bargaining process, recklessly charged that the board had "compromised the plan" to hold teachers to a rigorous performance review.[10]

At this point, it seemed that Vitale was not making anyone happy. The union had even staged a peaceful, if noisy, rally outside his home. Wearing the by then ubiquitous red CTU-support T-shirts, a modest crowd was visible to his seventeen-year old daughter, Mia. The sidewalk protest generated a family conversation, where Mia proceeded to show her dad a blog that referred to the strike. Commenting on the apparent union unhappiness with the school board, she matter-of-factly pointed out "They don't like you." Vitale did not, however, disappoint everyone. Mia also shared with him that some of her friends at Walter Payton College Preparatory High School had told her to "thank your dad for the vacation." Comforted by the knowledge that he had at least earned the gratitude of many of his daughter's friends, Vitale complained to Emanuel that the Performance Counts coalition was responsible for "giving them [CTU] more of the public microphone." The board president then made one strong request of the mayor: "Make them stop."[11] By all accounts, Emanuel at least applied the advice to himself. After his prestrike news conference, "the mayor was pretty quiet," the *Sun-Times*' Kate Grossman mused.[12]

Despite Vitale's efforts to tone down the public bashing of CTU, Monday's session and the competing public statements seemed to portend a war of attrition, with both sides digging into deep trenches. The parties had been engaged in dueling diatribes and narratives for several months. Grossman found it hard to sort the rhetoric from the truth. "Both CPS and CTU were on a public relations campaign," she charged. On one hand, "CPS was very willing to talk and spin; their communications team was unlike any I've ever seen—always in campaign mode." On the other hand, she argued, the union, ever prepared to immediately answer each allegation from the employer, "exaggerated and mischaracterized, casting CPS as a villain."[13]

With the parties now exchanging rhetorical blows, bargaining appeared to be locked down, but then the dynamic quickly shifted. The union's massive downtown march and rally late Monday afternoon signaled the beginning of another phase of its contract campaign. It also powerfully reinforced the CTU's position in the negotiations at a crucial time. Perhaps it was the sight of thousands of CTU members wearing red T-shirts while walking picket lines at nearly every school in the city and marching in the late afternoon through the Chicago Loop, but Franczek realized that something had changed. "We were now having the kinds of conversations needed to break through" the impasse.[14]

On Tuesday night, near the end of a long and frustrating second day of strike bargaining at Bloch's office, the employer made an important concession. It altered the formula of the rating categories, decreasing the size of the "developing" and "unsatisfactory" bans. CPS also agreed that the inclusion of student performance scores in teacher evaluations would gradually escalate over the life of the contract, but not exceed more than what state law required. Some positive movement was also made on the contentious issue of recall rights for laid-off teachers.

In presenting new proposals on recalls and evaluations, Vitale asked that CTU provide a "comprehensive proposal of [its] own."[15] Lewis said that the board's offer would be reviewed. She acknowledged that the day's negotiations had resulted in "compromise on some level," but she dismissed as "lunacy" Vitale's statement that an "end to the stalemate was near."[16] Talks were set to resume at 11 a.m. on Wednesday. They would move into a conference room at the Hilton Chicago on Michigan Avenue. Hopes for a settlement ran high in city hall. The union was less confident that a deal was in sight but reported progress on one critical area to its members: "We are closer to an agreement on evaluations, however CPS has only moved inches when they should be moving yards."[17]

Day Three

When the third day of strike-week meetings broke off after 11:30 p.m., the parties remained optimistic. Most of the discussions were between Sharkey and Swanson, who, Lewis said, talked "for hours." For the first time since the previous Thursday, Vitale and Lewis were smiling when the talks concluded. Vitale said that they had "really good discussions and proposals on the most difficult issues that we face."[18] NBC News reported, "School officials were holding out hope that teachers and students could return to class Thursday while the negotiations continued."[19] Emanuel had been imploring the union to go back to work. "My staff, as well as the Chicago Public Schools leadership team," he declared, "is committed to working through these issues, never leaving the table, to get this job done, and those issues can be negotiated simultaneously while our kids are in the classroom learning."[20] Unfortunately for the mayor, the media had begun to construct a narrative that blamed Emanuel for the school closings. In a testy exchange with reporters outside one of the school holding centers, Emanuel assertively dismissed any notion that the bargaining impasse and strike reflected how well he was doing his job. "Don't worry about the test of my leadership," he stated.[21]

When Wednesday brought further bargaining progress, the mayor thought that there was an opportunity to stop the bleeding. Near the end of the Wednesday session, during a conference call with his negotiators, Emanuel directed the team to continue bargaining in the hope of persuading CTU to suspend the work stoppage. In reply, Franczek recalls that "Vitale demurred and said 'We're tired and we're going home.'"[22] It was a smart move. While the union had favorably viewed a new set of board proposals on recalls, there was still too much distance between the parties. The union had no intention of ending the strike until every contract article was approved. "We were making progress, but there were a lot of articles left hanging, and we wanted more," Sharkey said.[23] The strike would go into a fourth day.

Day Four

Negotiations at the Hilton resumed at 9:30 a.m. on Thursday. The union had exchanged its latest proposals in response to the board's Tuesday evening offer. While discussing the differences between the proposals, the employer made another profound move. Recognizing the union's insistence that laid-off teachers be given strong consideration for rehiring, the employer recommended that 50 percent of all new hires be required to come from a pool of qualified displaced teachers. It was a plan that, Franczek said, "broke loose new ideas."[24]

On the employer's side the rehire proposal was lent gravitas by Barbara Byrd-Bennett, who began attending the meetings in early August. She had been working as a CPS leadership development consultant prior to the start of negotiations. She was a former teacher, principal, and CEO of the Cleveland Public Schools, and her presence for the first time in the nearly eight months since bargaining began added to the employer's team someone with education credentials and experience.

Byrd-Bennett's entrance into the bargaining immediately triggered questions about its timing. Suspicions that Emanuel was unhappy with Brizard and planning to fire him were widespread. Byrd-Bennett was a likely replacement, but, while Brizard remained as school CEO, it was politically awkward to appoint a subordinate to the bargaining team. When, however, it had become clear to CPS that a labor agreement might not transpire without a strike, Vitale had asked Bennett to join the bargaining table.[25]

It no doubt figured into CPS's thinking that Lewis had been complimentary toward Byrd-Bennett.[26] The two seemed to have a warm relationship and held many one-on-one conversations over the course of the bargaining. Before working in Chicago, Byrd-Bennett knew nothing about the union president, but contacts she had made working with other AFT officials advised her that Lewis was "incredibly smart, incredibly strategic." On arriving at her first bargaining session, Byrd-Bennett was nearly embarrassed when Lewis genuinely exclaimed, "finally somebody [on management's side] who may actually know something about education!"[27] While Byrd-Bennett and Lewis were able to talk respectfully to each other, the union leadership still cast a suspicious eye at the outsider. In *On the Line*, the union cautioned that Byrd-Bennett's presence was not going to easily change the tenor of the negotiations. "We don't know Barbara Byrd-Bennett (but we're learning)."[28]

As the school board representatives caucused from a session focused on the mechanics of the rehiring plan, they were interrupted by a knock on their conference room door. They were surprised when the Reverend Jesse Jackson Sr. entered the room. The two-time presidential candidate and Chicago-based civil rights activist had stopped by the hotel to offer his assistance in mediating the dispute. Not certain at first how to respond, the board's negotiators kindly declined the offer of help. Jackson then asked them to join him in a prayer. "Everyone then clasped hands, we bow our heads and he says a prayer," explained Franczek. "It was a bizarre moment."[29] Jackson also spoke with the CTU group, but instead of praying, they simply talked pragmatically about the importance of reaching an agreement. His visit and the prayer circle were symbolic of the strike's social and psychological impact. Upon entering negotiations that day, Lewis effusively exclaimed, when asked if a deal was possible by the next Monday, "Oh, I'm praying, praying, praying. I'm on my knees for that, please." As he left the hotel, Jackson told reporters, "There's a sense of urgency today" to arrive at a settlement.[30]

The union shared the reverend's assessment. CTU Vice President Jesse Sharkey emerged from negotiations bolstered by the "We Ask America" poll, which showed that more than 66 percent of parents with children in the public schools supported the strike. The poll of 1,344 voting Chicago households asked, "In general, do you approve or disapprove of the Chicago Teachers Union's decision to go on strike?"[31] In contrast to Vitale's claims about the dangers of going public, Sharkey proudly declared, "We are winning in the court of public opinion and winning at the bargaining table."[32] The union's bold contract campaign not only had moved community opinion, but it had also apparently knocked the board off its prestrike, preferred positions. "This is tremendous and unprecedented. We are winning." A settlement was beginning to look very possible because "the Board is finally moving in the right direction."[33] The next day held great promise; workers were encouraged to return to their pickets.

Day Five

On Friday, day five of the strike, the negotiations appeared to have finally produced the basic outline of an agreement. The union had scheduled a delegates meeting for later that day. There were still about twenty articles out of forty-nine that needed to be negotiated, and final draft language had to be prepared on the items tentatively settled, but, with a weekend push, it was possible that a deal could reopen schools on Monday. "We thought we had worked out the hard parts," explained Bloch.[34]

At Friday's emergency House meeting, delegates did not receive a written summary of the proposed contract but instead heard Sharkey recap the negotiations. His message also included a note of realism and resignation: "We all know that there are an abundance of concerns, including class size, charter expansion, school closings, woefully inadequate staff-to-student ratios among clinicians, and a lack of air-conditioning, playgrounds, and libraries." Unlike the union's previously unwavering insistence that it wanted the new contract to cover all the 4.5 work issues, Sharkey's late Friday update signaled that bargaining had reached a terminal point. "While the new contract won't be able to resolve all of these issues, we currently have a framework that the leadership believes will reflect our bottom-line concerns and demands."[35] Any sizable modification beyond the arrangement outlined by Sharkey, the union leadership believed, would only produce a less favorable outcome. Vitale had informed the union that the board would not engage in any further negotiations beyond Sunday. It was nearly time to get a deal done.

Days Six and Seven

Heading into the weekend and with a major rally planned, the union felt confident enough about the contract terms to schedule a special House of Delegates meeting for three o'clock Sunday afternoon. Under the union's bylaws, the delegates had the final authority to suspend the strike and recommend the final contract to the membership for a ratification vote. Knowing that a session was going to occur helped to move the process forward. "That put pressure on both sides," Franczek recalled, because it raised "hopes to have the strike called off before Monday."[36] Negotiations on Saturday started by 8:30 a.m.; with the House meeting looming, the parties had a hard deadline to meet. Fully aware of the implications of not grasping the opportunity to reach an agreement, Franczek told his team on Friday, "If we don't take charge here we lose the weekend and the strike stretches into a second week."[37]

The mayor's attorney was going to do everything he could to avoid another week of school closings. "CPS had anticipated a two-week strike," Franczek revealed. But he feared that, if the struggle went into a second week, the dispute would freeze into a dangerous standoff. What he did not know at the time was that CTU had made preparations for a four-week strike, like extending their use of Teamsters Local 705's auditorium. "That," Franczek declared, "would have been an unholy mess." With both sides sensing an opening to make a deal but worrying that the moment might be ephemeral, as Franczek recalled, "a whole frantic series of discussions" broke out.[38] The goal was to have a written agreement to present to the delegates by late Sunday afternoon.

Shifting back to Bloch's office, round-the-clock bargaining commenced on Saturday morning and ended Sunday afternoon. By the weekend, the parties had arrived at an understanding on all the remaining issues. What remained to do was to translate the agreement, all forty-nine articles, into actual contract language. It was no small task. Representatives from the board and the union committed themselves to one final long session to craft wording that accurately reflected the parties' understanding and could be presented to the delegates on Sunday. Franczek, however, did not participate in the weekend session that he colorfully characterized as the "marathon of hell."[39] The honors for the employer went to Joseph Moriarty and Franczek's law partner, Stephanie Donovan, who had once been the chief labor negotiator for the Chicago Transit Authority. Beginning on Saturday morning, the two board representatives were an almost constant presence until roughly 3 p.m. on Sunday.

Moriarty had three words for the experience: "It was awful." Trying to find the precise phrase that honestly expressed what both parties had agreed to in principle was hard enough, but, Moriarty admitted, trying to get the "language right" after one day turned into another made it "hard to think clearly."[40] Their involvement was an act of intellectual and physical endurance that impressed even the union. "Their butts did not leave those seats," noted Kristine Mayle, one of the CTU negotiators who stayed at the bargaining table that weekend. "They grabbed dinner and they went to the bathroom. That's the only time they left. It was crazy."[41]

Sharkey and Bloch joined Mayle that weekend, but Lewis was largely absent. The union decided that the CTU president would be inundated by media requests and needed to be well prepared. Mayle explained, "We sent her home because we knew she had to be good for the media." After speaking at the Saturday Union Park rally, Lewis obliged and "went home to get some rest."[42] Moriarty was not troubled by where Lewis was, but he was uneasy about who was coming and going. "Jesse and Kristine kept [alternately] leaving Saturday night," and they looked agitated when exiting the room. While their tag team–like behavior was never explained, Moriarty sensed that "they were having trouble with their folks."[43] CTU's "folks" were delegates and members who, Moriarty believed, were already raising objections about ending the strike.

Working without sleep, the negotiators rushed to complete the deal, but the bargaining on Sunday went long, finishing forty-five minutes past the time when CTU's leaders needed to leave in order to prepare for the union meeting. The parties separated with a good-faith handshake, expecting to get approval from the House of Delegates but feeling, according to Franzcek, a "great deal of anxiety."[44] After a bruising thirty-hour session, the board and union emerged with a final proposal. When the negotiators stopped talking, they were mostly finished, but, according to Bloch, "not completely finished."[45] The distinction was monumental, but Lewis agreed to bring the agreement to the union's governing body.

Sunday House of Delegates Meeting

Delegates met at the large and modern International Union of Operating Engineers Local 399 Union Hall and Training Facility pinched in between Cermak Road, South Grove, and Canal Street. Prior to addressing the House, the union's Executive Board and staff gathered in a side room to meet with the rank-and-file bargaining team. During the marathon weekend bargaining sessions, rank-and-file representatives remained a collective presence, prepared to offer counsel as proposals were feverishly written and rewritten. CTU officers reviewed the tentative deal with their rank-and-file brothers and sisters. They made it clear that while the contract offer had flaws, it was very good and the best that likely could be negotiated.

The leadership intended to recommend to the delegates that the strike be suspended. But a majority of the members expressed reservations about ending the strike. Objections were not about the substance of the tentative contract, but members wanted time to read the summaries before going back into the classroom. The attitude of most delegates, said one teacher, was that

> there is no way in heck you can expect us to vote on this right now. We need to read it and then we need to go back and discuss it at our school. I told my colleagues at my school, you need to read this. I do not want you to come back to me and say, "You gave us a bad contract." You will have the opportunity to read this, discuss this, have a conversation about this, and they you tell me how you want to vote. I represent you, and if every one of you says no to the contract and I like it, I'll vote no. If every one of you guys says yes to the contract, and I don't like it, I'll vote yes.[46]

Sharkey reflected, "We agreed with that desire and made it known that it wouldn't be a disaster if the strike didn't end then."[47] After a brief discussion about the merits of the two options, the rank-and-file representatives voted 20 to 10 to remain on the picket line for at least one more school day. Before adjourning, the full team agreed that the officers would go forward with their recommendation to suspend the walkout and present the dissenting view registered by membership representatives.

The House attendees gathered in the Operators' main hall were excited, energized, and still in a combative spirit. Union leaders meticulously went over a thirty-four-page document that summarized the agreement reached on key issues.[48] Officers were unequivocal in recommending that the delegates approve the tentative agreement. "But," Sharkey made clear, "we were conscious of not overselling the deal." He was privately concerned about "a deal like this getting overripe" and not happening. As promised, the leadership shared the vote and advice of the membership bargaining representatives. Sharkey explained, "We felt confident that if they read it after we voted to suspend the strike it would be as we faithfully presented it."[49] Nonetheless, skeptical voices came from among the delegates, who raised questions about voting for a summary that the membership had not seen.

The contract had indeed addressed many of the issues important to the membership, but the tentative deal being recommended still left too much to faith. Majority support for suspending the strike was lacking. The extent of the membership's distrust of CPS was high, and Bloch realized that delegates were wary that CPS "would undermine the deal."[50] During the three-hour discussion, recalled one delegate, "We had an open debate about whether we should stay on strike. Some schools were very strong for staying on strike and some schools were against it. It was a really great debate."[51] The attitude of most delegates, said one teacher, was that "there is no way in heck you can expect us to vote on this right now. We need to read it and then we need to go back and discuss it at our school."[52] After what the CTU officially characterized as a "civil and frank discussion," the delegates stunned city residents and national followers of the dispute by voting 61 to 39 percent not to suspend the strike.

Mayle was not surprised by the decision, but she was also feeling the strain of round-the-clock bargaining. At the moment of the vote, "it wasn't what I personally wanted," she frankly revealed. "But I knew it was good for the whole group."[53] In a press release issued after 6:00 p.m., Lewis emphasized, "This union is a democratic institution, which values the opportunity for all members to make decisions together. The officers of this union follow the lead of our members." Expecting some public backlash, she further explained, "The issues raised in this contract were too important, had consequences too profound for the future of our public education system and for educational fairness for our students, parents, and members for us to simply take a quick vote based on a short discussion. Therefore, a clear majority voted to take this time and we are unified in this decision."[54]

In a move that sent shock waves through the city and outraged city hall, the delegates voted to continue the strike until Monday, when a contract summary would be disseminated among the membership. Delegates and members would have Monday to assess the agreement and, if they were satisfied with the terms, vote to go back to work on Tuesday. Allowing the extra time for digesting the agreement would delay reopening schools but provide an opportunity for the membership to know what the deal included. It was a genuine act of union democracy. Franczek, however, claimed that it was "absolute unadulterated bullshit."[55] He understood that the union was "big on industrial democracy," but argued that on Sunday the delegates had sufficient opportunity to assess and recommend passage of the deal.

After the vote, however, an unidentified delegate yelled from the floor, "What about Rosh Hashanah?" Despite having a Jewish woman as president and an attorney at the bargaining table who was Jewish, the union had overlooked the start of the holiday. For observant Jews, Rosh Hashanah would begin at sunset on Sunday, September 16, and continue for two days until sunset on Tuesday, September 18. As is the custom with major religious observances, Rosh Hashanah prohibits certain behaviors. First among them is that no work should be conducted during the two days. Attentive to religious diversity, the delegates amended their previous vote and approved continuing the strike until Tuesday. Since the mayor was also Jewish, the union leadership assumed that he would understand the need for the one additional day before delegates voted on the contract. They were wrong.

Bloch called Moriarty with the news, and the two attorneys spoke briefly. Moriarty thanked Bloch for the call and then immediately contacted Swanson. She was with the mayor and explained that the union was not ending the strike before Wednesday. Emanuel was furious. He did not accept the Rosh Hashanah rationale. Lewis claimed that upon hearing about the holiday delay, Emanuel angrily declared, "I can get fifty fucking rabbis to say it's OK to work through Rosh Hashanah."[56] Franczek neither confirmed or denied Lewis's account, but he agreed with the mayor that "it was the most bullshit excuse I ever heard."[57] The mayor was also angry that the union leadership had not convinced the delegates to end the strike on Sunday. Emanuel then decided to try to legally compel the teachers to return to the classroom.

Day Eight

After the CTU meeting, while driving within blocks of his Oak Park home, Bloch received a phone call from a CPS attorney. The counsel informed him that the mayor was going to request immediately that a temporary restraining order

(TRO) from the Circuit Court of Cook County be issued to block the strike. City Corporation Counsel Steve Patton had actually filed the lawsuit the week before but had agreed not to pursue the injunction until the union refused to suspend the strike. As he had done several times before, Emanuel once again characterized the union as putting innocent school children at risk. "I will not stand by while the children of Chicago are played as pawns in an internal dispute within a union."[58] In a statement the union quickly denounced the mayor's "vindictive act . . . to trample our collective bargaining rights and hinder our freedom of speech and right to protest."[59]

Mayor Emanuel charged that the strike was illegal because the union was in part striking over nonstrikeable issues, such as class size. But Emanuel's position contradicted the rhetorical stance he had taken throughout the dispute. After months of charging that the teachers cared only about themselves, now he was publicly stating that the teachers were willing to strike, not over money, but over class size and other learning conditions. Evidence in the mayor's paperwork requesting an injunction, for example, included the accurate assertion that at "CTU informational picketing" in late August, "CTU picket signs demanded 'smaller class sizes' and increased staffing levels for 'nurses, counselors, and social workers.'"[60]

It was not the union but the CTU's community allies who quickly called a widely covered press conference to denounce the injunction. One hundred community supporters, teachers, and clinicians chanted outside the mayor's fifth-floor city hall office before the press conference began.[61] Jitu Brown, head of the Kenwood Oakland Community Organization and a longtime activist against school closings, stated that the strike is "the result of fifteen years of the abuse of teachers and demonizing teachers." High school student Sarah Johnson, a member of the Albany Park Neighborhood Council and the student group VOYCE, spoke in support of the strike extension. "I'm only 17 years old and I know that I will not sign a contract that I have not fully read yet or that I have not even fully received." Maria Torres of the Pilsen Alliance neighborhood group said, "If saving public education has to wait a day or two, so be it."[62]

Union leaders had discussed the possibility that the mayor would try to have the strike declared illegal or a threat to public health and safety. They were confident that the city would fail on either ground to get the TRO. Moriarty was certain the "strike was illegal" but thought it "was going to be a struggle to get the injunction."[63] CTU had legitimate issues to strike over and had been very careful in publicly explaining why it was on strike. Lewis argued that the union had a "completely legal work stoppage" and had "followed every rule."[64]

As careful as the union was, navigating around the contours separating legal from illegal actions was a challenge. CTU staff coordinator Jackson Potter knew firsthand how narrow the legal space for resisting was. "We had to be careful about explaining our reasons for striking." For example, the union could state, "we want this (i.e., 4.5 items) changed," but it "couldn't say we're striking" over this same thing. "It was a constant tug of war that limited our ability to articulate our reasons for fighting so hard."[65] The court could order an injunction shutting down a legal strike but only when it was legitimately a danger to public health. While there was no evidence that after only five days the community was at any risk of harm, upon receiving the call Bloch promptly turned his car around and drove back to his Michigan Avenue office. He waited to hear from a judge. The phone never rang.

The implications of filing a lawsuit were problematic. Even in the unlikely event that the city were to prevail, the consequences hardly seemed to favor the mayor. Teachers would be forced back to work, but they would be infuriated by the action. A contract would still have to be negotiated with a workforce further enraged by the questionable use of a court procedure to break their strike. In effect, the city would have labeled its schools' teachers, social workers, and nurses as lawbreakers. And what would happen if the union refused to honor the injunction? Community activists had many informal conversations about what actions they could take if the injunction went through and the delegates voted to continue striking, including engaging many hundreds or even thousands of people in nonviolent civil disobedience. Was the city willing to arrest picketing school librarians? Criminalizing the nonviolent action of union workers in Chicago would be a perilous political act, and yet, Emanuel had gone to court. Hours passed on Monday morning and still nothing happened.

Wanting to have a better idea of what was taking place, Bloch called city attorney Patton. He informed Patton that there was a high probability that if the union was not tied up in preparing to respond to a TRO, the labor agreement would be finished and voted upon on Tuesday. Circuit Court Judge Peter Flynn had declined to set a hearing for Monday, suggesting that he might schedule it for later in the week. The last thing Judge Flynn, up for reelection in November, wanted was to rule on the case. He used the fact that the House of Delegates was meeting again Tuesday night to postpone hearing arguments from both sides until Wednesday, September 19.

Day Nine

On Monday and Tuesday, at 580 schools across the city, instead of picketing, the teachers and staff sat in circles on plazas and sidewalks outside their schools and discussed the contract proposal.[66] "It was the antithesis of back room deals" that you hear about, said one delegate. "It gave every member of the union a chance to think about what we were going to do, should we continue to strike or come off the strike."[67] The debates over those two days were not much about whether the union had won big enough raises. There was discussion about the improvements in the teacher evaluation language, the layoff and recall policies, and how the language could have been stronger. But the central issue under debate was whether or not to continue the strike to win more gains for the parents and the students.

The spontaneous appearance of sidewalk union democracy was Lewis's "proudest moment." Months of membership engagement had affirmed the idea that the union belonged to its rank and file. Mayle was not surprised by the two-day delay. "We had activated people to the point they didn't want to vote until they had read the whole thing."[68] After two days of review, the final deal was better understood than what the delegates had rejected on Sunday, and there was little reason to believe that the delegates would not recommend suspending the strike.

As members discussed the deal, the *Chicago Sun-Times* quoted a parent who perfectly captured what they were debating. CPS parent Jeanne Marie Olson told the paper, "I would never want to sign a contract I didn't fully understand. The teachers I know want the things I want for my kids." But, at the same time, she said, "if they don't go back Wednesday they better have a damn good reason."[69] Still, there was a lingering feeling among many members that now was not the best time to go back to work. The tentative agreement had much to recommend it, but it was not without serious concessions, and, for the first time in many years, teachers and staff were in a position to genuinely affect the direction of public education in Chicago. The AFT's Mark Richard underscored just how empowering this must have looked to observers. In relative terms, "here was a fringe group without any [bargaining] skills that had taken on a great power elite with unlimited resources—and [the union] rocked Rahm's people."[70]

But the sense of power came with complications. CTU organizer Matt Luskin explained that while the tentative deal was being picked over, the union's biggest concern was "whether they had delivered real change for the community." As the strike drew closer to an end, CTU leaders feared that, according to Luskin, "we would disappoint the community by not winning things like air-conditioning." The union's education and mobilization campaign had managed to convince its members that "community interests are essential to a settlement." Would CTU's community partners see the collective bargaining agreement as a necessary step to achieving a greater community movement to defend public schools, one that started with CORE and was absorbed by the union? Luskin recognized that, despite CTU's more visionary attempt to redefine how Chicago's school children would be educated, in the end the union had to vote for a contract that, while containing substantial practical achievements, "had not brought about an end to corporate-style reform."[71]

The union tried to use the bargaining agreement as a vehicle to engineer a massive shift in school policy. Bargaining, Luskin explained, was used as an opportunity to disrupt established practices and relationships. It was a juncture at which CTU could mobilize its members, assert worker rights, and speak with moral authority to the community. Bargaining became a platform to lift up racial and economic issues by allowing the union to publically demand that CPS address the inequality that existed within the district. The legal parameters were narrow and the time brief, but as long as the union had the right to bargain and strike over mandatory subjects, during that moment, negotiations could actually improve public education. By building an unprecedented relationship with community-based school advocacy groups, CTU had forced Mayor Emanuel to consider the interests of Chicago's school children and their parents. In the end, however, Luskin admitted, "the law would only allow us to force CPS to accept a contract that improved [a limited range of] working conditions for our members."[72]

Knowing when to end the strike required performing a complicated three-part calculus. The union had first to pragmatically assess the present value of the tentative contract terms against any possible future improvements. In addition, CTU had to determine its ability to sustain membership activism. Lewis consulted all the union's organizers and asked them, "If we have to stay out, how long can we stay out?" Lewis revealed that she favored a longer strike, but if the delegates said "they were ready to go back" she would listen to the members.[73] The union would also have to judge the community's support for a prolonged strike. If, as Luskin suggested, the union had a moral obligation to its community allies that encouraged a fight to the bitter end, it also had to worry about losing public support. The public's affinity was not without limits. Investing in a neighborhood-by-neighborhood grassroots strategy produced a blade that cut both ways. The union was empowered by what Grossman called the "uprising of the masses" but, because it solicited that broader community of allies, CTU was also partly beholden to the opinions of those forces.[74]

Bloch explained that, until the school strike, he had never participated in a work stoppage that the public supported. More revealingly, he recognized an unintended consequence of being on the receiving end of favorable public opinion. At some point, the positive public attitudes would be put at risk by a longer work stoppage. Where parents had been unconditionally on the teachers' side, willing to endure some degree of inconvenience for a short while, they would certainly not be as cooperative if the situation remained frozen for too long. By the union's internal estimation, public support would begin to drain away after the second week. Aware that a shift in community opinion could occur on Tuesday,

September 18, the union passed out a leaflet expressing "profound gratitude for your support in our fight for quality public education and a fair contract."[75]

There was a related question that CTU wrestled with. What if, after two weeks, the school board and the mayor were even more desperate to for the kids to go back to school? With each passing day the dispute crept closer to the fall Democratic Convention and presidential election. Union leaders were confident that Emanuel had received phone calls from Washington pressuring him to end the strike, but the mayor was unequivocal in denying that any calls had occurred. "I have not received any pressure, and no pressure would work." Emanuel had bet heavily on being an "education mayor," and his poll numbers were tumbling, especially with black voters. Chicago political strategist Don Rose commented that the school labor negotiations were the "first issue that's gone out of control for Rahm."[76]

There were indications that a longer dispute would have produced resistance from other city unions; support for a strike among the labor community had never been unanimous. Some unions had predicted disaster and withheld support, while others attempted to persuade and even push CTU into settling. Sharkey was offended by one local labor leader who, at a breakfast meeting, lectured him about the need for the union to give in to the board. It is unlikely that opposition from other city unions would have deterred CTU from its path. All things considered, it was conceivable that in two weeks CTU could be less popular with the community but, paradoxically, in a stronger bargaining position. Membership unity was unprecedented, and Bloch referred to CTU as a "strike machine."[77] But respectful of its school leaders and uncertain of the durability of their community relationships, the union decided to recommend approving the tentative agreement.

On Tuesday evening, the seventh day of the work stoppage, ebullient, anxious, and tired delegates packed the Operators' Hall. As whistles blew and rhythmic clapping rafted up from the floor, the meeting was gaveled to order. Union leaders then took turns carefully reviewing and explaining specific provisions of the tentative contract. Delegates in the hall then heard members of the union's bargaining team admit that, while there were educators in some schools who did not want to end the strike, the negotiations committee was unanimous in recommending that the contract be brought to the membership for a vote.

Delegates and rank-and-filers then heard Lewis speak eloquently in support of the deal and about respecting the will of the membership. Before taking a voice vote to determine whether to suspend or continue the strike, the CTU president said simply, "It's time to go back."[78] After approximately thirty minutes of discussion, the CTU president finally asked the school representatives to vote on the contract items that had mobilized the union from the moment the CORE slate was elected. The response was deafening. By nearly unanimous acclamation, the assembled delegates offered their approval to end the strike. Students would be back in school on Wednesday.

In explaining an estimated 98 percent affirmative voice vote, Lewis was circumspect about what the union had accomplished. "We said that it was time—that we couldn't solve all the problems of the world with one contract, and that it was time to suspend the strike."[79] In a news conference, Emanuel called the settlement "an honest compromise" and, to the surprise of reporters, "choked up" in speaking about the role of schools in Chicago. Perhaps it was the strain of the long months of conflict, but the mayor was emotional in stating that the classroom was where students learned that they "have a place in the future of this city." Vitale praised the agreement by pointing out that it will "transform the way we run this district, for the benefit of the teachers and the kids."[80] He also extended a kind gesture to Lewis by sending her a "nice text" congratulating her, and stating that he "looked forward to working together to find solutions."[81]

In addition to ending the strike, the delegates recommended that the agreement be submitted to the members for a ratification vote. Two weeks later, on October 4, the contract was ratified with an 80 percent yes vote.[82] It was the highest approval rate ever recorded for a teachers' contract. Franczek, of all people, proudly pointed out that 82 percent of the membership had voted. To his recollection, it was also a record turnout for a contract vote.

2012–15 CTU Contract Terms

Although the three-year contract was publicly praised, labor and management held divergent views on how well their respective sides fared. Franczek acknowledged that the union had won on many valuable school-level working conditions or "nitty-gritty issues." However, from the vantage point of having bargained nearly two decades of school labor agreements, he had an unvarnished opinion about the respective advantages of this one: "It was the shittiest contract CTU ever negotiated."[83]

Many working and learning conditions were not adjusted. The contract did not provide for school air conditioners or libraries.[84] Elementary school guidance counselors were still being primarily used as case managers to coordinate the special education program for students with learning disabilities and were not free to actually counsel students. Class size was not reduced. While never a deeply contested issue, salary increases of 3, 2, and 2 percent, when adjusted for a 2 percent cost-of-living increase, meant that the employees received only a 1 percent real pay increase. Despite endorsing the agreement, Lewis frankly admitted that it was an "austerity contract" for "austerity times."[85] Additionally, on the major transformational issues like the length of the school day, teacher evaluations, layoffs, and compensation, Vitale claimed, "We won the contract."[86]

The union scoffed at the idea that it had lost the contract. Lewis pointed out that everything CPS obtained was "handed to them on a platter" by statute.[87] But even where CTU was handicapped by legal proscriptions, it still forced CPS to negotiate on the substance and impacts of most items. Franczek unintentionally offered a backhanded affirmation of the union's accomplishments. Despite the legal distinctions between permissive 4.5 and mandatory non-4.5 issues, the "union ran roughshod over the law."[88]

No one could deny that the union prevailed in shaping the final outcomes on the contested permissible items and in preventing more draconian results. Aware that school closings were imminent, the union had preserved the recognition of seniority in layoffs, and, for the first time, it also achieved recall rights for laid-off teachers. Sharkey explained, "In the past, there was a real propensity for principals to hire new people," but "now principals will have a reason to hire more veterans, or the district will face a financial penalty."[89]

In addition to the high-profile issues, many hours were spent negotiating numerous school-level items that defined the contours of an employee's workday. The contract included an antibullying provision deterring principals from treating employees harshly. It obligated CPS, for the first time, to provide textbooks to all students on the first day of school. Shops and laboratories would also be provided with any basic material or equipment as soon as school began. Funding to address work overload for teachers with disabled students was won. Teachers would also have new control over the organization, format, length, and other aspects of their lesson plans. When the lesson plan provision was discussed at the Delegates meeting, Lewis said, the "crowd went crazy with joy!"[90]

What the union accomplished included significant gains negotiated after the strike began. Recall rights, the creation of a teacher rehiring pool, the step salary schedule, resetting the rating bans, and the length of the contract were among the formative items that were approved late in the strike week. In reflecting on the impact of the strike on the final contract terms, Vitale insisted that the poststrike settlement closely tracked the prestrike proposals, except in two critical areas: teacher evaluations and, by implication, job security. "On the longer school day we would have ended up where we did, for instance, but not sure about the evaluation policy."[91]

Moriarty, however, was convinced that "CTU had a grand design to strike" and never really got around to genuinely negotiating until late in the summer.[92] Michael Brunson, recording secretary of the CTU, dismissed the notion that it was the CTU that was dodging the negotiations. The truth, he insisted, was that the employer "didn't take us seriously until they saw that a strike was imminent."[93]

Brunson thought he knew the exact moment when attitudes changed. Following a bargaining session at the union's offices, the school district's team wanted to avoid running the gauntlet of press representatives that had set up camp outside the union's offices. Instead of leaving through the front door, the union negotiators led their counterparts down a hall toward a side exit. As they "walked through the office, we went past an area where we were staging our strike material," Brunson chuckled. "Picket signs were all ready . . . that was an aha moment."[94]

Although the combatants of the 2012 bargaining round understandably promoted their own analysis of the outcome, they were not without the graciousness to appreciate what their opponents had done. No one better exemplified that point than Jim Franczek. On the occasion of the union's contract ratification, he sent a flattering personal note to his counterpart, Robert Bloch. The message was in part a respectful nod from one attorney to another. Yet Franczek's words embodied a genuine recognition of just how well the union did:

> Now that this contract is over I can tell you what I really think. Measured against what could have been and where we started, the final contract from CTU's perspective is exceptional. You have every right to take great pride in a job well done. . . . . I am thankful for your patience in enduring the occasional eruptions of a grouchy old man. New adventures no doubt await us, but at least for the moment I hope you savor the satisfaction of a really remarkable accomplishment. Maybe in the next few weeks, I can buy you a good bottle of wine accompanied by some decent food.[95]

Conclusion

The CTU's 2012 strike victory sent shock waves across the labor movement. In the first two decades of the twenty-first century, US unionists had precious little to cheer about. Year after year, the news was mostly depressing. The unionized percentage of the workforce steadily declined, with private sector unionism at just 6.5 percent of the workforce, or less than one-fifth of its peak size sixty years prior. US workers were afraid to strike out of fear they would be fired, and the annual number of major strikes was minuscule. Public-sector unions were demonized and assaulted.

Right-to-work (RTW) legislation, which sought to curtail unions, passed in historically strong labor states like Michigan (2012), Indiana (2012), and Wisconsin (2015). With its passage in West Virginia (2016), there are, in 2016, twenty-six RTW states, and a dozen other state legislatures have considered the legislation. In 2014, Illinois citizens elected billionaire hedge fund manager Bruce Rauner to be their governor. Governor Rauner promptly proposed local RTW laws in the guise of "empowerment zones" and declared his opposition to public-sector bargaining laws. Nearly two-dozen states had at least one Republican-controlled assembly pass restrictions on public-sector bargaining. Between 2010 and 2013, state legislators affiliated with the corporate-funded American Legislative Exchange Council (ALEC) sponsored more than one hundred bills to strip union bargaining rights and benefits from private- and public-sector workers. The business lobbying group also wrote numerous bills to privatize public education.[1]

The assault on union rights also ramped up at the federal level. Following their stunning Congressional electoral gains in the 2014 midterm elections, the

Republican Party held more than sixty hearings on efforts to defund or discredit the National Labor Relations Board.[2] On the verge of a historic organizing victory in the south, the United Auto Workers union lost a close election at a Volkswagen plant in Tennessee, not because of company opposition, but because the state's senior Republican political leadership threatened political retribution. There seemed to be no end to the forms of opposition to unions.

Since the early 1980s, unions negotiated concessionary contracts with stagnant or declining real wages, cuts in pension plans, two-tier pay compensation plans that paid new hires far less than other employees, and increased employee health-care contributions. Rarely was a union contract an improvement on the previous one. It is not an exaggeration to state that there were extremely powerful forces who wanted to see an end to organized labor in the United States, and that they had great momentum toward achieving that goal.

In most of the country in the quarter century after World War II, organized labor and management ended their seventy-year war. When that social accord came to an end, with President Reagan's destruction of the air traffic controllers union in 1981, labor began a steady decline; in response, a minority within labor began to call for a return to labor's militant past. When, rarely, workers rose up in struggle, labor's militant wing hailed it as an example: the United Food and Commercial Workers (UFCW) Hormel workers in Austin, Minnesota, in 1985–86; the United Mine Workers of America (UMWA) Pittston mine workers in 1989–90; the United Paperworkers International Union (UPIU) Staley workers in Decatur, Illinois, in 1992–95; the United Parcel Service (UPS) Teamsters workers in 1997; the Republic Windows factory occupation in Chicago in 2008; or the hundreds of thousands in Wisconsin who protested antilabor legislation in 2011.

Nevertheless, for the most part, labor had not changed. Albert Einstein is widely credited with having said that the definition of insanity is doing the same thing over and over and expecting different results. Yet for most of labor, their tactics have not changed over the past six decades despite a radical shift in labor relations.

Will future historians look back on the CTU strike as another militant blip in the otherwise steady downfall of labor? Or will the CTU prove to be an inspiring example that leads to a rebirth of a militant US labor movement, akin to the 1934 citywide strikes in Toledo, San Francisco, and Minneapolis, or the 1937 Flint, Michigan, autoworker sit-down strikes, all of which helped galvanize a labor upsurge that transformed US labor relations? We'll return to the question of the strike's legacy at the end of this chapter.

When the strike ended in September 2012, the CTU leadership did everything they could to make the second prophecy come to fruition, by sending union leaders and activists across the country to tell their story. *New York Times* journalist

Steven Greenhouse was accurate to argue, as the strike began, that a defeat for the CTU would be "a major setback for teachers unions nationwide" that would allow so-called education reformers to "declare that if Chicago's mighty union was willing to accept such changes, so should teachers union locals across the nation."[3] But the reverse was also true: the Chicago victory opened a discussion within labor about replicating the CTU's experience. Wherever they went, CTU speakers found an audience of union members eager to hear how the CTU transformed its union, took on a big city mayor, and won. As they traveled the country, they drew six lessons from their experience.

Internal Organizing

The first outcome of the 2012 Chicago teachers campaign was affirmation for those within labor who argued that there is no substitute for educating, organizing, and mobilizing the members in a democratic union. CTU's experience revealed that it is possible for a union leadership with determination and the right skills to turn a top-down bureaucratic organization into a bottom-up social movement.

When they took power, in June 2010, the new CTU leadership began a systematic effort to change the culture of their union. Seeking narrower goals and with far less community involvement, the CTU had been a militant union in the 1970s and 1980s, going on strike five times in eight years in the 1980s alone. But, by 2010, the union's militant history was a distant memory for most members. Teachers and staff understood the importance of having a union. But they did not see it as an important part of their daily lives. The union staff handled all grievances. There was no mentoring of members into leaders. There was no education of the members. There was no expectation that the members involve themselves with the union.

To flip this status quo, the new CORE leadership implemented one of the most successful contract campaigns in postwar labor history. Despite their positive track record, contract campaigns were not the norm in the AFL-CIO. The daily mass marches during the nine-day CTU strike, and the strike victory, would not have been possible without the previous two years of hard work to transform the union in nearly six hundred schools.

At every level of the organization, the CTU sought to encourage and mentor teachers and staff to become organizers and to see themselves as leaders. The three delegates conferences were instrumental in pushing that process forward. In the 2011–12 school year, thousands of members of the contract campaign committees engaged in tens of thousands of conversations with the members.

They changed despair into hope and a sense of helplessness into a feeling of empowerment.

So when the strike authorization vote came, no CTU activist was surprised that 98 percent of the members voted to strike, and that 92 percent of the members turned out to vote. No CTU activist was surprised that the bulk of the 26,500 members showed up for the daily downtown mass marches.

The mantra of CTU officers and staff was consistently to trust the members. They viewed union democracy as a fundamental, unbending principle. It's easy for union leaders, especially one who gets the press attention Karen Lewis did, to begin—as they say of Hollywood celebrities—to believe their own press and grow outsized egos. But Lewis, the officers, and the staff held their egos in check.

Lewis and the leadership were not saints; they sometimes made mistakes, and so sometimes there were significant tensions and fiery arguments. CORE did not close up shop when its slate was elected in 2010 or implode in internal divisions but continued to be a watchdog on the leadership and led the union's rank-and-file activism, which made the union doubly strong. And the caucus drove the May 2013 reelection campaign that resulted in an 80 percent win for the Lewis team. The support for the CORE leadership was so strong that no opposition candidates challenged them in 2016.

A Broader Vision of Labor

A second outcome of the Chicago teachers' experience was that it added new vigor to a very old debate in US labor about the purpose and goals of unions.

During the Industrial Revolution from the 1870s to the 1940s, which saw continuous labor battles against sweatshop conditions, two perspectives were hotly debated. The American Federation of Labor (AFL) argued for a "pure and simple unionism" approach that defined labor narrowly as seeking improved conditions and labor contracts for its own members. AFL leader Adolph Strasser, testifying to a Senate committee in 1883, stated it thus: "We have no ultimate ends. We are going on from day to day. We are fighting only for immediate objects—objects that can be realized in a few years. We are opposed to theories. We are all practical men."[4]

The Knights of Labor in the 1870s and 1880s, then the Industrial Workers of the World (IWW) in the 1900s and 1910s, then the Congress of Industrial Organizations (CIO) in the 1930s and 1940s, challenged this approach. They saw their purpose as extending far beyond protecting their own members. They fought equally hard to improve the lot of all working people.

When the AFL merged with the CIO in 1955, after a CIO purge of radicals induced by a wave of anticommunism, the new AFL-CIO for the most part returned to pure and simple unionism. The AFL-CIO and most of its affiliates stood by the sidelines as the 1960s and 1970s brought forth popular movements for civil rights, women's rights, peace, student rights, and gay rights.

A phrase capturing the debate, raised by labor's militant wing, was whether labor should fight for "just us" or for "justice" for all working people.

Most commonly since the 1970s, when unions strike their picket signs read "On Strike" or "Unfair to Labor," two slogans that do not resonate with the public. Progressive unions broke that mold; in the 1997 UPS strike, the Teamsters' slogan was "A part-time America won't work." A Teamster, quoted in a national news story, said, "We're striking for every worker in America. We can't have only low service-industry wages in this country." Similarly, the Republic Windows workers' slogan in 2008, when the company broke the law by suddenly shuttering the factory and moving machinery to a nonunion plant, was not "Pay us our money" but instead the broadly appealing slogan "The banks got bailed out, we [America's working people] got sold out."

The CTU loudly and defiantly rejected a "pure and simple unionism" approach. As Lewis put it, "While unions have been busy advocating for the rights of our members and institutions, we have made a mistake by forgetting to relate to and advocate for everyone else."[5] Mayor Emanuel and the Board of Education approached labor negotiations taking for granted that the new CTU leadership would negotiate as CTU leaders—and most union leaders nationally—had done for decades. The central issues, they assumed, would be a modicum of job control but mostly wages and employee contributions to health care and pensions.

Chicago power brokers were stunned when the CTU successfully turned the strike into, as Lewis repeatedly put it, a "fight for the soul of public education." Both CTU-printed and teachers' handmade signs focused on learning conditions: smaller class sizes, new texts, air-conditioning, libraries, and nurses and social workers in every school. The union declared its goal to be "the schools Chicago students deserve." They adopted a phrase and strategy that came out of the Minneapolis teachers union: "bargaining for the common good."[6]

Legally, the union could strike over compensation and some working conditions, like a grievance procedure, and health and safety issues. Therefore, every union flyer and strike bulletin read: "The union is not on strike over matters governed exclusively by IELRA Section 4.5 and 12(b)." But there was no legal constraint on the members' expressing the range of issues that motivated them to strike, and they were articulate in stating their opinions to the press and in their handmade signs.

Public-sector unions in particular, CTU argued, must see as central to their identity the defense of government as a positive good for society and the defense of social services for working people against the pushers of austerity. That expression was simultaneously the moral stance to take and the only stance that could win public support against the assault on the right of public-sector employees to unionize and bargain.

This debate within labor arose in another form in Chicago's 2015 mayoral elections. Seventy local unions, most of them in the building trades but also Teamsters joint Council 25 and UNITE HERE Local 1 (hotel and hospitality workers), endorsed Mayor Emanuel's reelection campaign and gave large donations. When no strong candidate emerged to challenge Emanuel, Lewis stunned the political establishment by announcing that she would run. But when she was struck by brain cancer and had to withdraw, the CTU, the national AFT, the SEIU Healthcare union, and several other unions encouraged Jesus "Chuy" Garcia to enter the race. Garcia shocked the political establishment by forcing a runoff in February but lost to Emanuel 55.7 to 44.3 percent in April 2015. Exit polling revealed that slightly more than half of the voters from a union household voted against the mayor.[7] However, a survey of CTU members revealed that 91 percent of them voted for Garcia.[8]

CTU members were aghast that unions would endorse and generously fund a mayor who had tried to cripple their union. But for the unions supporting the mayor it was an easy decision: Emanuel had, they said, been good to their members. Most of these unions would agree that social change was needed, and some have championed progressive causes, but fundamentally, in their view, the union is first and foremost a labor market organization that speaks for its own workers on the job.

To CTU and the few other unions that backed Garcia, however, unions must simultaneously defend their members and assertively speak out and organize for social change on behalf of all workers and the poor. To analysts of the labor movement's political role in society, the Chicago election signified a national schism between those in labor who, although committed to workplace justice, had "no ultimate ends and fight only for immediate objects," as Adolph Strasser put it, and those who saw labor's purpose and very existence as linked to a broader social justice fight for the rights of all working people.

Union supporters of Rahm Emanuel viewed the CTU and other unions that backed Garcia as having a radical, ideological agenda, whereas a grounded, pragmatic, winning approach to electoral politics was required. But for the CTU and other union supporters of Garcia, union busting cannot be forgiven, and labor will stop its disintegration, and once again thrive, only by aggressively advocating for all working people.

Labor and Community in Coalition

A third outcome of the Chicago teachers' experience was that the teachers embraced the idea of a labor-community coalition. They would not simply seek public support through advocating for their students; they would actively seek allies who shared their goals. A creed of bargaining for the common good made possible a strategy of organizing strong alliances for the common good.

Most unions are afraid to strike. Among those who do strike, they most often view the key to success as the unity of their members. But the CTU saw the path to victory as also linked to the depth of active support they could win from the public. From the moment the new leadership took office, in June 2010, it redirected the union toward building relationships with the community. It did not happen quickly, easily, or without tensions, but the CTU's Community Board brought together more than a dozen neighborhood and community groups that sought to end school closings, improve funding for neighborhood schools, and achieve an elected Board of Education that would welcome parents, teachers, and neighborhood groups as partners.

It was no accident that parents joined the picket lines during the strike and fed the teachers, that neighborhood groups initiated and led the downtown mass march on the fourth day of the strike, or that community groups assembled a press conference on the eighth day of the strike denouncing Mayor Emanuel's efforts to convince a judge to declare the strike illegal. Those actions were the fruit of two years of labor-community coalition building.

As CPS chief Brizard, who was fired by Mayor Emanuel soon after the strike, admitted, "We severely underestimated the ability of the Chicago Teachers Union to lead a massive grassroots campaign against our administration."[9]

Challenging Racism and Injustice

A fourth outcome of the strike was linked to the previous two, bargaining and organizing for the common good, but went deeper. The CTU argued not only that the goals of parents, students, and teachers were identical—that the students' learning conditions were the educators' teaching conditions. They bargained and struck not only for themselves and for their students.

The CTU also exposed and denounced institutional racism and poverty as central roadblocks to moving Chicago's students toward a great education. First among their own members, and then across the city, the union used the powerful phrase "education apartheid" to describe Chicago's public school system. As CTU organizer and African-American leader Brandon Johnson put it, "If this struggle and this fight does not have a moral consciousness about the obvious racism, we do not have a fight."[10] No large teachers union local—and only a handful of all local unions—in the country in current decades had ever put so much emphasis on challenging society's racism.

In addition to the many external factors that result in union decline, the CTU argued, there is a factor of labor's own making: too often unions are disconnected from the daily lives, problems, and aspirations of the majority of non-union working-class people, especially women and people of color. The idea that civil rights and union rights are the same struggle has a deep history in the labor movement. The Knights of Labor and the IWW denounced the AFL's racism a century ago, and the CIO succeeded only because it convinced black workers and black community leaders that the CIO was an ardent foe of racism.

For decades, the AFL-CIO has supported civil rights. But in Chicago, in 2011, few nonunion members—and for that matter, few union members—if they were asked, "Who are the leading voices challenging racism in this city?" would have answered "the AFL-CIO." But far more would have answered "the Chicago Teachers Union." And the union's prioritization of a challenge to racism and poverty did not diminish in the years immediately following the strike. For example, speaking to the city's political and business elite at the City Club of Chicago, in 2013, Lewis held nothing back:

> Members of the status quo, the people who are running the schools and advising the mayor on how best to run our district, know what good education looks like because they have secured it for their own children in well-resourced public and private institutions. When will there be an honest conversation about poverty and racism and inequality that hinders the delivery of an education product in our school system? When will we address the fact that rich white people think they know what's in the best interest of children of African Americans and Latinos, no matter what the parents' income or education level? And when did all these venture capitalists become so interested in the lives of minority students in the first place? There's something about these folks who love the kids but hate their parents. There's something about these folks who use little black and brown children as stage props at one press conference while announcing they want to fire, lay off, or lock up their parents at another press conference.[11]

They may not have stated it plainly in public meetings, but behind the scenes there were loud voices within labor who argued that there was no consensus in the AFL-CIO or its affiliates for taking stands on most social issues, let alone for acting on those stands. They argued that taking stands on social issues was divisive and would split the AFL-CIO. They argued that unions should stay away from controversial issues.

Yet the debate about whether unions should challenge injustice in US society reverberates throughout the early twenty-first-century labor movement. The CTU was not the only union to send a bus or carloads of members to Ferguson, Missouri, in 2014, to join protests against the institutional racism that too often leads police officers to kill unarmed black people and the court system that too often finds the officers not guilty of excessive force.

In a November 2014 speech to Missouri unionists, AFL-CIO president Richard Trumka powerfully denounced racism in US society. Trumka asserted that the labor movement must "clearly and openly discuss the reality of racism in American life. We must take responsibility for the past. Racism is part of our inheritance as Americans. Every city, every state, and every region of this country has its own deep history with racism. And so does the labor movement."[12] Yet the words that Trumka spoke, if put in resolution form, could not have been passed by the Greater St. Louis Labor Council, AFL-CIO. Some union leaders considered bringing forth a resolution, but dropped it when it was clear it would not pass.[13] In the CTU's sister AFT local in New York, some white teachers denounced their union's support for a rally against excessive police force.[14]

Should unions educate their members and put resources into building a group like the Earned Sick Time Chicago coalition, which sought a City Council ordinance mandating paid sick days? After all, nearly every union in Chicago had paid sick days in its contract. The CTU contract guaranteed twelve paid sick days a year. The Earned Sick Time coalition listed a dozen unions on its website, including the CTU—but that left out about fifty. And many of those included paper endorsements, not commitments to take action.[15]

Should unions educate their members and put resources into turning out members in solidarity with the Fight for $15 movement of fast-food workers, which sought to raise fast-food workers' pay—and all low-wage workers' pay—to at least $15 an hour? After all, most unions in Chicago had union contracts that guaranteed their members a higher rate of pay. A starting Chicago public school teacher who worked, as the University of Illinois study noted, fifty-eight hours a week for ten months made at least $23 an hour. The CTU joined this coalition but was one of only a handful of unions to do so. And at the Fight for $15 protests in Chicago, which labor journalist Steven Greenhouse called "the largest labor protests in the nation in years," far more visible than unions were the contingents of hundreds of members of neighborhood and community groups.[16]

In the Streets

A fifth outcome of the CTU strike is renewed debate within labor about the question, Where does our power lie? From the 1870s through the 1940s, the answer would have been: Labor's power lies in strikes, rallies, and marches. But as labor won a place at the table after the upsurge in the 1930s and 1940s, and as violence nearly disappeared from picket lines, the answer labor officials increasingly gave to that question became: Our power lies in our ability to elect prolabor candidates to office and in our lobbying efforts. The CTU rejected that strategy. Although it had a Legislative Department and, in 2015, threw itself into the mayoral and City Council elections, its organizing staff is much larger than its political staff. The CTU's emphasis, from challenging school closings to the contract fight, has always been mobilizing its members, parents, and supporters at Board of Education meetings and in the streets, including, when necessary, in nonviolent civil disobedience. As Lewis said, in 2012, "Our best tool is our ability to put people in the street, a mass movement, organizing."[17]

The union sent buses to join the mass worker protests in Wisconsin in early 2011 and welcomed the Occupy Wall Street movement in late 2011. And while CTU strikes in the 1970s and 1980s solely consisted of morning picket lines, the CTU was insistent that the 2012 strike must center on daily mass marches in downtown Chicago. Those marches contributed greatly to a sense of power that CTU members felt; a confidence, as labor's anthem "Solidarity Forever" proclaims, that "we can bring to birth a new world."

Of course, a decision not to rely on the good graces of elected officials became easier when the union's primary political adversary was the Democratic Party. It was Democrats in Springfield who passed Senate Bill 7 with the intent of preventing the CTU from striking, and it was Democrat Rahm Emanuel who first insulted teachers, then attempted to cripple their union. Teachers union activists across the country see a surprising convergence of the Democratic Party (including President Obama and his first secretary of education, Arne Duncan) and the Republican Party on education policies that aim to transform public schools into charters, replace creative teaching with teaching to constant standardized tests, end teachers' due process against unjust discipline and firing, and, overall, to weaken teachers unions.

Nevertheless, there were loud voices among the affiliates of the Chicago Federation of Labor (CFL) and the national AFT who cautioned the CTU leaders not to strike, to make whatever compromises were necessary with the mayor. They urged the CTU not to give ammunition to Republican presidential candidate Mitt Romney or embarrass President Obama by striking against his former chief of staff in the president's hometown just eight weeks before the election. The CTU leaders and members shrugged off these admonitions.

Bargaining and the Public Good

A final outcome emerged from the formal bargaining process. Before the strike was settled and the contract ratified, the parties held sixty-four formal and thirty-seven informal sessions. They spent roughly the equivalent of 138 days together in ten months, and they needed every minute. CTU and the board submitted, exchanged, and discussed 5,755 written proposals. There were so many ideas that Franczek retrospectively admonished each side for being unrealistic. "We fucked this up . . . too many proposals, too many changes, too many issues."[18]

CTU did not bargain like it had in the past. In fact, it could not. To begin with, there were two new imposing education laws that took a measureable degree of negotiating freedom away from the union. Previous contracts had also incrementally traded away the power teachers had over their working lives. Along with forfeiting the right to shape educational practices, the union had failed to consider the needs of the community. Critical of the past and recognizing that, since 2010, the national political climate had turned ferociously against public-sector unions, CTU committed to a broader bargaining approach.

Upon taking office, Lewis announced that a different "conversation" about public schools had to emerge in order to protect "what we love—teaching and learning in publicly-funded public schools."[19] Whereas, in the past, CPS defined the meaning of education reform and CTU focused exclusively (except briefly during Deborah Lynch's term) on compensation issues, under CORE the union injected pedagogical concerns and social impacts into the bargaining process. "The key is that we are trying to have people understand that when people come together to deal with problems of education, the people that are actually working in the schools need to be heard," Lewis said."[20]

According to CORE, the problem with previous bargaining rounds was a lack of rank-and-file and parental involvement. Teachers unions urgently needed to mobilize a network of people deeply committed to public education. CTU started this process with its members, by inviting them to submit contract proposals. Hundreds of proposals were sent in, and many were adopted. Unlike the case in past bargaining, all of the highest-ranked proposals focused on school children and learning conditions. CTU's approach equated student needs with the needs of workers, and what it proposed aimed at advancing "public goods." To the union, education, affordable housing, safe neighborhoods, mass transit, a livable minimum wage, and other city services were examples of public goods that should be available to all members of society as a basic right of citizenship. These benefits and services raised everyone's wellbeing and were not commodities to be bought and sold in a marketplace. Here was a public-sector union signaling that making common cause with the people one serves was not only a legitimate bargaining practice, but one that was essential for warding off accusations of self-interest. This time the membership would ensure that educational advocates and neighborhood groups would have a voice at the table.

CTU also fortified its lead negotiators by instituting the big bargaining team to bring the voices of classroom workers into the negotiations. The large group provided deep insights into what was being proposed at the table and made sure that lead negotiators remained true to the interests of the members. Those interests, however, were not limited to narrow contract clauses. They had evolved to include using bargaining to build a more dynamic union capable of affecting educational practices. Collective bargaining in 2012 featured the union's giving substantial weight to the interests of largely minority and working-class parents who were sending their children to neighborhood schools. The message for other state and local government-employee unions was that bargaining had to be about more than the pay and benefits of their members; it had to be in the name of a larger common good.

A transformative approach to public-sector bargaining, especially in education, was badly needed. The United States was engaged in an intense public policy debate about government employee unionism and collective bargaining. Education was at the forefront of a fevered rethinking about public-sector labor relations. In Illinois, the union had to navigate around the restrictions of SB 7. The law circumscribed the ability of CTU to negotiate on items like the length of a school day, class size, and social services that were central to a quality education. In response, the union consciously decided to go public with the issues at stake and use school-level and community research to promote a bargaining position.

Despite the legislative handcuffs, CTU astutely employed published reports to buttress its bargaining positions during both the fact-finding process and negotiations. It was an atypical use of relevant research data by a public-sector union to justify its demands and demonstrate its fealty to the recipients of government services, in this case the parents of Chicago school children. Publicly displaying its bargaining issues and not embargoing the talks by keeping them secret contributed to an empowered set of negotiating tactics. In the negotiations, the union managed to force the board to discuss the schools Chicago students deserve. CPS asserted its right under the law not to bargain over the substance or the impact of numerous issues CTU insisted on discussing—about teachers' working conditions, including the longer school day, teacher evaluations, and layoff recall. The union successfully maneuvered to conflate compensation issues with the substance and effects of working conditions and thus forced CPS to negotiate what it had no legal obligation to bargain over.

Fact-finding was another example of how CTU used the design of SB 7 to insert its interests into the bargaining process. The mediation step was supposed to be part of the negotiations, but not precisely in the way the opponents of the union intended. Despite the employer's contention that the longer school day was outside the neutral chair's jurisdiction, the union made the question of how many hours teachers worked a compensation issue. The fact finder agreed and ruled for the union. The ruling shoved the problem of paying for the hours that teachers worked into the negotiations where it rightly belonged. Once the item became negotiable, the union crafted a solution very much in the favor of its members and of parents.

SB 7 further compelled CTU to think immediately about how bargaining would end. Forced to cope with demands that the union submit stalled negotiations to mediation and then a fact-finding process before being free to legally strike, the union mastered the art of timing. Critical to its bargaining success was being able to control the time frame in which the process unfolded, opening the door to a possible strike at the moment that CTU determined. Setting the dates that would, nine months later, prove critical to the union's bargaining power occurred at the very outset of bargaining, when the parties agreed to the negotiation protocols. Along with taking the "early" strike authorization vote, CTU's awareness of the timeline drove the course of bargaining.

In 2012, the law imposed deadlines, and the union so successfully used them to their advantage that, in the 2015–16 bargaining, the school board balked at setting dates. The employer's slow-walking of the 2015–16 negotiations was designed to thwart CTU's ability to control the bargaining calendar and, if needed, pick its preferred strike date. CTU recognized the board's ploy in the successive bargaining round and charged that CPS was negotiating in bad faith.[21] If bargaining in 2012 and 2015 taught the parties anything, it was that deadlines mattered and that whoever controlled the calendar dictated the conditions under which negotiations would end.

After an exhausting set of talks, in September 2012 the parties signed a three-year labor pact that included many conventional and some unconventional elements. Every article, clause, and word that was fought over as if it were a sacred totem was actually a platform upon which the CTU launched a counterattack against the corporatization model of public education. Despite facing great odds and limited statutory rights, CTU had forced CPS to negotiate over many of the issues the membership identified as meaningful. In most cases, the union found a way to make fairer the real lived experience of classroom teachers, clinicians, and school paraprofessionals.

National Impact

On the day they voted to end the strike, CTU delegates were greeted outside the union hall by Chicago Teachers Solidarity Campaign activists who were waving red-and-white signs that symbolized how teachers felt and what they had accomplished. One read simply, "CTU: We're Proud of You." Another proclaimed a prophetic message that resonated with historical meaning: "CTU Shows U.S. Labor How to Fight."[22]

Since the 2012 CTU strike, there have been deep rumblings in labor about the intensifying threat to labor's existence and how to respond. The CTU's action was but a finger in the dike while water burst through dozens of other holes in the dam. A single local union cannot stop the flood of a government drive to cripple or eliminate public-sector unions, or a corporate wave to emasculate private-sector unions. In the nineteenth-century fable of the Dutch boy who stayed up all night in the freezing cold to plug the leaking dike with his finger, the village rallies in the morning and everyone joins the little boy in repairing the dam. Indeed, it will take the whole village—a reinvigorated national workers movement—to stop the onslaught.

But one union can inspire and teach by example. A measure of the national and international impact of the Chicago bargaining and strike was the way it situated the CTU as a model for teachers unions committed to social justice. In the United Teachers of Los Angeles, the second largest teachers union in the country, the United Power reform caucus, built on the CORE model, won office in April 2014. It began to replicate Chicago's experience by educating, organizing, and mobilizing the members; reaching out to parents and community allies; publishing a study, *The Schools That L.A. Students Deserve*; and preparing for a strike. After fifteen thousand teachers demonstrated in February 2015, the Los Angeles Unified School District Board of Education negotiated a fair contract.[23]

Modeled after CORE, rank-and-file caucuses formed in Newark, Philadelphia, New York City, and other cities. In 2015, the Educators for a Democratic Union caucus won the presidency of the United Educators of San Francisco teachers union, and a Seattle caucus came within a few dozen votes of winning in 2014. Three statewide rank-and-file caucuses formed in National Education Association (NEA) affiliates in Massachusetts, Colorado, and North Carolina, and, in 2014, the Massachusetts Teachers Association elected as its state head the fiery Barbara Madeloni, a leader of the Educators for a Democratic Union caucus. She was re-elected in May 2016.

CORE initiated three national conferences of the United Caucuses of Rank-and-File Educators, in an effort to replicate the CTU experience in AFT and NEA locals across the country, helped lead workshops with scores of teachers at the bi-annual Labor Notes conferences, attended by two thousand unionists. "CORE was definitely a blueprint for other caucuses around the country and the world," said a Newark teachers unionist at a CORE-initiated conference. "I was really in awe to see how they organized their members and aligned their members with the community."[24] In 2013, the conference attendees included Beth Davies, then president of the National Union of Teachers in England. Its 350,000 members were preparing for a national strike and had been inspired by CTU.

After the Chicago strike, Illinois schools saw a surge of teacher strikes. Districts in Lake Forest, Evergreen Park, Highland Park, Crystal Lake, and Waukegan settled contracts after walkouts, and unions in Carpentersville, Geneva, Grayslake, Huntley, and Hinsdale authorized strikes. Local disputes came with their own sets of issues, and the bad economy may have triggered some of the walkouts; perhaps these actions would have occurred without the CTU strike. But the almost complete absence of school work stoppages in the state since the 1980s is suggestive of a relationship between the success of Chicago teachers and the occurrence of strikes in other districts.[25]

In the spring of 2013, the Portland (Oregon) Association of Teachers (PAT) waged a successful contract struggle featuring a vision of "the schools our children deserve," patterned after the CTU's manifesto. Portland teachers worked closely with parents and community members to win contract demands that addressed the concerns important to each group. Organized support for the teachers came from religious leaders, the National Association for the Advancement of Colored People (NAACP), and the Portland Student Union.[26] The PAT expressed the aspirational effect of the CTU bargaining by placing on its Facebook page a summary of what the Chicago teachers had achieved under the heading "Chicago Teachers Union agreement shows how teachers advocate for students through bargaining."[27]

Postscript Chicago

Despite its victory, the CTU had no reprieve. Soon after the strike the Chicago Board of Education announced the largest school closings in US history. In early 2013, more than twenty thousand parents packed dozens of community meetings to tell the board they wanted their neighborhood school to be fully funded, not closed. The CTU and the community groups on its Community Board organized the massive turn-out, then initiated a three-day march of hundreds of parents and teachers through affected neighborhoods. Ignoring their protests, in May 2013 the board closed fifty schools and fired the entire staff (in so-called turnarounds) of seventeen others. The CTU denounced the racial character of the closings: 90 percent had a majority black student population, and 25 percent of all CPS schools with both majority black students and staff were closed. The closures resulted in three thousand more layoffs of CPS teachers and staff and escalated CPS's steady layoff of black teachers; 71 percent of the affected schools had a majority black teaching staff. Instead of opening new charter schools, said the CTU, the board should fully fund neighborhood schools.

Meanwhile, teachers reported that many principals ignored the "no bullying" language in the new contract. Angry at the excessive number of days spent on standardized tests, teachers and parents organized boycotts on test days at several schools.[28] The longer school day took its toll; teachers had already been exhausted by their average fifty-eight-hour workweek before more hours were tacked onto their workday. Teachers reported principals telling them, in violation of the contract, that as a result of too-low test scores, either no teachers or only a small quota would receive the highest evaluation ranking, regardless of how well they performed.

Lewis had repeatedly declared she would never run for mayor of Chicago. But, in early 2014, her appearances before teachers were met with chants of "Run, Karen, Run!" In July 2014, the city was stunned when a *Chicago Sun-Times* poll had Lewis beating Chicago Mayor Rahm Emanuel in a hypothetical contest by 45 percent to 36 percent. Among black voters, Lewis led 52 percent to 34 percent, and among Latinos, Lewis led 41 percent to 37 percent. An August 2014 *Chicago Tribune* poll showed Mayor Emanuel's approval rating was just 35 percent, down from 50 percent in May 2013. Only 26 percent of black voters approved of the mayor's performance. Asked "Is he in touch with people like you?" 62 percent responded that he was not. In the same poll, Lewis had the backing of 43 percent of city voters compared to 39 percent for Emanuel, close to the results of the *Sun-Times'* poll. Among CPS parents, 57 percent backed Lewis while 27 percent supported Emanuel; and 56 percent of union household members backed Lewis while 31 percent supported Emanuel's reelection.

Starting in late August, Lewis organized town hall meetings, dubbed "Conversations with Karen," in a number of neighborhoods across the city. She began to hire staff and plan a campaign; in August, meetings attended by hundreds of supporters initiated a petition drive. Then, in early October, it was reported that Lewis was hospitalized, and two weeks later word came that it was brain cancer. She was out of the race.

Within the month, Lewis, now recovering from emergency brain surgery, and other progressive labor leaders persuaded Jesus "Chuy" Garcia, a member of the Cook County Board of Commissioners who had advised Lewis on her precampaign strategy, to enter the race. It was an uphill battle, despite the mayor's poor poll numbers, because Garcia had low name recognition, was entering the race late, and had no big donors. Emanuel collected $8 million in campaign contributions by January 2015 and $15 million by February. With his Chicago Forward PAC, by early March he had reached $30 million, overwhelmingly from one hundred donors, and by April he had $40 million.

When Garcia forced Emanuel into a runoff in February 2015, the CTU threw its money, staff, and members into the campaign. The union also campaigned for a group of progressive incumbents and candidates, including two of its own members, in aldermanic (City Council) campaigns. Garcia lost the April 7 election, but twelve progressives, including Tenth Ward CTU member Sue Sadlowski Garza, won, doubling the size of the progressive caucus.

The decision to ramp up its political engagement meant the union had to take resources from its contract campaign, despite the contract's expiring on June 30, 2015. But throughout the spring the union held press conferences and issued press releases to highlight its primary contract demands.[29] Their program echoed what they had called for in 2012: smaller class size, more support staff in every school, adequate preparation time for teachers, and enforced paperwork limits. In addition, the union went far beyond traditional contract demands to request that the board retrieve $1 billion from the banks by renegotiating high interest rates on deceptive loan deals, divert tax increment funds to the schools, freeze charter school expansion, school closings, and turnarounds, and significantly reduce the number and duration of standardized tests.

Soon after the April election, the board announced it would not extend the contract one year (the union had not taken a public stance on the issue), claiming that it could not afford the negotiated 3 percent raise. Negotiations had begun in the spring but were far behind where they'd been at the same time in 2012. By conscious design, CPS attorney Franczek was stalling the process to prevent a September 2015 strike where tens of thousands could again sport red T-shirts in the warm weather. The union's April demand for mediation, as mandated in SB 7, would not occur until August, and fact-finding could not begin until after mediation concluded.[30] In May 2015, the board told the union it would soon force members to pay 7 percent more toward their pension, in effect a 7 percent pay cut. In 1981, CPS, along with scores of other school districts across the state, had agreed in bargaining to pick up most of individual teachers' pension payments in lieu of a more expensive increase in wages.[31]

On June 9, five thousand teachers and supporters converged in downtown Chicago in another sea of red as the union escalated its contract campaign. "When the wealthiest in our city tell us that our schools are broke, we say that our schools are broke on purpose," said CTU's Sharkey. "Walk two blocks in any direction from where we stand now and you will see untold wealth . . . and yet we are told we don't have the money for a nurse in every building."[32]

If another strike occurred, CTU would confront the additional challenge of newly elected Republican governor Rauner, who vilified the teachers union and had brought the anti-union group Stand for Children to Illinois. In 2014, Rauner narrowly defeated Democrat incumbent Pat Quinn and immediately demanded the legislature enact anti-union laws. The Democratic majority in the Senate and House refused, and Rauner in turn refused to agree to a budget until they acquiesced, further driving the state into fiscal crisis and leading to deep cuts in social service programs.[33]

CPS borrowed heavily to make a required $634 million pension payment and claimed that, without financial assistance from the state legislature, more than one thousand workers would lose their jobs and $200 million would be cut from school budgets. Governor Rauner stated his unwillingness to support financial assistance to Chicago without severe limitations on CTU's ability to bargain. The combative relationship between state government leaders suggested that the board was unlikely to receive any external funding help during this bargaining round.

Recognizing the dysfunctional situation in Springfield, the union and the school board came close to negotiating a one-year contract in August 2015. CTU members would have accepted a freeze in base salary in exchange for modifications in the teacher evaluation system and grading practices. Reflecting parents' concerns about the time consumed in meeting testing requirements, the union proposed that the district reduce the number of standardized student assessments. CTU also echoed community concerns by demanding that the mayor make a public pledge not to open any new charters or turnaround schools and that no neighborhood school would close. The pledges would be good only for the life of the contract, but they were substantive issues for the union. Emanuel had steadfastly refused to make any promises about further such school actions.

But at the next negotiation session the board withdrew its support for the contract extension. At the core of the school board's reversal was its renewed demand, first raised in May 2015, that union members begin to pay the entire cost of their pension contribution. If the union conceded, teachers and staff would incur a 7 percent annual pay cut. Such an action would "force us into a strike," declared Lewis.[34]

As bargaining continued, however, other political developments severely weakened the mayor. In April 2015, reports surfaced that the federal government was investigating CPS head Barbara Byrd-Bennett for corruption. Resigning on May 31, she admitted to making a deal to get $2.3 million in kickbacks in return for giving more than $23 million in no-bid contracts to her former employer, Supes Academy, to administer training for principals. Byrd-Bennett pled guilty in October 2015 and faced prison time. In July 2015, Emanuel appointed his chief of staff, Forrest Claypool, who was widely viewed by union leaders as bitterly adversarial, to be the new CPS head.

Then, on November 24, 2015, a judge ordered the release of a video showing that, thirteen months earlier, a Chicago police officer shot sixteen bullets into black teenager Laquan McDonald. Coming after a series of police shootings across the country that began in August 2014 in Ferguson, Missouri, and the subsequent rise of the Black Lives Matter movement, the video prompted repeated demonstrations in downtown Chicago. Emanuel promised changes and fired Chicago Police Department Superintendent Garry McCarthy, but the protests continued. Activists demanded the resignation of Cook County State's Attorney

Anita Alvarez, who had suppressed the video for thirteen months; she was badly beaten in the Democratic primary in March 2016. The Black Lives Matter movement was widely credited with her receiving just 29 percent of the vote in a three-way race. The mayor appointed a task force, which released a scathing report in April, agreeing with "the widely held belief the police have no regard for the sanctity of life when it comes to people of color. Stopped without justification, verbally and physically abused, and in some instances arrested, and then detained without counsel—that is what we heard about over and over again."[35]

A January 2016 poll found Emanuel's approval rating had fallen by half in two months to just 27 percent. Nearly three-quarters of voters believed Emanuel lied when he said he had not seen the McDonald shooting video, and four in ten wanted him to resign. A February 2016 *Chicago Tribune* poll found, as surveys had shown since 2012, that three times as many Chicagoans thought the CTU had a better plan to improve public schools than did Mayor Emanuel. In households with CPS students, 73 percent supported the teachers union while just 14 percent backed the mayor. A May 6, 2016, *New York Times* article, "In Deeply Divided Chicago, Most Agree: City Is Off Course," reported similar dismal poll results for Emanuel.[36]

On November 23, 2015, the union and its allies again held a large demonstration in downtown Chicago on a bitterly cold Monday evening, with an eye to warning CPS that its members were not afraid of a winter strike. Three weeks later, the CTU again held a three-day strike authorization vote, nearly matching its 2012 results, with 88 percent of its members giving its leaders the go-ahead to call a strike. 92 percent of the union's 24,752 eligible members voted, with 97 percent of those voting yes. "That's overwhelming," said CTU's Sharkey. "Rahm, Forrest Claypool: Listen to what teachers and educators are trying to tell you. Do not cut the schools anymore."[37]

Unlike in 2012, when the union's strike vote had taken the board by surprise, this time Franczek filed an unfair labor practice charge with IELRB. The employer claimed that a strike vote could happen only after the fact-finding process had ended and that the vote had to be administered by IELRB. On both counts, CTU prevailed. IELRB ruled that the education labor relations act did not grant it jurisdiction over a strike authorization vote. Additionally, in what must have triggered a very curious reaction from the union, in light of the way that SB 7 dictated the threshold level of support needed to strike legally, the decision stated that "strike votes are internal union matters and do not concern matters under the act."[38]

On February 15, 2016, the CTU leaders brought a contract proposal to their big bargaining team, which unanimously rejected it, saying they did not trust CPS. In the proposal, CPS promised, but was not legally bound, not to lay off teachers "for economic reasons" during the life of the contract or to increase the number of charters. Teachers would get modest pay hikes that would be matched by the loss of the pension pickup.[39] The union leadership did not express anger that the bargaining team had rejected what Lewis had called "a serious offer." Sharkey said, "When asked, 'Is it worth actually taking a pay cut for that?' people said 'no way.' Because the skin that we put in the game is concrete and will definitely be extracted from us, and the skin which they put in the game is something which is abstract, in the future, and can't be guaranteed."[40]

One of the lessons of the CTU experience is that a union cannot always be on the defensive and expect to win. A boxer holding his gloves to protect his face, cowering in the corner while getting pummeled by his opponent, will never win the match. To advance their cause, a union under attack has to go on the offensive.

Bargaining was at a stalemate after sixteen months of meetings. CPS made it clear that it would impose a 7 percent pay cut by ending the pension pick-up.[41] Every school faced annual cuts and layoffs. CPS threatened repeatedly to lay off up to 5,000 more teachers and staff. The Board of Education and the mayor continued to ignore or belittle CTU's demands that they form a united front to demand new funding through a graduated state income tax, shifting TIF funds to schools, a financial transactions tax, forcing the banks to renegotiate unfair loan rates, and an end to charter expansion. As CTU attorney Bloch put it, "CPS finances have surpassed the danger zone and are now nearly at meltdown. We need revenue solutions to finance public education, not more cuts to the system, which has already been cut well past the bone and now threatens the vital organs."[42]

The CTU determined, in early 2016, to call a major action for April 1. The first part of the action would be a one-day strike of CTU's 25,000 members. Under SB 7, the union could not engage in an open-ended strike until thirty days after the fact-finders' report was issued and rejected by one or both parties—and the fact-finder's report was not expected for another month. The union argued that there was no such legal restraint on a one-day unfair labor practices (ULP) strike. A ULP strike happens when a union calls a strike not over contract issues but in response to an employer's illegal actions. CTU encouraged other unions to walk off the job. The CTU flyer called for "all concerned Chicago citizens to unite in a day of action by withholding your labor, withholding your dollars, boycotting classrooms, boycotting the Magnificent Mile" and joining protests across the city.

The union declared that Claypool's threat unilaterally to end, in the middle of contract negotiations, the pension pick-up in April constituted an unfair labor practice and was thus a legal basis for a one-day strike. CPS attorney Franczek adamantly insisted that there was no legal basis for a strike under SB 7, but the union was undeterred. On March 4, Claypool withdrew his threat, hoping to avert the strike. The CTU, with organizing already at a full-steam, argued that CPS's unilateral action, in September 2015, to stop paying teachers' step and lane pay increases constituted a legal basis for a ULP strike.[43]

The second part of the April 1 action was to broaden the coalition of community groups that had been so visible during the 2012 strike. The April 1 Coalition meetings drew four dozen organizations and new unions into the mix. Students and unions at public colleges facing closure due to the budget stalemate in Springfield joined the effort. Several Black Lives Matter groups that had been in the streets demanding Emanuel's resignation opted in. Half a dozen public sector unions, mostly representing college teachers and health care workers, embraced the actions. CTU leaders privately admitted that organizing this broader community-labor coalition was far more complex and difficult than in 2012, but it was seen as the inevitable and necessary next step in the union's drive for educational and social justice.[44]

Broadening the coalition dovetailed with widening the focus. If the 2012 strike had caught CPS and Mayor Emanuel off guard by going far beyond compensation issues to demand fully funded neighborhood schools in a battle to defend public education, the April 1, 2016, strike and protests went much further, demanding that the city and state governments fully fund all public services by raising taxes on the wealthy. The strike's slogan was "Broke on Purpose: Fund Our Future."

Eighty percent of the unionists at the union's March 4 House of Delegates meeting, after a lengthy debate, endorsed their leadership's call for a one-day strike and day of actions. Much of the dissent came from activists who argued that the proposal was too timid—that, with no contract after nine months, it was time for an open-ended strike, law or no law. A minority of members worried about whether they could retain parents' support and feared CPS reprisals against strikers. 20 percent of CTU members were new hires who had not experienced the 2012 strike. And there was some confusion that the union was proceeding with the action even though CPS had backtracked on immediately ordering members to pay an additional 7 percent toward their pensions.

On April 1, 2016, after the CTU picketed at schools in the morning, three dozen actions, initiated by non-CTU community groups and unions and involving more than five thousand protesters, happened across the city. The day culminated in a downtown rally and march with 15,000 participants. April 1 showed that teachers were far from alone in their willingness to act. The multiple protests throughout the city were a collective anguished cry of unreserved defiance from the city's marginalized population.

At the evening rally on April 1, speakers representing an unprecedented collection of community organizations raged against the city and particularly the state political system. The result was a black-brown-white-queer-straight-immigrant-millennial-working-class consensus that the democratic system was failing the neediest. April 1 showed that, although they experienced oppression in different ways—deep cuts in social services, racism, colleges facing closure, or attacks on union contracts—members of diverse groups embraced the CTU's call for unity under the umbrella of challenging an austerity agenda. As CTU's Jackson Potter put it after the action, "When we fight, we win. CTU has shown the path to coalesce a political block with allies like SEIU, Grassroots Collaborative, Fight for 15, GEM, #BlackLivesMatter, and many others to create a political opposition to austerity, growing economic/racial disparities, and neoliberalism—with an alternative vision of robust community schools, democratic control of public education and the police, progressive taxation, free and universal childcare and higher education, $15 an hour, and a society that values schools over prisons."[45]

The *Chicago Tribune*, true to form, editorialized twice deriding the April 1 protests as "tantrum day," and Claypool denounced the "blatantly illegal strike" and filed charges against the union with the IELRB.[46] Meanwhile, CPS, as in 2012 seemingly unaware or unmoved by the growing political and union upheaval engulfing them, announced on May 17, 2016, that schools would face an additional 27 percent cut. That same day, CTU was unshaken by the release of the fact-finder's report endorsing CPS's last contract offer, the one that CTU's big bargaining team had voted down.[47] It rejected the fact-finder's report. The union, finally freed from the SB 7 restraint on their right to an open-ended strike, announced that it would not strike before the school year ended. But it prepared its members and allies for yet another showdown when schools opened in September 2016.

A Twenty-First-Century Community-Union Labor Model

The CTU story is emblematic of the complicated ways that unions in the public and private sectors have grappled with diverse levers of power in their search for the most effective strategy to wield against powerful opponents. The choices are not novel; nor are they endless. To confront the rising wave of antilabor political ideology, ignited in the late 1970s and supercharged since 2010, unions have employed strikes, bargaining tactics, electoral politics, regulatory action, and public support. Most unions have opted not to resist and made the best bad deal they could. As previously noted, teachers unions were more apt to accommodate "reform" than try to stand it down.

The CTU experience, however, provides labor students and labor relations practitioners with a unique lens through which to understand how working people and organized labor can create a more equitable society. Operating within difficult political, economic, and legal contexts, CTU conceptualized struggle differently from most unions. To Chicago teachers and staff, the fight was about how corporate interest and the hegemonic logic of the market was perverting the purpose of public education and undermining democracy. CTU, like other unions, had the authority to negotiate for its members, but to stand a chance at improving the lives of children of working and poor families, it needed a mechanism to develop and articulate power in multiple forms. In order to use different kinds of power to reinforce one another, CTU relied on an unconventional approach to an unlikely vehicle to represent workplace and working-class interests: the collective bargaining process.

Though circumscribed by law, CTU had the legal right to bargain over all compensation matters as well as most working terms and conditions. It also had the right to strike. Cognizant of what the law allowed, the union effectively translated its rank-and-file enhanced bargaining capacity into the public arena. The bargaining structure provided CTU with the opportunity to reach out to and mobilize allies. When it did so, the issues and actors engaged in the contract fight expanded and shifted. Parents acted as if the fight were theirs, and the bargaining claims broadened to include neighborhood survival. As conducted by CTU, bargaining became an instrument for bringing about social change. And therein lay the threat to corporate power.

As long as labor has the right to negotiate and strike over managerial control of the workplace, it has the potential to translate that capacity into the means of achieving more substantive social change. The demand of governors like Scott Walker and Bruce Rauner for an evisceration of the items that workers—particularly in the public sector—can negotiate over is not primarily about reducing state expenditures. It is about blocking the ability of organized labor to translate workplace representation power into social and political power. That the CTU strike did not in 2012 change the structural inequality of the public school system does not alter the significance of the threat.

Also, as prescribed by legal dictates, bargaining is a technical function with a set of expected behaviors and rules. It is one of the primary reasons workers organize and an essential service that unions provide. But bargaining is also a product of the labor-management relationship and therefore externally focused on changing the employer's behavior. It is not principally designed to attend to internal organizational needs. While the membership is often solicited about demands, unions do not typically use negotiations to transform the identity of the membership. Consequently, in the vast majority of cases, unions simply fulfill a functional duty to bargain. Contracts get settled and, in the best of situations, workers' material lives are dramatically improved, but rarely are union members or the public changed by the experience.

CTU, however, approached bargaining in a radically different fashion. In the run-up to and throughout the 2012 contract fight, CORE used negotiations as a membership development and institution-building tool. It did this in two ways. First, the union leadership engaged in a school-by-school educational program. Rank-and-file members were provided with the insights and language to speak out courageously for racial equality, economic stability, and educational equity. They were also trained to assume school-level leadership positions and to build trusted ties with neighborhood school leaders. Bargaining presented opportunities for member activism and involvement. Teachers, clinicians, and paraprofessionals joined the big bargaining team, and the district supervisors were turned into school and contract campaign organizers. Here is a contemporary example of a union's seriously attempting to exemplify historian Staughton Lynd's "we are all leaders" ideal of a popularly mobilized democratic rank-and-file.[48]

Additionally, unlike the majority of labor negotiations, including CTU's prior to 2012, CORE sought to expand on the private interests of individual members that typically characterize conventional bargaining. Central to confronting the limitations imposed by antilabor public policy and a softening of union political influence, CTU prioritized raising public consciousness about educational justice. Instead of narrowly focusing on the job-related concerns of CPS employees, the union addressed issues that resonated within the largely minority communities that suffered from inadequately supported public schools. Instead of focusing only on workplace conditions, CTU campaigned for an end to the economic inequities that were responsible for bad learning conditions. Even more significant, it tied an end to poverty to improving schools and raising the opportunities for working-class children.

Union bargaining typically treats building community alliances as irrelevant or, at best, a last-resort tactic, but CTU actively recruited community supporters. Instead of viewing its objective as reaching agreement on the bounded legal parameters of a contract, the union addressed the wider needs of workers and the working class. Sustaining a social movement is not without difficulties. But as Jeff Helgeson's *Crucibles of Black Empowerment: Chicago's Neighborhood Politics from the New Deal to Harold Washington* recounts, in places like Chicago it is the school system that constantly agitates public consciousness.[49] The education of children has been igniting intense debate since the founding of the first common school. The Chicago strike revealed that education issues are at the heart of the nation's commitment to the idea of an egalitarian public square. There is no more valuable good for union workers to defend than one that binds the community.

At the bargaining table, the issues that prolonged the bargaining and produced the 2012 strike were related to teacher job security. Despite CTU's efforts to negotiate over parental concerns like school closings, class size, and inequitable school resources, ultimately the legal and political context provided the board with a wall behind which it could retreat. Though the union made some gains in the final contract for parents and students, they fell far short of their goals. Nevertheless, the public endorsed the strike, accepted the inconveniences the work stoppage caused, and supported the union over the mayor during and after the strike. Why? The answer could be found on city and neighborhood streets, and represented in daily television broadcasts and newspaper articles and on social media platforms. While CTU bargained at the table what they could, everywhere else the union inserted community issues into the public consciousness. They did it so brazenly that the board accused it of waging an illegal strike. And the union made it clear that the 2012 strike was just one battle in a long fight for well-funded, high-quality neighborhood public schools.

CTU used the power of its mass community mobilization to popularize the importance of items like air-conditioning, the need for more libraries and counselors, and well-resourced neighborhood schools. The union identified these problems during bargaining and, in a robust way, asserted them in the streets of Chicago to expose the inequities within the system, which were the real reasons why so many Chicago students were at risk of being left behind. These actions had the effect of drawing their members' interests closer to the community's grievances. Teachers' school-level job issues and parental demands for quality neighborhood schools began to morph into a common interest. For all its creative efforts, however, CTU could not overcome the restrictions in the bargaining law to compel the board to negotiate more than they had to. But to anyone paying attention—and literarily millions were—there was no doubt that the union had put the corporate public education reform agenda on trial. And in the court of public opinion, the teachers won.

Moral support did not stop school closings, but it did move voters. When, in the fall 2014 elections, nearly 90 percent of voters approved a nonbinding resolution calling for an elected school board, there was no doubt that CTU was responsible for the popular effort to give parents a voice in how the school system was governed. CTU's efforts in the poststrike city elections were illustrative of what may be possible on a larger scale. Imagine what teachers unions could pragmatically accomplish if they regularly defended public education by first building, then activating, a strong relationship with the parents of the students they educate. Teachers unions in Minneapolis, St. Paul, Denver, and Los Angeles have in fact initiated campaigns where labor and community are working together to build public support for revenue solutions that would allow their communities to adequately fund public services like schools. And, in May 2015, thousands of Seattle teachers walked off the job in a political strike to protest legislation slashing school budgets. "We were using the Chicago strike as a model," Seattle Education Association President Jonathan Knapp told the *Seattle Times*.[50]

The approach is not limited to schools. Imagine union bus drivers all over the country acting within a "public transit coalition," like the one in Pittsburgh that links bargaining demands to the restoration of services to poorer neighborhoods.[51] Imagine child- and home-care providers across the United States, like those at SEIU Healthcare Illinois and Indiana, being perceived as the first line of defense for low-income families and people with disabilities.[52] Imagine illuminating to the nation's recipients of public services that the most aggressive defenders of those services are unions, as AFSCME 1989 has done in its efforts to build a broad labor-community coalition to demand Northeastern Illinois University be fully funded by the state.[53] To be clear, education and moral appeals are not sufficient. Resistance is still necessary. But fighting back with the community at your side would nourish a purpose large enough to stand a chance of succeeding.

The CTU example further demonstrates that bargaining with the common good in mind and the public at your side will still require the salutary benefits of political influence. CTU called on its political allies to minimize the worst impacts of a restrictive bargaining policy. Admittedly the lack of support from a Democratic governor put CTU in a legal bind, but the collar could have choked the life out of the union if not for the intervention of political allies in Springfield. In addition, in defiance of the majority of the city's labor unions, which solidly supported Mayor Emanuel, the union built an independent political infrastructure that placed educational issues at the forefront of local elections.

Although Garcia lost the mayor's election, the lesson is that large urban-based unions can build alliances with voters affected by public services to break away from narrow, interest-based politics. CTU was at the forefront of a labor-led politics that was committed to an inclusive and broad representation of working-class interests. Built primarily with public-sector unions representing transit, municipal, educational, and health-care employees, the strategy has the potential to upend austerity politics.

In Chicago, for example, prior to the election, a $13 hourly minimum wage was passed, and the city's living wage ordinance was extended to airport employees. Cab drivers also obtained substantive relief from oppressive licensing and administrative regulations and chartered the first taxi drivers union since the 1930s.[54] In the summer of 2015, the mayor appointed a task force that included, among others, representatives from labor, worker centers, and low-income advocacy organizations to propose legislation on earned sick time, fair scheduling, and additional family supports.[55] Chicago remains a place with deep fissures between its haves and have-nots, but the city's poststrike policy agenda is more humane than what preceded it.

What the CTU experience reveals is that a coalition of public service unions, allied with like-minded community organizations that advocate for communities of color and the poor, has the potential to serve as a focal organizing point to improve the lives of working people. If private-sector unions with memberships similar to the underserved populations in most cities (i.e., hotel and restaurant and manufacturing), as well as those attempting to diversify the industries they represent (i.e., building trades), embraced even a slightly broader working-class agenda, then municipal elections would more likely produce outcomes that would allow labor to support the candidates they genuinely need and want, and not the ones that seem best positioned to win.

In addition to pursuing enhanced independent political power, CTU's campaign strongly suggests that a coalitional approach organized around defending public services has real potential for helping labor navigate future bargaining and policy debates. Despite conservative rhetorical and actual assaults on public budgets, government continues to play a vital role in the lives of working- and middle-class people. As post–2008 recession state austerity plans coarsened the lives of working people, the importance of government was magnified. State public policy, from educational funding to child-care support for low-income working parents, touches the lives of all working-class citizens. Additionally, few if any private industries, from high tech to construction, do not benefit from public investment or tax abatement. The point is that work, whether done by employees of firms, government agencies, or school districts, is a public good with extreme importance for communities. Through either policies or services, government and market entities create "publicly valuable outcomes," like educating a child, paving a highway, processing a car registration, or taking care of a disabled adult.[56]

What the CTU experience reveals is that labor unions can best represent the shared interests of the community because they are the most effective institution for creating publicly valuable outcomes relating to work. The challenge for labor is to position itself as a creator of goods that are valued by the community. In 2012, despite the legal limitations, CTU emphatically carried the mantle of defender of educational justice, quality, and equity into its struggle with CPS. Especially important, the union acted on behalf of and with the support of the community it intended to represent. CTU was unquestionably strengthened by the relationship because it helped the union to draw from the different contextual sources of power previously discussed.

Every product of work has a community of interest that can provide moral, political, and organizational capacity to the people providing the labor. Conversely, labor movements have the capacity to build a more egalitarian order at work, in the community, and within the larger polity. The only question is whether a union-community coalition will form in order to translate gains across contexts. If it does so in other struggles, then CTU will be the embodiment of a labor movement empowered to represent the public good. If not, then Chicago 2012 is a shining example of what labor knew was possible but never fully realized.

Notes

INTRODUCTION

1. Karen Lewis, interviewed by Robert Bruno, March 12, 2013.
2. Lyndsey Layton, "Study Says Standardized Testing is Overwhelming Nation's Public Schools," *Washington Post*, October 24, 2015, https://www.washingtonpost.com/local/education/study-says-standardized-testing-is-overwhelming-nations-public-schools/2015/10/24/8a22092c-79ae-11e5-a958-d889faf561dc_story.html?tid=a_inl.
3. Take, for instance, the following by one of the nation's foremost public school and teachers union critics, Terry M. Moe:

> In the American public school system, the vested interests are the teachers unions.... The teachers unions have been masters of the politics of blocking for the past quarter century. Major reform is threatening to their vested interests in the existing system, and they have used their formidable power—leveraged by checks and balances—to repel and weaken the efforts of reformers to bring real change. Collective bargaining is also profoundly important for another reason: it has enabled the unions to impose ineffective forms of organization on the schools, thus exacerbating the very problems the reform movement has been trying to correct.

Terry M. Moe, "Teachers Unions, Vested Interests, and America's Schools," posted at http://www.hillsdale.edu/file/outreach/free-market-forum/archives/2013/Terry-Moe.pdf. These same ideas are laid out more explicitly in his book *Special Interest: Teachers Unions and America's Public Schools* (Washington, DC: Brookings Institution Press, 2011).

4. Margaret Haley's speech, "Why Teachers Should Organize" (National Education Association Addresses and Proceedings, Forty-Third Annual Meeting, Saint Louis, 1904) is included in Appendix B in *Battleground: The Autobiography of Margaret Haley*, edited by Robert L. Reid (Champaign-Urbana: University of Illinois Press, 1982), 279–87.
5. Lois Weiner, "Teacher Unions and Professional Organizations: Re-Examining Margaret Haley's Counsel on Councils" (paper presented at the Annual Meeting of the American Educational Research Association, San Francisco, April 20–24, 1992), p. 3.
6. Ibid., 4.
7. "1904 Margaret Haley Calls for Teachers to Organize," *History of Education, Selected Moments of the 20th Century*, ed. Daniel Schugurensky, Ontario Institute for Studies in Education, University of Toronto, http://schugurensky.faculty.asu.edu/moments/index.html.
8. Haley, "Why Teachers Should Organize."
9. Weiner, "Teacher Unions and Professional Organizations," 7.
10. Ibid., 9.
11. Haley, "Why Teachers Should Organize."
12. Weiner, "Teacher Unions and Professional Organizations," 12.
13. Ibid.
14. Alexander Thompson, *National Journal of the NEA* 2, no. 1 (Sept. 1917): 70.
15. John Budd has termed these goods "publicly valuable outcomes." John Budd, "Implicit Public Values and the Creation of Publicly Valuable Outcomes: The Importance of

Work and the Contested Role of Labor Unions," *Public Administration Review* 74, no. 4 (July/Aug. 2014): 506–16.

16. Weiner, "Teacher Unions and Professional Organizations," 14.

17. Ibid., 19.

18. Ibid., 16.

19. David Harvey, *Brief History of Neoliberalism* (New York: Oxford University Press, 2007), 3.

20. According to Professor of Education Policy Studies Pauline Lipman, the city was an "incubator, test case, and model for the neoliberal urban education agenda." *The New Political Economy of Urban Education: Neoliberalism, Race, and the Right to the City* (New York: Routledge, 2011), 19.

1. EDUCATION REFORM FROM WASHINGTON TO CHICAGO

1. *CPS Stats and Facts*, April 2016, http://cps.edu/About_CPS/At-a-glance/Pages/Stats_and_facts.aspx; Illinois State Board of Education, *Illinois School Report Card*, April 2016, http://www.illinoisreportcard.com.

2. National Commission on Excellence in Education, *A Nation at Risk: The Imperative for Educational Reform* (Washington, DC: US Department of Education, April 1983).

3. D. C. Berliner and B. J. Biddle, *The Manufactured Crisis: Myths, Fraud, and the Attack on America's Public Schools* (Reading, MA: Addison-Wesley, 1995); J. I. Goodlad, "A Nation in Wait," *Education Week*, April 23, 2003, 36–38; P. E. Peterson, *Our Schools and Our Future . . . Are We Still at Risk?* (Stanford, CA: Hoover Institution Press, 2003).

4. John E. Chubb and Terry M. Moe, *Politics, Markets, and American Schools* (Washington, DC: Brookings Institution Press, 1990), 2, 12.

5. Joseph Lieberman, "Schools Where Kids Succeed," *Readers Digest*, Jan. 1999, 145–51.

6. Milton Friedman, "The Role of Government in Education," in *Economics and the Public Interest*, ed. Robert Solo (New Brunswick, NJ: Rutgers University Press, 1955), 123–44.

7. Milton Friedman, "Public Schools Make Them Private" (*Washington Post*, Feb. 19, 1995; repr., Washington, DC: Cato Institute Briefing Paper 23, June 23, 1995).

8. Diane Ravitch, *The Death and Life of the Great American School System: How Testing and Choice Are Undermining Education* (New York: Basic Books, 2010), 98.

9. Alexandra Usher, *AYP Results for 2010–11* (Washington, DC: Center on Education Policy, Dec. 2011), http://www.cep-dc.org.

10. *Condition of Schools Report, 2011*; *Revenues for Public Elementary and Secondary Schools, by Source of Funds: Selected Years, 1919–20 through 2009–10* (Washington, DC: Institute of Education Sciences, National Center for Education Statistics, May 2015), http://nces.ed.gov/programs/digest/.

11. The average reading score in 2008 for 13-year-olds was higher than it was in 1971. Reading scores for 13-year-olds were actually climbing in the years before *A Nation at Risk* was published, and thirty years of reform efforts later they were still getting better. Math scores revealed a similar trend. In 2008 math scores for 9-year-olds and 13-year-olds were higher than in all previous assessment years and had been improving steadily all along beginning with 1973. *National Assessment of Educational Progress* (Washington, DC: Institute of Education Sciences, National Center for Education Statistics, 2013), http://nces.ed.gov/programs/digest/.

12. On the International Mathematics and Science Study which assesses students at the 4th and 8th grade levels, the Program for International Student Assessment which measures 15-year-olds, and the Progress in International Reading Literacy Study which tests 4th graders, US students score better than or as well as all but a few countries.

National Assessment of Education Progress: International Comparisons (Washington, DC: Institute of Education Sciences, National Center for Education Statistics, September 27, 2013), http://nces.ed.gov/programs/digest/.

13. About 3,192,000 public high school students graduated at the end of the 2012–13 school year. The number of high school graduates exceeded the high point during the baby boom era in 1975–76, when 3,142,000 students earned diplomas. Data from the early 1970s does not support a so-called dropout crisis in the years before *A Nation at Risk* or later. By the 2012–13 school year, graduation rates had reached an all-time high at 81 percent. *High School Graduates, by Sex and Control of School: Selected Years, 1869–70 Through 2021–22*, Digest of Education Statistics (Washington, DC: Institute of Education Sciences, National Center for Education Statistics, 2012), http://nces.ed.gov/programs/digest.

14. Sean F. Reardon, "Faces of Poverty: The Widening Income Achievement Gap," *Educational Leadership* 70, no. 8 (May 2013): 10–16; Sean Reardon, "The Widening Academic Achievement Gap between the Rich and the Poor: New Evidence and Possible Explanations," in *Whither Opportunity? Rising Inequality and the Uncertain Life Chances of Low-Income Children*, ed. R. Murnane and G. Duncan (New York: Russell Sage Foundation Press, 2011).

15. Thomas Piketty and E. Saez, "Income Inequality in the United States, 1913–1998," *Quarterly Journal of Economics* 118, no. 1 (2003): 1–39.

16. Reardon, "Faces of Poverty."

17. S. Kornrich and F. Furstenberg, "Investing in Children: Changes in Parental Spending on Children, 1972 to 2007," *Demography* 50, 1 (2013): 1–23.

18. Reardon, "Faces of Poverty," 10–16.

19. Deborah Lynch, interviewed by Robert Bruno, Chicago, Feb. 7, 2014.

20. Jitu Brown, Eric Gutstein, and Pauline Lipman, "Arne Duncan and the Chicago Success Story: Myth or Reality?" *Rethinking Schools* (Spring 2009), rethinkingschools.org/archive/23_03/arnc233.shtml.

21. Stephanie Simon, "Privatizing Public Schools: Big Firms Eyeing Profits From U.S. K–12 Market," Huffington Post, August 2, 2012, http://www.huffingtonpost.com/2012/08/02/private-firms-eyeing-prof_n_1732856.html.

22. Dennis Rodkin, "Charting a New Course," *Chicago Magazine*, April 2009, http://www.chicagomag.com/Chicago-Magazine/April-2009/Charting-A-New-Course/.

23. Gates's investment included a partnership with the textbook publishing company Pearson to develop a national test to measure school performance.

24. Letter to Terence Bell, Secretary of Education, US Department of Education, part of National Commission on Excellence in Education, *A Nation at Risk*, 2.

25. William Testa, "Groundhog Day for Chicago's Economy?" Federal Reserve Bank of Chicago Feb. 1, 2010, http://midwest.chicagofedblogs.org/archives/2010/02/questioning_chi.html.

26. Marc Doussard, Jamie Peck, and Nik Theodore, "After Deindustrialization: Uneven Growth and Economic Inequality in 'Postindustrial' Chicago," *Economic Geography* 85, no. 2 (April 2009): 183–207, quotes on 183.

27. Ibid., 187.

28. Ibid., 201.

29. United States of America v. Board of Education of the City of Chicago, No. 80 C 5124, 88 F. Supp. 132 (US District Court, N.D. Illinois, E.D., June 8, 1984). As Amended July 17, 1984, https://www.courtlistener.com/ilnd/9BeV/united-states-v-board-of-educ-of-city-of-chicago. According to Shawn L. Jackson, in 1980, an elaborate "Comprehensive Student Assignment Plan" was designed and directed by a court order to racially balance the schools. But changes in population patterns were following economic dislocations, and the schools largely retained their demographic one-dimensionality. Despite a

modification of the original consent decree and more than a half century after the *Brown v. Board of Education* case affirmed the idea that "segregation eliminated the possibility of equality, the Chicago Public Schools found itself supporting a social pattern that encouraged it." *An Historical Analysis of the Chicago Public Schools Desegregation Consent Decree, 1980–2006: Establishing Its Relationship with the Brown v. Board Case of 1954 and the Implications of Its Implementation on Educational Leadership* (PhD diss., Loyola University Chicago, 2010), http://ecommons.luc.edu/luc_diss/129.

30. Based on an analysis by Andrew Papachristos, the rate hit 10,647.9 per 100,000 people. "48 Years of Crime in Chicago: A Descriptive Analysis of Serious Crime Trends, from 1965 to 2013," working paper, Institution for Social and Policy Studies, Yale University, New Haven, CT, Dec. 9, 2013, 1–20.

31. As reported by Alina Tugend, a 1985 study by the social research organization Designs For Change found that approximately half of all Chicago's high school freshman class in 1980 failed to graduate, and that only a third of those who did were able to read at or above the national twelfth grade level. "Half of Chicago Students Drop Out, Study Finds," *Education Week*, March 6, 1985, http://www.edweek.org/ew/articles/1985/03/06/05130008.h04.html.

32. Mary O'Connell, "School Reform Chicago Style: How Citizens Organized to Change Public Policy," special issue, *The Neighborhood Works* (Chicago: Center for Neighborhood Technology, Spring 1991), 9.

33. Michael Martinez, "For Schools, It's Only a Start: 'Worst in America' in the Past, Its Problems Remain Deep-Rooted," *Chicago Tribune*, Feb. 12, 1999, http://articles.chicagotribune.com/1999–02–12/news/9902160027_1_private-schools-admission-lottery-whitney-young.

34. O'Connell, *School Reform Chicago Style*, 11.

35. Neil Steinberg, "1987 Teachers Strike Is an Ugly Lesson for Mayor Emanuel," *Chicago Sun-Times*, Sept. 9, 2012, http://chicago.suntimes.com/?s=Neil+Steinberg%2C+"1987+Teachers+Strike+is+An+Ugly+Lesson+for+Mayor+Emanuel%2C"+.

36. Ibid.

37. O'Connell, *School Reform Chicago Style*, 2.

38. Ibid.

39. Ibid., 3.

40. Jean Latz Griffin et al., "No Progress in School Strike Despite Pleading from Parents," *Chicago Tribune*, Sept. 13, 1987, http://articles.chicagotribune.com/1987–09–13/news/8703090114_1_chicago-teachers-union-mediator-bad-faith-bargaining.

41. O'Connell, *School Reform Chicago Style*, 10.

42. Ibid., 3.

43. Jean Latz Griffin, et al., "No Progress in School Strike," 1987.

44. Well after the strike had concluded, its deleterious impacts were still being felt. In order to meet the state Board of Education's required number of days that schools be in session, the school year was extended to June 30, 1988. The week before classes finally ended, daily temperatures broke 100 twice, topping out at 102, and included days at 97 and 91 degrees. Teachers and students were both overcome by the oppressive heat. Some students simply stopped coming to school, and by the last week of class, attendance had fallen to a fraction of enrollments.

45. "A Dismal End to a Sorry School Strike," *Chicago Tribune*, Oct. 6, 1987, http://articles.chicagotribune.com/1987-10-06/news/8703150231_1_school-strike-teachers-school-supt, accessed on Nov. 29, 2015.

46. Linda Lenz, interviewed by Robert Bruno, Chicago, June 26, 2014.

47. O'Connell, *School Reform Chicago Style*, 11.

48. Ibid.

49. Suzanne Davenport, interviewed by Robert Bruno, March 18, 2014.

50. Ibid.

51. Donald Moore, "Voice and Choice in Chicago," in *The Practice of Choice, Decentralization and School Restructuring*, vol. 2 of *Choice and Control in American Education*, ed. William H. Clune and John F. Witte (New York: Falmer Press, 1990), 169.

52. Ibid., 187.

53. Ibid., 189.

54. A late 1980s study done by Designs For Change (DFC) found that "81 percent of Chicago high school students ended up in nonselective high schools, while 19 percent attended academically selective high schools." Moore, "Voice and Choice in Chicago," 170.

55. Moore, "Voice and Choice in Chicago," 170.

56. Ibid.

57. O'Connell, *School Reform Chicago Style*, 24.

58. Donald Moore, *The System Matters: Chicago Activists Win District-wide Change*, Designs For Change, Chicago 1995), 1–9.

59. Daniel Egler and Rudolph Unger, "Thompson to Amend School Reform Plan," *Chicago Tribune*, Aug. 27, 1988, http://articles.chicagotribune.com/1988-08-27/news/8801250867_1_veto-school-reform-bill-madigan.

60. Ibid.

61. O'Connell, *School Reform Chicago Style*, 1.

62. Quoted in Donald Moore, *Chicago's Local School Councils: What the Research Says* (Chicago: Designs For Change, Jan. 2002), 2.

63. Brown, Gutstein, and Lipman, "Arne Duncan and the Chicago Success Story."

64. O'Connell, *School Reform Chicago Style*, 14.

65. Lenz, interview.

66. Ann Bradley, "Job Freeze Cited as Chicago Delays Opening of Schools," *Education Week*, Sept. 15, 1993, p. 5, http://www.edweek.org/ew/articles/1993/09/15/02chic.h13.html.

67. Associated Press, "Chicago Teachers Reach Tentative Agreement," *New York Times*, Oct. 10, 1993, http://www.nytimes.com/1993/10/10/us/chicago-teachers-reach-tentative-agreement.html.

2. THE ERA OF MAYORAL CONTROL BEGINS

1. John Kass and Rick Pearson, "Daley Quickly Flexes School Muscle," *Chicago Tribune*, May 25, 1995, http://articles.chicagotribune.com/1995-05-25/news/9505250228_1_mayor-richard-m-daley-chicago-public-schools-chicago-teachers-union.

2. Thomas Hardy, "Daley Now Has to Win Over State GOP," *Chicago Tribune*, April 6, 1995, http://articles.chicagotribune.com/1995-04-06/news/9504070030_1_daley-aide-mayor-richard-daley-republican-legislators.

3. Rick Pearson and John Kass, "GOP Beats Daley to the Punch on Schools; Its Plan Forbids Teacher Strikes," *Chicago Tribune*, May 11, 1995, http://articles.chicagotribune.com/1995-05-11/news/9505110332_1_mayor-richard-daley-school-year-gop-lawmakers.

4. Contracts had included a maximum class size provision as early as 1967. That number, however, was defined as a school board "goal," and CTU did not object to the employer's unilateral control of the matter. In 1970, union president John Desmond wrote in the contract that "our members appreciate the fine maximum class size provision (CTU-CPS 1970 contract)." It was not until 1976 that the labor agreement included negotiated mandatory class size for both elementary and high schools. (Copies of the CTU-CPS contracts from 1967–1995 are in the possession of the authors.)

5. State of Illinois, 89th General Assembly, House of Representatives, Transcription Debate, 68th Legislative Day (May 24, 1995), 45–46, http://ilga.gov/search/iga_results.asp?target=chicago+schools&submit1=Go&scope=hsetran89.

6. Ibid, 57–58.

7. Ibid., 60.

8. James Franczek, interviewed by Robert Bruno, April 2, 2013.

9. Lonnie Harp, *Education Week*, "Governor Signs Bill Putting Mayor in Control of Chicago Schools," June 7, 1995, http://www.edweek.org/ew/articles/1995/06/07/37ill.h14.html.

10. Franczek, interview.

11. Jacquelyn Heard, "Businesses Tell State to Boost School Funding," *Chicago Tribune*, March 21, 1995, http://articles.chicagotribune.com/1995-03-21/news/9503210081_1_basic-education-funding-civic-committee-chicago-public-schools.

12. Ann Bradley, "Daley Names Team in Takeover of Chicago Schools," *Education Week*, July 12, 1995, http://www.edweek.org/ew/articles/1995/07/12/40chic.h14.html.

13. George N. Schmidt, "Millionaire School Board Members Vote Themselves a Pay Raise," *Substance News*, March 26, 2009.

14. Linda Lenz, interviewed by Robert Bruno, June 26, 2014.

15. Franczek, interview.

16. Schools had to have at least 50 percent of their students for three years in a row fail to meet state standards on the Illinois Goals Assessment Program (IGAP) tests. The tests covered math, reading, writing, science, and social studies. School scores also needed to be declining rather than improving.

17. Franczek, interview.

18. The state law is at http://www.iga.gov/legislation/ilcs/ilcs5.asp?ActID=1005&ChapterID=17.

19. Reconstitution was a short-term school intervention plan, applied to seven low-performing high schools, which required firing all the faculty and staff members. In a study of how the schools fared, G. Alfred Hess concluded that "reconstitution did not prove to be a successful school improvement strategy." G. Alfred Hess, "Reconstitution: Three Years Later: Monitoring the Effect of Sanctions on Chicago High Schools," *Education and Urban Society* 35, no. 3 (2003): 300–327.

20. "School Overcrowding Report Issued," *Catalyst Chicago*, News Brief, Nov. 15, 1999, http://catalyst-chicago.org/2011/08/1999-news-briefs.

21. Franczek, interview.

22. Michael Martinez, "Teachers Get a Say on Fixing 12 Schools," *Chicago Tribune*, Nov. 28, 1999, http://articles.chicagotribune.com/1999-11-28/news/9911280221_1_chicago-teachers-union-re-engineering-worst-schools.

23. Ibid.

24. Joann Podkul, at the time a social studies teacher at Bowen High School and a Lynch ally, recalled the indignities a person had to endure in challenging the union leadership. While union delegates were meeting at the Bismarck Hotel, Lynch handed out campaign literature in front of the building. Podkul noted, "It was freezing cold, and they wouldn't let her inside. There she stood, looking perfect in her little high heels, and they treated her like a mutineer." Grant Pick, "Deborah Lynch and the Making of an Upset," *Catalyst Chicago*, Sept. 1, 2001, http://catalyst-chicago.org/series/2001-09-deborah-lynch/.

25. "At Issue," WBBM/WLS Radio, March 4, 2001; Greg Hinz, "Teacher Union's Leadership Fight," *Crain's Chicago Business*, April 30, 2001.

26. Lynch had been a CPS special education teacher, an adjunct university professor, and a professional development instructor; she had worked on educational issues at the AFT in Washington, earned a PhD, and helped launch and then direct the union's teacher leadership program, the Quest Center.

27. Kate Grossman, interviewed by Robert Bruno, July 11, 2013.

28. Pick, "Deborah Lynch and the Making of an Upset."

29. Jody Temkin, "What Some Teachers and Reformers Want," *Catalyst Chicago*, Sept. 1, 2001, http://catalyst-chicago.org/2005/07/what-some-teachers-and-reformers-want/.

30. Pick, "Deborah Lynch and the Making of an Upset."

31. Ibid.

32. Linda Lenz, "Lessons from Chicago," *Catalyst Chicago*, Nov. 7, 2011, http://catalyst-chicago.org/2011/11/lessons-from-chicago/.

33. Ibid.

34. "New School Board President," *Catalyst Chicago*, News Brief, June 7, 2001, http://catalyst-chicago.org/2011/08/2001-news-briefs.

35. "Exit Vallas," *Catalyst Chicago*, News Brief, June 6, 2001, http://catalyst-chicago.org/2011/08/2001-news-briefs.

36. "New Schools CEO," *Catalyst Chicago*, News Brief, June 26, 2001, http://catalyst-chicago.org/2011/08/2001-news-briefs.

37. Pick, "Deborah Lynch and the Making of an Upset."

38. Deborah Lynch Walsh, *Labor of Love: One Chicago Teacher's Experience* (New York: Writers Club Press, 2000), 166.

39. "New Budget," *Catalyst Chicago*, News Brief, June 26, 2002, http://catalyst-chicago.org/2011/08/2002-news-briefs/.

40. Dan Weissmann, "Lots of Will, Few Ways to Provide Staff Raises: A Financial and Political Analysis," *Catalyst Chicago* (Feb. 2003), 4.

41. George Schmidt, "CTU Shows New Strength at LEAD," *Substance News* 27, no. 3 (Nov. 2001): 7.

42. Lynch's meeting with House Speaker Michael Madigan pulled back the curtain on how the law would be changed. Madigan, according to Lynch, said, "If the mayor has a brick on it (i.e., the requested amendments), it doesn't move." The Speaker then picked up the phone and called the fifth floor at city hall to speak to Daley. A short time later the brick was gone, at least for the House caucus that Madigan controlled (Lynch, interview).

43. The proposed legislation failed to pass in the fall veto session of the General Assembly when CTU antagonist Senate President Pate Philip refused to let the bill be called for a vote.

44. Franczek, interview.

45. Lynch Walsh, *Labor of Love*, 146.

46. George Schmidt, "Chicago's Veteran Teachers Now Lowest Paid in Region," *Substance News* (April 2001): 9–10.

47. Dan Weissmann, "Salary Reform a Growing Rumble," *Catalyst Chicago*, July 28, 2005, 7.

48. Ibid., 6.

49. Sharon Schmidt, "Chicago's Veteran Teachers Now Lowest Paid in Region," *Substance News* 26, no. 8 (April 2001): 4.

50. Robert Bruno, *Study on the Causes of Teacher Flight from Chicago's Public Schools*, Executive Summary, unpublished manuscript, 2003.

51. Dan Weissmann, "CPS Pay Starts High, Ends Low: An Analysis of the Competition," *Catalyst Chicago*, Aug. 22, 2005, 8.

52. Jesse Sharkey, "Could Chicago Teachers Union Win More?" Socialist Worker.org, Oct. 3, 2003, http://socialistworker.org/2003-2/470/470_11_ChicagoTeachers.shtml.

53. Lori Olszewski, "Teacher Vote against Pact Also Message to Union Chief," *Chicago Tribune*, Oct. 18, 2003.

54. Ibid.

55. *Substance News* 27, no. 2 (Oct. 2001): 8.

56. Ibid.

57. Franczek, interview.

58. Kelly Quigley, "Duncan Tries to Sell CPS Health Plan," *Crain's Chicago Business*, Nov. 5, 2003.

59. Ana Beatriz Cholo, "City Teachers Spurn 1st New School Offer: Class Day, Health Plan Addressed but Not Resolved," *Chicago Tribune*, Nov. 7, 2003.

60. Lynch, interview.

61. Lori Olszewski, "New Tentative Teachers Pact," *Chicago Tribune*, Nov. 13, 2003, http://articles.chicagotribune.com/2003-11-13/news/0311130119_1_strike-vote-teachers-schools-chief-arne-duncan.

62. Lori Olszewski and Ana Beatriz Cholo, "Teacher Vote Count Goes into the Night: Tally Expected to Be Very Close on Ratification," *Chicago Tribune*, Nov. 19, 2003, http://articles.chicagotribune.com/2003-11-19/news/0311190401_1_vote-count-chicago-teachers-union-support-workers.

63. Ibid.

64. Lori Olszewski, "Crowded Field Could Force Runoff for Teachers Union," *Chicago Tribune*, May 21, 2004, http://articles.chicagotribune.com/2004-05-21/news/0405210077_1_teachers-union-contract-dispute-lynch.

65. Alexander Russo, "Gates, AUSL, & Closed Schools," *Catalyst Chicago*, Jan. 31, 2008, http://catalyst-chicago.org/2008/01/gates-ausl-closed-schools/.

66. Ibid.

67. Alexandra Bradbury et al., *How to Jump-Start Your Union: Lessons from the Chicago Teachers* (Detroit: Labor Notes, 2014), 11. What proved bad for teachers was no less traumatic for students. In a 2009 multipart exposé, *Catalyst Chicago* reported that, in Chicago, "elementary schools and high schools are suspending and expelling students at alarming rates, and African-American male students are bearing the brunt of these punishments." Black males made up 23 percent of the students but nearly twice as many of those who were suspended (44 percent) and a startling 61 percent of those who were expelled. In elementary grades, black males were being suspended at five times the rate that white males were suspended. When assessing the system's treatment of discipline problems, *Catalyst Chicago* Editor in Chief Veronica Anderson concluded that "the district's scales of justice tilt toward discrimination." Veronica Anderson, "Lopsided Discipline Takes Toll on Black Male Students," *Catalyst Chicago In Depth* 20, no. 5 (May/June 2009): 2.

68. Maureen Kelleher, "The Changing Face of CPS Teachers," *Catalyst-Chicago*, September 11, 2015, http://catalyst-chicago.org/2015/09/the-changing-face-of-cps-teachers/.

69. *The State of Teacher Diversity in American Education*, Albert Shanker Institute, September 2015, http://www.shankerinstitute.org/resource/teacherdiversity.

70. Sarah Karp and Rebecca Harris, "Bridging Differences," *Catalyst In Depth* 22, no. 2 (March 9, 2011): 6–19, 15.

71. Stephanie Banchero, "Daley School Plan Fails to Make Grade," *Chicago Tribune*, Jan. 17, 2010, http://articles.chicagotribune.com/2010-01-17/news/1001160276_1_charter-schools-chicago-reform-urban-education.

72. Ryan Blitstein, "Numbers Man," *Chicago Magazine*, July 21, 2009, http://www.chicagomag.com/Chicago-Magazine/August-2009/Numbers-Man/.

73. "What's wrong with CPS's Renaissance 2010??" *PUREPerspective*, undated, www.pureparents.org/data/files/WhatsWrong2008.pdf.

74. Lawrence W. Lezotte, "Revolutionary and Evolutionary: The Effective Schools Movement," 2001, http://www.lakeforest.edu/library/archives/effective-schools/Historyof EffectiveSchools.php.

75. In identifying the school as an agent of change and articulating jargon-free criteria of school effectiveness, the movement diverged from the teacher-blaming privatized school reform drive unfolding in Chicago. There were seven basic "correlates" of effectiveness: (1) a clearly articulated mission for the school; (2) a safe physical atmosphere; (3) a

climate of high expectations for students and staff; (4) classroom time sufficient for instruction; (5) the principal's role as the school instructional leader; (6) multiple methods of assessing academic progress, including teacher-made tests; and (7) the opportunity for parents to play an important role in helping the school achieve its mission. Ronald R. Edmonds, National Institution of Education, Teaching and Learning Program, Washington, DC, "Programs of School Improvement: An Overview" (paper presented at the National Invitational Conference, Research on Teaching: Implications for Practice, Warrenton, VA, Feb. 25–27,1982).

76. Suzanne Davenport, e-mail to Robert Bruno, March 26, 2014.

77. The deal was announced shortly after the city reached a historic ten-year agreement with building trades unions representing 8,000 members. Mayor Daley was in a very generous frame of mind because he was actively courting the International Olympic Committee to bring the 2008 Summer Games to Chicago. He anticipated starting numerous large construction projects and badly wanted to secure labor peace. In defense of the lucrative deal with the building trades that secured benefits and escalating incomes, the mayor was at his labor-ingratiating best: "There's nothing wrong with men and women earning a decent salary and prevailing wages." Fran Spielman, "Daley Not Backing Off Prevailing Wage Pact; Ten-Year Deal Placates Organized Labor, but Skirts Issue of Funding Pensions, Health Care, Budget Gap," *Chicago Sun-Times*, Aug. 8, 2007.

78. Abdon M. Pallasch and Rosalind Rossi, "Chicago's School Day Will Get Longer, Rahm Emanuel Pledges," *Chicago Sun-Times*, April 15, 2011.

79. Theresa D. Daniels, "Delegates Return to House Meeting Angry, Confused, and Threatened," *Substance News* (Nov. 2007), http://www.substancenews.net/articles. php?page=294.

80. John Myers, "Teachers Ratify 5-Year Contract," *Catalyst Chicago*, Jan. 18, 2008, http://catalyst-chicago.org/2008/01/webextra-teachers-ratify-5-year-contract/.

81. George N. Schmidt, "Final Days of Negotiations Were Key to Daley Deal . . . Stewart's Sellout," *Substance News* (May 2008), http://www.substancenews.net/articles. php?page=94.

82. Daley repeated the charge of a short school day: "We are going to be still talking to the teachers union about that because six hours a day . . . is not much." Carlos Sadovi and Gary Washburn, "Deal Reached with City Teachers," *Chicago Tribune*, Aug. 30, 2007, http://articles.chicagotribune.com/2007-08-30/news/0708291055_1_city-teachers-teachers-union-school-day.

83. Franczek, interview.

3. CHICAGO SCHOOL TEACHERS AND CORE

1. Maria Guerrero, letter to the editor, *Chicago Tribune*, Jan. 17, 2011, http://articles. chicagotribune.com/2011-01-17/opinion/ct-vp-0117voicelettersbriefs-20110117_1_ magic-pill-educational-troubles-fellow-teachers.

2. Robert Bruno, Steven Ashby, and Frank Manzo IV, *Beyond the Classroom: An Analysis of a Chicago Public School Teacher's Actual Workday*, Labor Education Program, School of Labor and Employment Relations, University of Illinois at Urbana-Champaign, April 9, 2012, https://ler.illinois.edu/?page_id=145.

3. Stand Up! Chicago and CTU, *Fight for the Future: How Low Wages Are Failing Children in Chicago's Schools*, Dec. 2012.

4. Ibid.

5. Helen L. Ladd and Edward B. Fiskedec, "Class Matters. Why Won't We Admit It?" *New York Times*, Dec. 11, 2011. Also see David C. Berliner, "Poverty and Potential: Out-of-School Factors and School Success," National Education Policy Center, Boulder, CO,

March 9, 2009; "Teaching through Trauma: How Poverty Affects Kids' Brains," KPCC Radio, June 2, 2014, http://www.scpr.org/blogs/education/2014/06/02/16743/poverty-has-been-found-to-affect-kids-brains-can-o/; Mark Santow and Richard Rothstein, *A Different Kind of Choice: Educational Inequality and the Continuing Significance of Racial Segregation*, Economic Policy Institute, Washington, DC, Aug. 2012.

6. Stephen Franklin, "Why the Chicago Teachers Won," *American Prospect*, Sept. 20, 2012, http://prospect.org/article/why-chicago-teachers-won.

7. Alex Kotlowitz, "Are We Asking Too Much from Our Teachers?" *New York Times*, Sept. 14, 2012, http://www.nytimes.com/2012/09/16/opinion/sunday/can-great-teaching-overcome-the-effects-of-poverty.html?_r=0.

8. Unpublished interview done for Bruno, Ashby, and Manzo, *Beyond the Classroom*.

9. Bruno, Ashby, and Manzo, *Beyond the Classroom*, 13.

10. Stand Up! Chicago and CTU, *Fight for the Future*.

11. Eduardo Porter, "Equation Is Simple: Education = Income," *New York Times*, Sept. 11, 2014, http://www.nytimes.com/2014/09/11/business/economy/a-simple-equation-more-education-more-income.html.

12. Unpublished interview done for Bruno, Ashby, and Manzo, *Beyond the Classroom*.

13. Also see Jesse Hagopian, editor, *More Than a Score: The New Uprising Against High-Stakes Testing* (Chicago: Haymarket Books, 2014); Kevin Russell, *The Impact of Early Childhood Testing*, CTU Report, 2013, http://www.ctunet.com/quest-center/research/Impact-of-Early-Childhood-Testing.pdf; and *Debunking the Myths of Standardized Testing: A CTU Position Paper*, CTU, 2012, http://www.ctunet.com/quest-center/research/CTU_Testing_Position_Brief_web-1.pdf.

14. Sarah Karp and Melissa Sanchez, "Conversations with Teachers: Testing," *Catalyst Chicago*, Sept. 2, 2014, http://catalyst-chicago.org/2014/09/conversations-teachers-testing/.

15. Unpublished interview done for Bruno, Ashby, and Manzo, *Beyond the Classroom*.

16. Ibid.

17. Bruno, Ashby, and Manzo, *Beyond the Classroom*, 13.

18. "CTU Analysis Shows Chicago's School Class Sizes Are among the Highest in the State," CTU analysis, http://www.ctunet.com/media/press-releases/ctu-analysis-shows-chicagos-school-class-sizes-are-among-the-highest-in-the-state.

19. Ben Joravsky, "The School Model That's Good Enough for President Obama and Mayor Emanuel," *Chicago Reader*, May 7, 2013, http://www.chicagoreader.com/chicago/uofc-university-lab-schools-respect-teachers-ucls/Content?oid=9579479.

20. Bruno, Ashby, and Manzo, *Beyond the Classroom*, 10

21. Dana Markow and Andrea Pieters, *The MetLife Survey of the American Teacher: Teachers, Parents, and the Economy*, March 2012, http://files.eric.ed.gov/fulltext/ED530021.pdf.

22. Richard M. Ingersoll, "Beginning Teacher Induction: What the Data Tell Us," *Education* Week, May 16, 2012, http://www.edweek.org/ew/articles/2012/05/16/kappan_ingersoll.h31.html.

23. Elaine Allensworth, "Teacher Performance in the Context of Truly Disadvantaged Schools in Chicago," *Issues of Voices in Urban Education* (Fall 2011): 36–43; Lorraine Forte, "Slowing the Revolving Door," *Catalyst Chicago*, May 17, 2014, http://catalyst-chicago.org/2014/05/slowing-revolving-door/.

24. Sarah Karp, "At Turnarounds, a Revolving Door for Most Teachers," *Catalyst Chicago*, April 17, 2014, http://catalyst-chicago.org/2014/04/turnarounds-revolving-door-most-teachers/.

25. Sarah Karp and Melissa Sanchez, "Conversations with Teachers: Evaluations," *Catalyst Chicago*, Sept. 3, 2012, http://catalyst-chicago.org/2014/09/conversations-teachers-evaluations/.

26. Bruno, Ashby, and Manzo, *Beyond the Classroom*, 21.

27. Abdon M. Pallasch and Rosalind Rossi, "Chicago's School Day Will Get Longer, Rahm Emanuel Pledges," *Chicago Sun-Times*, April 15, 2011.

28. The average nationally is 6 hours and 38 minutes. Sara Neufeld, "A Longer School Day in Chicago, but with What Missing?" *Hechinger Report*, Jan. 21, 2014. Also see n.a., "Chicago Public Schools Recess: District Offers Guidelines for Bringing It Back," Huffington Post, May 24, 2011, http://www.huffingtonpost.com/2011/05/24/chicago-public-schools-re_n_866101.html; and Rosalind Rossi, "CPS Gives Recess Advocates a Victory," *Chicago Sun-Times*, May 23, 2011.

29. Neufeld, "A Longer School Day in Chicago."

30. David Schaper, "The Lasting Impact of the September 2012 Chicago Teachers Strike," National Public Radio website, March 3, 2014, http://www.npr.org/2012/04/23/151047543/chicago-wants-longer-school-day-foes-want-details.

31. *White Paper on Chicago Public Schools' Extended Day Proposal: The Best Education, or Just the Longest?*, Chicago Parents for Quality Education, April 9, 2012, http://blogs.chicagotribune.com/files/best-not-longest-final.pdf.

32. Ibid.

33. Bruno, Ashby, and Manzo, *Beyond the Classroom*, 18.

34. Ibid, 14.

35. Ibid, 16.

36. Stephanie Simon, "Special Report: Class Struggle—How Charter Schools Get Students They Want," Reuters, Feb. 13, 2013, http://www.reuters.com/article/us-usa-charters-admissions-idUSBRE91E0HF20130215. Reuters notes, "There are now more than 6,000 charter schools in the United States, up from 2,500 a decade ago, educating a record 2.3 million children."

37. Noreen S. Ahmed-Ullah and Alex Richards, "CPS: Expulsion Rate Higher at Charter Schools," *Chicago Tribune*, Feb. 26, 2014, http://articles.chicagotribune.com/2014-02-26/news/ct-chicago-schools-discipline-met-20140226_1_charter-schools-andrew-broy-district-run-schools.

38. "How to Analyze False Claims about Charter Schools," *Diane Ravitch Blog*, Feb. 28, 2014, http://dianeravitch.net/2014/02/28/how-to-analyze-false-claims-about-charter-schools/.

39. Unpublished interview done for Bruno, Ashby, and Manzo, *Beyond the Classroom*.

40. Becky Vevea, Linda Lutton, and Sarah Karp, "The History of School Closings in Chicago 2002–12," WBEZ Radio, Jan. 16, 2013.

41. After tens of thousands of parents attended scores of hearings, CPS closed forty-nine schools, the largest single school-closing action in US history. See Noreen S. Ahmed-Ullah, John Chase, and Bob Secter, "CPS Approves Largest School Closure in Chicago's History," *Chicago Tribune*, May 23, 2013, http://articles.chicagotribune.com/2013-05-23/news/chi-chicago-school-closings-20130522_1_chicago-teachers-union-byrd-bennett-one-high-school-program.

42. Mary Wisniewski, "Chicago Teachers Fear Wave of School Closings after Strike," Reuters, Sept. 15, 2012, http://in.reuters.com/article/usa-chicago-schools-closing-idINL1E8KF03T20120915.

43. Anonymous interviews, Interviewee "MP1," *Sea of Red* interviews. The authors are grateful for the transcripts shared from thirty-seven interviews that were conducted in researching the *Sea of Red* report; the names of interview subjects were kept anonymous. Sean Noonan, Stephanie Farmer, and Fran Huckaby, *Sea of Red: Chicago Teachers Union Members Reflect on How the Social Organizing Model of Unionism Helped Win the Union's 2012 Contract Campaign*, CTU, Feb. 2014, http://www.ctunet.com/research/a-sea-of-red.

44. Noreen S. Ahmed-Ullah, "CPS: Poorer-Performing Schools Less Likely to Get Funds," *Chicago Tribune*, Dec. 15, 2011, http://articles.chicagotribune.com/2011-12-15/news/ct-met-cps-buildings-20111215_1_urban-school-leadership-cps-operating-officer-tim-cawley.

45. Carol Caref et al., *The Black and White of Education in Chicago's Public Schools*, CTU, Nov. 2012, http://www.ctunet.com/quest-center/research/black-and-white-of-chicago-education.pdf.

46. Noonan, Farmer, and Huckaby, *Sea of Red* interviews, Interviewee "PP2."

47. Caref et al., *Black and White of Education*.

48. Ben Joravsky, "Public Schools, Private Budgets," *Chicago Reader*, July 21, 2011.

49. CTU bylaws stated that charter teachers, whose direct employers were charter owners and not CPS, could not be members of the CTU, and state law held that unionized charter teachers had to have a separate CPS contract from the CTU.

50. Karp and Sanchez, "Conversations with Teachers: Testing."

51. Rob Heise, interviewed by Steven Ashby, Sept. 2014.

52. Tim Novak and Chris Fusco, "Inside Bruce Rauner's Charter Schools," *Chicago Sun-Times*, Feb. 4, 2014, http://chicago.suntimes.com/uncategorized/7/71/158113/inside-bruce-rauners-charter-schools. Also see Anastasia Ustinova, "Charter-School Growth Fuels Chicago Teacher Fears," *Bloomberg News*, Sept. 12, 2012, http://www.bloomberg.com/news/articles/2012-09-13/charter-school-growth-fuels-chicago-teacher-fears.

53. Caref et al., *Black and White of Education*.

54. Illinois Network of Charter Schools, accessed Dec. 2014, http://incschools.org/charters/charter-school-data-finder/data-illinois-charter-overview/comparative_teacher_and_staff_compensation_data; and Caref et al., *Black and White of Education*.

55. Sarah Karp, "Many Chicago Charter Schools Run Deficits, Data Shows," *New York Times*, Aug. 13, 2010, http://www.nytimes.com/2010/08/13/us/13cnccharters.html.

56. Heise, interview.

57. Chris Baehrend, interviewed by Steven Ashby, Sept. 2014.

58. These salary increases are referred to as "steps and lanes." *Steps* refer to how many years a teacher has taught, and *lanes* refer to the level of education the teacher has attained.

59. Cassie Walker Burke, "The Rise and Fall of Juan Rangel, the *Patrón* of Chicago's UNO Charter Schools," *Chicago Magazine*, Jan. 8, 2014, http://www.chicagomag.com/Chicago-Magazine/February-2014/uno-juan-rangel/.

60. Ben Joravsky, "Fighting for the Right to Fire Bad Teachers—and Good Ones Too," *Chicago Reader*, Sept. 26, 2012, http://www.chicagoreader.com/chicago/uno-charter-school-fires-teacher-without-hearing/Content?oid=7514850.

61. Joel Bleifuss, "Charter Schools: The Promise and the Peril," *In These Times*, April 10, 2013, http://inthesetimes.com/article/16401/charter_schools_the_promise_and_the_peril.

62. Jim Vail, "Aspira [*sic*] Whistle Blower Teacher Was Fired, CPS Covered Up Aspira Corruption . . . Who Is Holding Chicago's Charter Schools Accountable for Anything?" *Substance News*, June 24, 2009.

63. Rosalind Rossi, "Mom: I Don't Send My Kids to School to Be Strip Searched," *Chicago Sun-Times*, Jan. 7, 2009.

64. Independent journalist Ben Joravsky also covered a story that occurred at a UNO school in November 2009 prior to unionization. Gym teacher David Corral reported a mock rape of a boy in the locker room. At first the school director praised Corral, but, within days, he was fired by UNO CEO Juan Rangel, who heard about the incident while vacationing in Mexico. Without a union, there was no grievance procedure to ensure due process. The gym teacher was an at-will employee, so he could be fired without explanation or justification and was made a scapegoat because the boss was embarrassed that the sexual assault happened. Corral filed a lawsuit under whistle-blower protections for

reporting sexual assault, UNO failed to get a federal judge to dismiss it, and, in June 2014, UNO paid Corral $150,000 to settle the case. Joravsky, "Fighting for the Right to Fire Bad Teachers," and Dan Mihalopoulos, "UNO Charter Schools Paid Fired Teacher $150K to Settle Case, Records Show," *Chicago Sun-Times*, May 12, 2014.

65. This quotation appeared in the Comments section of Susan Volbrecht, "Don't Put Down Teachers Who Choose Charters," *Catalyst Chicago*, March 3, 2014. The Chicago ACTS union AFT Local 2323 had it easier when the law held that they were public education employees, and, under the IELRA, to get a union they needed only to turn in membership cards signed by a majority of a charter school's staff. When UNO CEO Juan Rangel—who was Rahm Emanuel's 2011 mayoral campaign cochair—was exposed for corruption and nepotism, he tried to rescue his job and his organization by agreeing not to fight the union at UNO's sixteen schools, which had about 7,600 students. Eighty-seven percent of the staff rapidly signed union cards, and the union was recognized. But in January 2013 the National Labor Relations Board (NLRB) held that all charter school staff were private-sector employees, and therefore that charter school unions must go through the process of an NLRB-sponsored election, giving the employer time to threaten and intimidate staff into opposing the union.

66. 1980: 10-day strike; 1983: 15-day strike; 1984: 10-day strike; 1985: 2-day strike; 1987: 19-day strike. The union struck nine times between 1969 and 1987.

67. "Union Leader Jacqueline Vaughn" (obituary), *Chicago Tribune*, Jan. 23, 1994. The first UPC president of the CTU was Robert Healey, who left union office in 1984—thus leading to his vice president Jackie Vaughn's becoming president. In 1987, he became the secretary-treasurer of the Chicago Federation of Labor (CFL).

68. In the June 2004 election, Marilyn Stewart received 11,566 votes (51.1%) and Deborah Lynch received 11,006. In the June 2007 election, Stewart received 15,734 votes (75.6%) and Lynch received 5,036 votes.

69. *Sea of Red* interviews, Interviewee "AV3."

70. *Sea of Red* interviews, Interviewee "AP1."

71. *Sea of Red* interviews, Interviewees "AV3," "AV9," "WA1," and "Ella."

72. Jackson Potter, interviewed by Steven Ashby, March 2013.

73. "A Cauldron of Opposition in Duncan's Hometown: Rank-and-File Teachers Score Huge Victory," *Rethinking Schools* (Fall 2010), http://www.rethinkingschools.org/archive/25_01/25_01_petersonsokolower.shtml.

74. Jackson Potter, interview.

75. "A Cauldron of Opposition."

76. Among Pauline Lipman's books are *The New Political Economy of Urban Education: Neoliberalism, Race, and the Right to the City* (New York: Routledge, 2011); *High Stakes Education: Inequality, Globalization, and Urban School Reform* (New York: Routledge, 2004); and *Race, Class, and Power in School Restructuring* (Albany: State University of New York Press, 1998).

77. For further details on the formation of CORE, see "Rank and Filers Start Doing the Union's Job," in Alexandra Bradbury et al., *How to Jump-Start Your Union: Lessons from the Chicago Teachers* (Detroit: Labor Notes, 2014); Micah Uetricht, *Strike for America: Chicago Teachers against Austerity* (Brooklyn, NY: Verso Press, 2013), 17–37.

78. Jen Johnson, talk given at the "Lessons from the Chicago Teachers' Strike" forum, sponsored by the Chicago branch of Solidarity, Chicago, Sept. 29, 2012, http://www.solidarity-us.org/site/node/3707.

79. "A Cauldron of Opposition."

80. Anthony Cody, "Chicago Strike Lessons: Teacher Activists Explain How It Was Done," *Education Week Teacher*, Sept. 24, 2013, http://blogs.edweek.org/teachers/living-in-dialogue/2012/09/chicago_strike_lessons_teacher.html.

81. "A Cauldron of Opposition."

82. Jody Sokolower, "Lessons in Social Justice Unionism: An Interview with Chicago Teachers Union President Karen Lewis," *Rethinking Schools* 27, no. 2 (Winter 2012–13), http://www.rethinkingschools.org/archive/27_02/27_02_sokolower.shtml.

83. *Sea of Red* interviews, Interviewee "PP1."

84. *Sea of Red* interviews, Interviewee "LS3A."

85. "A Cauldron of Opposition."

86. Jen Johnson, talk at "Lessons from the Chicago Teachers' Strike."

87. Ibid.

88. Paul Abowd, "Teacher Reformers Prepare for Battle over Public Education," *Labor Notes*, Sept. 9, 2009.

89. "A Cauldron of Opposition"; and Jen Johnson, talk at "Lessons from the Chicago Teachers' Strike."

90. At a June 2009 CORE conference, Karen Lewis and Jackson Potter were elected CORE cochairs. Chosen for the Steering Committee were Kenzo Shibata, Carol Caref, Jennifer Johnson, Lois Ashford, Norine Gutekanst, Kristine Mayle, and Jesse Sharkey.

91. Ben Goldberger, "Karen Lewis: Street Fighter," *Chicago Magazine*, Oct. 2012, http://www.chicagomag.com/Chicago-Magazine/November-2012/Karen-Lewis-Street-Fighter/. Also see "CTU President Karen Lewis' Address before the City Club of Chicago: 'On Baseball & Budgets,'" CTU press release, June 18, 2013.

92. Lisa Furlong, "Karen (Jennings) Lewis '74," *Dartmouth Alumni Magazine*, May/June 2011, http://dartmouthalumnimagazine.com/articles/karen-jennings-lewis-%E2%80%9974.

93. Karen Lewis, "CORE's Coming Out Party," *Jacobin* magazine, Apr. 7, 2014, https://www.jacobinmag.com/2014/04/cores-coming-out-party/

94. Ibid.

95. Ibid.

96. Ibid.

97. For a detailed discussion of CORE's election campaign, see "The Caucus Runs for Office" in Bradbury et al., *How to Jump-Start Your Union*.

98. Nate Goldbaum, "Thousands Jam Loop Streets Protesting Attacks on Public Schools, Board of Education Budget Cuts," *Substance News*, May 26, 2010.

99. In the first round PACT won 18.2%, SEA 6.2%, and CSDU 3.1%. In the runoff CORE not only won the top four offices in the union but also the other nine citywide offices and all six of the vice presidencies for high schools and elementary schools.

100. Lee Sustar, "Winds of Change in Chicago," posted by Hyde Park Johnny at *Daily Kos*, June 10, 2010, http://www.dailykos.com/storyonly/2010/6/10/870687/-Winds-of-Change-in-Chicago.

101. Lee Sustar, "A New Day in the Chicago Teachers Union," *Socialist Worker*, June 14, 2010, https://socialistworker.org/2010/06/14/new-day-for-chicago-teachers.

102. Bradbury et al., *How to Jump-Start Your Union*, 45.

103. *Sea of Red* interviews, Interviewee "IN3."

104. "Karen Lewis Election Victory Press Conference," Labor Beat videos, June 12, 2010, http://www.youtube.com/watch?v=42TtWpO9vf0; and Sustar, "A New Day in the Chicago Teachers Union."

105. Emanuel won 59% of the wards in black neighborhoods, 59% of the white wards, 38% of the Latino wards, and 55% of "mixed" wards in the 2011 election (Angela Caputo, "Voters in Black Wards Supported Rahm More than All Other Candidates Combined," *Chicago Reporter*, Feb. 23, 2011). The 2010 census showed that Chicago had a population of 2.7 million, with a racial breakdown of 32.4% African-American, 31.7% white, and 28.9% Hispanic or Latino.

106. For a biography of Rahm Emanuel, see Kari Lydersen, *Mayor 1%: Rahm Emanuel and the Rise of Chicago's 99%* (Chicago: Haymarket Books, 2014).

107. In addition to Teamsters Joint Council 25, Ironworkers Local 63, Plumbers Local 130, and Bricklayers District Council 1 endorsed Emanuel in 2011.

108. "Emanuel Education Platform—Speech, Policy Paper," *Chicago Sun-Times*, Dec. 13, 2010, http://blogs.suntimes.com/sweet/2010/12/emanuel_education_platform_spe.html.

109. Peter Baker and Jeff Zeleny, "Emanuel Wields Power Freely, and Faces the Risks," *New York Times*, Aug. 15, 2009, http://www.nytimes.com/2009/08/16/us/politics/16emanuel.html?pagewanted=all.

110. Mark Karlin, "The Rise of Chicago's 99% against Rahm Emanuel, Mayor 1%," *Truthout*, Nov. 5, 2013, http://www.truth-out.org/opinion/item/19810-the-rise-of-chicagos-99-against-rahm-emanuel-mayor-1.

111. Joe Nocera, "In Chicago, It's a Mess, All Right," *New York Times*, Sept. 10, 2012, http://www.nytimes.com/2012/09/11/opinion/nocera-in-chicago-its-a-mess-all-right.html.

4. EVALUATING TEACHERS AND POLITICAL OPPORTUNISM

1. "A 'Burnham Plan' for Schools," *Chicago Tribune*, May 21, 2007, http://articles.chicagotribune.com/2007-05-21/news/0705200335_1_student-outcomes-school-funding-proposal-induction-programs.

2. Education Policy Planning Committee of the Whole, Wednesday, June 20, 2007, http://www.isbe.state.il.us/board/meetings/2007/june07/eppc.pdf, 1.

3. Naomi Klein, *The Shock Doctrine: The Rise of Disaster Capitalism* (New York: Picador, 2008).

4. Darren Reisberg, interviewed by Robert Bruno, Aug. 14, 2013.

5. Ibid.

6. Daniel Weisberg et al., *The Widget Effect: Our National Failure to Acknowledge and Act on Differences in Teacher Effectiveness*, 2nd ed. (Washington, D.C.: New Teacher Project, 2009); quoted in Elliot Regenstein, "Illinois: The New Leader in Education Reform?" *Center for American Progress*, July 2011, https://www.americanprogress.org/issues/education/report/2011/07/13/9977/illinois-the-new-leader-in-education-reform/.

7. Regenstein, "Illinois: The New Leader," 4.

8. Weisberg et al., *The Widget Effect*, 2.

9. Ibid., 30.

10. Steven Tourkin et al., *Documentation for the 2007–08 Schools and Staffing Survey*, Appendix J, "Focus Group Findings and Recommendations: Principals' Attitudes toward Teacher Evaluation and Dismissal," US Department of Education, Washington D.C. 2010, http://nces.ed.gov/pubs2010/2010332_4.pdf.

11. National Center for Education Statistics (NCES) Symposium on Data Issues in Teacher Supply and Demand, Washington, D.C., March 26, 2007; Michael Long, *Teacher Dismissals: A Review of the Literature and Thoughts for the Future*, paper prepared for the Teacher Supply and Demand Symposium for NCES, and with support from NCES and the American Institutes for Research, paper available by contacting NCES https://nces.ed.gov/whatsnew/commissioner/remarks2007/06_20_2007.asp; Joan Baratz-Snowden, Education Study Center, "Fixing Tenure: A Proposal for Assuring Teacher Effectiveness and Due Process," paper prepared for the Center for American Progress, (June 2009), 29, n. 4, http://www.americanprogress.org/issues/2009/06/pdf/teacher_tenure.

12. The Illinois panel also included Cordelia (Dea) Meyer, executive vice president of the antiunion and pro–charter school Civic Committee of the Commercial

Club of Chicago, as well as attorney Charles P. Rose from Franczek Sullivan P.C. The panel, however, had no one from the IFT or CTU. See http://widgeteffect.org/panel-members/.

13. Weisberg et al., *The Widget Effect*, http://widgeteffect.org/panel-responses/.

14. Liza Featherstone, "Empowerment against Democracy: Tinseltown and the Teachers' Unions," *Dissent: A Quarterly of Politics and Culture* (Sept. 26, 2012), https://www.dissentmagazine.org/tag/education-reform. A large empirical study also revealed that unions raise the dismissal rate of "underperforming" teachers and lower the quit rate of "high ability" teachers. Eunice Han, "The Myth of Unions' Overprotection of Bad Teachers: Evidence from the District-Teacher Matched Panel Data on Teacher Turnover," National Bureau of Economic Research, Labor Studies Working Group Paper, 2016, www.nber.org/confer/2016/LSs16/Han.pdf.

15. Weisberg et al., *The Widget Effect*, http://widgeteffect.org/panel-responses/.

16. Ibid., 29.

17. Jonathan Baron and M. F. Norman, "SATs, Achievement Tests, and High-School Class Rank as Predictors of College Performance," *Educational and Psychology Measurement*, 52 (1992): 1047–55.

18. Reisberg, interview.

19. Mitchell Roth, interview by Robert Bruno, Aug. 27, 2013.

20. Mitchell Roth, "SB 7: A Union Perspective," *Illinois Public Employee Relations Report* 29, no. 2 (Spring 2012).

21. Audrey Soglin, interview by Robert Bruno, Aug. 27, 2013.

22. Regenstein, "Illinois: The New Leader?" 6.

23. Soglin, interview.

24. Roth, "SB 7: A Union Perspective."

25. Robin Steans, interviewed by Robert Bruno, July 2, 2013.

26. Roth, "SB 7: A Union Perspective."

27. Steans, interview.

28. Advance Illinois "History and Mission," http://www.advanceillinois.org/about-us/mission-history/.

29. Ibid.

30. Reisberg, interview.

31. Ibid.

32. Ibid.

33. Ibid.

34. "Stand Up to the Fat Cats," posted by Move Chicago Schools Forward and the CTU, Dec. 9, 2012, http://www.youtube.com/watch?v=g1eV8EHII5Q.

35. In Colorado, Stand for Children had "aggressively pushed through legislation making significant changes to teacher tenure, dismissal and layoffs." The parent organization was also operating in Arizona, Massachusetts, Indiana, Washington, Tennessee, and Texas. In each state, its actions were heavy-handed and backed by hefty political contributions. Roth, "SB 7: A Union Perspective."

36. "A Fiscal Rehabilitation Plan for the State of Illinois: An Analysis of the State's Fiscal Crisis and Actionable Recommendations for Governor Pat Quinn and the Illinois General Assembly," Institute for Fiscal Sustainability at the Civic Federation, Feb. 22, 2010, http://www.civicfed.org/sites/default/files/IllinoisFiscalRehabilitationPlan.pdf.

37. Ibid., 42.

38. Jamey Dunn, "Pension Reform Bill Passes Both Chambers," *Capitol Fax*, March 24, 2010, http://illinoisissuesblog.blogspot.com/2010/03/pension-reform-passes-both-chambers.html.

39. Shahien Nasiripour, "Illinois Pension Reform: Legislature Approves Massive Overhaul," Huffington Post, May 25, 2010, http://www.huffingtonpost.com/2010/03/25/illinois-pension-reform-l_n_513174.html.

40. National Institute on Money in State Politics, *Follow the Money*, http://www.followthemoney.org/database/StateGlance/state_contributors.phtml?s=IL&y=2008.

41. The PAC is officially called the Friends of Michael J. Madigan.

42. Quote on Ken Griffin from Rich Miller, "Rauner and Madigan," *Capitol Fax*, Nov. 25, 2013, http://capitolfax.com/2013/11/25/rauner-and-madigan/.

43. Rich Miller, "How Stand for Children Snuck into the Statehouse," *Illinois Times*, July 21, 2011, illinoistimes.com/article-8899-how-stand-for-children-snuck-into-the-statehouse.html.

44. Education and Society Panel, Aspen Institute Speech, http://www.youtube.com/watch?v=kog8g9sTDSo.

45. Education and Society Panel, Aspen Ideas Festival, June 27–July 3, 2011, http://www.youtube.com/watch?v=kog8g9sTDSo.

46. Rich Miller, "Who Are You and What Do You Want?" *Capitol Fax*, Oct. 18, 2010, capitolfax.com/2010/10/18/who-are-you-and-what-do-you-want.

47. "Stand for Children Raises $3 Million," *Catalyst Chicago*, April 12, 2011; National Institute on Money in State Politics, *Follow the Money*, http://www.followthemoney.org/database/StateGlance/state_contributors.phtml?s=IL&y=2008; Rich Miller, "Stand for Children has Wealthiest PAC in Illinois," *Capitol Fax*, Jan. 24, 2011, http://capitolfax.com/2011/01/24/stand-for-children-has-wealthiest-pac-in-illinois. "Non-leadership" refers to state representatives who do not hold a leadership position like Senate president.

48. Miller, "Stand for Children."

5. SENATE BILL 7

1. Information about Maywood can be found at http://www.maywood-il.org/Community/Our-History.aspx.

2. George N. Schmidt, "Illinois Governor Pat Quinn Signs 'School Reform' Law (SB7) At Huge Media Event," *Substance News*, June 13, 2011.

3. Kerry Lester, "Testing Teachers," *Illinois Issues*, April 5, 2014.

4. Rich Miller, "Stand for Children Has Wealthiest PAC in Illinois," *Capitol Fax*, Jan. 24, 2011, http://capitolfax.com/2011/01/24/stand-for-children-has-wealthiest-pac-in-illinois/.

5. Mitchell Roth, "SB 7: A Union Perspective, *Illinois Public Employee Relations Report* 29, no. 2 (Spring 2012):1–42.

6. Civic Committee, Commercial Club of Chicago, *Left Behind: Student Achievement in Chicago's Public Schools*, July 2003, http://civiccommittee.org.

7. "School Reform Bill Needs Teacher Input," *Chicago Sun-Times*, Dec. 15, 2010, http://www.ibhe.org/NewsDigest/NewsWeekly/121610.pdf, 52.

8. Education and Society Panel, Aspen Ideas Festival, June 27–July 3, 2011, http://www.youtube.com/watch?v=kog8g9sTDSo.

9. Mitchell Roth, interviewed by Robert Bruno, Aug. 27, 2013.

10. Miller, "Stand for Children has Wealthiest PAC in Illinois."

11. Kimberly Lightford, interviewed by Robert Bruno, Sept. 9, 2013.

12. Ibid.

13. Ibid.

14. Jessica Handy, interviewed by Robert Bruno, April 2, 2013.

15. Ibid.

16. Stephanie Banchero, "Illinois Attempts to Link Teacher Tenure to Results," *Wall Street Journal*, Jan. 4, 2011, http://www.wsj.com/articles/SB10001424052748704111504576060122295287678.

17. Roth, "SB 7: A Union Perspective."

18. Lightford's notes reveal that negotiating the Reduction In Force language was "complicated by pending litigation" between the Chicago school board and the union over the dismissal of more than 1,000 teachers in the summer of 2010. She penned in the margins of her session notes, "Let courts decide."

19. To be exact, as Mitchell Roth explained, teachers in Illinois did not actually earn tenure. What they earned was "contractual continued service," commonly called "tenure," under the state school code. Roth, "SB 7: A Union Perspective."

20. Ibid.

21. George Schmidt, "From Houston's 'Four More Years' to Houston's 'Three More Years' to Hours and . . . CPS and Rahm's Lies about 'Longer School Day' Have Evolved since They Were First Spouted Last Spring," *Substance News*, Sept. 28, 2011, http://www.substancenews.net/articles.php?page=2643.

22. Beth Swanson, interviewed by Robert Bruno, June 17, 2013.

23. James Franczek, interviewed by Robert Bruno, April 2, 2013.

24. *Agreement Between the Chicago Public Schools and the Chicago Teachers Union*, June 10, 2003, http://www.nctq.org/docs/4-05.pdf.

25. Franczek, interview.

26. Robert Bloch, interviewed by Robert Bruno, May 1, 2014.

27. *Application for New Grants under the Teacher Incentive Fund Program*, CFDA #84.385APA/Award #S385A100127 (Washington, DC: US Department of Education), June 1, 2010.

28. Ibid., Abstract.

29. Ibid., 11.

30. Karen Lewis, interviewed by Robert Bruno, March 12, 2013.

31. Stephanie Gadlin, "CTU President Calls for Inspector General Investigation into CPS' Fraudulent Use of $35 Million Federal Grant," CTU Press Release, May 31, 2012, http://www.ctunet.com/blog/ctu-president-calls-for-inspector-general-investigation-into-cps-fraudulent-use-of-35-million-federal-grant.

32. Roth, "SB 7: A Union Perspective."

33. Ibid.

34. Jonah Edelman spoke on the Education and Society Panel at the Aspen Ideas Festival, June 27–July 3, 2011; complete transcript of talk at http://www.substancenews.net/articles.php?page=2917.

35. In 2016, the state's largest public employees union, AFSCME Council 31, was engaged in a very hostile bargaining relationship with Governor Bruce Rauner. AFSCME believed that the governor had no intention of negotiating a deal and was actually trying to force the union to go on strike. In this situation, it took the unusual step of lobbying for an interest arbitration bill to settle the contract dispute. The bill passed the General Assembly but was vetoed by the governor, and later his veto was sustained by two votes.

36. Martin H. Malin, "Two Models of Interest Arbitration," *Ohio State Journal on Dispute Resolution* 28 (Jan. 14, 2013): 145–169; http://ssrn.com/abstract=2200502.

37. Roth, "SB 7: A Union Perspective."

38. Ibid.

39. Jessica Handy, interviewed by Robert Bruno, June 10, 2013.

40. Dan Montgomery, interviewed by Robert Bruno, Oct. 28, 2013.

41. Roth, SB 7: A Union Perspective."

42. Joy Resmovitz, "Illinois Education Reform Bill Passes with Union Support, for the Most Part," Huffington Post, May 13, 2011, http://www.huffingtonpost.com/2011/05/13/illinois-education-reform_n_861806.html.

43. Audrey Soglin, interviewed by Robert Bruno, Aug. 27, 2013.

44. Fred Klonsky, "Is Audrey Soglin a Bully? The IEA General Counsel Writes Me a Letter," June 13, 2012, http://preaprez.wordpress.com/2012/06/13/is-audrey-soglin-a-bully-the-iea-general-counsel-writes-me-a-letter-ui/.

45. Ibid.

46. Lee Sustar, "CORE Facing Internal Dissent over Response to Union-Busting Legislation in Illinois . . . A Crisis for Teacher Union Reformers?" *Substance News*, April 22, 2011.

47. "Senate Bill 7, Letter from President Lewis," *CTU Blog*, April 14, 2011, http://www.ctunet.com/blog/sb7letter.

48. Sustar, "CORE Facing Internal Dissent."

49. *Chicago Teachers Union Governing Body Supports Changes to SB7*, CTU Press Release, May 5, 2011, http://www.ctunet.com/blog/press-release-chicago-teachers-union-governing-body-supports-changes-to-sb7.

50. Karen Lewis, "President's Message," *Chicago Union Teacher* 74, no. 7 (May 2011): 3.

51. *Chicago Teachers Union Governing Body Supports Changes to SB7*.

52. Ibid.

53. Roth, "SB 7: A Union Perspective."

54. *Chicago Teachers Union Governing Body Supports Changes to SB7*.

55. Rich Miller, *Capitol Fax*, May 6, 2011, http://capitolfax.com/wp-mobile.php?p=13598&more=1.

56. Illinois General Assembly, Amendment to House Bill 1197, Senate Amendment 1, Senator Kimberly Lightford, filed May 24, 2011, http://www.ilga.gov.

57. "SB7's Trailer Bill Passes Senate Education Committee," *CTU Blog*, May 25, 2011, http://www.ctunet.com/blog/sb7s-trailer-bill-passes-senate-education-committee.

58. "Legislators Address Teachers Union Objections to Bill on Strike Rights, Tenure," *Catalyst Chicago*, May 25, 2011, http://catalyst-chicago.org/2011/05/legislators-address-teachers-union-objections-bill-strike-rights-tenure/.

59. Abdon M. Pallasch and Rosalind Rossi, "Chicago's School Day Will Get Longer, Rahm Emanuel Pledges," *Chicago Sun-Times*, April 15, 2011.

60. Karen Lewis comments at the Labor and Employment Relations Association, Annual Meeting, Saint Louis, June 7, 2013.

6. THE CONTRACT CAMPAIGN

1. Sea of Red interviews, Interviewee "AV6."

2. Sea of Red interviews, Interviewee "PP5."

3. Jackson Potter, "Reformers in Chicago Teachers Union Grapple with Leadership Challenges," Labor Notes, Jan. 13, 2011, http://labornotes.org/2011/01/reformers-chicago-teachers-union-grapple-leadership-challenges.

4. Norine Gutekanst, interviewed by Steven Ashby, March 13, 2014. Organizer Matt Luskin is credited with initiating the discussion about this issue in the union's Organizing Department and with the officers.

5. Sarah Chambers, "Building Power from the Bottom Up: How CTU Members Transformed Their Union," Chicago Teachers Solidarity Campaign poststrike forum cosponsored with the CTU, Oct. 20, 2012, https://www.youtube.com/watch?v=usw6g Ce3EWg, transcription by Steven Ashby. Chambers's comments were made in the discussion after her speech. Also see Kati Gilson, "Explaining to Students Why Unions Matter," *Chicago Union Teacher*, June 2011, 13.

6. In Feb. 2012, 65 workers at Serious Materials (formerly Republic Windows and Doors) occupied their plant for a second time to fight against its closing; the first occupation took place in Dec. 2008 and galvanized the city, with a thousand supporters picketing

downtown in a weekday rally called on short notice. For the 2012 reoccupation of the plant, scores of union, community, student, Occupy Chicago, and CTU members quickly gathered outside the plant to show their solidarity and donate food, and Occupy members put up tents outside the occupied factory. The workers won management's agreement to a 60-day period during which the plant would remain open while the United Electrical union sought a new buyer or capital that would enable the workers to run the factory themselves.

7. Labor Notes was formed in 1979 "to be the voice of union activists who want to put the movement back in the labor movement. Through our magazine, website, books, conferences and workshops, we promote organizing, aggressive strategies to fight concessions, alliances with workers' centers, and unions that are run by their members." In addition to holding biannual conferences, the organization publishes a monthly magazine and books. Its 2014 book *How to Jump-Start Your Union: Lessons from the Chicago Teachers* is cited in these notes.

8. Cynthia Smith, interviewed by Howard Ryan, shared with the authors, Sept. 9, 2012. Smith was a CTU district supervisor.

9. A member's salary was set at the level the member had earned as a CPS employee, prorated to twelve months. According to *Substance News*, the 2009 salaries of the top CTU officers, led by President Marilyn Stewart, ranged from $170,000 to $183,000, and Stewart also received $95,000 as an officer of the IFT. CTU field representatives who handled grievances, in addition to average 2009 pay of $140,000, had "a $240 per month cell phone allowance, a $1,000 per month car allowance, 85% reimbursement for car expenses and a 21 percent annuity on top of their regular teacher pension plan." Jim Vail, "Teacher Union Aims to Cut Perks," *Substance News*, Feb. 9, 2011.

10. Because all CPS public schools were organized by CTU, the union's organizing department was not focused on nonunion sites but on the education and organizing of existing members, community outreach, and planning public actions. ACTS, an AFT affiliate like the CTU, organized nonunion charter schools in Chicago. See the ACTS website at http://www.chicagoacts.org/.

11. *Meeting Challenges, Past and Present* video, http://www.ctunet.com/media/video or http://vimeo.com/22625871?ab. The video was produced with the technical assistance of the local CAN TV public television station, an independent nonprofit established by the City of Chicago in 1983 as "the public's space on cable television free of commercials, filters, and censors."

12. Matt Luskin, interviewed by Steven Ashby, March 2014.

13. According to the CTU Constitution, "One Delegate shall be elected for the first twenty regular members. An additional Associate Delegate shall be elected for every forty regular members thereafter in a particular school. Schools with less than twenty members shall be combined to form representational units." The *Chicago Union Teacher* printed, at the back of each issue, the names of delegates who did not attend the previous month's House of Delegates meeting.

14. The CTU Constitution and By-Laws explained that it was "the duty of the District Supervisors to maintain and increase the Union membership and to see that Delegates are elected and that they function effectively in all of the schools within their respective districts." Kristine Mayle recalled, "They would have a monthly district supervisor meeting the night before the House of Delegates meeting, but I don't know what they would talk about because they weren't talking about organizing or contacting their delegates. Then they would check in delegates at the monthly House meeting. They would get paid $75 for attending the meeting and a free dinner. But nothing ever came out of it. Everybody always saw it as the cushy job that everyone wants, as a ladder up to a staff job." Kristine Mayle, interviewed by Steven Ashby, March 2014.

15. Mayle, interview.

16. Gutekanst, interview.

17. The *Power at Work* video can be accessed at http://www.youtube.com/watch?v=VNNy5kbMHi0.

18. Sea of Red interviews, Interviewee "AV3."

19. Teachers whose schools voted for the longer-school-day waiver were promised one-time bonuses equal to roughly 2 percent of the average teacher's salary in the district, or about $1,250. In addition, schools would receive $150,000 in discretionary funds.

20. John Kugler, "How STEM Became 'The Mayor's Pet School' . . . . Chicago Teachers Union's Unfair Labor Practice Complaint is Comprehensive," *Substance News*, September 11, 2011.

21. Jackson Potter, interviewed by Steven Ashby, March 3, 2014.

22. Jody Sokolower, "Lessons in Social Justice Unionism: An Interview with Chicago Teachers Union President Karen Lewis," *Rethinking Schools* (Winter 2012–13), http://www.rethinkingschools.org/archive/27_02/27_02_sokolower.shtml.

23. "An Open Letter to the Longer Day Committee," *CTU Blog*, Feb. 7, 2012, http://www.ctunet.com/blog/an-open-letter-to-the-longer-day-committee.

24. Sea of Red interviews, Interviewee "AV6."

25. Chambers, "Building Power from the Bottom Up."

26. Alexandra Bradbury et al., *How to Jump-Start Your Union: Lessons from the Chicago Teachers* (Detroit: Labor Notes, 2014), 113.

27. Sea of Red interviews, Interviewee "LS3A." The CORE flyer can be accessed at http://www.coreteachers.org/wp-content/uploads/2012/03/CORE-Strike-Preparations-Flyer-new-2012–12.pdf.

28. Bradbury et al., *How to Jump-Start Your Union*, 116.

29. Sea of Red interviews, Interviewee "PP3." An afternoon plenary panel featured Gutekanst asking questions of key community leaders and two high school student activists.

30. Luskin, interview.

31. Jackson Potter, interview.

32. Sea of Red interviews, Interviewee "IN2."

33. Sea of Red interviews, Interviewee "AV6."

34. Sea of Red interviews, Interviewee "UP1."

35. Noreen S. Ahmed-Ullah, "Teacher Union Cites Support for Walkout," *Chicago Tribune*, April 6, 2012; Rosalind Rossi, "Union: Teachers Prepared to Support Strike," *Chicago Sun-Times*, April 6, 2012; and Karen Lewis, "Teachers Threaten Strike for Sake of Kids' Schools," *Chicago Sun-Times*, May 9, 2012.

36. CTU poll questions are in the authors' possession. The UIUC Labor Education Program was asked by CTU for advice on wording the questions.

37. "Poll of More than 25,000 Chicago Teachers and Other CTU Members Shows Overwhelming Support for a Strike If Necessary, Constitutes Another 'No Confidence' Vote in Administration of Jean-Claude Brizard," *Substance News*, May 11, 2012.

38. Luskin emphasized the importance of constant assessments drawn from his experiences organizing workers into unions as an organizer with the Service Employees International Union's Healthcare Illinois local union in Chicago led by President Keith Kelleher; the local was a strong CTU ally.

39. Bradbury et al., *How to Jump-Start Your Union*, 126.

40. Sea of Red interviews, Interviewee "LS3A."

41. Mayle, interview.

42. Sea of Red interviews, Interviewee "PP2." Songs played over the loudspeakers included Dolly Parton's "Nine to Five" and Aretha Franklin's "Respect."

43. Jen Johnson, talk given at the "Lessons from the Chicago Teachers' Strike" forum, sponsored by the Chicago branch of Solidarity, Chicago, Sept. 29, 2012, http://www. solidarity-us.org/site/node/3707.

44. Author Steven Ashby was in the front section of the May 23 Roosevelt Auditorium rally and interviewed participants during the march.

45. "Teachers Ready for Battle," *Chicago Tribune*, May 24, 2012.

46. George N. Schmidt, "'A historic beginning in the battle for the soul of public education . . .' Huge crowds rally and march unions and public schools in Chicago. 'Mayor One Percent' tries a publicity stunt Sox Park, while mayor's puppet school board runs away in the face of democracy," *Substance News*, May 24, 2012.

47. Noreen S. Ahmed-Ullah and Naomi Nix, "Thousands of Teachers Rally in Chicago," *Chicago Tribune*, May 23, 2012; Rosalind Rossi and Fran Spielman, "Teachers Ready for Battle," *Chicago Sun-Times*, May 24, 2012; Twitter feed live from the rally, "CTU Shows Strength at May 23 Rally," *Catalyst Chicago*, https://storify.com/CatalystChicago/ctu-shows-strength-at-may-23-rally; and "Massive Chicago Teachers Union Rally Takes Over Downtown," *Daily Kos*, May 24, 2012, http://www.dailykos.com/story/2012/5/24/1094420/-Massive-Chicago-Teachers-Union-Rally-Takes-over-Downtown.

48. Sea of Red interviews, Interviewee "AP4."

49. Sea of Red interviews, Interviewee "PP1."

50. Sea of Red interviews, Interviewee "IN3."

51. "The War on Teachers: Pick a Side" (interview with Karen Lewis), *In These Times*, Oct. 19, 2012, http://inthesetimes.com/article/14006/the_war_on_teachers_pick_a_side; and "CTU's Karen Lewis: People Don't Always Get Everything They Want in a Contract," WBEZ Radio, Sept. 18, 2012.

52. Luskin, interview.

53. Sea of Red interviews, Interviewee "IN2."

54. "Chicago Teachers Union President Karen Lewis: Deal Ending Strike a Victory for Education," *Democracy Now!* Sept. 19, 2012, http://www.democracynow.org/2012/9/19/chicago_teachers_union_president_karen_lewis.

55. Sea of Red interviews, Interviewee "LS3B."

56. *"The Schools Chicago's Students Deserve,"* CTU Blog, Feb. 16, 2012, http://www.ctunet.com/blog/schools-chicagos-students-deserve-presents-comprehensive-plan-to-improve-student-academic-performance-and-strengthen-neighborhood-schools.

57. Luskin, interview.

58. Norine Gutekanst, "How Chicago Teachers Got Organized to Strike," Labor Notes, Oct. 19, 2012, http://www.labornotes.org/2012/10/how-chicago-teachers-got-organized-strike.

59. Sean Noonan, Stephanie Farmer, and Fran Huckaby, *A Sea of Red: Chicago Teachers Union Members Reflect on How the Social Organizing Model of Unionism Helped Win the Union's 2012 Contract Campaign* (Chicago: Chicago Teachers Union, Feb. 2014), 10.

60. Carol Hayes, interviewed via e-mail by Steven Ashby, Sept. 2014.

61. Sea of Red interviews, Interviewee "PP7."

62. Hayes, interview.

63. Sea of Red interviews, Interviewee "PP8."

64. Luskin, interview.

65. Sea of Red interviews, Interviewee "MP2B."

66. *Wall Street Journal*/NBC poll conducted by Hart/McInturff, Feb. 24–28, 2011, http://issuu.com/wsj.com/docs/wsj-nbcpoll03022011.pdf?mode=window&pageNumber=6; and "New Poll Finds Overwhelming Support for Chicago's Teachers," *CTU Blog*, Sept. 13, 2011, http://www.ctunet.com/blog/press-release-new-poll-finds-over whelming-support-for-chicagos-teachers.

67. Sea of Red interviews, Interviewee "AV4."

68. Sea of Red interviews, Interviewee "AV5."

69. Mary Schmich, "Mayor's Home Turf Is Fair Game for Protesters: Demonstration Outside Emanuel House Was Unusual, Yet Respected Privacy Boundary," *Chicago Tribune*, Feb. 22, 2012; and Noreen Ahmed-Ullah, "Protestors Gather at Emanuel's Home to Protest CPS Plans," *Chicago Tribune*, Feb. 21, 2012.

70. Rev. Jesse L. Jackson Sr., statement to CPS Board meeting, Feb. 22, 2012; copy provided to authors by CTU staff.

71. George N. Schmidt, "Community, Teachers Begin Sit-In Outside Mayor Emanuel's City Hall Office Demanding an End to Threatened School Closings, Turnarounds, Phase Outs and Other Attacks on Public Schools," *Substance News*, Jan. 4, 2012; James Warren, "Marie Antoinette, I'd Like You to Meet David Vitale," *New York Times*, Dec. 17, 2011; Al Ramirez, "'You pray at the altar of greed . . .' Substance video of Dec. 14, 2011, Chicago Board of Education meeting shows context to the Mic Check and some Board security trying to stop reporters and cameras from covering the stories unfolding," *Substance News*, Dec. 15, 2011; "Parents, Teachers, and Community Leaders Hold Sit-In at City Hall," *Chicago Union Teacher*, Feb. 2012; "Full text of the 12-14-2011 Board of Education 'Mic Check'" and "In defense of the Mic Check," *Chicago Union Teacher*, Jan. 2012; and five-minute video footage of part of the "mic check" at http://vimeo.com/33673152.

72. Joel Hood and Rick Pearson, "Poll Shows Support for Longer School Day: But Voters Generally Side with Teachers Union over Emanuel," *Chicago Tribune*, May 15, 2012.

73. Rosalind Rossi, "'Enough Is Enough': Chicago Teachers Union to Hold Strike Authorization Vote," *Chicago Sun-Times*, June 2, 2012.

74. Noreen S. Ahmed-Ullah, "CTU Shares Some—Not All—of the Results of Its Poll," *Chicago Tribune*, May 11, 2012; and Sea of Red interviews, Interviewee "LS3B." The leader of the main antiunion group pushing the legislation, Jonah Edelman of Stand for Children, bragged that "In effect they wouldn't have the ability to strike, even though the [legal] right was maintained. . . . The unions cannot strike in Chicago. They will never be able to muster the 75% threshold necessary to strike," in a video at an antiunion conference that soon went viral among CTU members. Sarah Karp, "For the Record: Chicago Teachers Union Strike Votes," *Catalyst Chicago*, July 11, 2011, http://www.ctunet.com/media/in-the-news/for-the-record-chicago-teachers-union-strike-votes; Edelman speech at https://www.youtube.com/watch?v=kog8g9sTDSo.

75. The last day of CPS classes was Wednesday, June 13, 2012; the strike authorization vote occurred on the previous Wednesday, Thursday, and Friday.

76. Noreen Ahmed-Ullah and Joel Hood, "CTU: Nearly 90 Percent of Teachers Vote to Authorize Strike," *Chicago Tribune*, June 11, 2012.

77. Chambers, "Building Power from the Bottom Up."

78. "Video: Surgery Will Not Stop Solidarity," June 6, 2012, https://www.youtube.com/watch?v=67k3C_fm4TQ, also posted on the CTU website, http://www.ctunet.com/blog/surgery-will-not-stop-solidarity-video.

79. Stephanie Gadlin, "Chicago Teachers Vote Overwhelming for Strike Authorization as Contract Negotiations Continue," CTU blog, June 11, 2012, http://www.ctunet.com/blog/members-vote-yes-to-authorization; and Rosalind Rossi and Fran Spielman, "It's a Landslide: Nearly 90 Percent of Chicago Teachers Authorize Strike," *Chicago Sun-Times*, June 12, 2012.

80. Mark Brown, "Eyes on Chicago in Battle of Teachers Unions vs. 'Reformers,'" *Chicago Sun-Times*, June 12, 2012.

81. Steven Ashby, "Standing Up to Corporate School Agenda, Chicago Teachers Greenlight Strike," Labor Notes, June 12, 2012.

82. Rossi and Spielman, "It's a Landslide."

83. The statement that "nearly all those discarded ballots were yes votes" is based on the personal observation of author Steven Ashby as a ballot-counting observer on June 6, 7, 8, and 9, 2012. Ashby was the only nonclergy, non-CTU member or employee present to monitor the counting.

84. Sea of Red interviews, Interviewee "UP1."

85. Luskin, interview.

86. Rosalind Rossi, "No Pay Hike for CPS Teachers, but Executives Are Getting Raises?" *Chicago Sun-Times*, June 22, 2011.

87. Sea of Red interviews, Interviewees "MP1" and "IN1." Also see Carol Marin, "Rahm Emanuel Picked This Fight with Teachers," *Chicago Sun-Times*, Sept. 11, 2012.

88. Sea of Red interviews, Interviewee "AV9."

89. Mayle, interview.

90. Sea of Red interviews, Interviewee "IN2."

91. Sea of Red interviews, Interviewees "IN2" and "AV9."

92. "That was a turning point for me to understand that I wasn't just Karen Lewis, schoolteacher, any longer," Lewis told an interviewer in 2012. "That this was serious and that there are people who are trying to destroy public education and would use me to do that for them." Ben Goldberger, "Karen Lewis: Street Fighter," *Chicago Magazine*, Oct. 2012.

93. At their second and last one-on-one meeting on Aug. 2, 2011, Emanuel, reported Lewis, yelled at her "Fuck you, Lewis!" Rosalind Rossi, "Teachers Union President Says Mayor Emanuel 'Exploded' at Her," *Chicago Sun-Times*, Sept. 9, 2011; Goldberger, "Karen Lewis, Street Fighter."

7. EMANUEL PROVOKES, TEACHERS PREPARE TO BARGAIN

1. Karen Lewis and James Franczek, comments at Chicago Labor and Employment Relations Association Chapter Program, Marshall Law School, Chicago, March 20, 2013.

2. *Resolution Delegating the Authority to the Chief Executive Officer to Honorably Terminate/Dismiss Tenured and Probationary Appointed Teachers Displaced as a Result of Cost Saving Measures Implemented to Address Financial Exigencies for the 2010–2011 and 2011–2012 School Years, Including as a Result of Increases in Class Sizes*, Chicago School Board, June 15, 2010, http://www.cpsboe.org/meetings/board-actions/119.

3. "CPS Firings Target Highly Qualified Tenured Teachers," *CTU Blog*, Aug. 27, 2010, http://www.ctunet.com.

4. *Chicago Teachers Union v. Board of Education of the City of Chicago, No. 10 C 4852*, slip op. at 14, Northern District. Illinois. Oct. 4, 2010, http://www.illinoiscourts.gov/opinions/supremecourt/2012/112566.pdf.

5. Section 1 of the Fourteenth Amendment, known as the "Due Process Clause," reads as follows: "All persons born or naturalized in the United States, and subject to the jurisdiction thereof, are citizens of the United States and of the State wherein they reside. No State shall make or enforce any law which shall abridge the privileges or immunities of citizens of the United States; nor shall any State deprive any person of life, liberty, or property, without due process of law; nor deny to any person within its jurisdiction the equal protection of the laws."

6. *Chicago Teachers Union v. Board of Education*, 2010.

7. See the story and full decision at John Kugler, "Chicago Teachers Union Upholds Teachers' Tenure Rights . . . Judge Coar's Decision Shows How Completely CPS Has Lost (Again) in Federal Court," *Substance News*, Oct. 5, 2010.

8. Beth Swanson, interviewed by Robert Bruno, April 30, 2013.

9. Kate Grossman, interviewed by Robert Bruno, July 11, 2013.

10. Karen Lewis, interviewed by Robert Bruno, March 12, 2103.

11. Robert Bloch, "The 2012 CTU Strike from Legal Counsel's Perspective," notes from presentation to American Federation of Teachers National Lawyers and National Leadership Conference, Washington, DC, April 22, 2013.

12. Jesse Sharkey, interviewed by Robert Bruno, March 23, 2013.

13. Lewis, interview.

14. Sharkey, interview.

15. James Franczek, interviewed by Robert Bruno, April 2, 2013.

16. Rosalind Rossi, "No Pay Hike for CPS Teachers, but Executives are Getting Raises?" *Chicago Sun-Times*, June 22, 2011, http://www.ctunet.com/media/in-the-news/no-pay-hike-for-cps-teachers-but-executives-are-getting-raises.

17. Robert Bloch, "The 2012 CTU Strike from Legal Counsel's Perspective."

18. Mayor Emanuel, under Senate Bill 7, could impose the longer school day without discussion or negotiation with the union when the contract ran out in June 2012, but he could not legally do so before then.

19. Swanson, interview.

20. Bloch, "The 2012 CTU Strike from Legal Counsel's Perspective."

21. Leah Hope and Michelle Gallardo, ABC 7 News, "School Board Approves Property Hike," Aug. 24, 2011, http://abc7news.com/archive/8324887/.

22. Noreen S. Ahmed-Ullah, "Schools Gearing Up for Longer Days: 13 Now on Board with Minutes-Adding, Bonus-Laden CPS Initiative," *Chicago Tribune*, Sept. 21, 2011, http://articles.chicagotribune.com/2011–09–21/news/ct-met-cps-longer-day-imple ment-20110921_1_chicago-teachers-union-jackson-potter-schools-ceo-jean-claude-brizard.

23. Mayle was quoted in Alexandra Bradbury et al., *How To Jump-Start Your Union: Lessons from the Chicago Teachers* (Detroit: Labor Notes, 2014), 96. Teach For America (TFA) is a controversial program that places high-achieving college graduates with no formal teacher training in low-income schools around the country. Teachers unions found TFA personnel typically badly prepared for the classroom, ill informed about teachers unions, and often hostile to unionization.

24. "Teachers Express Concern as CPS Implements Its Ill-Planned 'Longer School Days,'" Sept. 26, 2011, CTU press release, http://www.ctunet.com/media/press-releases/teachers-express-concerns-as-cps-implements-its-ill-planned-longer-school-days.

25. Bloch, "The 2012 CTU Strike from Legal Counsel's Perspective."

26. Jackson Potter, interviewed by Steven Ashby, Oct. 14, 2014.

27. Letter from Jean-Claude Brizard, Chicago Public Schools, Sept. 16, 2011, http://www.cps.edu/Programs/DistrictInitiatives/LongerDay/Documents/LongerSchoolDay AndWaiverProcess.pdf.

28. Robert Bloch, oral argument, IELRB Hearing, Chicago, Oct. 20, 2011, http://www.ctunet.com/blog/text/CTU-Oral-Argument-to-IELRB-102011.pdf.

29. No author, *Chicago Sun-Times*, "Hearing Set on Teachers' Allegation of Pressure on Longer Days," Oct. 14, 2011.

30. Stephanie Gadlin, "Illinois Education Labor Relations Board Votes 5–0 to Seek Injunction Blocking Unlawful Implementation of 'Longer School Day,'" *CTU Press Release*, Oct. 20, 2011, http://www.ctunet.com/media/press-releases/illinois-education-labor-relations-board-votes-5–0-to-seek-injunction-blocking-unlawful-implementation-of-longer-school-day.

31. Jorge Ramirez, interviewed by Robert Bruno, May 20, 2013.

32. Ibid.

33. Jesse Sharkey, interviewed by Robert Bruno, May 24, 2013.

34. Ramirez, interview.

35. Illinois Official Reports, Supreme Court, *Chicago Teachers Union, Local No. 1 v. Board of Education of the City of Chicago*, 2012, IL 112566, Feb. 17, 2012, http://www.illinoiscourts.gov/opinions/supremecourt/2012/112566.pdf.

36. Bloch, "The 2012 CTU Strike from Legal Counsel's Perspective."

37. Franczek, interview.

38. Lewis, interviewed by Robert Bruno, March 25, 2013; Rosalind Rossi, "CTU Chief: Rahm Gives Up on Many Chicago Kids," *Chicago Sun-Times*, Feb. 29, 2012, http://www.ctunet.com/media/in-the-news/body/CTU_InTheNews_2012_03_09.pdf.

39. "Emanuel Denies Saying He'd Given Up on Some Schoolchildren," *CBS Local 2 News*, Feb. 29, 2012, http://chicago.cbslocal.com/2012/02/29/emanuel-denies-saying-hed-given-up-on-some-schoolchildren/.

40. Lewis, interview, March 25, 2013.

41. BJ Lutz and Mary Ann Ahern, "Emanuel Rejects CTU's '25 Percent' Anecdote," *NBC Chicago*, Feb. 29, 2012, http://www.nbcchicago.com/blogs/ward-room/rahm-emanuel-karen-lewis-ctu-cps-25-percent-140957593.html.

42. Lewis, interview, March 25, 2013; Rosalind Rossi, "Teachers Union President Says Mayor Emanuel 'Exploded' at Her," *Chicago Sun-Times*, Sept. 9, 2011, http://www.ctunet.com/media/in-the-news/body/CTU_InTheNews_2012_03_09.pdf.

43. Rossi, "Teachers Union President Says Mayor Emanuel 'Exploded' at Her."

44. Ibid.

45. James Franczek, interviewed by Robert Bruno, Feb. 6, 2014.

46. Robert Bloch, interviewed by Robert Bruno, June 23, 2013.

47. Franczek, interview, April 2, 2013.

48. Lewis, interview, March 12, 2013.

49. Robin Potter, interviewed by Robert Bruno, Oct. 13, 2014.

50. Lewis, interview, March 12, 2013.

51. Ibid.

52. Rosalind Rossi, "Teachers Union Accuses Ousted Member of Being a 'Spy' for CPS," *Chicago Sun-Times*, May 15, 2012.

53. Swanson, interview.

54. Lewis, interview, March 12, 2013.

55. Franczek, interview, April 2, 2013.

56. Bloch, interview, March 10, 2013.

57. Sharkey, interview, May 24, 2013.

58. Lewis, interview, March 12, 2013.

59. *Negotiation Protocols for Successor Bargaining between the Board of Education of the City of Chicago and the Chicago Teachers Union, Local No. 1, American Federation of Teachers, AFL-CIO, Board Counter-Proposal*, Dec. 8, 2011, in possession of authors.

60. Sharkey, interview, May 24, 2013.

61. *Member Contract Proposals*, 2011, in possession of authors.

62. Ibid.

63. Ibid.

64. Ibid.

65. Ibid.

66. Lewis, interview, March 25, 2013.

67. Editorial, "CTU Hopes Too High," *Chicago Sun-Times*, June 6, 2012.

68. Grossman, interview.

69. Kate Grossman, comments at Labor Employment Relations Association, Annual Meeting, Saint Louis, June 7, 2013, from notes taken by the authors.

70. Lewis, interview, March 12, 2013.

71. Mark Richard, interviewed by Robert Bruno, June 25, 2013.

72. Lewis, interview, March 12, 2013.

73. Richard, interview.

74. Bloch, interview, June 23, 2013.

75. Richard, interview.

76. Joseph Moriarty, interviewed by Robert Bruno, Sept. 12, 2014.

77. Swanson, interview.

78. Moriarty, interview.

79. Lewis, interview, March 12, 2013.

80. George N. Schmidt, "$7 Million to One Law Firm is not a 'budget buster' when CPS Faces another 'deficit' According to the *Sun-Times* . . . And the Winner is . . . Jim Franczek?" *Substance News*, Oct. 8, 2012.

8. THE START OF 2012 CONTRACT NEGOTIATIONS

1. *Summary of Successor Bargaining for the 2012–2015 Labor Agreement, Board of Education of the City of Chicago and the Chicago Teachers Union, Local No. 1, American Federation of Teachers, AFL-CIO,* undated, prepared by Franczek-Radelet law firm, in authors' possession.

2. Robert Bloch, "The 2012 CTU Strike from Legal Counsel's Perspective," notes from presentation to American Federation of Teachers National Lawyers and National Leadership Conference, Washington, DC, AFT, April 22, 2013.

3. CPS Proposal, Jan. 17, 2012, *Framework for Modern Successor Agreement* in authors' possession.

4. Karen Lewis, interviewed by Robert Bruno, March 25, 2013.

5. Robin Potter, interviewed by Robert Bruno, Oct. 14, 2014.

6. Lewis, interview.

7. Ibid.

8. Joseph Moriarty, interviewed by Robert Bruno, Sept. 12, 2014.

9. James Franczek, interviewed by Robert Bruno, April 2, 2013.

10. Lewis, interview.

11. Noreen S. Ahmed-Ullah and Joel Hood, "Chicago Teachers Asking for 30% Raises over Next 2 Years," *Chicago Tribune*, Feb. 17, 2012, http://articles.chicagotribune.com/2012–02–17/news/ct-met-ctu-proposals-0217–20120217_1_contract-negotiations-contract-proposal-president-karen-lewis.

12. Jesse Sharkey, interviewed by Robert Bruno, May 24, 2013.

13. *Summary of Successor Bargaining.*

14. Robert Bloch, interviewed by Robert Bruno, March 10, 2013.

15. *Summary of Successor Bargaining*, point 15, 3.

16. Bloch, "The 2012 CTU Strike from Legal Counsel's Perspective."

17. Bloch, interview, March 10, 2013.

18. *Summary of Successor Bargaining.*

19. Robin Potter, interview.

20. Ibid.

21. *Summary of Successor Bargaining.*

22. Stephanie Gadlin, "CTU Sets Strike Authorization Vote Date," CTU Press Release, June 1, 2012, http://www.ctunet.com/blog/chicago-teachers-union-sets-strike-authorization-vote-date.

23. Mitchell Roth, interviewed by Robert Bruno, Aug. 27, 2013.

24. Mark Richard, interviewed by Robert Bruno, June 25, 2013.

25. Bloch, "The 2012 CTU Strike from Legal Counsel's Perspective."

26. Ibid.

27. Franczek, interview.

28. Kimberly Lightford, interviewed by Robert Bruno, Sept. 9, 2013.

29. Ibid.

30. Jackson Potter, interviewed by Steven Ashby, Oct. 14, 2014.

31. IELRA, Section 12, Impasse Procedures, 4, I, http://www.ilga.gov/legislation/ilcs/ilcs3.asp?ActID=1177.

32. Titled *Beyond the Classroom: An Analysis of a Chicago Public School Teacher's Actual Workday*, April 9, 2012, the report was co-authored by Robert Bruno and Steven Ashby and research assistant Frank Manzo for the Labor Education Program, School of Labor and Employment Relations, University of Illinois at Urbana-Champaign, April 9, 2012, https://ler.illinois.edu/wp-content/uploads/2015/01/Springfield-Teachers-Study-Final.pdf. Bruno also testified at the hearing.

33. *CPS Instructional Time Comparison*, document created by the Office of the Chief Executive Officer, https://www.google.com/?gws_rd=ssl#q=From+kindergarten+through+high+school%2C+a+Chicago+child+will+receive+nearly+3+years+less+instructional+time+than+a+peer+student+in+Houston.

34. CTU, *Schools Chicago's Students Deserve: Research-Based Proposals to Strengthen Elementary and Secondary Education in the Chicago Public Schools* (Chicago: CTU, Feb. 2012).

35. Eric Zorn, "Is It Time for More Time for City Students?" *Chicago Tribune*, April 29, 2011.

36. *2012 Fact-Finding Procedure between the Board of Education of the City of Chicago and the Chicago Teachers Union*, Presentation by the Board, June 13, 2012, p. 3, prepared by Franczek-Radelet law firm, in authors' possession.

37. Ibid.

38. In a letter circulated to school officials by a vice president of municipal finance at Goldman Sachs, the deal's potential cost savings were highlighted, but an anonymous financial adviser claimed that the products had "no downside." The *Tribune* further noted that David Vitale, then the chief administrative officer at CPS, presided over the bulk of the auction-rate deals and that "no other school district in the country came close to CPS in relying so heavily on this exotic financial product." Jason Grotto and Heather Gillers, "Risky Bonds Prove Costly for Chicago Public Schools," *Chicago Tribune*, Nov. 7, 2014, http://www.chicagotribune.com/news/watchdog/cpsbonds/ct-chicago-public-schools-bond-deals-met-20141107-story.html. Records also show that a senior Bank of America official warned of a potential market "meltdown" but never shared the risk with the school district. Grotto and Gillers, "Banks Kept CPS in Shaky Bond Market," *Chicago* Tribune, Nov. 10, 2014. A study done by the Roosevelt Institute pegged the district's total cost to be nearly half a billion. *Chicago's Dirty Deals*, undated report, http://rooseveltinstitute.org/wp-content/uploads/2015/11/Chicagos_Dirty_Deals.pdf.

39. Peter Dowd, "Don't Slash Teachers' Pensions," Opinion, *Chicago Tribune*, Feb. 13, 2004, http://articles.chicagotribune.com/2014–02–13/opinion/ct-ctu-chicago-teachers-union-pensions-perspec-021–20140213_1_chicago-teachers-pension-fund-cps.

40. *Fact-Finding Report, In the Matter of the Fact-Finding between the Board of Education of the City of Chicago, and the Chicago Teachers Union, Local 1, American Federation of Teachers, AFL-CIO*, Case No: Arb. Ref. 12.178, July 16, 2012, pp. 9–10, https://www.illinois.gov/elrb/Documents/Chicago-Public-Schools-CTU-Fact-Finding-Report.pdf.

41. Bloch, "The 2012 CTU Strike from Legal Counsel's Perspective."

42. *Fact-Finding Report*, 15.

43. Ibid.

44. Ibid., 37.

45. Ibid., 44.

46. Ibid., 39.

47. Ibid., 56.

48. Ibid., endnote, 83–84.

49. Bloch, interview.

50. *Fact-Finding Report*, 83.

51. Ibid., 83–84.

52. *Separate Opinion of Panel Member Joseph T. Moriarty at the Conclusion of Fact-Finding*, July 18, 2012, pp. 1–2, https://www.illinois.gov/elrb/Documents/Chicago-Public-Schools-CTU-Fact-Finding-Report.pdf.

53. Ibid., 2.

54. Ibid., 13.

55. Rosalind Rossi, Lauren Fitzpatrick and Maudlyne Ihejirika, "Fact Finder Gives Report—School Board, Teachers Say No Thanks," *Chicago Sun-Times*, July 18, 2012.

56. Kristine Mayle, quoted in Alexandra Bradbury et al., *How to Jump-Start Your Union: Lessons from the Chicago Teachers* (Detroit: Labor Notes, 2014), 130.

57. *Concurrence and Dissent, Jesse Sharkey-Chicago Teachers Union Appointed Member*, July 18, 2012, https://www.illinois.gov/elrb/Documents/Chicago-Public-Schools-CTU-Fact-Finding-Report.pdf.

58. Ibid.

59. Mark Brown, "Time to Get Back to the Bargaining Table," *Chicago Sun-Times*, July 17, 2012.

9. A BREAKTHROUGH AND PRELUDE TO A STRIKE

1. Robert Bloch, "The 2012 CTU Strike from Legal Counsel's Perspective," notes from a presentation to American Federation of Teachers National Lawyers and National Leadership Conference, Washington, DC, AFT, April 22, 2013.

2. Fran Spielman, "Analysis: Emanuel Learning a Lesson from Teachers in Union Contract Flap," *Chicago Sun-Times*, July 17, 2012, http://www.ctunet.com/blog/sun-times-analysis-emanuel-learning-a-lesson-from-teachers-in-union-contract-flap.

3. Linda Lenz, interviewed by Robert Bruno, June 26, 2014.

4. Spielman, "Analysis: Emanuel Learning a Lesson."

5. Noreen S. Ahmed-Ullah, "CPS Finds Few Wins after School Reform Legislation," *Chicago Tribune*, July 23, 2012, http://articles.chicagotribune.com/2012-07-23/news/ct-met-state-education-reform-20120723_1_chicago-teachers-union-teachers-walkout-strike-authorization-vote.

6. Karen Lewis, interviewed by Robert Bruno, March 25, 2013.

7. Alexandra Bradbury et al., *How to Jump-Start Your Union: Lessons from the Chicago Teachers* (Detroit: Labor Notes, 2014), 121.

8. Sea of Red interviews, Interviewee "LS3B," 2013.

9. James Franczek, interviewed by Robert Bruno, April 2, 2013.

10. *Fact-Finder Report, In the Matter of the Fact-Finding between the Board of Education of the City of Chicago, and the Chicago Teachers Union, Local 1, American Federation of Teachers, AFL-CIO*, Case No: Arb. Ref. 12.178, July 16, 2012, 9–10, 44, https://www.illinois.gov/elrb/Documents/Chicago-Public-Schools-CTU-Fact-Finding-Report.pdf.

11. Spielman, "Analysis: Emanuel Learning a Lesson."

12. E-mail from Robert Bloch to Edwin Benn, July 18, 2012.

13. E-mail from Edwin Benn to Robert Bloch, July 18, 2012.

14. Jesse Sharkey, interviewed by Robert Bruno, May 24, 2013.

15. *Interim Agreement Term Sheet*, document prepared by Franczek-Radelet law firm, in authors' possession.

16. Noreen S. Ahmed-Ullah and Kristen Mack, "Chicago Schools to Add 477 Teachers to Allow Longer Day," *Chicago Tribune*, July 24, 2012, http://articles.chicagotribune.

com/2012-07-24/news/ct-met-cps-longer-day-0725-20120724_1_teachers-union-school-day-president-david-vitale.

17. Ibid.

18. Beth Swanson, interviewed by Robert Bruno, April 30, 2013.

19. Bloch, "The 2012 CTU Strike from Legal Counsel's Perspective."

20. Franczek, interview.

21. Editorial, "A Good Deal for Teachers, School Kids," *Chicago Sun-Times*, July 24, 2012.

22. Sharon Schmidt, "CTU/CPS Interim Agreement Decreases CPS Previously Announced Teacher Work Day Hours, Opens Positions to Displaced Teachers," *Substance News*, July 24, 2012, http://www.substancenews.net/articles.php?page=3431.

23. Franczek, interview.

24. Editorial, "A Good Deal for Teachers."

25. David Vitale, interviewed by Robert Bruno, March 4, 2013.

26. Ibid.

27. Noreen S. Ahmed-Ullah, "Teachers, CPS Facing an 'Intense' Weekend," *Chicago Tribune*, Sept. 8, 2012.

28. Noreen S. Ahmed-Ullah and Joel Hood, "School Board Boss Joins Teacher Talks," *Chicago Tribune*, Sept. 7, 2012.

29. Vitale, interview.

30. Sharkey, interview.

31. Ibid.

32. The interim agreement had actually been aided by the school calendar. Unlike schools that follow a traditional September to June schedule, Track E schools were year-round operations that began in early August. Consequently, there were roughly 195 elementary and high schools gearing up to welcome students back to a new year when the fact-finding report was issued. Until otherwise directed, though, the length of their school day would be unchanged. In order, then, to have a reconfigured school day in place by the beginning of the term, a new schedule had to be arrived at. "Track E schools," therefore, according to Sharkey, "forced a deadline" for the interim agreement. Sharkey interview, May 24, 2013.

33. Rosalind Rossi and Fran Spielman, "Chicago Teachers Set September 10 Strike Date; CPS to Open Half-Day Schools," *Chicago Sun-Times*, Aug. 30, 2012.

34. Ibid.

35. Sean Kennedy, "Don't Back Down: Spare the Kids, Decertify the CTU," Opinion, *Chicago Tribune*, Aug. 31, 2012.

36. Bloch, "The 2012 CTU Strike from Legal Counsel's Perspective."

37. Kate Grossman, interviewed by Robert Bruno, July 11, 2013.

38. Vitale, interview.

39. Ibid.

40. Franczek, interview.

41. James Franczek, Comments at Chicago Labor and Employment Relations Association Program, Marshall Law School, Chicago, Illinois, March 20, 2013.

42. Ibid.

43. Franczek, interview.

44. Rosalind Rossi and Stefano Esposito, "New CPS Offer 'Unacceptable,'" *Chicago Sun-Times*, Sept. 6, 2012.

45. *Board of Education Proposal on All Outstanding Issues to Achieve Contract and Prevent Strike, Initially Presented on September 6, 2012, Modified on September 7 and 8, 2012, Further Modified on September 9, 2012*, document prepared by Franczek-Radelet law firm, in author's possession.

46. Ibid.

47. If a school closing occurred through a consolidation, with all students assigned to one "receiving school," tenured teachers with a sufficient performance rating would be reappointed to the transferring school. In this case, as the union requested, teachers would follow their students. CPS also agreed that tenured teachers who were rated proficient or better, who were not able to transfer to a receiving school, would be assigned to a "Quality Teacher Pool" for a maximum of one year. Principals would then be required to interview up to three candidates from the pool for an open position. While a principal retained the final authority to select the best applicant, if he or she rejected the applicants from the pool, the school chief had to provide reasons for the decision.

48. *Board of Education Proposal, September 9, 2012.*

49. Franczek, interview.

50. Karen Lewis, interviewed by Robert Bruno, March 12, 2013.

51. Rosalind Rossi and Tina Sfondeles, "CTU President Says Teachers Contract Talks Take 'Turn for the Better,'" *Chicago Sun-Times*, Sept. 6, 2012.

52. Robert Bloch, interviewed by Robert Bruno, March 13, 2013.

53. Rosalind Rossi and Tina Sfondeles, "Chicago Teacher Contract Talks Resume Saturday, Still 'Disappointed,' Says One," *Chicago Sun-Times*, Sept. 7, 2012.

54. Ibid.

55. Franczek, interview.

56. Lewis, Comments at Chicago Labor and Employment Relations Association Program, Marshall Law School, Chicago, Illinois, March 20, 2013. Rauner had a reputation for making particularly scathing comments about the CTU, but his rhetoric grew more strident during and after the strike. In a memorable appearance on the local public television newsmagazine *Chicago Tonight*, he referred to the teachers strike as the "nuclear option." Bruce Rauner, Comments on WTTW, *Chicago Tonight* program, "What's Next for Teachers and Students," Sept. 10, 2012, http://chicagotonight.wttw.com/2012/09/10/whats-next-teachers-and-students.

57. Ahmed-Ullah, "Teachers, CPS Facing an 'Intense' Weekend."

58. Barbara Byrd-Bennett, interviewed by Robert Bruno, Oct. 28, 2014.

59. Lewis, interview, March 12.

60. Lewis, Comments, Marshall Law School.

61. Lewis, interview, March 12.

62. Fran Spielman, "Rahm Emanuel 'Not in the Room,' but 'Very Well Tuned In,'" *Chicago Sun-Times*, Sept. 9, 2012.

63. Noreen Ahmed-Ullah and Kristen Mack, "CPS Chief Brizard on His Way Out?" *Chicago Tribune*, Aug. 31, 2012, http://articles.chicagotribune.com/2012-08-31/news/ct-met-emanuel-brizard-20120831_1_cps-chief-brizard-president-david-vitale-emanuel-spokeswoman-sarah-hamilton.

64. A June 11, 2012, letter to the school chief that accompanied his annual review stated, "The organizational effectiveness of CPS could be substantially improved with a more coherent and decisive management decision-making process." Ahmed-Ullah and Mack, "CPS Chief Brizard on His Way Out?"

65. Michael Brunson, interviewed by Robert Bruno, Sept. 22, 2014.

66. Vitale, interview.

67. Sharkey, interview.

68. Franczek, interview.

69. Vitale, interview.

70. Kristine Mayle, interviewed by Steven Ashby, March 2014.

71. Ibid.

72. Bloch, interview.

73. Sharkey, interview.

74. Mayle, interview.

75. Bloch, interview.

76. Sharkey, interview.

77. Ibid.

78. Fran Spielman, "Rahm Emanuel 'Not in the Room'"; Beth Swanson, interviewed by Robert Bruno, June 17, 2013.

79. Robert Bloch, interviewed by Robert Bruno, June 25, 2014.

80. Sharkey, interview.

81. Ibid.

82. Bloch, interview, June 25, 2014.

83. Sharkey, interview.

84. Bloch, interview, June 25, 2014.

85. Ibid.

86. Vitale, interview.

87. Sharkey, interview.

88. Bloch, interview, June 25, 2014.

89. Noreen S. Ahmed-Ullah, Joel Hood, and Kristen Mack, "Picket Lines Up after CPS, Teachers Fail to Prevent Strike: Walkout Is First in 25 Years," *Chicago Tribune*, Sept. 10, 2012, http://articles.chicagotribune.com/2012-09-10/news/chi-chicago-public-schools-chicago-teachers-union-contract-talks-strike_1_picket-lines-teachers-strike-president-david-vitale.

90. Ibid.

91. Franczek, interview.

10. THE STRIKE

1. Sea of Red interviews, Interviewee "IN2."

2. Alexandra Bradbury et al., *How to Jump-Start Your Union: Lessons from the Chicago Teachers* (Detroit: Labor Notes, 2014), 134.

3. Sea of Red interviews, Interviewee "UP2."

4. Sea of Red interviews, Interviewee "UP1."

5. "Chicago Teachers Union President Karen Lewis speaks to 18,000 supporters on Labor Day," video, Sept. 3, 2012, https://www.youtube.com/watch?v=QWIsvi7LOAk. Transcription by Steven Ashby.

6. Sea of Red interviews, Interviewee "IN2." The Sept. 14, 2012, CTU *On the Line* strike bulletin quoted a delegate and strike captain admitting, "I would be telling a lie if I said that prior to this CTU strike, I didn't have serious doubts and fears," but that the picket line and marches had brought members together and had overcome those fears. The CTU daily *On the Line* strike bulletins can be accessed at http://www.ctunet.com/for-members/strike-central/on-the-line.

7. Teamsters Local 705 union representative Richard DeVries was the Teamsters' liaison to the CTU during the strike.

8. The CTSC spent $1,300 from its "Stand with the Chicago Teachers Union" T-shirt sales on supplies for the union during the strike.

9. Sea of Red interviews, Interviewee "IN2."

10. John Byrne, Kristen Mack, and Noreen S. Ahmed-Ullah, "Strike Risky for Mayor, Union Chief," *Chicago Tribune*, Sept. 9, 2012; Kristen Mack and John Byrne, "Teachers on Strike," *Chicago Tribune*, Sept. 10, 2012.

11. Noreen S. Ahmed-Ullah, Joel Hood, and Kristen Mack, "Picket Lines Up after CPS, Teachers Fail to Prevent Strike," *Chicago Tribune*, Sept. 10, 2012.

12. Sarah Chambers, "Building Power from the Bottom Up: How CTU Members Transformed Their Union," Oct. 20, 2012, Chicago Teachers Solidarity Campaign poststrike

forum cosponsored with the CTU, https://www.youtube.com/watch?v=usw6gCe3EWg. Transcribed by Steven Ashby.

13. CTU, *On the Line*, Sept. 15, 2012.

14. Sea of Red interviews, Interviewee "UP1."

15. Sea of Red interviews, Interviewee "IN2."

16. Sea of Red interviews, Interviewee "PP1."

17. Chambers, "Building Power From the Bottom Up," and Sea of Red interviews, Interviewee "IN2."

18. Sea of Red interviews, Interviewee "MP1."

19. Valerie Strauss, "A Strike of Choices in Chicago," *Washington Post*, Sept. 13, 2012.

20. Sea of Red interviews, Interviewee "MP2A."

21. Aldermen signing the antiunion letter included Burnett, Ervin, Graham, Reboyras, Suarez, Mell, Colon, Austin, Mitts, Cullerton, Laurino, M. O'Connor, P. O'Connor, Smith, Tunney, Osterman, Moore, Moreno, Harris, Beale, Balcer, Cardenas, Burke, Thompson, Thomas, Lane, O'Shea, Cochran, Brookins, Zalewski, Chandler, Solis, and Maldonado. Alderman who publicly supported the CTU during the strike were: Fioretti, Hairston, Sawyer, Foulkes, Muñoz, Waguespack, Sposato, and Arena. In its Wednesday, Sept. 12, 2012, *On the Line* the union noted that "We especially want to thank Alderman Pope (10), Alderman Jackson (7), Alderman Sawyer (6), Alderman Hairston (5), Alderman Burns (4), Alderman Dowell (3), Alderman Fioretti (2), Alderman Quinn (13), Alderman Foulkes (15), Alderman Muñoz (22), Alderman Waguespack (32), Alderman Sposato (36), Alderman Cappleman (46), Alderman Reilly (42), Alderman Arena (45), Alderman Pawar (47) and Alderman Silverstein (50) for resisting the pressures in city hall and standing for educational justice." Chicago ward numbers are in parentheses.

22. CTU, *On the Line*, Sept. 14, 2012.

23. Sea of Red interviews, Interviewee "MP2."

24. CPS "Children First Site—Student Supervisor Toolkit," http://www.ctunet.com/blog/text/HoldingCenterLessons.docx.

25. Chambers, "Building Power from the Bottom Up."

26. Sea of Red interviews, Interviewee "CS1."

27. Sea of Red interviews, Interviewee "AV4."

28. Sea of Red interviews, Interviewee "AV3."

29. The Sept. 15, 2012, *On the Line* proclaimed, "Turnout at the mass rallies has been beyond our wildest dreams—tens of thousands of CTU members and our allies EVERY day! Easily the largest and most inspiring demonstrations that most of us have ever experienced."

30. Strauss, "A Strike of Choices in Chicago."

31. Gloria Steinem, "Gloria Steinem Supports Chicago Teachers on Strike," *CTU Blog*, Sept. 9, 2012, http://www.ctunet.com/blog/gloria-steinem-supports-teachers-in-chicago-strike; and interview with Gloria Steinem, *The Big Picture with Thom Hartmann*, RTTV, http://www.progressivefox.com/?tag=chicago-teachers-union.

32. Sea of Red interviews, Interviewee "IN3."

33. AFT, "AFT Statement in Support of Striking Chicago Teachers Union Members," press release, Sept. 10, 2012, http://www.ctunet.com/blog/text/AFT_Endorsement.pdf.

34. Lisa Donovan, "Labor Leaders Supporting Striking Teachers Invoke 9–11 Terrorist Attacks," *Chicago Sun-Times*, Sept. 11, 2012.

35. Donovan, "Labor Leaders Supporting Striking Teachers."

36. Speakers at the Sept. 11, 2012, press conference included leaders of SEIU Healthcare Illinois; Alliance of Charter Teachers and Staff; SEIU Local 1; Air Line Pilots Association; and Chicago Federation of Labor head Jorge Ramirez.

37. Andrew Gill, "Social Media Acts as Megaphone and Sword in CTU Strike," WBEZ Radio, Sept. 14, 2012, http://www.wbez.org/blogs/bez/2012–09/social-media-acts-megaphone-and-sword-ctu-strike-102437.

38. Shibata noted that 61% of Facebook users are 35 or older, and 64% of Twitter users are 35 or older. Citing social media studies is problematic, because the figures are growing so rapidly that they are soon outdated. But studies from 2012 and 2014 reported that the percentage of Americans saying that they saw news on a social networking site yesterday doubled—from 9% to 19%—since 2010, and the figure rose to 34% for those under age 24. In a poll asking whether people used Facebook or other media the previous day, 41% of all adults answered yes. Studies show that 50% of social network users share or repost news stories, images, or videos, while 46% discuss news issues or events on social network sites. A large and growing percentage of young people have turned away from traditional TV or newspapers for news; they get the bulk of their news from clicking on story links they see on Facebook or Twitter. Gill, "Social Media Acts as Megaphone"; n.a., "How Americans Get Their News," American Press Institute, March 17, 2014, http://www.ameri canpressinstitute.org/publications/reports/survey-research/how-americans-get-news/; and n.a., "In Changing News Landscape, Even Television Is Vulnerable: Trends in News Consumption: 1991–2012," Pew Research Center, Sept. 27, 2012, http://www.people-press. org/2012/09/27/in-changing-news-landscape-even-television-is-vulnerable/.

39. "Chicago Teachers Union versus Astroturf Billionaires" video at http://www. schoolsmatter.info/2012/08/chicago-teachers-union-versus-astroturf.html.   Shibata blogged about the video in "The Battle of Chicago Teachers Union vs. Out-of-Town Billionaires," Huffington Post, Aug. 22, 2012, http://www.huffingtonpost.com/knzo-shibata/ the-battle-of-chicago-tea_b_1812729.html.

40. Curt Hopkins, "Connecting with the Chicago Teachers' Strike," *Daily Dot*, Sept. 18, 2012, http://www.dailydot.com/news/chicago-teachers-strike-social-media/. Also see Kenzo Shibata's interview, *Take Action News*, Sept. 22, 2012, http://www.mixcloud.com/ weactradio/take-action-news-kenzo-shibata-september-22–2012/.

41. The Chicago media reported that, on the first day of the strike, Mayor Emanuel said, "Everything here is down to two final issues, and it's not air-conditioning, OK. It's 71 degrees outside. We don't go on strike for air-conditioning." "Emanuel on Chicago's Teachers Strike: Get It Done 'for Our Children,'" ABC News Radio, Sept. 20, 2012, http:// abcnewsradioonline.com/national-news/emanuel-on-chicagos-teachers-strike-get-it-done-for-our-chil.html.

42. "Chicago Teacher" video is at https://www.youtube.com/watch?v=3yN7cRZP58k. The Rebel Diaz website is at http://rebeldiaz.bandcamp.com/track/chicago-teacher. Also see "CTU Strike Song: 'Imma Keep Rhyming til Salaries Start Rising,'" *Chicago Sun-Times* blog, Sept. 13, 2012, http://chicagobeta.suntimes.wordpress-prod-wp.aggrego.com/news/ 7/71/794533/ctu-strike-song-imma-keep-rhyming-til-salaries-start-rising.

43. Singers were CTU teachers and staff from Uplift Community High School and Hayt, Peirce, Swift, and Burr elementary schools. Teachers and staff at a number of schools made their videos based on the "Call Me Maybe" lyrics and posted the videos on YouTube.

44. Editorial, "If Chicago Teachers Strike Now, It's the Union's Bad Call," *Chicago Sun-Times*, Sept. 6, 2012; and Editorial, "Don't Be Fooled by Teachers Strike Drama," *Chicago Sun-Times*, Aug. 23, 2012.

45. Editorial, "Hold Firm, CPS: This Is about the Future of Chicago," *Chicago Tribune*, Aug. 31, 2012; Editorial, "Don't Cave, Mr. Mayor: This Strike Is about Who Controls Chicago's Schools, Chicago's Future," *Chicago Tribune*, Sept. 11, 2012; and Editorial, "Chicago Teachers Union Fighting Inevitability of Education Reform," *Chicago Tribune*, Sept. 13, 2012.

46. Eric Zorn, "Kibitzing from the Sidelines of Life: Dear Warring Chicago Teachers and School Administrators," *Chicago Tribune*, Sept. 2, 2012.

47. "Chicago Tonight: The Week in Review: 7/20," WTTW-TV *Chicago Tonight*, July 20, 2012, http://chicagotonight.wttw.com/2012/07/20/chicago-tonight-week-review-720.

48. Monica Davey, "With No Contract Deal by Deadline in Chicago, Teachers Will Strike," *New York Times*, Sept. 9, 2012.

49. Charles Lane, "Students Are Victims in Chicago Fight over Clout," *Washington Post*, Sept. 10, 2012.

50. "We can no longer live in a society where the public employees are the haves and taxpayers who foot the bills are the have-nots," said Governor Walker. Steven Greenhouse, "Strained States Turning to Laws to Curb Labor Unions," *New York Times*, Jan. 11, 2011, http://www.nytimes.com/2011/01/04/business/04labor.html.

51. For example, Lewis used the phrase at a protest against school closings in Dec. 2011. See "CTU, Occupy Chicago Join Forces in School Protest," NBC 5 News, Dec. 11, 2011, http://www.nbcchicago.com/blogs/ward-room/chicago-teachers-union-public-schools-occupy-protest-135556183.html#ixzz3C5vqvtPf.

52. Dana Liebelson, "What Happened with the Chicago Teacher Strike, Explained," *Mother Jones*, Sept. 11, 2012, http://www.motherjones.com/politics/2012/09/teachers-strike-chicago-explained.

53. Xian Barrett, "Why I'm Striking," blog, Sept. 9, 2012, http://chiteacherx.blogspot.com/2012/09/why-im-striking-jcb.html.

54. Brandon Johnson talk, "Lessons from the Chicago Teachers' Strike," a forum sponsored by the Solidarity group, Sept. 29, 2012, http://www.solidarity-us.org/site/node/3707.

55. Noreen S. Ahmed-Ullah and Joel Hood, "Chicago Teachers Asking for 30% Raises over Next 2 Years," *Chicago Tribune*, Feb. 17, 2012.

56. "CPS CEO Brizard sent letters to teachers Tuesday criticizing the timing of the vote and the information being sent by the union to its members," ABC Channel 7 News, June 5, 2012, http://abc7chicago.com/archive/8689390/.

57. "Full Text of the 'Arbitrator's Fact-Finding Report,'" https://archive.org/stream/402394-arbitrators-fact-finding-report/402394-arbitrators-fact-finding-report_djvu.txt. The conclusion to the fact-finding report stated on p. 59: "The short but difficult solution to this dispute is that the Board cannot unilaterally restructure the Union's contract and further expect employees to work 20% more for free or without fair compensation."

58. Rosalind Rossi and Maudlyne Ihejirika, "Analysis: Emanuel Learning a Lesson from Teachers in Union Contract Flap," *Chicago Sun-Times*, July 17, 2012.

59. "Fact-Finding Report Goes Public, CTU House of Delegates Rejects Proposals!" CTU blog, July 18, 2012, http://www.ctunet.com/blog/fact-finding-report-goes-public; and Noreen S. Ahmed-Ullah and Kristen Mack, "Deal Keeps Longer Day, Adds 477 Teachers," *Chicago Tribune*, July 25, 2012.

60. James Franczek, interviewed by Bob Bruno, April 2, 2013.

61. Kim Janssen and Fran Spielman, "47% of Chicago Voters Back Teachers," *Chicago Sun-Times*, Sept. 11, 2012.

62. "No, Hugo, They're Not "Supremely Unhappy" . . . Yet," *Capitol Fax* poll report, Sept. 13. 2012, http://capitolfax.com/2012/09/13/no-hugo-theyre-not-supremely-unhappy-yet/; and "As Chicago teachers strike enters fourth day, a new poll proves majority of parents and taxpayers approve of fair contract fight," *CTU Blog*, Sept. 13, 2012, http://www.ctunet.com/blog/new-poll-shows-that-that-majority-of-the-public-supports-the-strike.

63. Melissa Harris-Perry, "Casualties in the Education Reform Wars: The Stakes Are High for Students Unlucky Enough to Be Caught in the Crossfire," *Nation* magazine, Oct. 8, 2012, http://www.thenation.com/article/casualties-education-reform-wars/. MSNBC hosts Ed Schultz and Chris Hayes, however, invited teachers and prounion panelists and were themselves sympathetic to the teachers and their strike issues.

64. Curtis Black, "Penny Pritzker's TIF," Community Media Workshop, *Newstips* blog, Aug. 8, 2012, http://www.newstips.org/2012/08/penny-pritzkers-tif/.

65. Laura Washington, "Shadow Strikers March with CTU," *Chicago Tribune*, Sept. 16, 2012.

66. "Chicago Teachers Union Community Board" (list), CTU website, http://www.ctunet.com/community.

67. Linda Lutton, "Union Opens 'Strike Headquarters,' Community and Parent Groups Line Up behind Teachers," WBEZ News, Sept. 8, 2012, http://www.wbez.org/union-opens-strike-headquarters-community-and-parent-groups-line-behind-teachers-102285.

68. "Tens of Thousands Rally to Support Striking Chicago Teachers," Real News Network video, Sept. 11, 2012, https://www.youtube.com/watch?v=9Dzb5Jg_qSA#t=263.

69. Linda Lutton, "Paid Protesters a New Force in School Closings Debate: Protesters Say They Were Paid $20, $25 to Attend Hearings," WBEZ Radio, Jan. 14, 2012, http://www.wbez.org/story/paid-protesters-new-force-school-closings-debate-95792;   Marty Ritter, "Crane Closing Hearing Sheds Light on Paid 'Protesters,'" *Chicago Union Teacher*, Feb. 2012; and Rosalind Rossi, "Two Say They Got Paid to Protest, Back Closing Chicago Schools," *Chicago Sun-Times*, Jan. 24, 2012.

70. Noreen S. Ahmed-Ullah and Kristen Mack, "Pro-Emanuel Education Groups Organized by Mayoral Ally," *Chicago Tribune*, Feb. 13, 2012.

71. Aug. 29, 2012, CTSC town hall speakers included Jitu Brown, Kenwood Oakland Community Organization; Father José Landaverde; Mack Julion, president, National Association of Letter Carriers Branch 11; students from Social Justice High School; Erica Clark, Parents 4 Teachers; and Michael Brunson, CTU Recording Secretary.

72. Photos of CTU strike headquarters can be found at Bob Simpson, "Spirits Were High at the Chicago Teachers Union (CTU) Strike HQ," *Daily Kos*, Sept. 9, 2012, http://www.dailykos.com/story/2012/09/09/1129514/-Spirits-were-high-at-the-Chicago-Teachers-Union-CTU-Strike-HQ.

73. CTU, *On the Line*, Sept. 13, 2012; "Solidarity Donations," CTU website, http://www.ctunet.com/for-members/strike-central/solidarity-donations.

74. Sea of Red interviews, Interviewee "LS2."

75. Hal Dardick, Ellen Jean Hirst, and Joel Hood, "Tentative Deal Reached with Striking Chicago Teachers," *Chicago Tribune*, Sept. 15, 2012.

76. Barack Obama, campaign speech in Spartanburg, South Carolina, Nov. 3, 2007, https://www.youtube.com/watch?v=SA9KC8SMu3o.

77. "Chicago Teachers Strike Headache for Democrats," *In These Times*, Sept. 11, 2012; and "Statement from U.S. Secretary of Education Arne Duncan," Sept. 11, 2012, http://www.ed.gov/news/press-releases/statement-us-secretary-education-arne-duncan-1.

78. After the strike President Obama continued to decline to take sides. He praised teachers but also praised the mayor's actions by adding that "It was very important, I think, for Mayor Emanuel to say let's step up our game." Lynn Sweet, "Obama Accuses Romney of 'Teacher Bashing' in Wake of Chicago Strike," *Chicago Sun-Times*, Sept. 25, 2012.

11. BARGAINING DURING THE STRIKE AND A DEAL REACHED

1. David Vitale, interviewed by Robert Bruno, March 4, 2013.

2. James Franczek, interviewed by Robert Bruno, April 2, 2013.

3. CTU, *On the Line: Daily Bulletin of Our Fight for Fairness at CPS*, Sept. 8, 2012.

4. "Chicago Teachers Strike Updates: Lewis, Others, End Talks for Night," *Chicago Tribune*, Sept. 10, 2012, http://articles.chicagotribune.com/2012–09–10/news/chi-strike-updates-pickets-up-as-more-talks-scheduled-20120910_1_ctu-president-karen-lewis-front-of-cps-headquarters-teachers.

5. Vitale, interview.

6. Joel Hood, Noreen S. Ahmed-Ullah, and Hal Dardick, "Teachers Strike Heads into Second Day," *Chicago Tribune*, Sept. 11, 2012, http://articles.chicagotribune.com/2012–09–11/news/ct—met-chicago-teachers-strike-0911–20120911_1_teachers-in-red-t-shirts-teachers-strike-teachers-walkout.

7. Vitale, interview.

8. Ibid.

9. Noreen S. Ahmed-Ullah and Diane Rado, "CPS Offer Gives Some Ground," *Chicago Tribune*, Sept. 14, 2012.

10. Vitale interview.

11. Ibid.

12. Kate Grossman, interviewed by Robert Bruno, July 11, 2013.

13. Ibid.

14. Franczek, interview.

15. Kim Vatis and Mary Ann Ahern, "School Board Gives New Offer to Union," NBC5 Chicago, Sept. 11, 2012, http://www.nbcchicago.com/news/local/chicago-teachers-strike-day-2-negotiations-169323346.html.

16. Phil Rogers and Rob Elgas, "Chicago Teacher Strike Goes into Second Day," *NBC Education Nation*, Sept. 11, 2012, http://www.nbcchicago.com/news/local/chicago-teachers-union-strike-day-one-negotiations.

17. *On the Line*, Sept. 12, 2012.

18. Rosalind Rossi, Lauren Fitzpatrick, and Fran Spielman, "CPS Makes 'Pretty Generous' Offer," *Chicago Sun-Times*, Sept. 13, 2012.

19. Kim Vatis and Mary Ann Ahern, "Chicago Teacher Strike Goes into Fourth Day," *NBC Education Nation*, Sept. 12, 2012, http://www.nbcchicago.com/news/local/Chicago-Teachers-Third-Day-of-Walk-Out.

20. Rosalind Rossi et al., "Chicago Public Schools Students Back in Class by Friday?" *Chicago Sun-Times*, Sept. 12, 2012.

21. Monica Davey, "Teachers' Strike in Chicago Tests Mayor and Union," *New York Times*, Sept. 10, 2012, http://www.nytimes.com/2012/09/11/education/teacher-strike-begins-in-chicago-amid-signs-that-deal-isnt-close.html?_r=0.

22. Franczek, interview.

23. Jesse Sharkey, interviewed by Robert Bruno, May 24, 2013.

24. Franczek, interview.

25. Less than one month after the strike ended, Barbara Byrd-Bennett was named the new CEO of the Chicago Public Schools.

26. Bennett, like Lewis, is an African-American woman. In a 2016 interview, Lewis acknowledged that the two women's similar cultural backgrounds made it easier for them to relate with one another. "I had a very good working relationship with Barbara. It was easier for us because we were two old Black women. That just cut down on a lot of barriers." Mary L. Datcher and Robert T. Starks, "Exclusive: CTU President Karen Lewis: Finding Peace in the Fight," *Chicago Defender*, Feb. 5, 2016, http://chicagodefender.com/2016/02/05/exclusive-ctu-president-karen-lewis-finding-peace-in-the-fight/.

27. Barbara Byrd-Bennett, interviewed by Robert Bruno, Oct. 28, 2014.

28. *On the Line*, Sept. 13, 2012. In a startling turn of events in 2015, Byrd-Bennett resigned because of her involvement in a CPS contracting scandal connected to her previous employer.

29. Franczek, interview.

30. Monica Davey and Steven Yaccino, "Fresh Hopes for End to Chicago Teacher Strike by Weekend," *New York Times*, Sept. 13, 2012, http://www.nytimes.com/2012/09/14/education/chicago-teachers-strike-fourth-day.html? r=0.

31. The survey was conducted by the Springfield, Illinois, interview and automated polling firm We Ask America at the request of Rich Miller, the author of the Illinois state politics blog site, *Capitol Fax*. Miller first reported the findings on his *Capitol Fax* site on September 13, and Chicago newspapers, along with national news services, followed with their own stories. CTU provided a detailed account of the survey in a blog post titled "As Chicago teachers strike enters fourth day, a new poll proves majority of parents and taxpayers approve of fair contract fight," Sept. 13, 2012, http://www.ctunet.com/blog/new-poll-shows-that-that-majority-of-the-public-supports-the-strike.

32. *On the Line*, Sept. 14, 2012.

33. Ibid.

34. Bloch, "The 2012 CTU Strike from Legal Counsel's Perspective." notes from presentation to American Federation of Teachers National Lawyers and National Leadership Meeting, Washington, DC, AFT, April 22, 2013.

35. *On the Line*, Sept. 15, 2012.

36. James Franczek, interviewed by Robert Bruno, Aug. 18, 2014.

37. Franczek, interview, April 2, 2013.

38. Ibid.

39. James Franzcek, interviewed by Robert Bruno, Sept. 10, 2014.

40. Joseph Moriarty, interviewed by Robert Bruno, Sept. 12, 2014.

41. Kristine Mayle, interviewed by Steven Ashby, March 2014.

42. Ibid.

43. Moriarty, interview.

44. Franczek, interview, Aug. 18, 2014.

45. Bloch, "The 2012 CTU Strike from Legal Counsel's Perspective."

46. Sea of Red, Interviewee "PP3."

47. Jesse Sharkey, interviewed by Robert Bruno, Sept. 6, 2014.

48. *On the Line*, Sept. 17, 2012.

49. Sharkey, interview.

50. Bloch, "The 2012 CTU Strike from Legal Counsel's Perspective."

51. Sea of Red, Interviewee "LS3A."

52. Sea of Red, Interviewee "PP3."

53. Mayle, interview.

54. "House of Delegates Votes to Continue Strike," http://www.ctunet.com/blog/house-of-delegates-votes-to-continue-strike (Sept. 16, 2012).

55. Franczek, interview, Aug. 18, 2014.

56. Karen Lewis, interviewed by Robert Bruno, March 12, 2013.

57. Franczek, interview, April 2, 2013.

58. Linda Lutton, "Mayor Seeks Legal Action as Chicago Teachers Union Votes to Continue Strike," WBEZ Radio, Sept. 16, 2012.

59. Jason Meisner and Hal Dardick, "Court Hearing Set for Wednesday, after Union Vote," *Chicago Tribune*, Sept. 17, 2012; the CTU statement is at http://www.ctunet.com/blog/chicago-teachers-continue-strike-as-mayor-cps-attempt-to-trample-free-speech-right-to-protest.

60. The filing asking for an injunction to end the strike is at http://posttrib.suntimes.com/csp/cms/sites/STM/dt.common.streams.StreamServer.cls?STREAMOID=eYeCDAdk1y6tUBfqeYW_aVtlnvLZEb1lj2q9UTOpesc5iB$GIhlg1CtTVovIm5vw4Aw$6wU9GSUcqtd9hs3TFeZCn0vq69IZViKeqDZhqNLziaXiKG0K_ms4C2keQo54&CONTENTTYPE=application/pdf&CONTENTDISPOSITION=injunction.pdf.

61. Because clinicians worked at multiple schools, they were asked to staff the picket line at CPS headquarters, and they marched to the CTSC press conference to show their support.

62. Lisa Donovan, Lauren Fitzpatrick, and Fran Spielman, "Judge Punts on Forcing Teachers Back; Union Delegates to Decide on Wednesday Return," *Chicago Sun-Times*, Sept. 17, 2012, CTSC website, http://ctscampaign.weebly.com/announcements.html. Author Steven Ashby emceed the event and stated, "I can tell you that over the past century injunctions have been used as a union-busting tool to suppress the democratic right to strike." Jitu Brown's speech is at https://www.youtube.com/watch?v=XiHwXJiAvQo, video produced by Mike Siviwe Elliott. Other speakers were from Parents 4 Teachers, National Nurses United, and National Association of Letter Carriers Branch 825.

63. Moriarty, interview.

64. Lewis, interview.

65. Quoted in Alexandra Bradbury et al., *How to Jump-Start Your Union: Lessons from the Chicago Teachers* (Detroit: Labor Notes, 2014), 159.

66. On those two days, instead of asking each school to send someone to strike headquarters to get the daily strike bulletin, as happened on the first five days of the strike, the union sent volunteers on routes throughout the city to deliver *On the Line* to the schools. Author Steven Ashby was one of those volunteers.

67. Sea of Red, Interviewee "LSB3."

68. Quoted in Bradbury et al., *How to Jump-Start Your Union*, 156.

69. Donovan et al., "Judge Punts."

70. Mark Richard, interviewed by Robert Bruno, June 25, 2013.

71. Matthew Luskin, comments at the Bargaining for the Common Good Conference, Georgetown University, Washington, DC, May 21, 2014.

72. Ibid.

73. Lewis, interview.

74. Kate Grossman, interviewed by Robert Bruno, July 11, 2013.

75. CTU, Sept. 18 flyer, http://www.ctunet.com/delegates/resources/text/Parent-flyer-Eng.pdf.

76. Monica Davey, "As Chicago Strike Goes On, the Mayor Digs In," *New York Times*, Sept. 17, 2012, http://www.nytimes.com/2012/09/18/education/chicago-teachers-strike-enters-second-week.html.

77. Robert Bloch, interviewed by Robert Bruno, March 10, 2013.

78. Noreen S. Ahmed-Ullah, Diane Rado, and Bill Ruthhart, "Back to School: Classes Resume Wednesday as Teachers Union Ends Strike," *Chicago Tribune*, Sept. 19, 2012, http://articles.chicagotribune.com/2012–09–18/news/ct-met-chicago-teachers-strike-0919–20120919–56_1_ctu-president-karen-lewis-teacher-evaluation-system-chicago-teachers-union.

79. Monica Davey and Steven Yaccino, "Teachers End Chicago Strike on Second Try," *New York Times*, Sept. 18, 2012, http://www.nytimes.com/2012/09/19/us/vote-scheduled-on-chicago-teachers-contract.html.

80. Rosalind Rossi, Stefano Esposito, and Lauren Fitzpatrick, "Emanuel: Deal Is 'Honest Compromise,'" *Chicago Sun-Times*, Sept. 18, 2012.

81. Rosalind Rossi, "Exclusive: CTU's Karen Lewis on Emanuel, Vitale and Steinem," *Chicago Sun-Times*, Sept. 19, 2012.

82. Greg McCune, "Chicago Teachers Union Ratifies Deal That Ended Strike," *Chicago Tribune*, Oct. 4, 2012, http://articles.chicagotribune.com/2012–10–04/news/sns-rt-us-usa-chicago-schoolsbre89309m-20121003_1_chicago-teachers-union-karen-lewis-part-on-student-performance.

83. Franczek, interview, April 2, 2013.

84. CPS did, however, commit to installing air-conditioning, after the contract was ratified, during the school year. CPS Press Release, 2014, http://cps.edu/News/Press_releases/Pages/PR2_08_19_2014.aspx.

85. Michael Pearson, "Wins, Losses, and Draws in Chicago School Strike," CNN, Sept. 19, 2012; "CTU's Karen Lewis: People Don't Always Get Everything They Want in a Contract," WBEZ Radio, Sept. 18, 2012, http://www.wbez.org.

86. Vitale, interview. In July of 2015 Vitale announced that he was stepping down as board president.

87. Lewis, interview.

88. Franczek, interview, April 2, 2013.

89. Rebecca Harris and Sarah Karp, "For the Record: Displaced Teacher Hiring," *Catalyst Chicago*, Oct. 19, 2012, http://catalyst-chicago.org/2012/10/record-displaced-teacher-hiring/.

90. Lewis, interview.

91. Vitale, interview, March 2013.

92. Moriarty, interview.

93. Michael Brunson, interviewed by Robert Bruno, Sept. 22, 2014.

94. Ibid.

95. E-mail from James Franczek to Robert Bloch, Oct. 4, 2012.

CONCLUSION

1. A list of such bills can be found at *Alec Exposed*, http://www.alecexposed.org/wiki/Bills_Affecting_Worker_and_Consumer_Rights_and_More, accessed on Aug. 5, 2015.

2. Robert Bruno testified at one of these hearings before the full House Education and Workforce Committee on June 3, 2015.

3. Steven Greenhouse, "In Standoff, Latest Sign of Unions Under Siege," *New York Times*, Sept. 10, 2012.

4. "'Pure and Simple': Making the Case for Unionism," History Matters website, http://historymatters.gmu.edu/d/5037/.

5. Karen Lewis, "Fight for the Whole Society," *The Nation*, Feb. 13, 2013, http://www.thenation.com/article/fight-whole-society/.

6. Mary Cathryn Rickert, president of the Saint Paul Federation of Teachers, Presentation at the Bargaining for the Common Good Conference, Georgetown University, Washington DC, May 12, 2014.

7. "How Chicagoans Voted and Why," *New York Times*, April 8, 2015.

8. Online survey of Illinois labor union members conducted by the Labor Education Program, School of Labor and Employment Relations, University of Illinois, survey results in possession of the authors.

9. Alex Parker, "Jean-Claude Brizard: We 'Underestimated' Teachers Union," *DNAInfo.com*, Aug. 22, 2013, https://www.dnainfo.com/chicago/20130822/downtown/jean-claude-brizard-former-cps-boss-we-underestimated-teachers-union.

10. Brandon Johnson, "Lessons from the Chicago Teachers Strike" (speech), Sept. 29, 2012, video and transcript at http://www.solidarity-us.org/site/node/3707.

11. "CTU's Lewis Rips Emanuel's 'Elite' Advisers," *Chicago Tribune*, June 19, 2013, http://articles.chicagotribune.com/2013–06–19/news/chi-ctus-lewis-rips-emanuels-elite-advisers-20130618_1_union-president-karen-lewis-education-financial-transactions-tax.

12. "At the 2014 Missouri AFL-CIO Convention," http://www.aflcio.org/Press-Room/Speeches/At-the-2014-Missouri-AFL-CIO-Convention.

13. "'Mike Brown Is Our Son,'" *Labor Notes*, Aug. 20, 2014, http://labornotes.org/2014/08/mike-brown-our-son.

14. "NYC Police, Teachers Union Chiefs Clash over T-shirt Statement," *Newsday*, Sept. 5, 2014, http://www.newsday.com/news/new-york/nyc-police-teachers-union-chiefs-clash-over-t-shirt-statement-1.9239268.

15. In response to public pressure, including a non-binding February 2015 referendum approved by more than 80% of Chicago voters, a few months after the April 2015 mayoral election, Mayor Emanuel set up a Working Families Task Force, which included representation from the Chicago Federation of Labor, to "study paid sick leave, scheduling predictability, and paid family and medical leave policies to address growing concerns about the juggling of work and family obligations." In April 2016 the task force recommended that the mayor and city council endorse legislation mandating five paid sick days. It became law in June 2016. Alexia Elejalde-Ruiz, "Task Force Proposes Chicago Employers Offer 5 Days of Paid Sick Leave a Year," *Chicago Tribune*, April 2, 2016, http://www.chicagotribune.com/business/ct-paid-sick-leave-ordinance-0414-biz-20160413-story.html.

16. "Strong Voice in 'Fight for 15' Fast-Food Wage Campaign," *New York Times*, Dec. 14, 2014, http://www.nytimes.com/2014/12/05/business/in-fast-food-workers-fight-for-15-an-hour-a-strong-voice-in-terrance-wise.html?_r=0.

17. "Lessons in Social Justice Unionism: An Interview with Chicago Teachers Union President Karen Lewis," *Rethinking Schools* (Winter 2012–13), http://www.rethinkingschools.org/archive/27_02/27_02_sokolower.shtml.

18. James Franczek, interviewed by Robert Bruno, April 2, 2013.

19. Karen Lewis, *CTU President-Elect Election Acceptance Speech*, June 13, 2010, http://www.coreteachers.org/karen-lewis-ctu-president-elect-acceptance-speech-2/.

20. Karen Lewis, interviewed by Robert Bruno, March 25, 2013.

21. *State of Illinois, Illinois Education Labor Relations Board Charge against Employer*, May 6, 2015, complaint filed by CTU against Chicago Board of Education available as a pdf at chicagotonight.wttw.com/.../Complaint%20Against%20.

22. Noreen S. Ahmed-Ullah, Diane Rado, and Bill Ruthhart, "Back To School," *Chicago Tribune*, Sept. 19, 2012.

23. Mario Vasquez, "Can Los Angeles Teachers Push Back the Corporate Education Reform Movement?," *In These Times*, April 15, 2015, http://inthesetimes.com/article/17849/los_angeles_teacher_strike; Karla Griego, "L.A. Teachers Escalate," *Labor Notes*, March 30, 2015, http://www.labornotes.org/2015/03/la-teachers-escalate; Howard Blume, "L.A. Unified Teachers Ratify Three-Year Contract," *Los Angeles Times*, May 8, 2015, http://www.latimes.com/local/lanow/la-me-ln-la-teachers-approve-contract-20150508-story.html.

24. Michelle Gunderson, "Teachers Compare Notes," *Labor Notes*, April 17, 2015, http://labornotes.org/2015/04/teachers-compare-notes; Samantha Winslow, "Chicago Teacher Organizing Lessons Go National," *Labor Notes*, Aug. 12, 2013, http://www.labornotes.org/blogs/2013/08/chicago-teacher-organizing-lessons-go-national; and Melissa Sanchez, "Teachers Unions Tackle Social Justice to Improve Schools, Communities," *Catalyst Chicago*, June 15, 2015, http://catalyst-chicago.org/2015/06/teachers-unions-tackle-social-justice-to-improve-schools-communities/.

25. Lisa Black, "Why the Sudden Crop of Teacher Strikes?" *Chicago Tribune*, Oct. 12, 2012, http://articles.chicagotribune.com/2012-10-21/news/ct-met-teacher-strikes-why-now-20121021_1_teacher-strikes-school-boards-public-schools-and-districts.

26. Bob Peterson, "A New Teacher Union Movement Is Rising," *Common Dreams*, May 25, 2014, http://www.commondreams.org/views/2014/05/23/new-teacher-union-movement-rising; Nicole Dungca, "Portland Teachers Strike Officially Suspended with Tentative Agreement," *Oregon Live/The Oregonian*, Feb. 19, 2014, http://www.oregonlive.com/portland/index.ssf/2014/02/portland_teachers_strike_offic.html.

27. "Chicago Teachers Union Agreement Shows How Teachers Advocate for Students Through Bargaining," Facebook, posted on Sept. 24, 2012, https://www.facebook.com/notes/portland-association-of-teachers/chicago-teachers-union-agreement-shows-how-teachers-advocate-for-students-throug/383356755066574.

28. Sarah Chambers, "Ice the ISAT: Boycotting the Test under Mayor Rahm Emanuel's Regime," in *More Than a Score: The New Uprising Against High-Stakes Testing*, ed. Jesse Hagopian (Chicago: Haymarket Books, 2014).

29. "Chicago Teachers Union Releases Transformational Contract Demands for the City Chicago's Students Deserve," CTU Press Release, March 26, 2015, http://www.ctunet.com/media/press-releases/chicago-teachers-union-releases-transformational-contract-demands-for-the-city-chicagos-students-deserve; "Broke on Purpose: Board of Education Continues to Peddle Budget Myths to Justify Its Starving of Classrooms," CTU press release, May 5, 2015, http://www.ctunet.com/media/press-releases/broke-on-purpose-board-of-education-continues-to-peddle-budget-myths-to-justify-its-starving-of-classrooms; "CTU Contract Talk Briefing," CTU press release, May 13, 2015, http://www.ctunet.com/media/press-releases/ctu-contract-talk-briefing.

30. On May 7, 2015, the CTU filed an unfair labor practice charge with the Illinois Educational Labor Relations Board, asserting that CPS had refused three formal requests for mediation "despite the lengthy period of bargaining and lack of agreement on any substantive issues." Melissa Sanchez, "CTU Files Unfair Labor Practice Complaint, Seeks Mediation," *Catalyst Chicago*, May 7, 2015, http://catalyst-chicago.org/2015/05/ctu-files-unfair-labor-practice-complaint-seeks-mediation/.

31. Since 1981, CTU members paid 2%, and CPS picked up the remaining 7% pension payment.

32. "CTU Leads Thousands in Downtown Rally for A Just Chicago and Fair Contract," CTU blog, June 9, 2015, http://www.ctunet.com/blog/ctu-leads-thousands-in-downtown-rally-for-a-just-chicago-and-fair-contract.

33. An election study of Illinois labor union members by the University of Illinois found that teachers strongly supported Quinn despite intense displeasure about his championing SB 7 and pension cuts for government employees. *Illinois State Governor Election 2014: Voting Patterns of IL AFL-CIO Union Members*, online study conducted by Robert Bruno and Brandon Grant, Labor Education Program, School of Labor and Employment Relations, University of Illinois, Urbana-Champaign, March 13, 2015. "Illinois Governor Pushes Anti-Labor Agenda Amid Budget Standoff," *The American Prospect*, March 14, 2016, http://prospect.org/article/illinois-governor-pushes-anti-labor-agenda-amid-budget-standoff.

34. Melissa Sanchez and Kalyn Belsha, "Back to Drawing Board for Contract Negotiations," *Catalyst Chicago*, Aug. 7, 2015, http://catalyst-chicago.org/2015/08/back-to-drawing-board-for-contract-negotiations/.

35. Monica Davey and Mitch Smith, "Chicago Police Department Plagued by Systemic Racism, Task Force Finds," *New York Times*, April 3, 2016, http://www.nytimes.com/2016/04/14/us/chicago-police-dept-plagued-by-systemic-racism-task-force-finds.html?version=meter+at+7&module=meter-Links&pgtype=article&contentId=&mediaId=&referrer=https%3A%2F%2Fwww.google.com%2F&priority=true&action=click&contentCollection=meter-links-click.

36. Rick Pearson and Bill Ruthhart, "Emanuel Job Approval Hits Record Low as Chicagoans Reject McDonald Video Explanation," *Chicago Tribune*, Feb. 1, 2016, http://www.chicagotribune.com/news/local/politics/ct-rahm-emanuel-laquan-mcdonald-poll-20160131-story.html; Monica Davey and Giovanni Russonello, "In Deeply Divided Chicago, Most Agree: City Is Off Course," *New York Times*, May 6, 2016, http://www.nytimes.com/2016/05/07/us/chicago-racial-divisions-survey.html. Asked "Whom do you side with in the debate over improving Chicago public schools?," 60 % sided with the CTU, 20 % with the mayor, and 20 % had no opinion or said neither. Bill Ruthhard and Juan Perez, Jr., "Teachers Union Has Triple the Public Support of Emanuel," *Chicago Tribune*, Feb. 4, 2016, http://www.chicagotribune.com/news/local/politics/ct-rahm-emanuel-schools-poll-met-20160203-story.html.

37. "CTU Details on Strike Authorization Vote: 96.5% of Educators Say 'Yes,'" CTU Press Release, Dec. 14, 2015, http://www.ctunet.com/blog/ctu-strike-authorization-96-5-percent-yes.

38. "CTU Details on Strike Authorization Vote: 96.5% of Educators Say 'Yes,'" CTU Press Release, December 14, 2015, http://www.ctunet.com/blog/ctu-strike-authorization-96-5-percent-yes.

39. Melissa Sanchez and Stephanie Choporis, "Citing Lack of Trust, CTU Rejects Latest Contract Offer," *Catalyst Chicago*, Feb. 1, 2016, http://catalyst-chicago.org/2016/02/citing-lack-of-trust-ctu-rejects-latest-contract-offer/.

40. Juan Perez, Jr., "Chicago Teachers Union Bargaining Team Rejects City's Contract Offer," *Chicago Tribune*, Feb. 2, 2016, http://www.chicagotribune.com/news/ct-chicago-teachers-union-contract-decision-met-0202-20160202-story.html. "I know people were expecting something completely different," Lewis said of the vote. "But that's not how we work as the Chicago Teachers Union. It doesn't matter what one person wants or what two people want or what three people want. People need to understand that our Big Bargaining Team is an extension of the officers, and the experts and the lawyers who come with us to have conversations with the board."

41. CPS announced on August 12, 2015, that it was phasing out over three years the 7 % pension pick-up for its more than 2,000 non-CTU members.

42. "Board of Ed's Zombie Budget Apocalypse Will Destroy Public Education," CTU Press Release, April 16, 2016, http://www.ctunet.com/media/press-releases/board-of-eds-zombie-budget-apocalypse-will-destroy-public-education. Also see Sarah Chambers and Micah Uetricht, "The Next Great Chicago Strike," *Jacobin*, March 31, 2016, https://www.jacobinmag.com/2016/03/chicago-teachers-union-strike-core-karen-lewis/.

43. The CTU took the issue to the Illinois Educational Labor Relations Board, but the IELRB, on February 18, 2016, refused to take a position, arguing that it would be inappropriate to do so while contract negotiations were in progress.

44. University Professors of Illinois Local 4100, representing faculty at seven public universities: Chicago State, Eastern Illinois, Governors State, Northeastern Illinois, Northern Illinois, Western Illinois, and University of Illinois at Springfield; Cook County College Teachers Union Local 1600; Alliance of Charter School Teachers and Staff 4343; Amalgamated Transit Union Local 308; United Electrical Workers Western Region; SEIU Healthcare Indiana, Illinois, and Missouri; Fight for $15; SEIU 73; and the Coalition of Black Trade Unionists. Steven Ashby participated in the April 1 coalition as one of the leaders of the reconstituted Chicago Teachers Solidarity Campaign, which held a March 9, 2016, town hall forum, attended by 250, entitled "Broke on Purpose: Fund Our Futures."

45. Jackson Potter, Facebook post, May 8, 2016.

46. "Mulling a Tantrum Day in Chicago: When Teachers Lock Out Their Students," *Chicago Tribune*, March 21, 2016, http://www.chicagotribune.com/news/opinion/editorials/ct-chicago-teachers-schools-walkout-ctu-cps-edit-0322-jm-20160321-story.html; "On Tantrum Day, Will Teachers Rebel against CTU?," *Chicago Tribune*, March 27, 2016, http://www.chicagotribune.com/news/opinion/editorials/ct-chicago-teachers-strike-emanuel-rauner-cps-edit-0328-20160327-story.html. In response, see Alison Eichhorn, "Why I Am Walking Out with The CTU on April 1," *Chicago Tribune*, letter to the editor, March 28, 2016, http://www.chicagotribune.com/news/opinion/letters/ct-why-i-am-walking-out-with-the-ctu-on-april-1-20160328-story.html. Melissa Sanchez, "CTU Ends One-Day Strike with Downtown Rally," *Catalyst Chicago*, April 1, 2016, http://catalyst-chicago.org/2016/04/liveblog-april-1-ctu-strike/.

47. Melissa Sanchez, "CTU Rejects Fact-Finder's Report, Can Strike in 30 Days," April 16, 2016, http://catalyst-chicago.org/2016/04/in-teacher-contract-talks-fact-finders-report-due-this-weekend/.

48. Staughton Lynd, *We Are All Leaders: The Alternative Unionism of the Early 1930s* (Urban-Champaign: University of Illinois Press, 1996).

49. Jeff Helgeson, *Crucibles of Black Empowerment: Chicago's Neighborhood Politics from the New Deal to Harold Washington* (Chicago: University of Chicago Press, 2014).

50. Maureen Kelleher, "Chicago's Brand of Teacher Organizing Goes Viral," *Catalyst Chicago*, Sept. 21, 2015, http://catalyst-chicago.org/2015/09/chicagos-brand-of-teacher-organizing-goes-viral/. School examples are taken from an ongoing collection of Bargaining for the Common Good campaigns being chronicled at Georgetown University's Kalmanovitz Initiative for Labor and the Working Poor, http://lwp.georgetown.edu/bcg/.

51. "Pittsburghers for Public Transit" is the website for a grassroots organization of transit riders, drivers, and supporters that advocates for mass transit for all residents of the Pittsburgh metropolitan region, http://www.pittsburghforpublictransit.org/2011/04/get-on-bus-transit-union-looks-to-ally.html.

52. "Pledged to Protect" is an example of one of many campaigns of SEIU HCII to defend programs that serve low-income families and people with disabilities against government cuts. A story of the union's activities can be found at chicago.cbslocal.com/2016/06/23/home-care-workers-boo-rauner-over-proposed-cuts/. The local's website is seiuhcilin.org.

53. "AFSCME Members, NEIU Students Rally for University Funding," AFSCME Council 31 website, Feb. 26, 2016, http://www.afscme31.org/news/afscme-members-neiu-students-rally-for-university-funding#sthash.fIfH4COG.dpuf; "Northeastern Illinois University Protests the Budget Death of Higher Education," *Chicago Monitor*, April 4, 2016, http://chicagomonitor.com/2016/04/northeastern-illinois-university-protests-the-budget-death-of-higher-education/.

54. The union was chartered on Aug. 1, 2015, as Cab Drivers United/AFSCME Local 2500; see http://www.cabdriversunitedafscme.org/#!/#post/55be3c414cc536972b75b315.

55. The group was officially known as the Mayor's Task Force on Working Families; Robert Bruno served on a subcommittee addressing fair scheduling issues.

56. We borrow the phrase "publicly valuable outcomes" from John Budd's article "Implicit Public Values and the Creation of Publicly Valuable Outcomes: The Importance of Work and the Contested Role of Labor Unions," *Public Administration Review* (July/Aug., 2014): 506–16.

Index

Academy for Urban School Leadership
(AUSL), 41, 111, 144
Accountability for All (bill), 91
achievement gap, 13–14, 18–19
Action Now, 63, 207
Adams, Monty, 49, 58
administrators, 78, 113–15; salaries, 131, 161.
See also principals
Advance Illinois, 73, 76, 80–82, 90, 92–93, 96,
98, 103, 205, 212
AFL-CIO, 234, 237–38
African Americans, 26, 57, 122, 204; layoffs,
122, 176, 204, 244; teachers, 21, 41, 195
Ahmed-Ullah, Noreen, 201
air-conditioning, 147, 155, 199, 217, 224, 227,
234, 254, 290n41, 295n84
Albany Park Neighborhood Council, 207, 222
aldermen, 192, 289n21
Alliance of Charter Teachers and Staff (ACTS),
57, 60, 269n65, 276n10
alternative public schools, 3, 24, 40–43
Alvarez, Anita, 248
Amendatory Act (1995), 30–32, 36
American Federation of Labor (AFL), 233–34,
237. *See also* AFL-CIO
American Federation of State, County, and
Municipal Employees (AFSCME), 83, 208,
255, 274n35
American Federation of Teachers (AFT), 14,
19, 149, 196–97, 235, 238–39, 269n65
American Legislative Exchange Council
(ALEC), 17, 230
Anderson, Veronica, 264n67
antiunion attitudes, 174, 178, 200–201, 205–6,
212, 251, 281n23, 287n56; groups, 129, 205,
279n74. *See also specific groups*
antiunion legislation, 85, 230–31
arbitration, 97–98, 155, 274n35
Arise Chicago, 126, 129, 208
Ashby, Steven, 208, 280n83, 295nn61, 66,
299n42, 299n44
ASPIRA charter schools, 59
auction-rate deals, 162, 284n38
austerity, 162, 227, 255–56

Baehrend, Chris, 58–59
Balanoff, Tom, 197
Bank of America, 162, 284n38
bargaining. *See* collective bargaining; contract
negotiations (2012); contracts
Baron, Hal, 21
Barrett, Xian, 64, 199, 203
Bayer, Henry, 83–84
Bell, Terrence, 11
Benn, Edwin "Ed," 155–57, 159–61, 163–67,
170, 172
Bennett, William, 19
Berman, Arthur, 25
Beyond the Classroom (University of Illinois),
47, 54–55
Bill and Melinda Gates Foundation, 2, 16, 41,
82, 259n23
Black Lives Matter, 247–48, 250–51
Blagojevich, Rod, 36
Bloch, Robert, 96, 102–3, 135–37, 139–40, 142,
144, 146, 149, 151–52, 154, 157, 163, 165,
168, 170, 172, 174, 176–78, 180–84, 209–10,
217, 220–21, 223, 225–26, 229, 249
Blocks Together, 63, 126, 207
Board of Education (Chicago), 21, 35, 39, 96;
hearings on school closings, 62, 69, 126–27
(*see also* school closings); Nominating
Commission, 26–27, 29; teacher layoffs,
134–36. *See also* Chicago Public Schools
(CPS); Illinois State Board of Education
bonuses, 71, 96, 138, 277n19
Born, David, 154
Boucek, Sara, 92
Brizard, Jean-Claude, 71, 116, 129, 138–41,
179, 203–4, 207, 215, 236, 287n64
Broad, Eli, 2
Brown, Jitu, 222
Brown, Mark, 129, 167
Bruno, Robert, 300n55
Brunson, Michael, 66, 146, 179–80, 182,
228–29
Budd, John, 300n56
bullying, 101, 111, 113–15, 138, 148, 169, 193,
228, 244

The Burnham Plan for a World-Class Education (Education Policy Dialogue Group), 73

Burrus, Clark, 20

Bush, George W., 12

business leaders, 2, 21, 24, 30, 34, 36, 82, 179

Business Roundtable, 90, 98, 103

business unionism, 60–61

Byrd-Bennett, Barbara, 178, 215, 247, 293nn25–26, 28

calendar: bargaining, 154–55, 242; school, 39, 160, 185, 286n32

Capitol Fax, 86, 89, 294n31

Caref, Carol, 108, 121, 159

Catalyst Chicago, 34, 37, 42, 51, 168, 264n67

Caucus for a Strong Democratic Union (CSDU), 66

Caucus of Rank and File Educators. See CORE

Cawley, Tim, 56–57, 144

Chambers, Sarah, 106, 112, 128, 191, 193

chants, 43, 118–19, 132, 186, 188, 191–92, 195–96

charter schools, 2, 15–16, 31–32, 40, 43, 55–60, 74, 132, 161; teachers, 31–32, 57–60, 268n49

Cheatham, Jennifer, 145

Cherkasky-Davis, Lynn, 159

Chicago: economic conditions, 17–19; mayoral control over schools, 26–33, 71; mayoral elections, 19, 28, 38, 70–71, 235, 245, 270n105; policy agenda, 255–56; racial demographics, 18; as union city, 196

Chicagoans United to Reform Education (CURE), 19, 23

Chicago Federation of Labor (CFL), 107, 140, 187, 239, 297n15

Chicago Federation of Teachers (CFT), 5

Chicago Panel on Public School Policy and Finance, 20

Chicago Public Schools (CPS): overview, 1–10; resource distribution, 53, 122, 127, 253–54; restructuring of schools, 3, 32–33, 40–41, 262n19; school-based management, 25–27; school board (*see* Board of Education); school closings, 40–41, 56–57, 61–62, 65, 124, 127, 131–32, 167, 203–4, 207–8, 244, 253, 267n41, 287n47; school district jurisdictions, 23–25; turnaround schools, 51–52, 56, 111, 126–27, 132, 244. *See also* administrators; charter schools; clinicians; contract negotiations (2012); contracts; funding; learning conditions; paraprofessionals; principals; students; teachers; working conditions

Chicago School Reform Act (1988), 23–25

Chicago Sun-Times, 34, 54, 60, 90, 116, 118, 129–30, 135, 137, 145, 148, 166–68, 172, 174, 186, 188, 200–202, 205, 207, 209, 245

Chicago Teachers' Pension Fund (CTPF), 162

Chicago Teachers Solidarity Campaign (CTSC), 189, 194, 208–9, 242, 288n8

Chicago Teachers Union (CTU): "big bargaining team," 121, 145–49, 169, 179, 181, 241, 248, 299n40; By-Laws, 276n14; Communications Department, 199; Community Board, 63, 236, 244; Constitution, 276nn13–14; delegates' conference, 113; House of Delegates, 37–38, 43–44, 61, 63, 68, 101, 109, 209, 217–21, 276nn13–14; lawsuits, 135; mobilization, 183, 232–33, 239, 252–53 (*see also* contract campaign); Organizing Department, 108, 185; research reports, 121–23; salaries, 108, 276n9; and SB 7, 88–104; as social movement for public good, 7–10, 63–70, 234–35, 240–42, 251–56; Solidarity Fund, 209; and teacher evaluation law, 74, 76, 80–82 (*see also* evaluations); weakened influence of, 28–32. *See also* contract negotiations (2012); contracts; job security; leadership; protests; strike (2012); strikes

Chicago Tribune, 38, 41, 54, 60, 86, 126–27, 129–30, 153, 160, 162, 169, 174, 179, 186, 190, 201, 245, 248, 251, 284n38

Chicago Union Teacher, 102, 108, 198, 276n13

Chico, Gery, 35

churches, 126

Clark, Erica, 207

class size, 41, 50–51, 128, 153, 160–61, 176, 201–2, 207, 222, 227, 253, 261n4; monitoring panel, 32–33, 176

Claypool, Forrest, 247–51

clinicians, 123–24, 147, 161, 169, 292n60

Clinton, Bill, 34, 70

Coar, David H., 135

collective bargaining, 4, 105; bargaining rights, 36–37, 83; laws restricting, 29–31, 89–92, 94–95, 100–101, 230; permissive subjects, 153, 160; and the public good, 240–42, 251–56; and right to strike, 90–92, 95, 98–100, 158; role of players, 146; rules and procedures, 143–45, 252. *See also* contract negotiations (2012); contracts

Colorado, 243, 272n35

Commercial Club of Chicago, 40; Civic Committee, 30, 36, 42, 90, 98, 271n12

Common Core, 16

Community Board, 206–7

community-labor coalition, 236, 251–56

community mobilization, 7–9, 45, 63–66, 124–27, 183

Congress of Industrial Organizations (CIO), 233–34, 237. *See also* AFL-CIO

contract campaign, CTU, 105–33; in 2015, 246; clinicians and paraprofessionals, 123–24; contract action committees, 110, 113, 118, 123, 130, 190–91; defined, 105–6; first steps, 108–10; leadership's democratic approach, 120–21; May 10 practice strike vote, 116–17, 132; May 23 rally and march, 117–19, 132; organizing in schools, 111–15; parents and communities, 124–27; research reports, 121–23; success of, 232. *See also* strike authorization

contract negotiations (2012), 44–45, 121, 128; bargaining calendar, 154–55, 242; contract duration, 166–67; CTU agenda, 137, 146–49, 201–3, 212, 253; CTU "big bargaining team," 121, 145–49, 169, 179, 181, 241; day before strike deadline, 178–83; final deal, 219–25; House of Delegates meeting, 219–21; interim agreement, 171–74, 286n32; and "public goods," 240–42; rules and procedures, 143–45; staffing proposal, 169–78; start of, 151–67; during strike, 211–29; during strike preparations, 189; "thin contract," 151–55. *See also* fact-finding process

contracts: 1991 contract, 27; 1995–1999 contract, 27–32; 1999–2003 contract, 32, 36–37; 2003 contract, 35–40; 2007 contract, 37–40, 43–44; 2012–15 contract, 227–29; 2015 contract, 242, 246–51

contract schools, 40, 70

CORE (Caucus of Rank and File Educators), 3, 8, 46, 62–66, 82, 104–5, 113, 118, 123, 146, 149, 212, 232–33, 240, 243–44, 253

corporate education reform, 2–6, 8, 15, 17, 41–43, 45, 68–71, 82, 143, 145, 147, 160, 183, 225, 251–54. *See also* charter schools; privatization

Corral, David, 268n64

Cotton, Nellie, 53

Cowlishaw, Mary Lou, 29

CPS. *See* Chicago Public Schools

crime, 18–19

Crown, Henry, 86

CTU. *See* Chicago Teachers Union

Cullerton, John, 24, 84, 89, 91–92

Daley, Richard J. "Boss," 27, 80

Daley, Richard M., 27–35, 37–38, 40–41, 44, 55, 70, 135, 144, 162, 263n42, 265n77, 265n82

Daley, William, 81

Dallas, Ted, 66

Darling-Hammond, Linda, 15

Davenport, Suzanne, 22, 42–43

Davey, Monica, 201

Davidoff, Al, 149

Davies, Beth, 243

Davis, Monique, 29

deindustrialization, 17–18

Democratic Party, 2–3, 23–25, 84–87, 89, 158, 187, 210, 226, 239

Democrats for Education Reform (DFER), 129, 205, 212

Designs For Change (DFC), 22, 42, 141, 260n31, 261n54

Desmond, John, 261n4

DeVries, Richard, 288n7

Donovan, Stephanie, 152, 218

Doussard, Marc, 17

due process, 135, 280n5

Duncan, Arne, 15–16, 35, 39–40, 42, 64, 71, 75, 144, 239

Durbin, Dick, 210

Early College High School (AEC), 59

Earned Sick Time coalition, 238

economic inequality, 13–14, 42, 163, 253, 255–56. *See also* poverty

economic recession, 2, 75

Edelman, Jonah, 86, 90–91, 97, 99–100, 131, 279n74

Edelman, Josh, 59

Edgar, Jim, 81

educational apartheid, 122, 127

educational justice, 4, 7–8, 45, 163, 250–56, 289n21

educational performance trends, 11–17

Education Policy Dialogue Group, 73

education reform movement, 1–17

Educators for a Democratic Union, 243

"effective schools" movement, 42, 264n75

elections, 7, 84–87, 230; CTU leadership, 33–35, 38, 40, 43–44, 66–70, 269n68, 270n99; mayoral, 19, 28, 38, 70–71, 235, 245, 270n105

Emanuel, Rahm, 2–4, 51, 91; 2012 contract, 154, 166–68, 171, 173, 177–82, 184, 214–15; and 2012 CTU strike, 184, 199, 205–7, 221–22, 226–27, 236, 290n41; approval rating, 248; and contract campaign, 106, 111–12, 119, 126–27, 131–32; educational policy, 55, 71, 135–36, 174, 207–8, 292n78; elections, 70–71, 245, 270n105; fear of strike, 98–99, 157–58, 175; longer school day proposal, 52–54, 94, 104, 111–12, 131, 136, 138, 143, 152, 159–60, 207; meetings with Lewis, 142–43; personality, 132;

Emanuel, Rahm (*continued*)
 protests against, 126–27; relations with teachers, 119, 178, 190, 239; and SB 7, 101, 111; union support for, 70, 235, 255
evaluations, teacher, 159, 201; in 2012 contract, 155–56, 166, 177, 182, 212–14, 227–28; and job security, 174–76 (*see also* job security); rating bans, 182, 212, 214, 228; and student test scores, 15–17, 69, 71–87, 93, 155–56

Facebook, 197–99, 208–9, 244, 290n38
fact-finding process, 155–57, 204–5, 249; hearings, 159–63; report, 128–29, 163–67, 170–71, 291n57
"failing schools" narrative, 42, 51–52
family stress, 48–49, 123–24
Feldman, Sandra, 14
Finnegan, Paul, 86
Flider, Bob, 86–87
Flynn, Peter, 223
"Framework for a Modern Successor Agreement," 152
Franczek, Jim, 33, 39, 73, 81, 95–97; 1995 contract, 27, 30–31; 2003 contract, 35–37; 2012 contract, 44–45, 134, 137, 140, 142–46, 150–54, 157, 160–65, 167, 169–72, 175–80, 182, 184, 240; and 2012 strike, 205, 211–18, 221, 227–29; 2015 contract, 246, 249
Franklin, Stephen, 48
Friedman, Milton, 12
funding, educational, 16, 27, 96, 138, 161–62, 164, 249, 276n19; federal, 35, 75, 81, 134–35; state, 12, 35, 75. *See also* Race to the Top
Furr, Jon, 92

gangs, 53, 57, 124
Garcia, Jesus "Chuy," 235, 245
Garza, Sue Sadlowski, 245
Gates, Bill, 2, 16, 41, 82, 259n23
Goldbaum, Nate, 68
Goldman Sachs, 162, 284n38
Goldner, Greg, 208
graduation rates, 13, 259n13, 260n31
Grassroots Collaborative, 63, 207, 251
Grassroots Education Movement, 65
Greenhouse, Steven, 232, 238
grievance procedures, 29, 114–15, 232, 268n64
grievances, 21, 137, 141, 147, 254
Griffin, Ken, 86
Grossman, Kate, 34, 135, 148, 174, 213, 225
Guerrero, Maria, 47
Gunderson, Michelle, 123
Gutekanst, Norine, 62, 106, 108, 110, 114, 123, 194, 208

Hajiharis, Ted, 66
Haley, Margaret, 5–9
Hamilton, Sarah, 179
Handy, Jessica, 82, 92, 94, 97, 99–100
Harbison, Victor, 129
Harissis, Stavroula, 209
Harris, Brian, 60
Harris-Perry, Melissa, 206
Hawkins, Jon, 34
Hayes, Chris, 291n63
Hayse, Carol, 123
Healey, Robert, 269n67
health care, 38–39
Heileman, John, 206
Heise, Rob, 58
Helgeson, Jeff, 253
Hess, G. Alfred, 262n19
Hickey, Susan, 123, 169
Higgins, Ryan, 86
higher education, 78–79
holding centers, 193
homelessness, 49, 122
Houston, 53, 159–60
Huberman, Ron, 42, 73, 80
Huffington Post, 198
Huffman, Rebeca Nieves, 129
Hyatt Hotel, 206, 208
Hynes, Dan, 14

Illinois: Chamber of Commerce, 98; Constitution, 25; governor, 25, 230, 298n33; Network of Charter Schools, 58; School Code, 91, 135, 138; Supreme Court, 141–42; teacher strikes, 243–44
Illinois Association of School Administrators, 92
Illinois Educational Labor Relations Act (IELRA), 29, 269n65; Section 4.5 items, 36–37, 93–96, 102, 153–55, 159–60, 170, 176, 182, 202, 212, 217, 223, 228; Section 12(b), 95, 102, 212, 234
Illinois Educational Labor Relations Board (IELRB), 112, 128, 139–41, 154, 251, 298n30, 299n43
Illinois Education Association (IEA), 23, 73–74, 79–80, 82, 84–85, 90, 92, 98, 100
Illinois Federation of Teachers (IFT), 23, 73–74, 82, 84–86, 90, 92, 99
Illinois General Assembly, 23, 25–26, 28, 89; education legislation, 73–87, 157–58; pension fund legislation, 83–86. *See also* Senate Bill 7
Illinois State Board of Education (ISBE), 37, 76, 79, 92

impact bargaining, 95, 153–54
Industrial Workers of the World (IWW), 233, 237
injustice, 236–38. *See also* economic inequality;
    educational justice; poverty; racism
interest arbitration, 98, 274n35

Jackson, Jesse, Sr., 127, 216
Jackson, Shawn L., 259n29
Jepsen, Carly Rae, 200
job loss, in manufacturing sector, 17–19
job security, 24–25, 44, 77–79, 93, 166–67,
    172–76, 182, 201, 212, 228, 253
Johnson, Brandon, 204, 236
Johnson, Jen, 63, 65–66, 107, 118, 198
Johnson, Sarah, 222
Joravsky, Ben, 57, 268n64
Joyce Foundation, 82

Katten, Wendy, 53
Katz, Michael, 26
Kelleher, Keith, 277n38
Kennedy, Hen, 49
Kenwood Oakland Community Organization
    (KOCO), 63, 126, 207, 222
Kerrey, Robert, 26
Klein, Naomi, 62, 75
Klonsky, Fred, 100, 199
Klonsky, Mike, 42
Knapp, Jonathan, 254
Knights of Labor, 233, 237
Koldyke, Martin, 41
Kotlowitz, Alex, 48
Kotsakis, John, 22, 26
Kristof, Nicholas, 206
Kustra, Robert, 24

labor-community coalition, 236, 251–56.
    See also community mobilization
Labor Day, 187
labor movement history, 196, 230–31.
    See also unions
Labor Notes, 107, 276n7
Lamme, Bill, 69
Lane, Charles, 201
Latinos, 26, 57, 122, 204; teachers, 21, 41, 195
layoffs, 93, 134–36, 171, 173–74, 176–77, 182,
    201–2, 227–28, 244, 248; African American
    and Latino teachers, 40–41, 122, 176, 204,
    244. *See also* job security; recall policy
leadership, CTU: district supervisors, 109–10,
    190, 276n14; elections, 33–35, 38, 40, 43–44,
    66–70, 269n68, 270n99; member-driven
    model, 65, 120–21, 131, 146–47, 169, 178,
    223–24, 232–33, 240–42 (*see also* CORE);

new media coordinator, 198; runoff elections,
    68–69, 270n99; strike coordinators, 190, 193,
    208; top-down, 64, 121; training, 149–50
learning conditions, 32–33, 147, 194,
    201–2, 222, 227–28, 234. *See also*
    air-conditioning; class size; school
    day, length of
length of school day. *See* school day, length of
Lenz, Linda, 22, 27, 31, 168
lesson plans, 4, 55, 148, 173, 228
Lewis, Karen: 2012 contract, 134, 136, 145–46,
    148–50, 152–53, 156, 158, 171–72, 175–78,
    180–82, 184, 204, 209, 212, 214, 218–20, 240;
    2012 contract terms, 227–28; 2012 strike,
    201–2, 210, 226–27, 234; 2015 contract, 247,
    249; 2016 contract, 299n40; contract cam-
    paign, 111, 116, 118, 120–23, 131–32;
    in CORE, 62–70; in CTU video, 108–9;
    democratic methods, 103; mayoral
    campaign, 245; meetings with Emanuel,
    142–43, 280n93; and merit pay system, 96; on
    mobilization, 239; on PC coalition, 90; per-
    sonal background, 67, 280n92;
    personality, 132, 233, 280n93; on racism,
    237; relationship with Byrd-Bennett, 215–16,
    293n26; and SB 7 law, 88, 99–104, 169; setting
    strike date, 174; sexist attacks against, 196;
    on SFC, 92; "Stand Up to Bullies" speech,
    188; strike authorization vote, 128, 130;
    on waiver vote, 139–40
libraries, 53, 58, 122–25, 127, 137, 153, 161,
    202, 217, 227, 234, 254
Lieberman, Joseph, 11
Lightford, Kimberly, 82, 88–96, 98–101, 103,
    158, 169, 274n18
Lindgren, Hugo, 206
Lipman, Pauline, 62, 258n20
Local School Councils (LSCs), 25–27
Logan Square Neighborhood Association, 207
Long, Michael, 77
Los Angeles, 160, 243, 254
lottery system, 24, 55
Love, Alvin, 208
low-performing schools, 31–33, 41.
    See also school closings; turnaround
    schools
Luchini, Jean, 129
Luechtfeld, David, 94
Luskin, Matt, 109, 113–14, 120, 122, 124, 126,
    131, 204, 224–25, 277n38
Lydersen, Kari, 71
Lynch, Deborah, 33–40, 43, 61, 64, 66–67, 240,
    262nn24, 26, 263n42, 269n68
Lynd, Staughton, 253

Madeloni, Barbara, 243
Madigan, Michael, 24–25, 83, 85–86, 89–92, 158, 263n42
magnet schools, 55–56
Malin, Martin, 98
Maloney, Ed, 94
Marin, Carol, 130
Massarsky, Pam, 152, 180
May, Audrey, 180
Mayle, Kristine, 66, 109, 118, 132, 138, 146, 166, 180–82, 218, 220, 276n14
Mazany, Terry, 172
McCarthy, Garry, 247
McDonald, Laquan, 247–48
McLeod, Rhonda, 56
mediation, 154, 241–42, 246
Meeks, James, 94
Meeting Challenges, Past and Present (CTU), 108–9
Mercado, Ana, 207
merit pay, 44, 71, 96–97, 152, 175
Meyer, Cordelia "Dea," 271n12
Michie, Gregory, 192
militancy, 231–32. See also protests; strikes
Miller, Rich, 86–87, 89, 294n31
Moe, Terry M., 257n3
Montgomery, Dan, 92, 100
Moriarty, Joseph, 140, 145, 150, 152, 165–66, 177, 180, 182, 218–19, 221–22, 228
Murphy, Matt, 94
Murphy, Maureen, 29

National Commission on Excellence in Education, 11
National Education Association (NEA), 5–9, 243
National Governors' Association, 16
National Labor Relations Board (NLRB), 231, 269n65
National Union of Teachers (England), 243
A Nation at Risk (National Commission on Excellence in Education), 11–12, 15, 17
Neighborhood Capital Budget Group (NCBG), 32
neoliberalism, 8, 251
New York City, 71, 160, 243
New York Times, 201, 206, 231, 248
Noble Charter schools, 56, 58
No Child Left Behind Act (NCLB), 12, 15–16, 35, 50
Nominating Commission, 26–27, 29
North Carolina, 243

Obama, Barack, 3, 14–17, 51, 70, 143, 149, 210, 239, 292n78

Occupy Chicago, 107, 117, 126, 156, 208, 276n6
Occupy Wall Street, 107, 126, 239
O'Connell, Mary, 20
Olson, Jeanne Marie, 224
On The Line (CTU strike bulletin), 189, 191, 193, 210, 212, 216, 288n6, 289n29, 295n66
Open Letter petition, 112, 125

Papachristos, Andrew, 260n30
paraprofessionals, 123–24, 169
parents: in Local School Councils, 25–27; mobilization, 20–23, 63–64, 124–27, 185–86, 192, 205, 236
Parents United for Responsible Education (PURE), 20, 42, 57, 141
Patel, Amisha, 207
Patton, Steve, 222–23
PC coalition. See Performance Counts Act
PEACE (Chicago Parents, Educators and Clergy for Education), 208
Peck, Jamie, 17
pensions, 83–85, 161–62, 246, 298n30, 299n41
Performance Counts Act (PC coalition), 90–99, 102–3, 157–58, 213
Performance Evaluation Reform Act (PERA), 74–82, 89, 154–56, 174, 182
perks, 61, 108, 276n9
Phalen, Molly, 78
Philip, James "Pate," 28
Pilsen Alliance, 63, 222
Pilsen-Little Village, 193, 196
Pioneer Program, 137–41
Pittsburgh, 255, 300n51
"Pledged to Protect" (SEIU HCII), 300n50
Podkul, Joann, 262n24
police brutality, 247–48
police union, 187–88
Pope, Debby, 68
Porter, Linda, 66
Portland (Oregon) Association of Teachers (PAT), 244
Potter, Jackson, 61–62, 66, 69, 106, 111, 115, 117, 139, 158, 222, 251
Potter, Robin, 144, 156
poverty, 17–19, 80, 122, 144, 160, 237, 255; impact on learning, 47–49, 123
Power at Work (video), 110
prep time, 50, 54–55
principals: bullying teachers, 111, 113–15, 138, 148, 169, 193, 228, 244; hiring authority, 171, 173, 287n47. See also administrators
Pritzker, Penny, and family, 71, 86, 203, 206
privatization, 3, 12, 15, 31, 41–43, 65, 82, 99, 137, 143, 207, 230, 264n75.

See also charter schools; corporate education reform

ProActive Chicago Teachers & School Employees (PACT), 33–34, 37–38, 43–44, 61, 64, 66–68, 270n99

protests, 68, 106–7, 126, 239; during 2012 strike, 191–92, 194–97, 209–10, 213–14, 239; in 2013, 244; April 1, 2016 action, 249–51, 299n44; Labor Day, 187–88; May 23 march, 117–19, 187; Occupy Chicago, 156; red T-shirt campaign, 112, 115, 118–19, 187, 193, 209, 213–14; "Save Our Schools" march, 68

public good, 7–10, 63–70, 234–35, 240–42, 251–56

public schools. *See* Chicago Public Schools (CPS)

Quest Center, 108, 121, 159

Quinn, Pat, 81, 84, 88, 91–92, 104, 246, 298n33

Race to the Top, 14–17, 71, 73–76, 79, 81–82, 87

racism, 29, 122, 163, 204, 236–38, 248, 264n67; "educational apartheid," 122, 127

raises, 20–21; in 1999, 32; in 2003, 37–40; in 2007 contract, 43, 131; in 2012 contract, 128, 152–53, 155, 159–61, 163–66, 175–76, 182–83, 201, 204–5, 227; cancellation of 4 percent raise, 131, 136–37, 141, 152, 176, 204–5; fact-finding report on, 163–64, 170–71, 204–5, 291n57; steps and lanes, 160–61, 175, 249–50, 268n58. *See also* salaries

Ramirez, Jorge, 140–41, 158

Rangel, Juan, 268n64, 269n65

rank-and-file members, 65, 120–21, 131, 146–47, 169, 223–24, 232–33, 240–44, 253. *See also* CORE

rating bans, 182, 212, 214, 228

Rauner, Bruce, 85, 178, 230, 246–47, 252, 274n35, 287n56

Ravitch, Diane, 12

REACH (Recognizing Educators Advancing Chicago) Students, 155–56, 182

Reagan, Ronald, 11, 231

Reardon, Sean, 13

Rebel Diaz, 200

recall policy, 135, 141, 171–72, 174, 176–77, 214–15, 228, 287n47

Reece, Thomas, 30, 32–34, 36–37, 60

Rehak, Jay, 40, 119, 190

Reisberg, Darren, 75–77, 79, 81–82, 92

Renaissance 2010 initiative, 40–43

Republican Party, 2, 7, 23–25, 28, 84, 86, 89, 158, 231, 239

Republic Windows, 231, 234, 275n6

Resnick, Rachel, 134–35, 144–45

Reuters, 16, 56, 267n36

Rhee, Michelle, 76

Richard, Mark, 149–50, 157, 224

right to strike, 90–92, 95, 98–100, 158

right-to-work (RTW) legislation, 230

Rivera, Arnaldo, 179

Roberts, Larry, 208

Romney, Mitt, 239

Rose, Charles P., 272n12

Rose, Don, 226

Rosenwasser, Amy, 52

Rosh Hashanah, 221

Rossi, Rosalind, 137

Roth, Mitchell "Mitch," 79–80, 90, 92–93, 97, 100–101, 157, 273n19

salaries, 37, 58, 78, 108, 166, 201, 265n77, 276n9; administrators, 131, 161; bonuses, 71, 138, 276n19; charter teachers, 58–59; merit pay, 44, 71, 96–97, 152, 175. *See also* raises

Santiago, Miguel, 29

SB 7. *See* Senate Bill 7

Schmich, Mary, 126

Schmidt, George, 44

Scholastic Aptitude Test (SAT), 79

school board. *See* Board of Education; Illinois State Board of Education

school choice, 24

school closings, 40–41, 56–57, 61–62, 65, 124, 127, 131–32, 167, 203–4, 207–8, 244, 253, 267n41, 287n47

school day, length of, 38–39, 43, 52–55, 92, 94–95, 128, 131, 267n28; in 2012 contract, 227; comparative studies, 159–60; compensation for, 163–68, 170, 241–42; Emanuel's proposal, 52–54, 94, 104, 111–12, 131, 136, 138, 143, 152, 159–60, 207; and Pioneer Program, 137–41; "Sharkey Plan," 169–78

School Employee Alliance (SEA), 66

School Reform Summit, 22

schools, public. *See* Chicago Public Schools (CPS)

Schools and Staffing Survey (SASS), 77

The Schools Chicago's Students Deserve (CTU), 121–23

school year, length of, 95

Schultz, Ed, 291n63

Scott, Michael, 35

Scott, Thaddeus, 207

Seattle, 243, 254

segregation, 122, 259n29

Senate Bill 7 (SB 7), 88–104, 151, 241–42; 75 percent strike vote requirement, 99–104, 116, 127–28, 130–31, 157–58; bargaining time frame, 154, 182; and fact-finding process, 155, 166, 170; on longer school day, 136, 168–69; Performance Counts (PC) coalition, emergence of, 89–91; special committee, 91–98; on strikes, 98–101, 157, 239, 249, 251

Serious Materials factory, 275n6

Service Employees International Union (SEIU), 107, 117, 208, 235, 255, 300n50; Healthcare Illinois, 130, 277n38, 300n50

sexism, 196

Sharkey, Jesse, 38, 62, 66, 110, 128, 136–37, 140, 144–46, 153, 159–60, 166–67, 183, 226, 248, 286n32; 2012 contract, 180–82, 214, 216–17, 219–20, 228; 2015 contract, 246, 249; "Sharkey Plan," 169–78

Shibata, Kenzo, 66, 197–99, 290n38

Shields, Michael, 188, 197

Simpson, Bob, 209

Sims, Jinny, 63

Slay, Joan, 19

slogans, 202, 234, 239, 250

Smith, Anthony, 119

Smith, Cynthia, 107

social media, 197–200, 208–9, 290n38

social-movement unionism, 3. *See also* public good

social workers, 123–24

Soglin, Audrey, 79–80, 92, 100–101

special education, 55–56, 148, 227

standardized testing: amount of, 4, 14, 46, 49–50, 125, 239, 247; as predictor, 78–79; preparation for, 13, 46, 78; use in teacher evaluations, 69, 74–82. *See also* test scores

Stand for Children (SFC), 82–83, 85–87, 89–93, 96, 98, 100, 103, 131, 158, 198, 205–6, 212, 246, 272n35, 279n74

Stand Up! Chicago, 107, 117, 119

Steans, Robin, 73, 80–82, 89, 92–94, 103, 145, 157, 178, 213

Steans Foundation, 80

Steinem, Gloria, 195

Stewart, Marilyn, 40, 43–44, 60–62, 66, 68, 74, 76, 81, 120, 149, 269n68, 276n9

Strasser, Adolph, 233, 235

strike (2012), 1–9, 44–45, 185–229; authorization vote, 127–33, 157–58, 168, 233; bargaining during, 211–29; community support for, 192–96, 205–9, 216, 224–26, 236; downtown marches, 192–97; end of, 226–27; goals of, 137, 146–49, 201–3, 212, 234, 253;

informational picket lines, 185–86; and Labor Day holiday, 186–88; legality of, 222–23, 236, 254; media coverage, 186, 188, 190, 194, 200–206, 212–14, 229, 290n41; national impact, 242–44; outcomes, 232–42; picket lines, 185–86, 190–94, 210, 292n60; practice strike vote, 116–17; preparation for, 189–90; press conferences, 184, 208; social media organizing, 197–200, 208–9; strike coordinators, 190–91, 193; strike lieutenants, 190; as "strike of choice," 184, 190, 201, 212; teachers' reactions to, 191–92, 195; temporary restraining order (TRO) injunction, 221–23; ten-day notice, 174, 186; threat of, 98–101, 165–66, 171–73; twenty-four hours before deadline, 178–83

strike authorization, 99–103, 116, 127–28, 130–31, 157–58; 2012 vote, 127–33, 157–58, 168, 233; 2015 vote, 248

strikes: in 1983, 21; in 1984, 21; in 1987, 19–24, 260n44; in 2003 (threatened), 37–40; in 2016 (ULP strike), 249–50; in Chicago history, 196; community support for, 234, 249–51, 254–56; by Illinois teachers, 243–44; legality of, 222–23, 236, 251, 254

students: discipline, 264n67; dropout rates, 18, 259n13; graduation rates, 13, 259n13, 260n31; racial demographics, 10, 41, 259n29; socioeconomic status, 10, 13–14, 41, 78 (*see also* poverty). *See also* learning conditions; test scores

Substance News, 37, 44, 68, 88, 101, 150, 276n9

Sullivan, Meg, 59–60

Swanson, Elizabeth "Beth," 94, 135, 138, 145, 150, 171, 177, 179–82, 214, 221

Swanson, Ken, 100

Tax Increment Financing (TIF), 117, 161, 203, 206, 249

teachers: attitudes toward, 2, 4, 46–52, 125, 131; at charter schools, 31–32, 57–60, 268n49; demoralization, 46–52, 130; "developing," 182, 212, 214; dismissal, 56, 76–79, 93, 97, 272n14, 274n18 (*see also* layoffs; recall policy); female, 195–96; minority, 21, 41, 195; professionalism, 5–6; seniority, 79, 93, 161, 174, 228; turnover rates, 37, 51–52; unions, 2–6 (*see also* Chicago Teachers Union); young, 59, 111, 115, 138, 186, 199. *See also* evaluation; raises; salaries; tenure; working conditions

Teachers for Social Justice, 63

Teach for America (TFA), 58, 138, 281n23

Teaching Assistant Association, 194

Teamsters, 146, 189, 193, 218, 234–35

tenure, 41, 76–77, 92–94, 273n19; and
    dismissal, 97, 134–35, 141, 176
    (*see also* recall policy)
test scores, 3, 11–13, 46, 69, 78, 93,
    258n11; and teacher evaluations,
    15–17, 69, 71–87, 93, 155–56.
    See also standardized testing
Theodore, Nik, 17
Thompson, James, 25–26
Thuet, John, 119
TNTP (The New Teacher Project), 76–80
Torres, Maria, 222
Travis, Leslie, 53
Trumka, Richard, 238
Tugend, Alina, 260n31
turnaround schools, 51–52, 56, 111, 126–27,
    132, 244
Twitter, 197–99, 208–9, 290n38

unfair labor practices (ULP), 139–40, 154,
    249–50, 298n30
unions: history, 196, 230–31; internal
    organizing, 232–33; political involvement,
    64–65, 84–85; power of protests, 239;
    purpose and goals of, 233–235 (*see also*
    public good); rank-and-file caucuses,
    243–244 (*see also* rank-and-file
    members); solidarity with CTU,
    187–88, 194, 197, 208, 226, 250,
    299n44. *See also* Chicago Teachers
    Union; *specific unions*
United Auto Workers (UAW), 71, 231
United Caucuses of Rank-and-File
    Educators, 243
United Progressive Caucus (UPC), 33, 38, 40,
    43, 60–62, 66, 68, 269n67
UNITE HERE, 206, 235
University of Chicago: Consortium on
    School Research, 42; Lab School, 51
University of Illinois, 37; Labor Education
    Program (LEP), 108–11
UNO charter schools, 59, 268n64

US Department of Education,
    75, 81, 96

Vallas, Paul, 32–33, 36–37
Vaughn, Jacqueline, 19–22, 24, 27, 30, 60
violence, 48–49, 53, 57, 124
Vitale, David, 71, 140, 150, 209, 284n38,
    296n86; 2012 contract, 172–73, 175,
    177–78, 180–81, 183–84, 211–15,
    227–28
Voices of Youth in Chicago
    Education, 207

Wagner, Alex, 206
waiver vote, 111, 138–40
Walker, Scott, 201, 252
Walton Family Foundation, 2, 16
Washington, Harold, 19–23
Watkins, Roosevelt, III, 207
WBEZ, 197
Weingarten, Randi, 149, 196–97
Weisman, Joel, 201
Wennlund, Larry, 29
Westerhoff, Julie, 57
West Virginia, 230
whistle-blowers, 59–60, 268n64
white teachers, 41, 238
The Widget Effect (TNTP), 76–80
Wigler, Marc, 145
Wisconsin, 106–7, 143, 158, 194, 201, 210,
    230–31, 239
Women's Rights Committee, 148
women teachers, 195–96
working-class agenda, 255–56
working conditions, 37–38, 46–55, 147, 178,
    225, 227–28, 241, 245
Working Families Task Force, 297n15

YouTube, 82, 198–200

Zell, Sam, 86
Zorn, Eric, 160, 201

Lightning Source UK Ltd.
Milton Keynes UK
UKHW012138260123
416027UK00003B/35/J